MAJOR FLYWAYS of NORTH AMERICA

Designed by Patricia Coyle Nicholson
Drawn by Irvin E. Alleman

Water, Prey
and
Game

BIRDS

of North America

329 species portrayed in color
and fully described

Water, Prey, and Game

A volume in the Natural Science Library prepared by
NATIONAL GEOGRAPHIC BOOK SERVICE
Merle Severy, Chief

Foreword by
MELVILLE BELL GROSVENOR
President and Editor, National Geographic Society

NATIONAL GEOGRAPHIC SOCIETY, WASHINGTON, D. C.

BIRDS of North America

By ALEXANDER WETMORE

Research Associate and former Secretary of the Smithsonian Institution
past President of the American Ornithologists' Union
Trustee of the National Geographic Society

AND OTHER EMINENT ORNITHOLOGISTS

Western gulls off the California coast
Bates Littlehales, National Geographic photographer

643 illustrations, 600 in full color

Photographs by FREDERICK KENT TRUSLOW, ARTHUR A. ALLEN, ELIOT PORTER, G. RONALD AUSTING, KARL W. KENYON, and others. Paintings by WALTER A. WEBER, ALLAN BROOKS, and others.

Chapters by

John W. Aldrich
Research Staff Specialist, U. S. Fish and Wildlife Service

Robert Porter Allen
Former Research Director, National Audubon Society

Dean Amadon
*Lamont Curator of Birds, American Museum of Natural History
President, American Ornithologists' Union*

Frank C. Craighead, Jr.
President, Environmental Research Institute

John J. Craighead
Leader, Montana Cooperative Wildlife Research Unit

Philip S. Humphrey
*Chairman, Department of Vertebrate Zoology
U. S. National Museum*

George H. Lowery, Jr.
*Director, Museum of Natural Science, Louisiana State
University; past President, American Ornithologists' Union*

Robert M. McClung
*Former Curator of Mammals and Birds
New York Zoological Society*

Alden H. Miller
*Director, Museum of Vertebrate Zoology, University of
California; past President, American Ornithologists' Union*

Robert Cushman Murphy
*Lamont Curator Emeritus of Birds
American Museum of Natural History*

Robert J. Newman
Curator, Museum of Natural Science, Louisiana State University

Roger Tory Peterson
Ornithologist, author of A Field Guide to the Birds

Olin Sewall Pettingill, Jr.
Director, Laboratory of Ornithology, Cornell University

Austin L. Rand
*Chief Curator of Zoology, Chicago Natural History Museum
past President, American Ornithologists' Union*

S. Dillon Ripley
Secretary, Smithsonian Institution

Alexander Sprunt, Jr.
Former Southern Representative, National Audubon Society

George Miksch Sutton
Research Professor of Zoology, University of Oklahoma

Frederick Kent Truslow
Photographer-naturalist

Paul A. Zahl
National Geographic Senior Staff (Natural Sciences)

This book was prepared under the editorial guidance of **MELVILLE BELL GROSVENOR** and **FREDERICK G. VOSBURGH** by the following staff:

MERLE SEVERY, *Editor and Art Director*
PATRICIA COYLE NICHOLSON, *Designer*
ANNE DIRKES KOBOR, *Picture Editor*
EDWARDS PARK, SEYMOUR L. FISHBEIN, *Associate Editors*

ROSS BENNETT, GOODE P. DAVIS, JR., JOHN J. PUTMAN, BERRY L. REECE, JR.,

STATELY COMMON EGRETS *vie for strategic*

DAVID F. ROBINSON, EDWARD C. SHEPHERD
Editorial Staff

JAMES P. KELLY, *Production;*
WILLIAM W. SMITH, JOE M. BARLETT,
Engravings and printing

BARBARA V. KETCHUM, ROBERT W. LANNI, JOYCE A. McKEAN, MARY E. RILEY, PAULA C. SIMMONS, JOCELYN C. WHITE, *Assistants;*
ANDREW POGGENPOHL, *Art;* **WERNER JANNEY,** *Style;* **DOROTHY M. CORSON,** *Index*

Biographies written by **DRS. ALDRICH, HUMPHREY, MILLER, PETTINGILL, RAND, SPRUNT, SUTTON,** *and the Book Service staff*

Composed by National Geographic's Phototypographic Division, **HERMAN J. A. C. ARENS,** *Director*
ROBERT C. ELLIS, JR., *Manager*
Printed and bound by R. R. Donnelley and Sons Co., Chicago. First printing 300,000 copies

fishing rocks in a pond in Florida's Everglades; smaller snowies scurry out of the way.

Foreword

I CAN STILL SEE those great blue herons, and hear their hoarse cries as they came winging in from the Bras d'Or Lakes in Nova Scotia, where I spent my boyhood summers. My father, Gilbert Grosvenor, often took us children to the birch and maple forest where the magnificent birds nested. Now as I turn the pages of this book and listen to heron calls on my record player, youthful memories awaken.

How clearly I remember the day we came upon a young heron that had tumbled from its nest. Unable to fly, it flopped about on the ground.

"Can we take it home?" we asked eagerly.

Father weighed the question. "All right," he said, "if you promise to feed it." This seemed little to ask, and we quickly agreed.

First we built a wire cage. Then we set up a supply line of perch, caught from the family pier. Our first offerings the heron rejected. Fearing the bird might starve, we pried open his beak and dropped morsels down his gullet. That first taste did it. He gulped eight or ten perch daily and squawked for more. I fished so much that summer that I felt I never wanted to see another hook and line!

SYMBOLS *of nature's majesty and a nation's pride, bald eagles glare from a Florida mangrove stub.*

Frederick Kent Truslow

As our heron grew in size and appetite his disposition got worse. We learned to approach him warily at feeding time—which was any time we had fish—and to dodge the jabbings of his rapierlike beak. Several weeks later, however, that beak was deftly catching live perch that we put in a tank inside the enclosure.

Realizing that the heron no longer needed our help, we opened the cage door. He stepped out with his mincing gait, a cold glare in his beady yellow eyes, his neck in a graceful "S". Then he spread his great wings, croaked, and sailed off to join his fellows feeding down by the shore. Glad as we were to see him go, we felt it had all been worthwhile. We knew our efforts had given this bird the chance to soar wild and free, to stalk frogs and minnows in the shallows, to find a mate and rear more herons that would gladden the hearts of nature lovers.

Many more people than we ever realize are moved by the grace and beauty of birds. I note this with increasing pleasure as I read the heartwarming letters that pour in from readers of our companion volume, *Song and Garden Birds of North America*. Together the two volumes cover all 656 major species of birds, big and little, to be found in the United States, Canada, and parts of northern Mexico.

In *Water, Prey, and Game Birds* you will find color pictures, life histories, breeding and winter ranges, lengths (covering male and female), and characteristics of 329 species—seabirds that roam the lonely oceans, sharp-eyed hawks and owls, soaring vultures, ducks and geese in all their colorful variety, plump grouse, tall and stately wading birds, little shorebirds that twinkle across our beaches.

Members who marveled at our initial venture into wildlife sound will be pleased with the album that eavesdrops for a full hour on 97 species, keyed in the text with the symbol ♪⁚ We have reproduced these calls with the same fidelity that caused one member to complain the songbird recordings were too realistic. In search of the tempting singers, his cat leaped into—and wrecked—a costly record player!

To me, the voices of the big, dramatic birds in this volume are even more varied and arresting than the melodies of the songsters. The clangor of wild geese flying over, the laughter of loons on a northern lake, the haunting cry of a limpkin in a southern swamp—these stir us all. One call may come as a surprise—the squeak of our national bird, the bald eagle, as out of character as a piping soprano voice issuing from the mouth of a giant! Hearing this again reminds me of the hours I spent crouched in an Everglades blind studying a bald eagle family with Frederick Kent Truslow. His unique close-ups stand out among the 480 photographs which complement the masterful paintings of Walter A. Weber.

Enlisting the best efforts of outstanding contributors, Book Service Editor Merle Severy and his staff outdid themselves in creating this beautiful and instructive volume. Once again the world-renowned ornithologist Alexander Wetmore served as chief author and consultant, checking each page of text for accuracy, every illustration for fidelity of color. Ornithologist John W. Aldrich and naturalist Robert M. McClung also checked the text. My associate, Frederick G. Vosburgh, reviewed proofs with the loving, ever-watchful eye of a lifelong bird enthusiast.

For species names, ranges, and general order of presentation we have followed the *Check-list of North American Birds*, published by the American Ornithologists' Union. The *Check-list* covers birds north of Mexico, also in Baja California, and lists them in order of increasing complexity. *Water, Prey, and Game Birds* portrays the more primitive species, from loons to swifts. *Song and Garden Birds* begins with the hummingbirds and proceeds to the most highly specialized birds, the sparrows.

All make up a fascinating, colorful world. As you delve into this book, may you share my delight in exploring this winged realm of beauty and sound.

Melville Bell Grosvenor

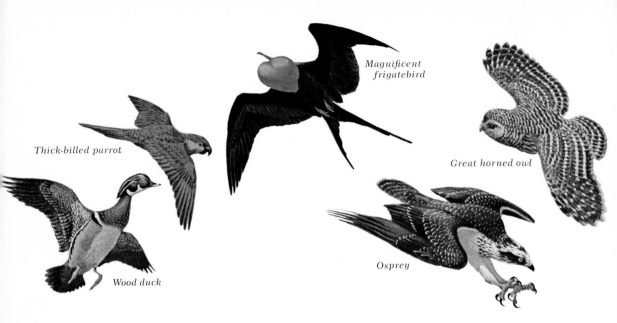

Thick-billed parrot

Magnificent frigatebird

Great horned owl

Wood duck

Osprey

Contents

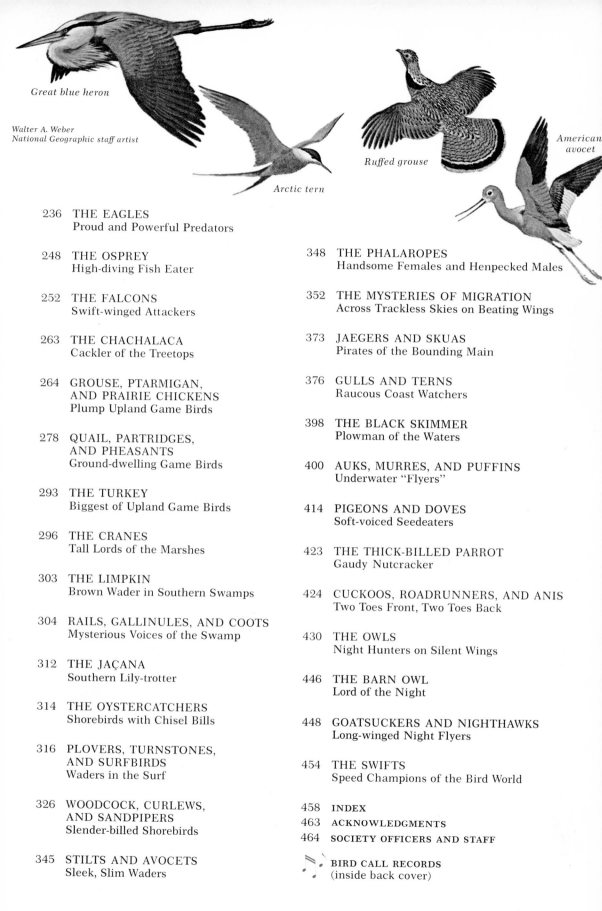

Great blue heron

Walter A. Weber
National Geographic staff artist

Arctic tern

Ruffed grouse

American
avocet

WINGED CREATURES THROUGH THE AGES

The World of Birds

By ALEXANDER WETMORE

I HEARD THE SONG in a rain forest high on a Haitian mountain. With a botanist companion I had climbed the steep north face of the Massif de la Selle and made camp beside the first spring beyond the crest. The following day I heard birds hidden in the trees whistling notes strange to me. I glimpsed one of the songsters — a bird the size of a robin, with slaty back and robin-colored breast — and realized at once it was an unknown species of thrush.

Though numerous, the birds were so shy that for three days I hunted them unsuccessfully. Finally, during a tropical downpour that the thrushes seemed to enjoy more than I, several came out into the open and I collected a specimen. I named the species *Haplocichla swalesi* in honor of a friend, ornithologist B. H. Swales.

Finding a new bird is no everyday occurrence. Ornithologists recognize some 8,660 living species in the world of birds and estimate that fewer than 100 others, of limited range in remote regions, remain undiscovered. Birds range everywhere on earth except at the heart of the Polar Plateau of Antarctica. Some course the open sea; some appear at tiny, remote islands. Migrating land birds have rested aboard ships on which I traveled, and drunk at desert springs where I camped.

Ornithologist Roger Tory Peterson calculates that at the close of the nesting season the North American bird population reaches 20 billion. His British colleague, James Fisher, puts the world's total at 100 billion. Vast colonies of seabirds on rocky islands impress the eye, but far greater numbers of smaller birds live inconspicuously in grassland and forest. Recently, during three weeks in a jungle camp in Panama, I released 20 or more antbirds daily that my nets trapped. Obviously these little birds abounded, but in that dense foliage I never saw one flying free.

Birds in all their wondrous variety developed, scientific evidence tells us, from lizardlike ancestors of the Triassic period — about 200 million years ago. These were the stem stock of the dinosaurs, which dominated the Age of Reptiles. They also gave rise to giant pterodactyls that glided on batlike wings, some spanning 25 feet — nature's experiments in reptilian flight. Certain of the Triassic reptiles ran birdlike on their hind legs; some dwelt in trees. Scientists theorize that ever so gradually they developed a protective coat of feathers and the evolving bird became warm-blooded, which enabled it to survive changing conditions of heat and cold that spelled death to the cold-blooded reptiles.

Our knowledge of prehistoric animals comes from fossils. Most birds have fragile bones, and their bodies usually fall prey to scavengers. Often only fragments of a skeleton remain to tell us of an extinct species. To me, each such piece of fossil bone seems a small window through which I may see, though indistinctly, something of the birdlife of past ages. "Bird watching" in this manner intrigues me as much as observing the living birds that come daily to the feeders in my garden.

What a view into the hidden past was unveiled in 1860 when a Bavarian quarry worker turned up a slab with the fossilized impression of a feather! The very next year a partial skeleton came to light nearby — a reptilian bird revealed in Jurassic limestone 150 million years old! A second, more complete skeleton, found in 1877, showed the form of the head. A third, also from southern Germany, was discovered in 1956. Christened *Archaeopteryx* — "ancient wing" or "ancient bird" — this strange

12   **ADAM OF THE BIRD WORLD,** Archaeopteryx *sailed from his primeval perch 150 million years ago. Dying, the crow-size creature sank into silt in Bavaria. This turned to stone, preserving the imprint of feathers (inset), not reptilian scales.*
Roger Tory Peterson. Inset: Paleontology Institute and Museum of Humboldt University, Berlin

LONG BEFORE THE DAWN *of history primitive men stalked birds for food. Here Ice Age Americans hunt stately whooping cranes. Grooved stone balls found at prehistoric sites suggested to artist Andre Durenceau the whirling bolas once used to entangle ostrichlike rheas on the Argentine pampas.*

creature remains the earliest bird
known. It had a crow-size body
and jaws armed with teeth instead of a bill. Claws on its wings
helped it climb about in trees.
Feathered wings and long, jointed
tail enabled it to fly.

Two of the skeletons agree in
size; the third has a smaller leg
and foot, with the toes—three forward and one behind—in different
proportion. On many occasions, in
the Natural History Museum in
London, I have studied the slab
with the first *Archaeopteryx* and
compared it with reproductions of
the others. I believe that the fossils show two distinct species.

The best known fossil bird of
the Cretaceous period that follows is *Hesperornis*—"bird of the
west"—from Kansas chalk beds
90 million years old. This huge

MIGHTY TERATORNIS *flaps in on wings that span 12 feet to feast on a bear trapped by the tar at La Brea. Mired himself, he leaves his bones in the California pit. From abundant fossil remains, scientists assembled a skeleton of this Ice Age scavenger (upper left). Teratornis or one of his condor kin may have been the "thunderbird" of Indian lore.*

Roger Tory Peterson. Inset: J. R. Eyerman

flightless diver with paddle feet is the latest bird known with certainty to have true teeth.

By the beginning of the Tertiary period, some 70 million years ago, mammals had replaced the great reptiles of previous ages. Birds, most of them favored by flight and with little competition from earthbound creatures, multiplied. Families existed that we know today. Some strange kinds also thrived: *Diatryma*, taller than a man, with fearsome beak and a skull the size of a horse's; and *Neocathartes*, a short-winged vulture that must have run about on its long legs as the secretary bird does in Africa today. *Neocathartes* is one of 80 birds that I have described from bone fragments.

By the start of the Pleistocene, a million years ago, birds had reached their high point. Then the great glaciers of the Ice Age edged south, drastically cutting down the habitat for northern hemisphere species. In eastern North America the ice reached the Ohio Valley. I have identified bones found in Virginia as belonging to the gray jay and the spruce grouse—both now found mainly in Canada. The ice had forced them south.

They have survived the rigors of the Ice Age. Many species did not. The unsuccessful ones could not adapt to new territory or to altered conditions in old surroundings. Some became too specialized, or could not compete with rising species, and departed from the living scene.

Much of our knowledge of Ice Age life comes from the La Brea tar pits, today flanked by Wilshire Boulevard in Los Angeles. Here hundreds of thousands of bones of Pleistocene creatures have been recovered, including fossils representing 92 bird species, 15 now extinct. Let imagination clothe these bones with the flesh and fur and feathers of life and we may witness the drama of La Brea:

Dust covers the surface of the death pits, concealing the viscous tar. Unwary animals come to drink at the scattered pools of water and get mired. Their struggles attract predators—saber-toothed cats, huge dire wolves, hawks, and eagles—and these too fall prey to the clinging tar. Carrion eaters come to feast on the bodies and they in turn blunder into the pit. As the victims slowly sink into the blackness, flesh disappears and tar impregnates the bones, preserving them.

Teratornis—"monster bird"—a vulture with 12-foot wingspan, probably weighing twice as much as a California condor, first emerged into the light of science from the tar pits. The giant scavenger ranged far beyond California. Its bones, and those of condors, have come to me from Florida for identification. Both birds lived there during the Pleistocene.

Man struck down some of the spectacular birds that survived the Ice Age. Two-gallon eggshells uncovered in Madagascar give mute evidence of *Aepyornis*—"high bird"—which towered ten feet and weighed, estimates ornithologist Dean Amadon, nearly half a ton. The legendary roc that Sindbad the Sailor met on his travels possibly was based on this great elephant bird of Madagascar.

New Zealand's giant moas may have survived to the 14th century, perhaps later. They were flightless, therefore defenseless against man's improving weapons. Prehistoric Indians on Caribbean islands ate a rail as large as a guinea fowl. We know this because of the discarded bones. Years ago in Puerto Rico I heard of a bird called

Strange birds of the Galapagos Islands, developing in isolation show nature's wonder of adaptation

"A LITTLE WORLD WITHIN ITSELF," *wrote Charles Darwin after visiting the Galapagos in 1835. Here wildlife differs oddly from that in South America, 600 miles away.*

Cormorants whose ancestors strayed to the islands ages ago found no need to fly for food or to escape. A plunge off any rock sufficed to fill their stomachs with the abundant fish. Ashore they can only run, fanning stubby wings (above), when chased.

Thirteen species of finch, all of common ancestry, have adapted to different foods. The woodpecker finch fills the role of the woodpecker, which never reached the islands. Lacking a long tongue, the finch uses a tool. Cactus spine in beak, he impales a wood borer, pries it out, holds his spear with a foot while he pulls off the grub. To Darwin these finches suggested a theory of evolution: animals must adapt to their environment to survive.

Irenäus Eibl-Eibesfeldt. Top: Don Ollis

the carrao that men used to hunt with dogs on dewy mornings. Once its feathers became soaked a hunter could catch it by hand. I wonder if the extinct rail, whose bones abound, somehow survived to relatively recent times. I wonder if it and the carrao were one.

To SURVIVE and exploit a wide diversity of habitats around the globe, birds developed in a number of special ways. Penguins, with their heavy streamlined bodies, waterproof feathers, and thick layers of blubber, are admirably adapted for pelagic life in the Antarctic. Though descended from flying birds, they lost the power of flight when their stubby wings evolved into efficient paddles for speeding underwater after fish.

Le Conte's thrasher dwells the year round in the hottest, driest deserts in the Southwest — without water to drink. It gets some moisture from the caterpillars it eats. Petrels and many other seabirds drink nothing but salt water; nasal glands over the eyes excrete salt concentrations from their bodies. Long, slender wings equip these ocean dwellers for endless gliding over the waves. Two years may pass before an albatross sets foot on dry land; then it flounders on weak legs, out of its element. More terrestrial species have stronger legs. The roadrunner can outpace a horse. Plovers, sandpipers, and other shorebirds scurry across sand and pebble beaches on short, sturdy legs.

Large wading birds such as storks, cranes, and herons have long, slender legs that serve as stilts as they stalk through shallows in marshes and bays. Their long necks and rapierlike bills flash downward to seize a fish or other aquatic animal. A great blue heron that I once raised could strike with the speed of a coiled snake, thanks to an internal triggerlike mechanism that herons have in their necks.

The exotic little jaçana almost seems to walk on water as it seeks its fare of bog insects and seeds. Nature's gift of greatly elongated toes distributes the weight as the bird treads on lily pads. It even raises its young out on the water, cradled in a cup of leaves amid the floating vegetation. Gallinules also have lily-trotting toes.

Ducks and most other swimming birds propel themselves with webbed feet. Coots and grebes swim with lobed feet. Auks and puffins actually "fly" underwater, pumping their wings and steering with their feet as penguins do. Though unrelated to penguins, they developed similarly for life in the Far North.

AMID THE TIMELESS WORLD *of the Everglades a snowy egret stands on golden slippers. Endowed with long legs and serpentine neck, this exquisite plumed wader fishes in swamps and sloughs.*

18

Charles Allmon, National Geographic staff

Purple gallinule, Eliot Porter

NATURE PUTS THE BEST FOOT FORWARD *to equip a water bird for its special function. Long toes that distribute weight evenly over a broad area permit the purple gallinule (above) to patter across lily pads in search of aquatic insects.*

A western grebe (below) displays a lobed foot that propels it underwater. The black duck (right), a surface feeder or dabbler, paddles with webbed feet. The redhead (far right) combines webbing with lobed rear toes—badge of membership in the group of diving ducks.

The well-named stilt stalks through shallows on pink pipestem feet with heels where you'd think his knees would be.

Western grebe, Frederick Kent Truslow

Black duck, Arthur A. Allen

I shall always associate these birds with my first memories of the Aleutian Islands of Alaska. I had found passage on a Coast Guard cutter, and we approached at half speed on a gray, misty day, feeling for a landfall. Occasionally an indistinct, heavy-bodied bird would blunder away from the ship. Then suddenly the fog lifted to reveal Tigalda Island, our destination, and on all sides I could see thousands of birds stretching away to the horizon. Puffins with large gaudy bills sat in pairs on the water. Tiny auklets rested in flocks. Groups of murres swam over the swell. As we bore down upon them, some dived with beating wings and darted away in submarine flight. Others pattered across the surface on their webbed feet until they picked up enough speed to launch into the air. Unlike penguins, these birds can fly. One relative, the great auk, could not. It became extinct a century ago.

Members of this fascinating family live in such remote places that many naturalists have little firsthand knowledge of them. So you can imagine my delight when a bird with white breast and black back swam through the surf as I walked along a Maryland beach one cold December morning. I recognized it as a razorbill, rare so far south. Without seeming to notice me the auk moved beyond the sea's wash, inching along on its breast with its wings and legs. Thinking it must be injured, I stepped forward to pick it up. To my astonishment it pattered off and flew back to the surf. There it rested buoyantly before swimming out to sea—the element to which nature had adapted it so well.

The sharply compressed beak of the razorbill makes an admirable tool for catching fish, shrimp, or squid. Mergansers have beaks with saw-toothed edges to help them grasp fish. Hooked tips on the bills of gulls, cormorants, and pelicans serve the same purpose. Pelicans, in addition, have huge gaping pouches in which they trap their catch.

Ibises and stilts use their long beaks as tongs or tweezers for grasping aquatic food. The anhinga, or snakebird, impales fish with its lancelike bill. The feeding avocet sweeps its slender, upturned beak sideways through the water in search of larvae and other tiny organisms. Curlews and snipe probe in the mud with slender bills for crustaceans and worms. With its strong chisel bill the oystercatcher pries shellfish loose from rocks with a twist of the head.

*Hind toe
of a dabbling duck*

*Lobe on hind toe
of a diving duck
acts as a paddle*

Black-necked stilt, Frederick Kent Truslow

Redhead, David G. Allen

The skimmer, with its lower mandible – the bottom part of the bill – longer than the upper, is an extraordinary specialist in the world of birds. Flying just above the water, the bird cuts the surface with this lower mandible as if it were plowing a field. When it strikes a small fish or other aquatic animal, the mandibles clamp and the bird's head moves down and back to swallow the tidbit.

Omnivorous feeders such as ducks and geese have broadened and flattened bills, usually with fine strainers along each side. The shoveler, for example, scoops up ooze and with a lateral shaking sifts out worms, tadpoles, shellfish, and seeds.

The flamingo, in contrast to most birds, has a movable upper mandible and a lower mandible that is fixed. But the long-necked bird eats with its head upside down, so the curved upper mandible scoops organic material from the bottom. The bird opens and closes its mouth, taking in and forcing out water. Tiny food particles are strained out by the grill along the beak edges and by rows of fleshy teeth on the sides of the thick tongue, which works to and fro like the piston of a pump. The flamingo slowly pivots until it clears out a complete circle, then moves to another spot.

Throughout the world of birds nature fashioned beaks for special purposes: the woodpecker's drill to dig for wood borers, hummingbird bills in many shapes for probing differently shaped flowers for nectar. A parrot's bill is designed to cut open nuts and fruit; its claws are adapted to hold this food and raise it to the beak.

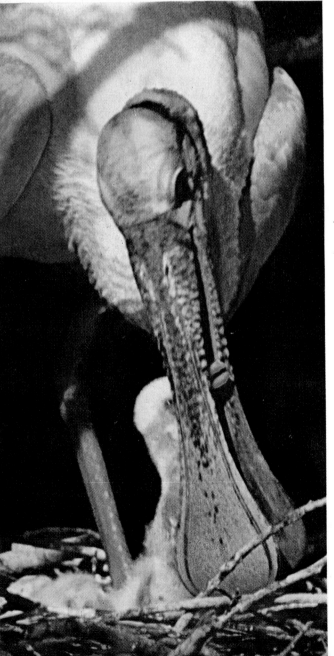

Frederick Kent Truslow

BIRDS OF PREY generally have long, curved talons for seizing their victims and strongly hooked beaks for tearing them apart. These birds, moreover, are masters of flight. Round-winged hawks excel at hedgehopping and tight maneuvering to get at their

BIZARRE BILLS *fit the feeding needs of these big waders. The American flamingo (opposite) probes shallows with inverted beak, sifting out tiny organisms with the strainers on its sharply curved mandibles.*

The roseate spoonbill (left) swings its banjo beak through the water till nerve endings inside detect killifish, crustaceans, or insects and signal the order to clamp shut. The bill opens to serve a chick a predigested meal from the gullet. The spoon-fed youngster soon cheeps for more.

prey. Unsurpassed at soaring, vultures and condors spiral for hours on motionless wings in their tireless search for food, often at such altitudes that these great birds appear as mere specks against the blue. Falcons, with their pointed wings, fly with the dash of fighter planes. The peregrine falcon may hit 175 miles an hour in a dive!

On the Bear River marshes, at the northern end of Great Salt Lake in Utah, I have spent many exhilarating hours watching this falcon hunt and play in the air. I have seen the predator dash through a closely massed flock of flying sandpipers, strike one with its claws, let the victim drop, then wheel swiftly and snatch it in midair. I have seen it streak down and knock a redhead duck to the ground.

On one occasion a pair of these duck hawks harried a helpless nighthawk, stooping, or diving, at it playfully until one in passing gave it a squeeze with one foot. The predator released its grip, the nighthawk fell—and the other duck hawk seized it. As the pair of hunters flew away, one would drop the booty and the other catch it.

Often I watched falcons fly along the river channels, driving ahead of them a motley flock of blackbirds, herons, avocets, and other birds. The predators, capable of killing almost at will, herded them like sheep but never harmed one.

Again, as night herons flew ahead of my launch, a duck hawk darted at them repeatedly, forcing them lower and lower until with squawks of protest they struck the water. They had to swim into the willows to escape their tormentor—but the duck hawk made no kill.

One pleasant afternoon I heard a roaring of wings overhead and looked up to see a cormorant that

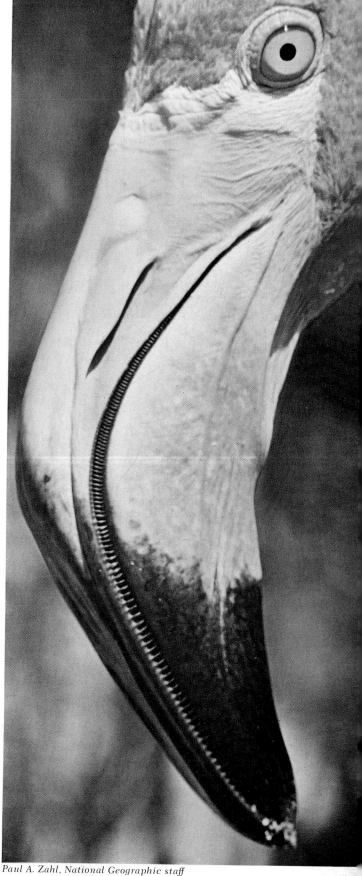

Paul A. Zahl, National Geographic staff

had been soaring peacefully high in the sky diving toward the river with wings set. A few feet behind it came a duck hawk. Just over the water the falcon suddenly accelerated, tapped the cormorant lightly on the back, then circled easily away while the frightened quarry took refuge in the water.

The duck hawk is one of some 270 birds of prey that hunt in daylight around the globe. Owls — more than 140 species in all — are the night raiders of the bird world. Fringed edges on their flight feathers enable them to slip through the air in silence to pounce on their prey. In some owls,

Skimmer by Luther Goldman. Heron sequence by Frederick Kent Trusl

SPEAR OR SCOOP, *the shape of the bill reflects a bird's food and how he gets it. With long lower mandible, a black skimmer (opposite) plows a Maryland bay. The furrow may roil minute aquatic life, luring small fish and shrimp. The skimmer retraces its course and scoops them up. In Florida a great blue heron stabs into an Everglades lake, impaling a catfish on its dagger bill (above). Usually this patient stalker seizes a small fish and gulps it on the spot. This large catch it took ashore, gave a coup de grace, and slowly swallowed whole, headfirst.*

as in certain hawks, the eyes are larger than those of a man – and a great deal keen-
er. Like a man's they look forward, toward the prey, instead of being set on the side
of the head as in most birds, to watch for enemies. The woodcock, which probes in
soft ground for food, has eyes set far back so that it can see a full 360° without moving its head. In fact, it can see better to the rear than ahead!

Experiments with some owls have proved that they can see in a tiny fraction of
the minimum light that a man requires. In what we would call total darkness these
owls flew directly to a dead mouse from six feet away, guided solely by their eyes.

What about an owl's hearing? To determine whether it helps the bird catch its
prey, scientists at the Hatheway School of Conservation, near Boston, Massachusetts, turned a live mouse loose among dead leaves in a room made absolutely light-
proof. "Wol," a barn owl, left his perch and the rustling stopped. A beam of light
showed Wol on the floor, grasping the mouse in his talons. The scientists repeated
the experiment several times with the same result, then tried it using a wad of
paper drawn by a string to make the rustling noise. This target had no scent and no
body heat to help guide Wol, but the barn owl homed in on it unerringly.

The oilbird of northern South America goes the barn owl one better: It navigates
in the ink-black caves where it nests by bouncing bill clicks off the rock walls. This
hawk-size relative of the goatsuckers possesses a sonar sense shared among birds,
so far as we know, only by cave-dwelling swifts of Southeast Asia, whose nests are
prized for bird's-nest soup. Bats also navigate by sound reflection – but their chirps
usually are inaudible to man, whereas we can hear the oilbirds' evenly spaced
clicks. To test this echolocation technique, scientists put several of the birds in a
room, where they safely flew about in the dark. When experimentally the birds' ears
were plugged with cotton, they crashed into the walls.

When oilbirds flock out of their caves in the evening, they feed only on the fruits
of forest trees, mainly palms and laurels. Many other birds have special tastes. The
Everglade kite preys only on a certain kind of large freshwater snail. The kite's
long, slender, hooked upper mandible serves to pry this dainty from its shell. The
bat-eating hawks, the honey buzzard, and the serpent eagles of the Old World are
named for the foods they prefer. The powerful harpy eagle feeds regularly on mon-
keys. So does the crowned eagle, even luring them into ambush with a soft whistle.

The osprey lives on fish. Pads under its toes are covered with spiny scales. These
help the bird hold its slippery catch. When a diving osprey strikes its prey, the talons

automatically lock. If the predator binds to a fish too large to lift, it may have difficulty releasing its grip and be dragged under. Skeletons of ospreys have been recovered from fishermen's nets — talons still locked in the fish that drowned them.

Compared to aquatic and predatory birds, most of our upland game birds — pheasants, quail, grouse, and the like — are relatively unspecialized, though bound to a definite way of life. They gather most of their food on the ground and take to the air only as a last resort. With short, stout bills they grub for their meals; on strong legs they run and

George Silk, courtesy Life, © Time, Inc.
Left: Frederick Kent Truslow

Walter A. Weber
National Geographic staff arti

TALONED FEET *and hooked beak mark birds of prey as meat eaters. Dagger claws locked in a ground squirrel's back, a golden eagle thrashes into the air from a California field (above). Three toes are forward, one back—the usual arrangement.*

The osprey (left) can rotate one outer toe either forward or back. When fishing it sets two toes in front and two behind. Spiny foot pads help ensure a firm grip on its catch. Talons pin the fish to a perch, sharp beak rips it. 27

scratch. Cock pheasants, like domestic roosters, have long sharp spurs on their legs. Anyone who has seen a cockfight knows what these are for!

Ruffed grouse in summer have smooth feet. But in winter a row of flat scales grows on each side of the toes to serve as snowshoes. The ptarmigan is feathered on its legs and toes right down to the claws. And, like snow buntings, ptarmigan wear white winter garb that helps conceal them in the snow.

On the leafy brown litter of the forest floor the whip-poor-will huddles motionless, so perfectly camouflaged that you might step on it before noticing it. The

CLOAKS OF COLOR *hide the hunted. Ptarmigan (left) time their plumage changes to nature's clock and blend into each season's face. Male wood duck (upper right) trades resplendent nuptial hues for drab shades of safety when molting leaves him flightless. Camouflaged by its mottled coat, the whip-poor-will (below) might pass for a stick among the fallen leaves.*

woodcock relies on the same kind of concealment. The killdeer and other plovers wear plumage in disruptive patterns that blend with fields and beaches.

As with songbirds, the males of many waterfowl assume bright colors, while their mates remain drab. Resplendent breeding plumages help them to attract females and advertise their presence to would-be rivals. Many of the females wear browns or grays, streaked or spotted to blend into the habitat. Since they bear the major burden of incubating eggs and rearing young, which ties them to the nesting grounds, they must have every protection that nature can afford.

Man, even in his most primitive state, long has been aware of the variety of the birdlife around him. Modern ornithologists probed a mountain range in New Guinea to study the little-known birds of the area. They discovered that the local

people—Stone Age tribesmen—recognized 137 different kinds and had names for each. After careful study the scientists classified the same birds: 138 species!

For tribal rites New Guinea natives wear fantastic headdresses made from plumes of the bird of paradise. African dancers use ostrich plumes. Polynesians in Hawaii wove sumptuous robes of brilliant feathers which only the nobility might wear. American Plains Indians prized eagle feathers for their warbonnets and ceremonial robes.

Long before the dawn of recorded history bird watchers depicted birds on the walls of caverns in France and Spain. The duck, crane, raven, ibis, spoonbill, flamingo, and stork can be recognized in these crude paintings, the earliest dating back more than 15,000 years.

The ancient Egyptians revered birds and used the vulture, swallow, sparrow, and others as characters in hieroglyphics. Archeologists excavating near the Step Pyramid at Saqqara have broken through into a series of underground passages filled with ibis mummies— thousands of them stacked like bricks. Scientists believe that the ibises, sacred to worshipers of Osiris, had been brought as offerings by pilgrims to a shrine.

WATERFOWL BURST *from a papyrus swamp on the Nile in this scene recorded 3,400 years ago at Thebes. Towering over wife and lotus-gathering daughter, the Egyptian noble grasps throwing-stick and three flailing herons. His hunting cat makes a midair catch under the eyes of hieroglyphic hawks.*

Hunting scenes and bird designs adorn the walls of Egypt's tombs. Six geese of three different species march across a beautiful fresco in the vault of Princess Itet at Maidum, dating from about 2700 B.C.

The Greeks depicted birds on their coins, pottery, and statues. In the New World stylized owls and vultures peer at us from Mayan sculptures, the raven and eagle from towering totem poles carved by Indians of the Pacific Northwest.

Through the ages the eagle has stood as an emblem of war and courage and power. This regal bird symbolized the Sumerian city of Lagash in the third millennium before Christ. It was engraved on the seal of the King of Ur, and continued in double-headed form in Hittite art. It graced Byzantine coins and the banners of Turkoman princes. A silver eagle topped the standards of Roman legions; today it decorates flagstaffs in many lands. The American bald eagle emblazons the Great Seal of the United States, many coins and decorations, and the President's flag and seal.

The Romans believed they could foretell the future by watching the flight of birds, listening to their songs, or examining their entrails. No vital enterprise was begun without consulting the birds to see if the omens were auspicious—a word that stems from the Latin *avis,* meaning "bird," and *spicere,* "to look at."

One old belief holds that gulls contain the souls of sailors lost at sea; another that an albatross following a ship betokens good fortune. The bird's slayer would be dogged with bad luck, as Coleridge portrays in his *Rime of the Ancient Mariner.* The raven, in

Tomb fresco from XVIII Dynasty; British Museum, London

Poe's famous poem, is an "ominous bird," a "thing of evil." In the Bible, however, the bird is shown in a kindly light when it brings food to the prophet Elijah in the wilderness. The Book of Genesis tells of Noah releasing a raven from the ark to bring tidings of dry land, but the bird never returned. A dove, sent on the same mission, flew back bearing an olive leaf in its beak. Since then the dove—and the olive branch—have symbolized peace and goodwill.

Similarly the bluebird depicts happiness, the peacock indicates pride and vanity, and the pelican symbolizes Christian charity. The owl sometimes signifies wisdom, sometimes evil. Pliny the Elder, in his celebrated *Natural History*, reported the bird as "an extremely bad omen . . . a direful portent"—but added that he knew of cases in which an owl had perched on someone's home without fatal consequences.

Aristophanes spoofs many such beliefs in his play *The Birds*, first performed in Athens in 414 B.C. Aesop used birds as characters in his fables to illustrate the foibles of mankind. Shakespeare's mention of the starling resulted in an act of far-reaching consequence: The bird was brought across the Atlantic and released in New York's Central Park in 1890 by enthusiasts seeking to introduce into the United States all the birds mentioned in Shakespeare!

STYLIZED BIRDS *date back more than 15,000 years to the cave art at Lascaux in France. Beside a fallen hunter, gored by a bison, a bird perches atop a rod (below)—as on Eskimo funeral posts. Egyptians honored Horus the hawk (right), protector of the pharaohs, and built a temple to him at Idfu, which this granite god surveys. Assyrians carved winged bulls (opposite, upper) to guard Sargon's palace at Khorsabad. On an Athenian vase (lower) Heracles slays the man-eating Stymphalian birds.*

Romain Robert. Right: Merle Severy
National Geographic staff

32

Another bird from England—the house sparrow, brought in to help control cankerworms in Brooklyn—also took hold only too well. Carried by man around the globe, the starling and the house sparrow have multiplied until it is believed they now outnumber any other bird except the domestic fowl.

Our many breeds of chicken trace back to one of the jungle fowls of the Indian area, ancestral stock also for the bantams, the Japanese silky, and the long-tailed fowl, raised mainly as ornamental birds. As early as 1400 B.C. records tell of the Chinese keeping chickens. Probably they had been doing so for a thousand years before that.

The goose, domesticated in eastern Asia from the wild greylag species, has a lineage just as venerable. Homer relates that Odysseus' wife Penelope had a flock of 20 geese. A favorite on farms all over the world, the goose also serves

ritish Museum, London. Above: the Louvre, Paris; Tel-Vigneau

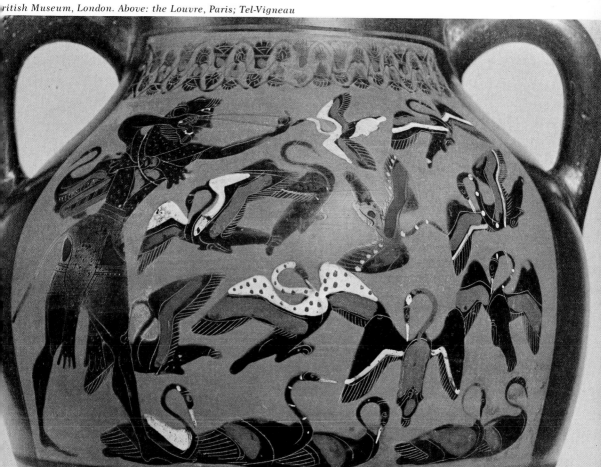

today as distillery watchman in Scotland, where gaggles cackle at intruders—just as geese warned ancient Rome of invading Gauls in 390 B.C. Perhaps a million geese waddle through cottonfields in the South, destroying weeds more efficiently than man, mechanical weeders, or herbicides.

Our domestic ducks stem from two wild species, the Muscovy duck of tropical America and the mallard. The turkey, strictly North American, was domesticated by the Aztecs of Mexico for hundreds of years before Spanish conquistadores took the bird home with them in the 1520's. Bird feathers as well as eggs and flesh form a valuable crop. And Peru bolsters its economy by mining the nitrogen-rich guano deposited by the millions of cormorants and other seabirds on offshore islands.

B IRDS PROVIDE SPORT as well as produce. Falconry, long a sport of kings, was practiced in the East as early as 1200 B.C. After the Norman conquest in 1066 it became the noble sport of England. A man's rank decided what species he could fly. Only the king rated the gyrfalcon; earls could sport with peregrines, yeomen with goshawks, and priests with smaller hawks. Today a handful of game birds fall prey to devotees of falconry; millions of birds drop before guns that bark over fields and waterways every fall. Happily, numbering even more than the hunters are those who find pleasure and adventure simply in watching or photographing wild birds.

Pigeon raising and racing attracts many fanciers. Famed as couriers in war, homing pigeons descended from the rock dove and may be the earliest domesticated birds. Pigeons have been bred into innumerable varieties, some for beauty, some for

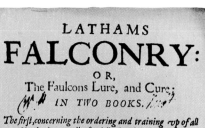

LATHAMS
FALCONRY:
OR,
The Faulcons Lure, and Cure;
IN TWO BOOKS.

The first, concerning the ordering and training up of all Hawkes in generall; especially the HAGGARD FAVLCON GENTLE.

The second, teaching approued medicines for the cure of all Diseases in them.

Gathered by long practice and experience, and published for the delight of noble mindes, and instruction of young Faulconers in things pertaining to this Princely Art.

By SYMON LATHAM. *Gent.*

THE HAGGARD FAVLCON IN OPEM ME COPIA FECIT

LONDON:
Printed by *Thomas Harper*, for *Iohn Harison*. 1633.

Hans Holbein, 1533; Mauritshuis, The Hague
Left: McGill Library, Montreal. Below: Estense Library, Modena, Italy

FALCON ON FIST, *men have hawked for meat or merriment some 3,000 years—ever since nomads on the steppes of Asia first feasted on the kills of birds they had trained.*

Spreading to medieval Europe, falconry became sport for gentry. Frederick II, Holy Roman Emperor in the 13th century, lost a battle when he left a siege operation to go hawking; his treatise on falconry remains a classic.

Ruling families coaxed, even abducted trainers from rival courts and collected manuscripts illuminated with scenes like that at left, from a 15th century Italian codex. A courtier of Henry VIII sat for a Holbein portrait with a gyrfalcon (above). Tudor monarchs decreed death to falcon thieves.

Today's small circle of devotees employs techniques little changed since Symon Latham penned Falconry *(above left), standard reference of the 17th century and one of more than 700 books dedicated to the art.*

Heirs to an ancient lineage, living birds of North America branch in 20 orders from the avian tree of life

FROM EARLY TIMES *man has marveled at the diversity of the birds around him and pondered the relationship of one kind to another. The Assyrians grouped them according to their habitat. Aristotle, father of natural history, dissected them and listed 170 kinds.*

Scientists today classify birds according to rules Linnaeus laid down in the 18th century in his monumental Systema Naturae. Ornithologists group birds through the combination of a wide variety of characters. External form of body, bill, and feet, internal anatomy, body chemistry, behavior—even parasites—provide clues to kinship. Similar birds have similar kinds of feather lice.

Closely related families are grouped in orders. Such seabirds as cormorants, frigatebirds, and boobies, as well as pelicans, belong to the Pelecaniformes. The Anseriformes include the waterfowl—ducks, geese, and swans. The earliest known relatives of our modern birds of prey, the hawks and vultures of the Falconiformes and the owls that make up the Strigiformes, appeared some 60 million years ago. North American fossil deposits of this era have yielded remains of rails of the order Gruiformes, and sandpipers which belong to the Charadriiformes along with gulls, plovers, and auks. The Passeriformes, largest and most highly developed order, contain about half the world's more than 8,600 avian species and include the true song birds.

Today, in field and laboratory, scientists add to the vast store of reference material on birds. In the forests of Panama the author (opposite) examines a parrot, one of the Psittaciformes. The lowest order, the Gaviiformes, has only one family, the loons, whose four species are presented in the next chapter.

Passeriformes — 27 334

Piciformes — 1 23

Coraciiformes — 1 3

Trogoniformes — 1 1

Apodiformes — 2 24

Caprimulgiformes — 1 6

Strigiformes — 2 18

Cuculiformes — 1 7

Psittaciformes — 1 1

Columbiformes — 1 15

Gruiformes — 3 16

Charadriiformes — 10 135

Galliformes — 4 21

Falconiformes — 4 38

Anseriformes — 1 62

Ciconiiformes — 4 23

Pelecaniformes — 6 18

Procellariiformes — 3 37

Podicipediformes — 1 6

Gaviiformes — 1 4

NUMBER OF FAMILIES
NUMBER OF SPECIES

speed, some for acrobatic ability. Tumbler pigeons can do backward somersaults.

Human pleasure in song, color, and sprightly movements helps explain why so many cage birds dwell in the homes of men. Parrots and cockatoos, brightly garbed mimics, have been favorites for centuries. The Australian budgerigar, or "budgie," now enjoys an equal vogue. The universally loved canary, a finch native to the Azores, Madeira, and Canary Islands, was first brought to Europe in the 16th century and has since been transported to countries throughout the world.

Birds as tame as cage birds often wander through the huts of primitive people. In the Gran Chaco of South America a baby rhea adopted me, staying so close that I never could get a good photograph of it. On cool mornings it lay across my slippered feet for warmth, and as I worked it leaned against my legs. I also recall a California gull that I cured of a sickness. Though free, it became as tame as any chicken. And a Canada goose once accepted me as an equal and followed me about like a dog.

Man's relationship with the world of birds is seldom as intimate as that. Yet our interest, expressed in many ways, has grown through the centuries. Fascinated by the variety of birds about us, we have studied them, classified them, sought to learn more about their intriguing ways. And with this knowledge has grown our understanding of our wild, winged neighbors. Our task now is to preserve and safeguard their world as part of our own.

M. Woodbridge Williams. Opposite: Walter A. Weber, National Geographic staff artist

DIVERS WITH EERIE VOICES

The Loons
Family Gaviidae

By GEORGE MIKSCH SUTTON

A BLIZZARD in early June put the finishing touch on the long winter. Afterwards a gentle south wind hurried the water birds northward – gulls, terns, guillemots, eiders, and a scattering of loons flying low above the icebound coast of Southampton, the big island at the mouth of Hudson Bay. The loons flew strongly, heads held low in their unmistakable fashion, big feet sticking straight behind, far beyond their tails. The red-throated loons, which the Eskimos call *kokshowk*, quacked like barnyard ducks. The larger Arctic loons, the *kudloolit*, gave a sort of growl. Both species were looking for open water, a place to rest. I watched eagerly as they passed. It was good to know that spring was returning.

All four species of the family Gaviidae are creatures of the northland. Since they spend most of their time afloat, they must migrate to find open water. But they do not leave the northern hemisphere. The common loon, southernmost of the species, ranges through the lake country of Canada and the northern United States. The smallest of the family, the red-throated loon, breeds northward almost to the limits of land. The largest, the yellow-billed loon, inhabits northern Eurasia and western regions of the American Arctic. In many parts of the Far North, in both the Old World and the New, you may find Arctic and red-throated loons, and in some places one of the others may occur as well. But nowhere do all four breed in the same area.

While breeding, and occasionally at other seasons, loons utter their famous cries. I know of few more beautiful sounds than the wild laughter of the common loon ringing through the night across a star-strewn lake. The courtship cries of red-throated loons remind me of college yells. Each bird calls *cocka-krah-oh, cocka-krah-oh* over and over. Several calling at once produce bedlam. The Arctic loon growls *kwuk kwuk kwuk* in anger or suspicion and sounds a puppy-like yelp just before he dives. Sometimes he calls *oo-loo-lee,* a sad, infinitely lonely cry.

With webbed feet set far back on his body and legs articulated to allow quick turns underwater, the loon is well adapted for catching fish. His legs are strong, his bill long and sharp. Special adaptations of his body enable him to dive deep. He waddles helplessly on land but knows how to handle himself in an emergency, as I saw on Jenny Lind Island in the Northwest Territories of Canada.

My companions and I discovered a red-throated loon's primitive nest at the edge of an islet in a tundra pond. As we came near, the loon slid off and dived, leaving a single egg. This gave two circling parasitic jaegers their chance. They alighted; one tapped the egg with his beak. We waved and shouted but neither of the jaegers paid much attention. Then came the surprise.

Out of the blue, swinging down in a magnificent curve, flew a loon — perhaps the one that had submerged, perhaps the mate. Any notions I had held about the awkwardness of loons vanished when I saw that one sweep in, feet spread, taut wings whistling. Striking the water, the loon sent up two great fans of spray. The jaegers left in a hurry. Seeing us, the loon dived.

Then the jaegers returned to the egg. Surfacing, the loon charged, racing across the water, wings flailing noisily. Barking and snarling, it stabbed at the jaegers with its bill, dashing back and forth, never leaving the water, the element where it was safe and effective. Presently the robbers acknowledged defeat and flew away. When last we looked, the loon was sitting quietly on that precious egg.

GRACEFUL BRACE *of common loons finds privacy in a spruce-rimmed northland lake*

John W. Taylor

Common loons, length 28-36"; Charles J. Ott, National Audubon Society. Below: juvenile, Allan Brooks

Common Loon
Gavia immer

FOR THOSE who know the wild lake country, who have lived with moonlit water, little campfires, long portages, and the solemn darkness of the spruce forest, one sound brings back the *feel* of the north woods. Call it mirthless "laughter" if you will. But the high, far-carrying, liquid tremolo of the common loon sets your spine atingle. Some who hear it feel a longing for the wilderness that is hard to dispel.

Spring after spring the loons move northward in twosomes—birds that may well have been paired for a long time. Resplendent in breeding plumage, they arrive on their home lakes. Here their calls echo. Sometimes two birds, perhaps rival males, work themselves into a vocal frenzy with a yodeling cry that carries far and sets off a chain of answering yodels from other loons.

Always the birds return to the same northern lakes to nest—usually one pair to a lake. They seek out their old nesting site—a mound of turf at the water's edge, a heap of debris requiring a bit of rebuilding, perhaps a muskrat house. They favor the lee side of an islet or the end of a peninsula. They want deep water, since they come and go secretively, below the surface.

Two eggs, long and dark brown spotted with black, lie an inch or so apart in the nest. They stay apart most of the time, for the incubation "pouches" in the adults' plumage do not adjoin. As with all loons, incubation starts when the first egg is laid. During the month-long chore the lake may become so quiet on a warm spring day that the sitting bird naps. But a hint of danger sends it off the nest and into the water.

The downy chicks, dark gray except for the white of the belly and undersides of the wings, take to the water as soon as the down dries. Aged one day, they are fed whole fish and crustaceans. Extremely buoyant, a chick swims close behind the head of the nearly submerged parent. When the broad back rises to the surface, the chick rides high and dry among the warm feathers.

The common loon swims very fast underwater, and like all loons can sink by compressing the feathers and squeezing air from the body.

The yellow-billed loon (*Gavia adamsii*), larger than the common, has a slightly upturned bill whose ivory color shows up from afar. It nests on rivers and large lakes in northwestern North

40

America and northern Eurasia. Eskimos still use its head as an ornament and give the bird a place in their folklore.

Far more familiar, the common loon may be seen in migration almost anywhere in the United States. It is the state bird of Minnesota.

Range: N. W. Alaska to Iceland, south to N. E. California, N. W. Montana, N. Ohio, and Newfoundland; winters mainly along coasts to N. W. Mexico, Gulf states, and S. Florida; also Great Lakes and Europe. *Characteristics:* straight black bill, black head and neck with greenish gloss, white-streaked collar; white underparts, black back checkered with white. Young and winter adults have gray upperparts, white throat.

Arctic loon, length 23-29"; C. G. Hampson

Red-throated Loon
Gavia stellata

SMALLEST OF LOONS, the redthroat wears a distinctive neck patch only during breeding season. But you can always identify the bird by the slight uptilt of the bill. This loon needs far less water for landing and takeoff than its cousins—indeed, it is the only loon that can fly from the ground. And it ranges farther north.

On a shallow tundra pond courting redthroats paddle furiously in unison, half standing in the water, heads bowed stiffly. Sometimes a pair swim slowly, bills agape and partly submerged, then suddenly dive, kicking up spray.

If the two dark brown, spotted eggs escape jaegers and foxes, the downy gray hatchlings make for the pond, often riding on a parent's back to reach it. In early fall the loons move south.

Range: Alaska to N. Greenland, south to S. W. British Columbia, N. Manitoba, S. Ontario, and Newfoundland; winters on the Great Lakes and along the coasts to N. Mexico and S. Florida. Also found in Europe and Asia. *Characteristics:* lower mandible slightly upturned, gray head, hindneck streaked with white; chestnut throat patch, blackish-brown back, white underparts. Young and winter adults have white throat, spotted back.

Red-throated loon, length 24-27"; Arthur A. Allen

Arctic Loon
Gavia arctica

IN REGIONS where the redthroat and the Arctic loon summer together, the redthroat usually breeds at a shallow pond and fishes in larger lakes or the sea. The Arctic loon, slightly bigger and with a straight bill, prefers to nest beside a deep lake well stocked with fish. The two loons have similar call notes, but the Arctic, just before diving, gives a doglike yelp.

Courting birds circle the lake, then plummet amid sheets of spray. The two spotted brown eggs lie in an unlined scrape at water's edge.

On bright windy summer days six or eight adults may gather to frolic amid the whitecaps. They lunge at each other, dive, pop up, and take to the air, wings slapping the waves. On a chill morning in early fall the lake falls silent. Most families, even those in northeast Canada, head for winter quarters on the Pacific coast.

Range: Alaska and N. Canada; winters along Pacific coast to N. Mexico. Also found in Europe and Asia. *Characteristics:* thin, straight bill, gray crown and nape, black throat streaked with white, black back checkered with white; white breast streaked at sides. Plumage of young and winter adults resembles that of common loon.

James P. Blair, National Geographic photographer

POWERFUL SWIMMERS AND DIVERS

The Grebes

Family Podicipedidae

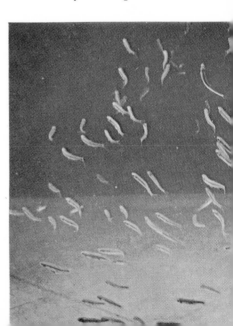

W HEN MILLINERS sought feathers for ladies' hats, North American grebes suffered. Their plumage is soft and silky – one of the features that distinguishes these diving birds from the loons.

Another difference is their feet. A grebe's feet are set far back on the body, like a loon's, so that the bird must jerk itself forward on land with the help of its wings. But the grebe's toes are not webbed together. Instead they have broad flaps that overlap and serve as paddles, as webbed feet do.

Afloat, the bird may remind you of a duck, but it sits higher in the water, has a longer and slenderer neck, and its beak tapers to a point. Grebes can dive in a flash if sudden danger threatens, or sink slowly out of sight if merely uncertain. To fly they must run and flap through the water for a great distance, and once airborne they labor along with rapid wingbeats, steering with their feet since they have practically no tail.

Some of the world's 18 species of Podicipedidae are confined to a single island or large lake. But three of the six North American species—the red-necked, horned, and eared grebes—occur in the Old World as well. Another, the pied-billed grebe, ranges from southern Canada to southern South America.

In North America grebes breed almost exclusively in fresh water, where vegetation provides cover and nest material. In migration and during winter many show up in salt water. Few water birds match the grebes for showmanship at mating time. With wails, brays, shrieks, mews, and chuckles both sexes dance intricate water ballets and race one another. Each species has its own repertoire.

After mating, both birds help build a floating home of plant debris. When the eggs have hatched, the parents carry the youngsters piggyback. Adult grebes even dive with their young held in place under the folded wings. But regularly the babies come loose and pop to the surface like downy corks.

Strangely, grebes eat their own feathers, retaining them in their stomachs in a tight ball until they disintegrate enough to pass through. The clumps may hold back such objects as fish bones until they are soft enough to digest.

COURTING WESTERN GREBES *(below) spar with bills, entwine necks, and take off on stylized chases. Lobed toes propel a horned grebe (right and bottom), diving for minnows in a laboratory tank. "Wait for me!" peeps a baby pied-billed grebe (opposite) who slipped off its parent's back.*

Frederick Kent Truslow

David G. Allen

43

Horned grebe, length 12-15"; Charles J. Ott, National Audubon Society

Horned Grebe
Podiceps auritus

BOTH SEXES of this handsome species wear horn-like reddish-yellow plumes that explain their name. And both participate in nuptial displays. Treading water, they rise upright and face each other, then circle, shaking plumes and touching bills. They dive together and soon pop up, one presenting a bunch of waterweeds to the other. More plume shaking and circling lead to mating.

At their secluded breeding ground in a northern marsh the cheeky little birds may not bother to hide their nest. But approach it and one rushes at you with horns elevated, rises to kick the water furiously, and gives an ear-splitting screech.

The soggy nest hardly seems worth all the fuss, yet it is a clever engineering feat—a raft of mud and plants, anchored usually to stalks of cattails or bulrushes. A shallow depression holds the four or five whitish eggs. For 24 or 25 days the birds take turns incubating them.

Both parents dive for tiny aquatic animals to feed the chicks. Often the youngsters scramble up on their parents' backs or under their wings and nap. As the young gain more independence the father loses interest and moves away. The mother remains until the brood is fully grown. Cool weather sends the grebes—now minus their feather horns—into winter quarters, mainly along the coasts but to some extent on the Great Lakes and other inland waters.

Range: W. Alaska to N. New York and Nova Scotia, south to E. Idaho and Wisconsin; winters along coasts to S. California and S. Texas. Also found in Europe and Asia. *Characteristics:* thin dark bill, tawny "horns," glossy blackish crown and cheek ruff, blackish back, chestnut throat, breast, sides, and rump; white belly and wing patch. In winter, white cheeks and underparts.

Red-necked Grebe
Podiceps grisegena

HEAD WEAVING to the rhythm of paddling feet, a shy bird in drab winter plumage swims off lonely headlands and beaches, just beyond the surf. At times the swimmer pauses to peer underwater, then dives after a fish or crustacean.

Spring turns this bird into a red-necked grebe with a cocky curl in its crown. Joining a flock, the redneck, also called Holboell's grebe, migrates far inland to secluded northern lakes. On an early May morn the waters resound to eerie

Red-necked grebes, length 18-22½"

Eared grebe, length 12-14"; Arthur A. Allen (also left)

voices—rednecks often sound like whinnying horses. As more flocks arrive on succeeding nights the chorus swells. Birds rush to and fro with a roar of beating wings and a thrashing of feet. Then abruptly they disperse in pairs to establish nesting territories.

Here male and female circle in courtship rites, black crowns raised like tricorn hats. They rise breast to breast, swim side by side, all the while uttering a tuneless duet of nasal rattles.

Their floating nest is always wet, and their four or five white eggs take on a brownish stain from its decaying plants. For 23 days the adults share incubation. Unlike horned grebes, nesting rednecks show no hostility to intruders, they simply retire out of sight. The hatchlings hide under the folded wings of their parents and ride along even when the adults dive for food.

Range: N. W. Alaska to N. W. Ontario, south to N. Washington and S. Minnesota, sporadically east to New Hampshire; winters along coasts to S. California and central Florida. Also found in Europe and Asia. *Characteristics:* yellowish bill, tufted black crown glossed with green; whitish cheeks, wing patches, wing linings, and underparts; dark gray back, reddish throat. In winter, brownish crown, white face crescent and throat.

Eared Grebe
Podiceps caspicus

ANY SHALLOW WESTERN LAKE or prairie slough may furnish a summer home for the eared grebe, provided it is reed-bordered and large enough to support many pairs. These dumpy little birds with perky crests and bright tufts behind the eyes congregate by the hundreds. They sound squeaky *poo-eep* cries as they court in mid-lake.

Eared grebes choose homesites only a few feet apart. Together they start building; they take off in a group to rest and feed; they even complete their well-hidden platforms in unison.

Each nest takes only a few hours to build—and the workmanship shows this. Shallow and fragile, it lies almost level with the water, so the three or four whitish eggs are partly wet. A bird arriving to incubate nearly upsets the nest at its reed mooring and threatens to tip out the eggs.

If disturbed, all sitting birds in a colony slip off their nests and disappear. Moments later they show up out on the lake. Danger over, they return underwater, all emerging almost simultaneously beside their nests and hopping on.

After the chicks appear, each adult takes part of the brood and goes its own way. In three weeks the young are independent too.

Range: British Columbia to W. Minnesota, south to Baja California, central Arizona, and S. Texas; winters to Colombia. Also found in Europe, Asia, and Africa. *Characteristics:* slightly upturned bill, crested black head, tawny "ears," black neck and breast, brownish-black back, white wing patch and belly, brownish sides. In winter, whitish cheeks, neck, and breast.

Western Grebe
Aechmophorus occidentalis

MAY BRINGS flocks of distinctively black-and-white grebes back to their northwestern breeding grounds—an azure lake, perhaps, where the colony nested the year before. Here these largest of North American grebes—sometimes called swan grebes because of their long, slender necks and stately swimming style—steal the show from ducks, coots, gulls, and terns.

The western grebes stab at the ducks, often from underwater. A canvasback, sailing serenely and minding its own business, rises suddenly, splashing frantically. Moments later the guilty grebe bobs up, all innocence, and glides away.

In nesting season western grebes engage in strange races. Two birds approach each other, heads low, throats swollen, red eyes bulging, crests erect. They dip their beaks in the water and shake them with a rapid clicking. Now, as if on signal, they turn sideways, rise upright, arch their wings, bend their necks in an S curve, and dash ahead, seeming to run on the water. Then they dive, emerge, and swim sedately abreast.

This strange race may be performed by birds of the same sex, and sometimes by more than two individuals. Apparently it is a sort of social ceremony that releases nervous energy.

Building the nest in the bulrushes, the male often brings the material; the female puts it in place. Both incubate the three or four eggs, which hatch in about 23 days. Incubation begins before the second egg is laid, so the chicks emerge on successive days. Yet the newest and smallest gets as much attention as the oldest.

Unlike chicks of other grebes, which are striped and spotted, these are uniformly pale gray with short, thick, velvety down.

October marks the departure of western grebes for Pacific coastal waters. In sounds, bays, and harbors they pass the winter, still in large flocks, still stealing the show.

Range: S. British Columbia to N. Alberta and S. Manitoba, south to central California, N. North Dakota, and locally from S.W. Colorado to S.W. Minnesota; winters along Pacific coast to W. Mexico. *Characteristics:* large size, long thin neck; yellowish bill, blackish upperparts; white face, throat, wing patch, and underparts.

Western grebe arriving to incubate, length 22-29"; Allan D. Cruickshank, National Audubon Society

Least Grebe
Podiceps dominicus

ONLY IN SOUTH TEXAS does the smallest of our grebes dwell within the United States. Dark and drab, with orange eyes, it stays on ponds and backwaters, breeding practically the year round.

Least grebes display modestly, except when they race and utter high-pitched, nasal calls. Both sexes build the floating nest, and until the four to six whitish eggs hatch they never cease remodeling it. Approach, and they circle you, beating the water, calling, feigning attack, then hastily retreating. They may actually strike larger birds such as pied-billed grebes.

Two weeks after a clutch hatches the female may lay again. Caring for young and incubating at the same time keeps the parents busy. Sometimes both tend the chicks, letting the sun warm the eggs. As soon as the young can fend for themselves, out they go. By this time chicks of the second brood are taking their first excursions, snug on the back of one parent while the other feeds them insect larvae and other morsels. Home again, the chicks tumble off to rest and preen. Earlier broods linger at the pond for a year or so until old enough to breed.

Range: Baja California to S. Texas, south to Argentina; also in West Indies. *Characteristics:* small size, short neck, orange eye, short straight bill, black crown and chin, slaty-brown back, white wing patch and underparts. When not breeding, brownish cap, golden eye, white chin.

Pied-billed Grebe

Podilymbus podiceps

HELLDIVER, water witch, dabchick—these are some local names for our commonest grebe. In summer it may frequent almost any reed-bordered pond from southern Canada south through the 48 states. Its pied bill, shaped like a chicken's, is distinctive. Close up, you may see the ring around it that explains the name.

Arriving on their northern range with most of the ducks, pied-billed grebes retire into fast-growing reeds to nest. All day and even at night you hear their loud *cow-cow-cow-cow-cow, cow-hu, cow-hu,* slow at first, then speeding up.

From a blind you can see a head emerge like a periscope beside a floating mass of vegetation. Slowly the bird rises, jumps on the nest, uncovers four to seven whitish eggs, and settles on them. If you wait the mate shows up—you cannot tell the sex—and takes a turn. If you make a sound the sitter covers the eggs, then dives.

In fall these shy birds lose the ring on their bills. Migrating, they sometimes land on wet pavement, mistaking it for open water, then cannot take off again. One got back in the air by running with flapping wings across a clipped lawn.

Range: S. British Columbia to N. Manitoba and Nova Scotia, south to Argentina; migratory in the north. *Characteristics:* black band around whitish, chickenlike bill; black throat patch, gray-brown upperparts, white underparts. In winter, whitish throat, dusky or yellowish bill.

east grebe, length 8-10"; Paul Schwartz

Pied-billed grebe, length 12-15"; Allan D. Cruickshank
National Audubon Society

47

The Albatrosses

Family Diomedeidae

By JOHN W. ALDRICH

EW SPECIES OF BIRDS have aroused more controversy than the famed albatrosses of the Midway Islands. Coleridge's Ancient Mariner ascribed supernatural power to the albatross, but the modern mariner of the United States Navy respects it for more tangible reasons—particularly if he has served at the Midway Naval Station in the North Pacific, where the birds nest by the thousands.

Over the years operations officers in Midway's control tower have sweated it out while great radar-equipped picket planes roared down the runway and took off through hundreds of soaring albatrosses, or "gooney birds." Before clearing the ground a plane might hit a goose-size albatross with seven-foot wingspan and have to return for repairs, leaving a gap in the network of our national defense.

In years of trying to drive albatrosses away from the runways, the Navy used just about every weapon except the Ancient Mariner's crossbow. Clubs, flares, rocket launchers, smoke, and ultrahigh-frequency sound waves failed to discourage the birds. I was in charge of a team of U. S. Fish and Wildlife Service scientists assigned to help, and we had the ticklish job of finding a solution agreeable both to the Navy, concerned about safety, and to conservationists who wanted the birds preserved.

Albatrosses have many admirers. Masters of the air currents, they follow ships for days, soaring effortlessly in S's and 8's, setting their narrow tapered wings with the precision of racing skippers trimming sail. Sometimes they are caught on baited fishhooks and pulled aboard ship. They waddle clumsily about the deck, often unable to take off over the gunwales because of cramped space. Paradoxically, these seagoing birds become as seasick as any landlubber.

Perhaps because of this ludicrous shipboard behavior, sailors call the larger albatrosses "gooneys" or "goneys," meaning dunce. Yet they look with respect upon the royal and wandering albatrosses, largest of all seabirds. Weighing as much as 18 pounds, these graceful rovers of the southern oceans spread their wings 11 to 12 feet, the longest span of any bird. One wandering albatross, bearing a note tied round its neck by the crew of a whaling vessel, flew 3,150 nautical miles in 12 days!

The 14 species of the albatross family roam all the oceans except the North Atlantic and the Arctic. Most of them stay in the roaring forties, the windy waters of the southern hemisphere, for the equatorial doldrums can becalm them, like the Ancient Mariner's vessel, "as idle as a painted ship upon a painted ocean." Three species have been reported ranging in North American waters. The gray-and-white Laysan albatross (*Diomedea immutabilis*), resembling an overgrown seagull, and the soot-colored black-footed albatross (*Diomedea nigripes*) cruise near our West Coast, riding winds that filled the sails of clipper ships. Bones of the short-tailed albatross, largest North Pacific species, abound in old Indian kitchen middens on the Oregon and California coasts, but this almost extinct bird no longer ventures there.

Midway's gooneys—the Laysan and the blackfoot—were little known until Pan American Airways built a base for its transpacific clippers on the mid-Pacific atoll in 1935. A hotel there was named Gooneyville Lodge, and a golf course received worldwide billing as the only one with gooney birds nesting on its fairways.

During the Battle of Midway in World War II these birds took Japanese bombings in stride. And they persevered when the defenders eliminated thousands of them to reduce hazards to aircraft. As Midway's postwar traffic grew, the rate of bird-plane collisions became alarming. When I arrived at Midway in 1956 our plane hit two Laysan albatrosses. In the passenger cabin, I was unaware of the impact until we landed and I heard of it from the crew. They showed me the dents in the plane's wings. This was mid-November, when albatrosses arriving on the nesting grounds in great numbers swarmed over the runways. Four out of ten planes operating in daylight struck birds. And about one in 15 collisions caused damage—broken windshields and antennas, dented radomes and cowling, torn wings and stabilizers, bent propellers. Some damaged planes nearly careened into the lagoon.

NAVY PLANE *tallies the Laysan and black-footed albatrosses it struck above its base on Midway atoll in the Pacific. Such blows were a bane— reminiscent of the curse that befell Coleridge's Ancient Mariner when he slew an albatross with his crossbow—for these collisions canceled missions and could wreck a plane. Gooneys long defied all attempts to move them from runways.*

Robert B. Goodman. Opposite: Karl W. Kenyon

SOARING DAY AND NIGHT,
*the albatross wanders
the world's widest ocean.
Black-footed gooneys
roam to the limits
of the flight range;
Laysans keep within
the dotted lines.
Homeward bound,
the tireless rovers
chart courses
fantastically true.
One banded bird
from Midway flew
all the way in
from Puget Sound,
some 3,200 miles,
in only ten days.
Another, released
in the Philippines,
found its way home
across 4,120 miles
of empty ocean.*

    *Sand Island (right),
Midway's air center
ringed with coral
reefs, was long
the battleground
for man and bird.
The gooney (below),
like the Navy planes
he threatened,
needs a run upwind
to get airborne.*

Robert B. Goodman

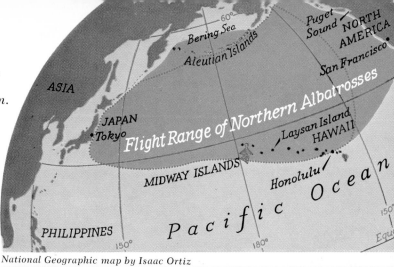

National Geographic map by Isaac Ortiz

Nobody wanted to slaughter the gooneys; we simply hoped to chase them away. But how? First we tried smoke. Daylight flares wafted orange clouds over 130 black-footed albatrosses. No birds moved. We placed a burning truck tire near five of the black gooneys; it produced an acrid black cloud. One gooney moved because of the heat but returned to its egg in a few minutes. No birds left the area.

Next, Marines fired a mortar. Birds no more than 200 feet from the mortar continued to sleep, and none of those any closer moved away. Bazookas did no better. The backflash ruffled the feathers of brooding birds, but none moved. Loudspeakers beamed sound waves of varying lengths at the albatrosses—without success. Disagreeable odors also failed. The smell of naphthalene, commonly used to repel insects, did not even cause the gooneys to turn up their noses.

Black-footed albatrosses, length 28-36"
Robert B. Goodman

Why do gooneys seem to fear neither man nor machine? Perhaps because the birds had no enemies on the oceanic islands until the turn of this century, when the trade in feathers for ladies' hats reached its peak. Man's first serious threat to gooneys probably came with the Japanese plume seekers who wiped out the albatrosses on several North Pacific islands. But U. S. authorities during the presidency of Theodore Roosevelt stepped in before hunters could complete their slaughter on Midway and other islands in the Hawaiian chain.

After World War II a survey calculated Midway's Laysan albatrosses at 110,000, its black-footed birds at 53,000. A more recent estimate showed populations of 200,000 Laysan and 17,000 black-footed gooneys, making Midway second only to Laysan Island—about 390 miles to the east—as an albatross nesting ground.

Plainly, we were confronted with two species lacking the usual nervous, or fear, responses. Before we could control the gooneys, we would have to make a thorough study of their life history and behavior—find their Achilles' heel.

On bicycles, our biologists began exploring every part of the great bird city. We grasped nesting birds by the neck—firmly, for their beaks can inflict painful wounds—and clamped numbered aluminum bands on their legs.

Albatrosses possess an extraordinary homing ability. To test it, two of our team members banded 18 Laysan albatrosses and shipped them by air to distant points in the North Pacific. Fourteen returned to their nests on Midway. The long-distance record went to one which made a 4,120-mile flight from the Philippines in 32 days. We abandoned all idea of exiling the nesting birds from Midway to other islands.

Evidence indicated that our two species begin to breed at about the age of five years, though seven is considered the more normal age. Adult birds spend the nine months of breeding season

LIKE A COUNTRY-DANCE COUPLE *bowing and stomping through the figures of a Virginia reel, black-footed albatrosses tread the measure of their courtship display on Midway. Mooing like a cow, one raises high his beak. Then the partners, identical to human eyes, "honor" each other, wings akimbo, and step sedately forward to bob heads, bill to bill.*

Laysan albatross, length 32"; Karl W. Kenyon

IT'S CHOWTIME ON MIDWAY *and a Laysan albatross regurgitates partially digested squids and oil into the eager bill of a chick. The parents stop these feedings after about 165 days, and soon the youngster soars away to sea.*

on Midway; they spend the other three months at sea, soaring on ocean winds and the updrafts created by waves. When calm weather brings them down, they sleep on the water like ducks. They range across the Pacific and north into the Bering Sea, feeding chiefly on squid. They must dine largely at night, since that is when squid are most active at the surface. Numbers of indigestible beaks and "cuttlefish bones" of these sea creatures, disgorged by the birds, lie around the nests. Albatrosses also may trail a ship for the sake of jettisoned garbage.

Like many other seabirds, gooneys drink only sea water. They have special glands in their heads which enable them to eliminate excess salt from the blood. In fact, the birds cannot remain healthy on fresh water alone. Those kept in zoos must be supplied with salt tablets to go with their food.

The gooneys start returning to Midway in late October – a great event for the islanders. In from the blue Pacific they glide, over the line of breakers on the barrier reef, across the green lagoon and the brush-covered dunes, along the beach and down the streets. Each heads unerringly for the nest site he has used for years. Down go the wing and tail flaps. Down go the broad, webbed feet. But can months at sea make a bird forget how to land? Perhaps.

Robert B. Goodman

Brakes aren't set soon enough. Speed's too great. Landing gear collapses. In a flurry of gyrating wings and disheveled feathers a bird sprawls across the ground. Each new albatross picks himself up with an embarrassed look as crowds of recent arrivals stand by, squealing, groaning, and clapping their bills.

Both species nest in colonies, black gooneys on the open beaches and whites near clumps of bushes or in the shade of ironwood trees. Areas near runways offer many such protected sites, so the far more numerous white gooneys are the main menace to fliers. Both species scoop shallow depressions in the sand, but the whites add weeds, sticks, and debris. Male and female take turns incubating their single pale, brown-blotched egg. For stints of two weeks or more the brooding parent never leaves the four-inch egg unattended—even though he may be buried up to his neck in windblown sand. He may lose a quarter of his weight for lack of food and sea water. The off-duty parent often roams thousands of miles over the North Pacific.

In January the albatross egg hatches. The fuzzy chick pokes his bill inside that of his parent to receive regurgitated food. By summer he has reached full size. Parental feeding visits become fewer and fewer, and finally stop. The young albatross lives on stored fat. Then, having exercised his wings for weeks, he takes off over the ocean. Should his wings fail now, he may fall to sharks waiting offshore. If he flies successfully, perhaps two years will go by before he sets foot on dry land again, another three to five years before he begins to breed.

Those gooneys that nested nearest the runways constituted the worst hazard. We began eliminating them. But to our surprise, the number of birds over the runways *increased*. Apparently the non-nesting birds seeking homesites were attracted by the depopulated strip in a thriving gooney colony. And since they were not yet tied down to nests or young, they spent most of their time cruising about. So we abandoned this plan too.

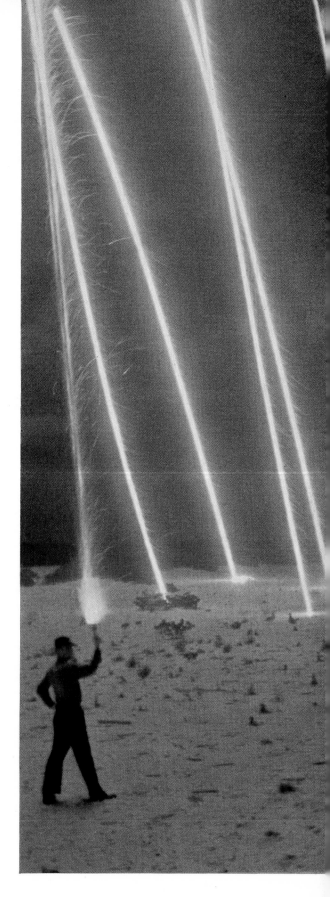

We kept looking. Finally we found the clue. Gooneys seemed to concentrate over parts of runways near uneven terrain.

The conclusion became inescapable — gooneys tend to soar over dunes and wartime revetments. These deflect winds up, producing currents ideal for gliding.

Seabees now swung into action. They leveled all the land near the most used runway. They also blacktopped 750-foot strips on both sides of that runway's center to prevent nesting. Immediately bird-plane collisions decreased.

At last the Navy had its answer. The leveling and paving continued. Unfortunately, birds nesting beside the runways had to be eliminated. Otherwise these homeless ones would soar aimlessly over the traffic zone, increasing the hazard. But the 17,000 gooneys involved — mostly Laysans — comprised only a fraction of the albatrosses on Midway and less than one percent of the world population.

Now, hopefully, modern mariners of Midway can view the autumn return of their gooneys without mixed emotions.

Black-footed albatross — *Range:* Tori Shima in the Izu Islands of Japan, Kaula and the Leeward Islands of Hawaii; wanders to E. Asia coast and coast of North America from Aleutians to S. Baja California. *Characteristics:* large blackish body, gray belly, whitish face, black feet. Young are dark brown.

Laysan albatross — *Range:* Leeward and Niihau Islands of Hawaii; wanders to Japan and coast of North America from Aleutians to Baja California. *Characteristics:* white head, neck, rump, underparts, and wing lining; blackish-gray back, wings, and tail; pinkish feet.

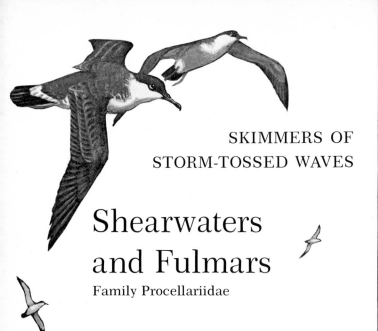

SKIMMERS OF
STORM-TOSSED WAVES

Shearwaters
and Fulmars

Family Procellariidae

A TROPICAL STORM rages against the East Coast of the United States and moves inland, leaving sullen surf to growl on the scoured beaches. Bird watchers appear, patrolling the sands to see what strange birds have been hurled ashore. Sometimes they find a short-bodied bird with long, tapered wings and mark it down as one of the Procellariidae — the shearwaters, petrels, and fulmars.

This may be the first such bird recorded since the last big storm, even though the Procellariidae are not rare. Charles Darwin, in fact, labeled the fulmars the world's most numerous species. But the 64 members of the family are relatively little known because they nest on remote islands and headlands and spend the rest of their lives on the ocean far from any land, skimming for hours on end above the waves, or resting upon them.

REMOTE ISLETS *of volcanic Tristan da Cunha archipelago comprise the*

No one could mistake these birds. All have cylindrical nasal tubes atop their beaks, a feature they share with albatrosses. In size these seabirds range from the three-foot-long giant petrel of Antarctic regions to petrels no larger than some of the sparrow-size storm petrels of the family Hydrobatidae. In plumage they vary from the drably garbed shearwaters, black, brown, or gray with light underparts, to the handsome gull-like fulmar. And though many of the species are abundant, two — the black-capped and Bermuda petrels — have barely avoided extinction.

In the air the birds share a graceful and distinctive manner of flight: a few rapid wingbeats, then an interval of gliding. They sweep so low over the ocean that they seem to cut the surface with their wing tips — hence the name "shearwater."

On land, however, these seabirds stumble and waddle ineptly, often falling forward on their breasts, sometimes shuffling with the aid of their wings. Approach one and it may vomit an oil whose reek generally drives off intruders. Inhabitants of the Hebridean island of St. Kilda, where thousands of fulmars nest, used to brave the stench to collect the oil for use as medicine.

James P. Blair, National Geographic photographer. Opposite: greater shearwaters, John W. Taylor

only known nesting sites for greater shearwaters. Villagers on the main *island (above) brave South Atlantic seas to collect eggs from the breeding places.*

Some of the family dig burrows for their nests; some settle in crevices or piles of rubble. Fulmars nest on cliffs, completely covering the rocky heights. When you try to get near such a headland it seems to dissolve in flying birds.

Members of the family migrate vast distances and exhibit extraordinary homing instinct. All the greater shearwaters nest only on three small islands, Nightingale, Inaccessible, and Gough, near Tristan da Cunha in the South Atlantic. In April most of them soar northward along the western side of the Atlantic.

Thousands swarm about the fishing fleets on the Grand Banks off Newfoundland, quarreling over scraps. They move on toward Davis Strait, between Canada and Greenland, and near its mouth spread out to the northeast. Then the shearwaters start funneling back toward their nesting grounds. In late August and early September millions of them sweep in to the little plots of land. Watchers on Nightingale tell of the birds tumbling into the tall grass or through the branches of trees, somersaulting and tripping as they crash-land. But once on the ground, they head purposefully for their own burrows among the millions that riddle the turf. They have nested here so long that the island rocks are scarred by their feet.

Fulmar
Fulmarus glacialis

TRANSATLANTIC PASSENGERS, braving the boat deck of their liner as it batters through cold, wind-ripped seas, note with astonishment a group of seabirds with pearl-gray wings and white bellies escorting the ship. Herring gulls? So far from land, and in weather like this?

A close look as one bird swings near reveals that it is smaller than a herring gull, has a stouter bill, and lacks the gull's black wing tips. This is a fulmar, sailing with its flock above the North Atlantic. Stocky yet sleek-looking, *glacialis* flies with graceful buoyancy.

Fulmars nest in colonies on bleak, rocky headlands. Around the coasts of the British Isles, where nesting is on the increase, the birds have scouted the crumbling walls of ancient castles for homesites. In a shallow depression lined with grass and herbaceous plants the female lays her single white egg. Both sexes incubate it. They feed their youngster by regurgitation.

If threatened the fulmar resorts to the unlovely habit of spewing odorous stomach oil at intruders. The musty smell clings to the bird even after it has entered a museum cabinet.

Silent most of the time, fulmars utter soft guttural croaks while on the nest and sometimes cackle and quack excitedly while feeding in flocks. They dine on plankton, jellyfish, and shrimp, and gather hungrily about the floating carcass of a whale. Old-time whalers reported that fulmars followed their ships for scraps.

The birds and their eggs serve as food for man in many places. Islanders have taken fulmars by the tens of thousands with little impact on the huge world population of the species. But Iceland bans their capture because some of the birds carry psittacosis, a disease harmful to man.

One subspecies ranges through the Bering Sea and North Pacific. As in the two Atlantic races, the birds may occur in light or dark color phases.

Range: Siberian, Alaskan, and Canadian Arctic islands to Novaya Zemlya, south to Norway and Great Britain; winters to waters off Japan, Baja California, New England, and France. *Characteristics:* stubby yellow bill, white head and underparts, pearl-gray back and wings. In dark phase, plumage is smoky gray.

Cory's Shearwater
Puffinus diomedea

LARGEST of our shearwaters and the commonest off New England shores in late summer and fall, the Cory's cruises with slow wingbeats as it searches for small fish and crustaceans.

Silent at sea, these birds wail harshly around their Old World breeding islands. Each female lays one white egg in a cliff crevice or burrow.

Range: islands off Portugal and N. W. Africa and in the Mediterranean; wanders over Mediterranean and Atlantic from latitude 44° N. to 36° S. Seen off North America from Newfoundland to South Carolina. *Characteristics:* large yellowish bill, grayish-brown upperparts blending to white underparts.

Pink-footed shearwater length 19-20"

Fulmar, dark phase length 17-20"

Cory's shearwater length 21"

Fulmar, light phase

Pink-footed Shearwater
Puffinus creatopus

A COASTWISE ROVER, the pinkfoot may sweep nearly the entire length of the Pacific shoreline of both Americas after nesting chores end.

In summer you'll find this heavy-bodied, thick-billed shearwater off the coast from California to Alaska. It flaps and sails on narrow, stiffly held wings, and dives for squid and small fishes.

In September–spring in the southern hemisphere–pink-footed shearwaters begin to arrive for nesting at a few Chilean islands. On one, Más a Tierra in the Juan Fernández group, a stranded Scottish seaman lived through adventures which inspired the Robinson Crusoe story.

Each nest burrow, 6 to 10 feet long, holds a single white egg. Unseen by day, the birds mill around at night, cackling and screaming.

Range: Chilean islands; wanders over E. Pacific to waters off S. E. Alaska. *Characteristics:* pale bill with dark tip; pink feet, grayish-brown upperparts, white throat and belly.

Pale-footed Shearwater
Puffinus carneipes

FROM THEIR NATIVE HAUNTS in the southwest Pacific, a few pale-footed shearwaters visit our West Coast. Perhaps more of them come than we know, for these dark-bodied birds can easily be mistaken for the more common sooty shearwaters. The light-colored bill and dark wing linings distinguish *carneipes*.

In its habits the palefoot resembles the pink-footed shearwater. Though they differ in plumage and nest far apart, they are regarded by some authorities as races of a single species.

Range: islands off Australia and New Zealand; wanders over W. Pacific and Indian Ocean. Sometimes seen off the Pacific coast of the United States and Canada. *Characteristics:* dark-tipped pale bill, pale pinkish feet, dark brown body.

Greater Shearwater
Puffinus gravis

FOR MONTHS the huge flocks roam the vast perimeter of the Atlantic. Then, in August and September, the entire breeding population of greater shearwaters converges on three islets in the Tristan da Cunha group, about midway between South America and Africa.

Some four million shearwaters squeeze onto the single square mile of Nightingale Island, where the nesting burrows average three to every two square yards. Another million of these birds occupy the two other islands. Nobody lives on Nightingale; when men visit, the honeycombed earth crumbles as they walk. In the evening clouds of shearwaters swarm in from sea. The air resounds with their croaking calls. Soon the ground is covered with the birds.

For about 55 days the two adults in each burrow take turns incubating the single white egg. The chick hatches in January, and by the end of May young and old are off for the "grand tour."

They move quickly up the western Atlantic; by June the early birds have reached New England and the Grand Banks off Newfoundland. They are easily recognized by the sharp contrast between the dark cap and white throat. Fishermen call them hagdons. At one time seamen "chummed up" the shearwaters with fish entrails. When the birds crowded round the boat to eat, they were hooked and used for food and bait.

Hunting small fish and squid, greater shearwaters fly close to the water. On windy days they can stay aloft for hours without a wingbeat.

They spread north and east over the Atlantic. As summer wanes the breeders swing south to complete the circuit to their tiny islands.

Range: Tristan da Cunha island group; wanders over most of the Atlantic. *Characteristics:* thin dark bill, blackish crown, grayish-brown back, whitish rump band, white underparts.

Pale-footed shearwater
length 19½"

Greater shearwater
length 18-20"

59

John W. Taylor

Sooty Shearwater
Puffinus griseus

RISE AND DIP, flutter and glide, over the wave and down the trough—on and on for hours on end fly hundreds, thousands, a hundred thousand birds! West Coast observers shake their heads in disbelief as hordes of sooty shearwaters pass by.

The flocks normally remain at least three to five miles from land, but they often follow schools of anchovies close to shore. Then from a headland you can watch the "black hags" scrapping and screaming and gorging on the fish. Sated, the birds settle on the water to rest, some with fish hanging from their bills.

Most abundant of the shearwaters off the Pacific coast, these birds sweep north in peak numbers in April and May and return in August and September. These southbound flocks apparently breed on opposite sides of the Pacific. One group of them continues south along the coast to breeding grounds in the Cape Horn region. Another eventually crosses the ocean to nesting territories in the New Zealand area, thus completing a clockwise circuit of the Pacific.

A third group, also nesting near Cape Horn, swings round the Atlantic. These birds appear off North America in May and June, swarming about trawlers to feast on oily fish livers.

Each pair tends a single white egg on a bed of grass in a burrow up to four feet long.

A white-bellied relative of the sooty, the New Zealand shearwater (*Puffinus bulleri*), visits our West Coast in small numbers.

Range: Tasmania and islands near New Zealand, also islands off S. Chile and in Cape Horn area; wanders over most of Pacific, Atlantic, and S. Indian Oceans. *Characteristics:* dark gray body, pale gray or whitish underwing.

Manx Shearwater
Puffinus puffinus

LONG AGO the Isle of Man resounded with the wheezy calls of breeding Manx shearwaters. But these white-bellied birds haven't nested on their namesake island since the 18th century.

They have an astonishing homing ability. One bird, taken from its nest in Wales and flown 3,000 miles to Boston, Massachusetts, in an airliner, made its way back to the burrow in 12½ days!

The single white egg hatches in about 51 days. A Pacific race called the black-vented shearwater visits our West Coast after breeding.

Range: islands off Baja California; wanders north to Vancouver Island. Also on islands of W. Europe and the Mediterranean; wanders to Argentina and N. Africa. *Characteristics:* dark bill, black upperparts, white underparts mottled on sides; white wing linings, pale legs.

Slender-billed Shearwater
Puffinus tenuirostris

DOWN UNDER, several kinds of shearwaters and petrels provide food for man. Among these "muttonbirds" the slender-billed shearwater, known as Tasmanian squab, is considered a delicacy. Controlled commercial slaughter claims up to 500,000 of them each year.

Both sexes incubate. During the 53-day period one bird may sit on the single white egg for as long as two weeks without food or water.

After breeding, the flocks fly clockwise round the Pacific to California, thence southwest to the nesting islands. In looks and habits these birds resemble the larger sooty shearwaters.

Range: islands off S. Australia; wanders widely over most of the Pacific. *Characteristics:* grayish-black upperparts, gray bill, feet, and underparts; dusky underwing.

Audubon's Shearwater
Puffinus lherminieri

AUDUBON encountered a flock of these small shearwaters off the tip of Florida. They pursued fish with great agility, he noted, and would "dive, flutter, and swim with all the gaiety of a flock of ducks, newly alighted in a pond."

A warmwater species, Audubon's shearwater flies with rapid wingbeats and glides less than most of its kin. In calm air its wheeling flight reminds some observers of a swift.

On Caribbean islands each nesting pair tends one white egg in a burrow or limestone cavity. During the nuptial season these birds fill the night air with catcalls and mournful cries.

Range: Bermuda and West Indies; often seen off Florida coast, sometimes wanders to Maine coast. Also found in Galapagos Islands and islands of south central and W. Pacific and Indian Oceans. *Characteristics:* like the greater shearwater but smaller and with sharper contrast between dark brown back and white underparts.

*Sooty shearwater
length 16-18"*

Bermuda Petrel
Pterodroma cahow

EXTINCT. That was the verdict on the Bermuda petrel for nearly three centuries. Settlers early in the 17th century found the bird "fabulously abundant" on the island, named it cahow for one of its calls, and slaughtered it in great numbers for food. Rats and pigs added to the destruction and the species succumbed.

So ran the story until 1906 when a live cahow was captured on Gurnet Rock off Bermuda. By 1951 several other specimens had turned up, and on January 28 of that year Robert Cushman Murphy and two associates aimed a flashlight beam into a burrow on a Bermuda islet. There at the end of a six-foot tunnel sat a nesting cahow!

Carefully extricated, the bird promptly nipped its captors. In the burrow lay a single white egg. Dr. Murphy's team estimated the total adult population as about 100 birds. More recent checks indicate fewer than 20 nest holes. Every effort has been made to preserve the species – the commander of a U.S. air base in Bermuda even declared a cahow nesting area off limits to his men.

Range: Bermuda; wanders over Atlantic in summer. *Characteristics:* dark brown crown and back, pale rump, white face and underparts.

Black-capped Petrel
Pterodroma hasitata

LIKE THE CLOSELY RELATED Bermuda petrel, the blackcap suffered great slaughter and became a rare species. In the late 19th century science lost track of its breeding grounds. But in 1963 ornithologist David B. Wingate discovered 11 nesting colonies in the forested cliffs of Haiti.

Range: Haiti and perhaps other West Indian islands; wanders over Caribbean and Atlantic from Florida to Brazil. *Characteristics:* like the Bermuda petrel but has a white nape and rump.

*Bermuda petrel
length 15"*

*Black-capped petrel
length 14-16"*

*Audubon's shearwater
length 12"*

*Slender-billed shearwater
length 16"*

*Manx shearwater
length 12½-15"*

John W. Taylor

MOTHER CAREY'S CHICKENS   The Storm Petrels

Family Hydrobatidae

THEY LIVE OUT most of their days above or on the oceans
far from land. Even when the wind turns ugly and
the sea cruel, they remain very much at home — scudding
through the wave spray and sheltering in the troughs. Medieval
sailors watched the safe passage of these swallow-size birds and
thought they saw in it the guiding hand of *Mater cara*, the Dear
Mother or Virgin Mary. Eventually the storm petrels came to be known
as Mother Carey's chickens. Another story holds that the way these birds
pitter-patter along the surface led to their common name — "petrel" being a
diminutive for Peter, the apostle who with divine help walked upon the water.

    The family Hydrobatidae numbers about 20 species, and they range over oceans
round the world. Six species are found regularly in or near North America, but the
name storm petrel comes from one, *Hydrobates pelagicus*, that lives exclusively

Photograph by Hans C. Engels, from The Skipper. *Painting of Wilson's petrels by John W. Taylor*

in the Old World. General identification of these birds is relatively easy. All have tubular nostrils and webbed feet, and most have sooty plumage which may be off-set by a white rump patch. Learning the flight style – for example, Leach's petrel bounces and glides – is probably the best way of marking individual species.

According to legend, the storm petrel carries her single white egg beneath her wing and hatches it in flight! Actually, both parents incubate the egg on an offshore island or a seacoast and it may take an amazingly long time – seven weeks – to hatch. Still, the legend is understandable, for storm petrels visit land only in breeding season, and even then those birds not tending the nest burrows spend their days at sea hunting small crustaceans and other aquatic creatures. But when night brings the foragers back, the breeding ground resounds with chatter and twittering cries. And when the birds flounder on weak legs into their tunnel homes, there to be met by mates and young, Mother Carey's flock sounds like elves talking in the earth.

Ashy Petrel
Oceanodroma homochroa

NOT EVEN the ear-splitting foghorn on South Farallon Island off California's Golden Gate can drive ashy petrels from their breeding grounds. The birds ignore the blasts and carry on their housekeeping chores in unlined burrows and rock cavities. While one bird incubates the single white egg wreathed with reddish-brown dots, the other hunts crustaceans at sea.

The foragers return at dusk, fluttering and zigzagging across the colony. Inside the nest chambers the birds call to each other with a sing-song twitter punctuated by a gasp.

Though some storm petrels rank as notable sea rovers, these dark-rumped birds stay relatively close to home, even when not breeding.

Range: Farallon, Channel, and Los Coronados Islands off the California coast; wanders south to waters off central Baja California. *Characteristics:* blackish body with pale mottling on wing lining; forked tail.

Wilson's Petrel
Oceanites oceanicus

WINGS UPRAISED and spindly legs thrusting forward and back, Wilson's petrels hop and patter and glide across the heaving ocean. On this grand stage generations of seamen have enjoyed the dance of these tireless birds.

Hour upon hour they follow a ship, crossing and recrossing the wake as they perform their little dances. They feed on plankton and ship's refuse but rarely come near enough for a voyager to note the square tail and the yellow webs between the toes that distinguish the species.

First described by pioneer ornithologist Alexander Wilson, these petrels follow the summery seasons. In October and November, springtime in the southern hemisphere, they arrive at their breeding grounds on subantarctic islands and even on the fringes of Antarctica itself. Banding records indicate that some use the same nest year after year—a rock cranny or burrow lined with plant stalks or penguin feathers. Both parents incubate a single white egg in 48-hour shifts. The chick frequently perishes when early snow blocks the nest entrance.

By April, with summer over, the northward migration has begun and many of these 1¼-ounce birds will cross 7,000 miles of ocean.

In July and August Wilson's petrels gather in swarms off Nova Scotia and New England.

Range: subantarctic islands to Antarctic coast; migrates to waters of Labrador and British Isles, Australia and Peru, and to the Red Sea and Persian Gulf. *Characteristics:* sooty-brown except for white rump and pale wing patch; square tail.

Fork-tailed Petrel
Oceanodroma furcata

AMONG HIS somberly clothed relatives the forktail stands out in his lovely pearl-gray coat. In sunlight he looks almost white; in evening shadows his plumage appears much darker.

He spends the daylight hours roaming the open ocean—a dumpy little bird with a thick head and a black bill that points down as he flies. He skims the water with wings angled up, dodging the big waves, cruising the troughs, twittering softly. He glides to the surface and alights to feed on fish, refuse, and oil from wounded seals or whales. Eskimos know him as *O-ku-ik*, "oil eater." To take off, he spreads his wings and lets the wind lift him from a rising swell.

Breeding forktails return at dusk to island colonies where each pair tends a white egg with dark specks at the larger end. The nursery is a burrow or rock crevice. As the homecoming birds mill about, you may hear their swishing wings and soft calls. At times they have flown accidentally into an observer's face.

Range: Kuril, Commander, and Aleutian Islands, southeast to N. California; wanders south to Japan and S. California. *Characteristics:* pearl-gray upperparts, whitish underparts, blackish eye patch and wing lining, forked tail.

Least Petrel
Halocyptena microsoma

ERRATIC, fluttering flight barely above the waves marks this pygmy of the storm petrels. In midsummer you may see him off San Diego, California, but he usually remains south of the border.

Often these birds share an island with black petrels, nesting in crevices and under boulders. Their call sounds like whizzing cogwheels.

Range: islands off Baja California; wanders to waters of southern California and Ecuador. *Characteristics:* small size, sooty-black body, indistinct buffy wing patch; wedge-shaped tail.

Leach's Petrel
Oceanodroma leucorhoa

OVER THE PEACEFUL blue sea a cloud of dark birds suddenly churns up behind a fishing boat. These petrels, named for English naturalist William E. Leach, ordinarily ignore vessels. But when fishermen clean the day's catch the sooty little seafarers gather for a feast of fish oil and discarded morsels. Ever on the move, these birds settle

Ashy petrel
length 7½"

John W. Taylor

on the surface only for a moment or so and do not patter on the water as do other storm petrels. In the North Atlantic, Leach's and the smaller Wilson's petrel are easily confused. Both have a white rump but Wilson's has a square rather than forked tail. The flight pattern provides the best clue. Wilson's petrel skims like a swallow; Leach's bounds over the water like a butterfly or nighthawk with slow, spasmodic wingbeats and abrupt changes in course.

In winter *leucorhoa* roams the equatorial waters of the Atlantic and Pacific. For breeding, many of his kind prefer islands in the higher latitudes. At some favored sites their one- to three-foot nesting tunnels honeycomb the earth, and their musky smell pervades the island.

When the chick breaks out of the single white or spotted egg, plaintive peeps rise from the ground. At sundown the island sky is alive with returning petrels calling to each other with staccato notes and trills. On bright evenings great black-backed and herring gulls wait along the shore to seize the arriving birds. And a dog or cat can wreck a breeding colony.

Range: N. Japan to the Aleutians, southeast to Baja California; wanders to Hawaii and the Galapagos. Also from Massachusetts to Labrador, Iceland, and the British Isles; wanders to equator. *Characteristics:* blackish brown except for white rump; forked tail.

Black Petrel
Loomelania melania

On slowly beating wings, these larger petrels fly in graceful, languid patterns. They dine on the young of spiny lobsters, other marine creatures, and floating garbage. Sometimes on a calm sea off California they gather in dense, dark rafts that extend a hundred yards or more.

Some black petrels spend the winter off the southern California coast. Others migrate south to equatorial waters. In spring all return to Baja California. Over their breeding islands these petrels sound weird *puck-a-ree, puck-puck-a-roo* calls. In a rock cranny or old auklet burrow each female lays one plain white or spotted egg.

Range: islands off Baja California; winters to waters off Peru. Wanders to central California coast. *Characteristics:* large blackish-brown body, pale bar on upper wing, forked tail.

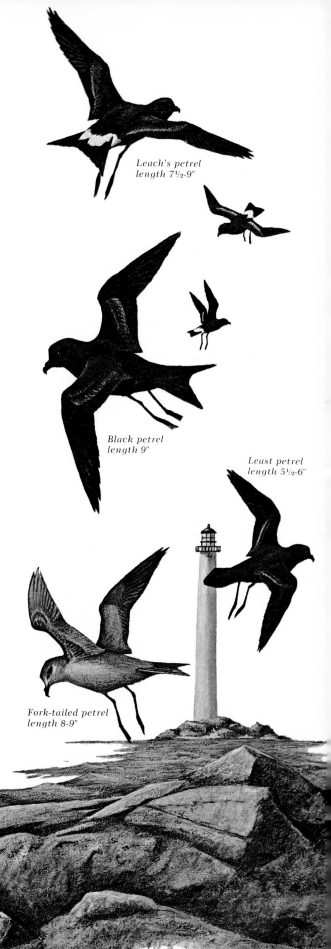

Leach's petrel
length 7½-9"

Black petrel
length 9"

Least petrel
length 5½-6"

Fork-tailed petrel
length 8-9"

Wilson's petrel
length 7"

The Tropicbirds

Family Phaëthontidae

THE FLEDGLING white-tailed tropicbird sits on the floor of the small cave. Here, 62 days ago, he cracked his way out of an egg spotted brown, black, and purple. Here he has taken regurgitated fish and other marine animals from the gullets of his parents until his pigeon-size frame is upholstered with fat. Now he waddles to the lip of the cliff, takes a few more practice flaps – he began exercising those large wings weeks ago – and eyes the restless Atlantic far below. Then, suddenly, he steps off the cliff and flutters away.

The tropicbird swims easily but he is a pitiful walker, shuffling on weak legs, using his wings as crutches. Airborne he is in his element. Flying high on strong wings, he sometimes veers off course to circle a ship. Then sweeping close to the waves, he reflects the sun-bright water and his white breast shimmers with iridescent greens and blues. Sometimes he calls – a harsh, grating note. His long tail recalled the marlinespike carried by boatswains, and sailors named him "bosun bird."

The scientific family name for the tropicbirds comes from Greek legend. Phaëthon, son of the sun god Helios, rode his father's solar chariot across the sky, lost control of the immortal steeds, and plummeted to his death. To catch a fish, a tropicbird arrows down, wings trailing, tail extended. Sometimes he spirals as he dives. He plunges deep, emerges with a fish or perhaps a small squid, and floats lightly on the surface to eat. He fishes alone, for these birds are not gregarious. They gather in numbers only during nesting season.

The white-tailed tropicbird (*Phaëthon lepturus*) is one of three species in the family. He is also known as the yellow-billed, though in maturity the bill turns orange-red. His best distinguishing mark is the large amount of black in his wings. He comes to North America's southern coasts and islands, as does the red-billed tropicbird (*Phaëthon aethereus*). This species has dark back markings which it retains

White-tailed tropicbird, length 32" (includes 16-19" tail);
Quentin Keynes. Opposite: red-tailed tropicbirds,
length 34" (includes 16" tail); Karl W. Kenyon, National Audubon Society

FLYING FREE, *red-tailed tropicbirds court through the blue Hawaiian sky, while half a world away on the isle of Mauritius, a whitetail endures his gentle prison.*

throughout adulthood. The third species is the red-tailed tropicbird (*Phaëthon rubricauda*), whose only contact with the United States occurs in the Hawaiian Islands. All three birds fly over warm seas and nest on remote isles and headlands. They normally lay but one egg a season, and it is during incubation that they are most vulnerable to their primary enemy – man. He takes eggs and sometimes feathers. On Polynesian and other Pacific islands native boys pull out the long tail shafts of sitting birds and present them to their girl friends.

When nesting season is over, the parent birds are quick to leave their young and set off on journeys that may take them hundreds of miles from land. Whitetails have been seen even in mid-Atlantic, in the heart of the Sargasso Sea.

White-tailed tropicbird – *Range:* Bermuda and tropical islands in Atlantic, Pacific, and Indian Oceans; seen off U. S. coast from Florida to North Carolina. *Characteristics:* white head, body, and tail streamers; black shoulder patch and eye stripe, orange bill. Young have barred back, short tail.

Red-billed tropicbird – *Range:* islands and coasts from Caribbean to Brazil and Gulf of California to Peru; also Red Sea and Persian Gulf. Seen off S. California and Newfoundland. *Characteristics:* black eye stripe, white head, underparts, and tail streamers; barred back, red bill. Young have yellow bill, short tail.

*Red-billed tropicbird
length 24-40" (includes 12-24" tail)
Lewis Wayne Walker*

67

AERIAL ACROBATS WITH HUGE BILLS

The Pelicans

Family Pelecanidae

By ROBERT CUSHMAN MURPHY

O N THE GROUND the pelican wins no beauty prize. Bulky and squat, he waddles awkwardly about, his enormous beak pointing down. His takeoff hardly improves the image. He flaps his wings through a wide arc and kangaroo-hops, feet together, to launch himself. But once airborne he becomes a different creature, no longer grotesque. Even his ponderous bill, reminiscent of that extinct flying reptile the pterodactyl, cannot mar the inexpressible dignity of his flight.

His powerful, sweeping wingbeats are about the slowest of any bird's. Once, watching from an island off the coast of Peru, I timed the strokes of passing pelicans—between one and one and a half seconds for a complete cycle.

Flying thus, a group of pelicans forms a file or a V formation, gliding steadily, then picking up the wingbeat from the leader. A short line flaps almost in unison; a long line seems to undulate as the strokes travel from front to rear.

Pelicans are the largest of the Pelecaniformes, the order of birds that includes tropicbirds, cormorants, anhingas, frigatebirds, gannets, and boobies. All are totipalmate, or "oar-footed," with webs uniting all four toes. Eight species comprise the family Pelecanidae, but it will do little violence to fact if we think of them as only two sorts: the white pelicans, with one New and several Old World representatives, and the brown, found only in the New World.

In North America the brown pelican (*Pelecanus occidentalis*) hugs the coast, fishing almost exclusively in salt water. In the west his range extends south to Chile, in the east to British Guiana. Beyond the Guianas so much silt pours from Brazilian rivers into the Atlantic that he could not see his prey.

Hurricanes may blow the brown pelican far offshore. Perhaps this explains how the species got to the Galapagos Islands. The 600 miles that separates the islands from the South American mainland is the widest water gap the bird has crossed.

This isolated population on the Galapagos is one of several races of brown pelicans. While on an expedition in 1941 I collected pelicans in Ecuador and on the Pacific coast of Colombia. I was unaware that these differed from the Caribbean race, but Dr. Wetmore, chief author of this volume, found that they represented a previously unknown subspecies. He honored me by naming it *Pelecanus occidentalis murphyi*. The range of this race adjoins that of the huge Peruvian pelican, one of the guano birds. In fact, in southern Ecuador the two ranges overlap and many people mistake the smaller Colombian birds for babies of the Peruvian race.

Seldom uttering a sound, brown pelicans often fly so low that their wings seem to brush the waves. Fishing, they may dive from as high as 60 or 70 feet. When they spot their prey they abruptly tip forward and fall with half-closed wings. They rotate as they dive and often slant into the water belly up and back down. Air sacs under the skin cushion the impact and help bring the birds up again like corks. They apparently twist or somersault underwater, for they often angle into the water traveling downwind and yet always emerge facing upwind, ready for takeoff.

CRANO OF SEABIRDS, *the brown pelican folds his great pouch against his beak. bled to nourish offspring with their own blood, pelicans symbolize charity.* 69

own pelicans, adult (foreground) and juvenile, length 45-54"; Luis Marden, National Geographic staff

ON TARGET, *a brown pelican hurtles down, strikes deep, and takes off into the wind. This remarkable sequence suggests the force with which the great bird smashes the sea to seize fish. One pelican clobbered a snorkel diver in a case of mistaken identity!*

Brown pelicans stirred patriotic ire in World War I when they were accused of ruining the food fisheries. Investigators proved they eat mostly trash fish such as the oily Gulf menhaden and the birds were spared.

The pouch serves as a scoop, not a storehouse. After a plunge, the water is drained between the mandibles. The bird points his bill skyward and the fish slides down his gullet. Capacity of the pouch? An ornithologist once poured in 3½ gallons of water before any spilled!

State bird of Louisiana, the brown pelican amuses visitors to Gulf and Florida coasts. Western relatives (right) flock to feed off the Pacific coast of Mexico.

Frederick Kent Truslow. Left: Hugo H. Schroder
Opposite: James P. Blair, National Geographic photographer

If a bird makes a catch, he pauses on the surface to drain the water from his huge pouch and swallow the fish. I have often seen a laughing gull alight on a pelican's head to snap up any fish that might wriggle out while the pouch is being drained. As visitors to Florida know, brown pelicans are notorious filchers and panhandlers themselves. They will catch scraps in midair as fast as you toss them.

Brown pelicans nest in colonies on the ground or in trees. The parents, which look alike, relieve one another incubating the two or three chalky eggs. In a month the hatchlings emerge, helpless but soon calling for food. Those born aloft usually sit tight until they are fledged—in about nine weeks. Below, the young investigate the strange new world as soon as they can walk—in about five weeks.

THE WHITE PELICAN of North America (*Pelecanus erythrorhynchos*) breeds mainly on islands in western lakes. But in winter he ranges south through Mexico to Guatemala and feeds in brackish and salt water. I first watched these big 20-pound birds feeding on a lagoon of the Snake River in Idaho. Unlike the brown pelicans they never dive for fish. In deep water beside the reed beds four or five birds swim abreast, gliding smoothly into shallow water. Here in a curved line they thrash the water with wings spanning nine feet. Then they scoop up startled fish that try to dart past. On such a foray a white pelican may eat a third its own weight before resting and digesting the catch.

When my wife and I visited Lower Klamath Lake along the border of California and Oregon in the spring of 1915, we found it full of floating mats of cattails and rushes through which green shoots were sprouting. These rafts of vegetation could hardly support a man, but they held hundreds of nesting white pelicans. The birds had raked up mounds of debris and laid their two to four dull white eggs on top. Some had hatched, and the featherless, flesh-colored, rubbery chicks seemed unreal to us – they had such short bills!

The baby pelicans fed on regurgitated "soup" in their parents' pouches. This is the only food pelicans hold in these great scoops, for they swallow their catch as soon as they have drained off the water. Soon the young began thrusting their fast-lengthening bills far into the adult gullets for fish that were less digested. By the end of two weeks they had sprouted white down that made them look like lambs. They bleated too, though the adults were as silent as brown pelicans.

*White pelicans
length 54-70"
Bob Davison*

A few years after our visit the Klamath marshes were drained to provide arable land for homesteaders. The birds vanished—and the exposed bottomland proved too poor to grow crops. In 1935 the U. S. Department of Interior restored 20,000 acres of the marsh and, happily, the white pelicans returned.

Today, soaring on high, they present a breathtaking sight. Their banks and turns catch the sun in a glitter of white. Then they half close their wings and swoop. An Oregon naturalist, William L. Finley, described their roaring descent: "They used the sky as a big toboggan-slide and dropped like meteors, leaving a trail of thunder."

Brown pelican—*Range:* Pacific coast from S. British Columbia to S. Chile; in east, coastal areas from North Carolina to British Guiana, including West Indies. *Characteristics:* huge grayish bill; brownish plumage streaked silvery gray and black; white markings on head and neck. Young have dark head, white underparts.

White pelican—*Range:* British Columbia to S. W. Ontario, south to S. E. California and N.W. Wyoming; also in S.E. Texas. Winters to Guatemala and Florida. *Characteristics:* huge yellowish bill; white plumage except for black on tip and trailing edge of wings. Breeding bird has short crest, yellowish tinge on plumage, orange or salmon bill with fibrous plate on upper mandible.

Otis Imboden, National Geographic photographer

NESTING *on Gunnison Island in Great Salt Lake, Utah, white pelicans (opposite) display the horny plates which adorn their bills from late winter until after eggs are laid. Some whites migrate southeastward to share a Florida beach with brown pelicans (above) in sight of Cape Kennedy's looming gantries.*

73

Gannets and Boobies

Family Sulidae

By ROBERT CUSHMAN MURPHY

FROM BONAVENTURE ISLAND in the Gulf of St. Lawrence to the Pentland Firth in Scotland, from the skerries off Ireland to as far south as the bird flies, I have pursued the king of the North Atlantic — the gannet. To me this magnificent seafowl with six-foot wingspread is the most majestic inhabitant of that ocean, and I can readily understand why the Anglo-Saxons came to regard the North Atlantic as the "Gannet's Bath." The Old English term conjures up the vision of a sparkling sea and this great bird wheeling through the air and plummeting from mast height upon its prey.

After folk from Scandinavia invaded and settled in England, the gannet was called the solan goose. "Solan" comes from *sula*, Old Norse for gannet, and "goose" from the bird's white plumage. Even today it is often called the sea goose. When the naturalist Linnaeus published the first scientific description of this northern gannet in 1758, he named it *bassanus*, after Bass Rock at the mouth of the Firth of Forth in Scotland, a breeding place from time immemorial.

On low, nearly rainless islands off Africa's Cape of Good Hope dwells a second species — the Cape gannet. During voyages of exploration in the 15th and 16th centuries Spanish and Portuguese sailors became acquainted with this brown-tailed gannet. It took another 250 years or so before explorers reached the hideouts of the third species — the Australian gannet — in southeastern Australia and New Zealand.

Of these three seabirds I have yet to meet the Cape species. But in New Zealand I have studied the Australian gannet. It was November, springtime in the southern hemisphere, when gannet pairs have their single eggs and young chicks. At Horuhoru in Hauraki Gulf I leaped from a dinghy to the sloping face of the islet and scrambled through the nests to the summit. On the way up, my wife (and best fellow fieldworker) was nipped through her corduroys but lost no blood. Adult birds streaked in from the sea, passing me at arm's reach, and applied brakes in the same abrupt manner as our northern gannets. Then they settled noisily beside their mates.

In February, when fledgling gannets were beginning to go through strenuous ground practice for flight, I landed on another island, off the Coromandel Peninsula, under a fearful overhanging cliff of volcanic ash. Again I crawled over perilous rock faces and through unyielding thickets to the open terraces on which the nests were packed almost base to base. Except for their distinctly tawny heads, these gannets looked like the familiar North Atlantic species.

ON QUEBEC'S BONAVENTURE ISLAND, *principal gannetry in the New World, cliffs sparkle with "sea geese." Fishermen once killed gannets for bait; now Canada protects them.*

Grant Haist

Until the era of the great voyages of exploration, from the 15th to the 18th centuries, no European could have guessed that the gannets had tropical relatives, the boobies. Columbus, during his voyage to the New World, noted several sightings of a bird he called *alcatraz*. This Spanish name now generally means pelican, but in those days it referred to the largest seabird in any particular region. Undoubtedly the birds Columbus sighted were boobies.

Six species of boobies roam the world's warm seas, and I have had the good fortune to live among all but one – the little-known Abbott's booby of the Indian Ocean. In the Cape Verde Islands, Hawaii, and the Philippines I have studied the red-footed, blue-faced, and brown boobies. And in the eastern Pacific the blue-footed booby and the Peruvian piquero have been my intimates for more than a year.

The piquero, one of the priceless guano birds along the mountainous coast of Peru,

Frederick Kent Truslow (also left and opposite)

Grant Haist

DANCING BEAK TO BEAK, *a pair of gannets celebrates mating season on Bonaventure. After stroking bills and preening come formal bows (above left). When one nesting bird relieves the other it sometimes brings feathers or plant material (left).*

A non-nesting bird or an intruder in another bird's territory may be set upon. Assailants pin down a trespasser (opposite), gripping his beak and plucking his tail. Peck lumps mark the wrestlers' heads. Locked, they may fall 200 feet into the sea.

nests on the ledges of sheer cliffs and on island rooftops. I recall my first climb, in 1919, to the crest of Guañape Sur, a lofty island occupied by these white-bodied boobies, whose deposits make a highly valued organic fertilizer. The young were attaining the fledgling state, and incredible numbers of adults seemed to be riding the wind for sheer joy. Scores of them stretched away until they looked like white specks in the sky. During a later visit to Macabí Island I watched these birds fish. They circled about looking for prey, then plunged down like hissing hailstones. Thousands struck the sea at the same time, vanishing in spurts of foam that appeared to leap up to meet them.

Like the gannets, with whom they comprise the family Sulidae, the boobies have streamlined, spindle-shaped bodies with a layer of air sacs beneath the skin to cushion the impact of their dives. Except for short stretches between their nests and the water, none of the family voluntarily fly over land.

The most notable difference between gannets and boobies concerns their breeding habits. None of the gannets nest near other species of the family. Yet I have seen several species of boobies breed on a single small island and, because of different feeding habits, capture their food without serious competition.

Gannet
Morus bassanus

WHILE EXPLORING the Gulf of St. Lawrence in the summer of 1534, the Breton navigator Jacques Cartier took note of an awesome sight on some red sandstone cliffs. "These Ilands," his journal stated in Hakluyt's early translation, "were as full of birds, as any field or medow is of grasse, which there do make their nestes: and in the greatest of them, there was a great and infinite number of those that wee call Margaulx, that are white, and bigger then any geese."

Cartier's journal begins the recorded history of the American breeding haunts of the bird known in English as the sea goose or gannet, a term that stems from the same Old English root as gander.

Nearly 300 years later Audubon rubbed his eyes in amazement at the same spectacle on the Bird Rocks, as they came to be known. From afar they seemed mantled in white. At closer range flying gannets resembled a swirling snowstorm.

Other men did more than look and wonder. Fishermen clubbed countless gannets to death and used the flesh as cod bait. In 1860 the colony on the Rocks numbered some 150,000. By 1904 fewer than 3,000 birds remained.

Then the Canadian government decreed an end to the wanton slaughter and *bassanus* revived. In the New World the awesome colonies of Cartier's day are no more, but perhaps 28,000 breeding birds flourish in six gannetries. Best known of these is on rugged Bonaventure Island, near the Gaspé Peninsula of Quebec, a mecca for bird lovers. Here at close range some 14,000 of these birds can be seen courting, nesting, and feeding their young.

The North Atlantic gannet has been a source of food for man since the dawn of history, and it is one of the few birds whose population is well known. In 1939 British ornithologists James Fisher and H. G. Vevers organized a painstaking census of every known gannetry in the North Atlantic. The count totaled 166,000 breeding adults. A check ten years later of the colonies on the east side of the Atlantic showed an increase of 18 percent.

Older gannets return to the breeding islands in spring to reclaim their nesting sites. These are usually on narrow ledges facing the sea. An unmated bird tries to attract the attention of each female that flies over. If one lands, the two birds stand face-to-face waving their heads and clacking their bills together like castanets. Then, uttering hoarse *urrah* notes, they curtsy to each other with wings half folded.

Gannet and young (left), length 35-40"; Walter Meayers Edwards, National Geographic staff

OFF TO FISH, *a sleek-nosed gannet flaps from a Bonaventure ledge on wings spanning six feet.*

The male may next escort his mate to the nest site, placing pellets of mud at her feet for the foundation of a mound. He soon starts gathering construction material. Together the pair fashions a pile of flotsam, generally seaweed.

Both sexes take turns incubating the single chalky bluish egg for six weeks. The adult covers the egg with one webbed foot, overlaps it with the other, then settles down. Thieving gulls are quick to devour unguarded eggs and chicks.

During their last weeks in the colony the season's offspring gather in groups and exercise their wings. Now they are clothed in the dark, spangled juvenile plumage; the change to adult plumage is not completed until the third year.

About the 11th week the parents stop feeding the youngsters. For a week or ten days the fledglings fast, living on accumulated baby fat. Finally, half flying, half falling, the juveniles flounder down to the sea. They paddle frantically away from the island, then drift with the tides for several weeks until their muscles are hard enough for flight. For at least three years a youngster remains at sea, and he may not begin nesting until he is six or seven.

A mature bird departing a gannetry raises his wings, stretches his neck, points his bill to the zenith, marches to the cliff edge, and bounds into the air. On level ground he may not succeed in taking off; if he drops in among his neighbors they peck him severely.

The great white bird wheels in wide circles over the open ocean, black-tipped wings beating rapidly. The body tapers to a point at both bill and tail. Usually these birds cruise in small groups anywhere from the line of breakers to the limits of the continental shelves.

They prey on school fishes – herring, mackerel, and menhaden. Where such food is plentiful, gannets continually bombard the sea in spectacular dives that send up spray as high as ten feet.

The plunge begins at altitudes up to a hundred feet. The deeper the fish the higher the starting point. Spotting prey, a gannet seems to stall in the air, then drops with nearly folded wings. The bird may descend 50 feet below the surface.

If the fish is not too large, the gannet often swallows it before emerging, probably from fear of having to give it up to raiding skuas.

Range: N. Atlantic islands from the Gulf of St. Lawrence to Iceland and the British Isles; winters to the Gulf of Mexico, N. Africa, and Syria. *Characteristics:* creamy-buff head, white body, black wing tips; throat feathered except for a narrow line at center. Young have slaty upperparts flecked with white, paler underparts.

79

Brown Booby
Sula leucogaster

THROUGH THE CENTURIES this brown fisherman has paused in his wanderings to rest on passing ships. Long ago sailors noted how foolishly tame he was and christened him "booby."

Even around their nests brown boobies do not fly from man but stand fast and try to drive off the intruder with their bills.

We hear the grunts and brays of nesting brown boobies on tropical islands that are bare or covered with low vegetation. Boobies favor cliff or hillside sites, for without a jumping-off place or a breeze they rise with difficulty.

For 40 days a pair take turns incubating their one or two chalky bluish eggs in a shallow scrape that passes for a nest. Newly hatched, a baby lies helpless and nearly naked, though it soon will be covered with white down. Only the shelter of a parent's body keeps it from being cooked by the sun. The hatchling feeds on regurgitated fish soup from a parent's gullet.

When not breeding the brown booby travels far from his nesting territory. Though he ranges over most warm ocean areas, he never crosses even so narrow a land strip as the Isthmus of Panama. Male brown boobies on the Pacific side have hoary heads, unlike those of the Atlantic side, indicating that the two populations came to their habitats by way of the two oceans.

This booby fishes mainly in blue water but may dart among breakers during a gale, feasting on flying fish, halfbeaks, and mullet. He plunges from as high as 60 feet and dives to a depth of 6 feet. Amid a school of fish he strikes repeatedly from a few feet above the water.

He often waits until dark before coming in to roost on his home island. Thus he avoids ambush by the frigatebird, which retires early after a day spent harassing other seabirds and forcing them to disgorge their catches.

At sea the brown booby may roost on coastal buoys, on a turtle's back, or in a ship's rigging. This is the booby species most likely to be seen off the southern coast of the United States. In the west the blue-footed booby (*Sula nebouxii*) nests on islands in the Gulf of California.

Range: tropical islands in Atlantic (from Bahamas to Brazil), Pacific, and Indian Oceans. Seen in S. E. California, along Gulf Coast and Florida's east coast. *Characteristics:* dark brown head, back, breast, and wings; white belly, yellowish feet. Young have grayish-brown belly.

Male (blue tinge at base of bill) and female brown boobies, length 28-30"

Blue-faced Booby

Sula dactylatra

OVER WARM SEAS where flying fishes play roams this dark-visaged mariner, often called the masked booby. He dives underwater for these fishes, often swallowing them before surfacing.

This booby frequently follows ships, gliding on air currents created by the vessel. In summer he often comes to the Dry Tortugas off Florida, though he does not nest there. In breeding colonies on tropical islands each pair incubates one or two chalky blue eggs.

Range: worldwide in tropical oceans; visits East Coast from South Carolina to Texas. *Characteristics:* slaty face, bare chin, white head and body; blackish wing tips, rear edges, and tail. Young have white patch on brownish back.

Blue-faced boobies, length 27"

Red-footed Booby

Sula sula

WHEN DUSK ends the day's fishing in tropical waters, the redfoot seeks new prey. He dives for squid that rise from the depths with the approach of night; his large eyes help him see in the waning light. When the moon shines bright, he may forage until daybreak.

Sated, he returns to his island home, as far as 50 miles from his feeding ground. Unlike most boobies, the redfoot nests in trees. He builds a platform of sticks from which he can take off to windward. A lone tree may support a dozen nests. Where there are no trees this bird builds on a clump of brush or a pile of rocks.

A redfoot incubating its single chalky blue egg sometimes droops its head over the side of the nest as if lifeless. When disturbed, the bird squawks loudly, thrusts its head out, and jabs at the intruder.

While the bright red feet provide a good field mark in all adults of this species, the plumage varies. In many birds it is predominantly white, in others largely brownish.

Range: worldwide in tropical oceans; sometimes seen off Texas and Louisiana. *Characteristics:* red feet, bare chin. White phase has white body, black on tips and trailing edges of wings. Brown phase is grayish brown except for white rump, belly, and tail. Young are grayish brown.

Red-footed booby, white phase, length 26-30"; Karl W. Kenyon, National Audubon Society

The Cormorants
Family Phalacrocoracidae

THE EARLY SUN sparkles on San Francisco Bay and silhouettes the dark shapes of a few double-crested cormorants, quietly rising and falling with the waves. These form the nucleus of a morning miracle. For as the sun climbs, more cormorants come to join those few. They fly singly, in groups, or in flocks of hundreds, stringing out in long, shifting lines or wedges like geese. They come fast, necks outthrust, legs held back, wings pounding the autumn air. As they see the growing numbers of their kind on the surface of the bay, they set their wings and glide in to enlist. Splash follows splash until a great black shoal of birds has formed — nearly 2,000 cormorants in a living line that stretches hundreds of yards across the water and counts its ranks four or more deep. Above gulls circle, screaming.

Now the great raft of birds begins to move across the water. Schools of smelt and other small fish are swimming near the surface, and the cormorants form a long, ragged harvester to reap them. Individual birds lunge toward riffles that mark the gleaming prey, then dive and hunt underwater. They suddenly reappear, twisting their long necks to swallow the catch, and set off on a half-fluttering race to the front rank for still another dive. Sometimes a bird trying to swallow a large fish is pursued and robbed by his neighbors.

Voracious? The name cormorant comes from the Latin *corvus marinus*, "sea raven"; Shakespeare called the birds "insatiate"; and salmon fishermen in the Gulf of St. Lawrence once put a price on their heads. Yet they do not seem to eat appreciably more fish than many other seabirds. They also dine on crustaceans, and the fish they eat are mostly "trash" – commercially unimportant – not salmon.

Their skill at stalking and seizing fish, however, has been exploited in Asia for centuries. Held on long leashes and wearing collars that prevent them from swallowing their catch, domesticated cormorants in Japan, China, and India fish for their masters. In Britain cormorant fishing, like falconry, was a gentleman's sport for many years. And cormorants serve man in other ways.

In fact, writing in *National Geographic*, ornithologist Robert Cushman Murphy countered the old slanders about the family Phalacrocoracidae by calling one of its 30 species, the guanay cormorant, the world's most valuable wild bird. The South American fisher leaves an immense tonnage of guano on rocky islands off the coast of Peru. This natural resource has buttressed that nation's economy since

TETHERED *to a Japanese master (opposite), cormorants nab the fish his beacon lures. A bird can catch 150 an hour – a collar prevents swallowing. Nabbed himself (below), a nestling pelagic cormorant in the Aleutians eyes his captor.*

Karl W. Kenyon. Opposite: J. Baylor Roberts, National Geographic staff

GREEDY GUANAYES *fish for anchovies off the fog-draped guano islands of Peru. A colony of these cormorants may eat 1,000 tons of fish a day. Their droppings make the world's best organic fertilizer—rich in nitrogen, potassium, and phosphorus.*

This guano once lay 150 feet deep, the lower layers deposited some 2,500 years ago. In this almost rainless climate it retains its richness. The Incas valued it and decreed death to disturbers of breeding birds. But when guano began earning big revenues more than a century ago the deposits were mined so extensively that the birds' nesting was disrupted.

Today Peru protects the cormorants and limits the taking of anchovies by the growing fish meal industry. On the island sanctuaries workers (right) now collect guano only two or three months in a year.

Robert Cushman Murphy and Grace E. Barstow Murphy. Lower: Bates Littlehales, National Geographic photographer

the early 19th century, when world demand for this mineral-rich fertilizer made it an export commodity more precious to Peru than gold.

Six species of cormorants live in North America. They are generally similar in appearance and behavior. Most adult birds have dark iridescent plumage, a partially naked face and throat patch colored yellow, blue, or red; a stiff, wedge-shaped tail, and a strong bill sharply hooked at the tip. They are at home in either fresh or salt water, swimming half-submerged as do the grebes. They paddle along with necks raised and bills angled skyward. Underwater, cormorants propel themselves rapidly with their broad, webbed feet. They surface or go ashore to eat, for they cannot or do not swallow underwater.

Whether waddling clumsily about on land, perching upright, flapping and soaring through the air, or searching for the next meal in the water, these birds seem to enjoy each other's company. When undisturbed, cormorants are usually silent much of the year. In breeding season, however, the nesting grounds resound with their cries and croaks. Here tens of thousands of birds may gather to build homes of seaweed and guano on rocks, cliffs, or in bushes.

Such places soon become noxious to humans — slimy and evil-smelling. But after a 25-day incubation the hatchlings arrive and thrive in these surroundings. Feeding on regurgitated fish from their parents' gullets, the young are soon big enough to wander about the nesting area. At mealtime, territories become defined again as, prodded by adults, the youngsters scurry back to their nests.

Double-crested Cormorant
Phalacrocorax auritus

EVERYONE HAS his own idea of home. For the double-crested cormorant it may be an island, a reef, a cliff, or a swamp. It may be along the coast or far inland; it may be bare or forested. But always there will be good fishing nearby.

Finding a spot fit for raising families, the migrating squadrons pour in, sometimes by the thousands. Their shape and flying formations – oblique lines and ragged V's – may remind you of geese. A close look quickly dispels any doubt. The cylindrical bill hooked at the tip, the bright orange pouch underneath, and the dark glossy plumage distinguish the cormorant. Both male and female have the crests on either side of the head for which this species was named. These disappear soon after nesting begins.

You can recognize a cormorant, or shag as he is often called, by the way he perches on a rock, stub, or buoy – body upright and neck forming an S. Sometimes he strikes a spread-eagle stance. When he flies off he usually drops almost to the surface before lifting; hence the belief that the "shag must wet its tail before it can fly."

A courting male pounds his wings in the water near his prospective mate, then hurls himself along the surface in a series of jumps and dives. The two birds may toss a bit of weed to each other, and sometimes the female spreads her wings and spins about. Soon the male flies off to claim a nest site in a tree or on a cliff ledge or rocky islet. At the site he crouches, wings beating, and pours forth a croaking serenade of *ok ok ok ok* notes. The female alights nearby and housekeeping begins. They may build a new nest or rebuild an old one. Several refurbishings with trash, seaweed, sticks, and grass can produce a platform two feet high and two feet in diameter. Both incubate the three or four pale blue eggs.

The naked, coal-black hatchlings look like animated rubber toys, but they soon grow a thick coat of down. In a few weeks they band together and troop through the colony. By now the nesting area is strewn with eggshells and bits of fish, coated with droppings and swarming with flies.

By about the tenth week the youngsters can dive for fish, can fly, and are thoroughly independent. Like their elders they swim low in the water, heads erect and bills tilted upward.

Range: S. W. Alaska to Newfoundland, south to S. Mexico, Florida, and the West Indies; winters to Central America. *Characteristics:* hooked bill, orange throat pouch, bronze upper back; head, neck, and lower back are black with green gloss. Breeding birds have double crest. Young are brownish with whitish breast and dark belly.

Great Cormorant
Phalacrocorax carbo

"CORMORANTS," wrote New Englander William Wood in 1634, "bee as common as other fowles which destroy abundance of small fish."

The great, or European, cormorant is still common over much of the Old World, but only in certain places in the New. Along the New England coast he usually is seen only in winter.

Bigger than the double-crested, the great cormorant has a stouter bill and a yellow instead of an orange throat pouch. In late winter and spring he sports white feathers on his head and nape and a white thigh patch. The two species have a similar flight style: rapid and direct, with the neck thrust out and slightly upward.

The great cormorant also thrives on fish and crustaceans but, unlike the double-crested, rarely fishes in cooperative fleets. Plunging from the surface, he strokes both feet in unison in underwater forays that often last half a minute. Small fishes he swallows on the spot. Larger ones he carries to the surface, maneuvers to a headfirst position, and swallows. In the Far East he is trained for commercial fishing (page 82).

Nesting birds incubate three or four blue eggs on a mound of sticks and seaweed placed on a cliff, a rock, or in a tree.

Range: S. E. Quebec, Newfoundland, Nova Scotia, Greenland, and much of Europe, Asia, Africa, and Australia; in U. S. winters to Long Island, occasionally to Georgia. *Characteristics:* hooked bill, yellow throat pouch bordered with white; blackish-blue neck and underparts, blackish upperparts with bronze tints. Young are brownish with white belly and undertail.

Great cormorants, length 34-40"; Arthur A. Allen

DOUBLE-CRESTED CORMORANTS *nest off the Maine coast.*
Length 30-36"; Eliot Porter. Inset: juvenile, Frederick Kent Truslow
Detail at top: crests at start of breeding season, Allan Brooks

Brandt's cormorant, length 33-35"
Robert C. Twist, U. S. Fish and Wildlife Service

Brandt's Cormorant
Phalacrocorax penicillatus

ALONG THE WEST COAST you may find Brandt's cormorants in any season. In spring, colonies of these big black birds jam rocky headlands and gently sloping islands, with nests so close together that you may not be able to walk between them. In the cold months the cormorants retire to sheltered inlets where great numbers sleep through the nights on sandy beaches.

Often these birds mingle with gulls, pelicans, murres, and with other cormorants. In San Francisco Bay, when Brandt's cormorants leave their rocky roosts in the morning to go fishing, doublecrests take over their perches. The daytime tenants have a much brighter throat pouch.

Brandt's cormorants sweep the fishing grounds in lumbering, low-flying V's. Finding a school of small fish, they settle in a great black raft on the sea and sound their sharp *kauk* notes. Their huge feet propel them far below the surface in pursuit of prey. One fisherman reported finding dead Brandt's cormorants trapped in nets set at more than 30 fathoms.

Nesting birds wear long white plumes at the sides of the neck. One parent bird always stands guard at the seaweed nest, for western gulls find the four bluish eggs appetizing.

Range: Pacific coast from Washington to Baja California. *Characteristics:* black plumage glossed with purple, green and bronze; slaty or bluish throat pouch, brownish band under pouch. Young are brownish.

Olivaceous Cormorant
Phalacrocorax olivaceus

IN THE UNITED STATES this slim, small cormorant finds living conditions suitable only along the brackish coastal waterways and nearby lakes of Texas and Louisiana.

Farther south you'll find him fishing in quiet Mexican streams, in equatorial swamps, near arid islands and marshy seashores, in icy Andean lakes more than 14,000 feet high, and off the storm-swept barrens of Tierra del Fuego. Since the olivaceous is the only cormorant found throughout the Neotropical region – South America, the West Indies, and tropical North America – some authorities call him the Neotropic cormorant. He is also known as the Mexican or Brazilian cormorant.

The olive tinge in his back and wings can be seen only at close range. Usually his feathers appear all black. He looks and acts much like a double-crested cormorant but is smaller, has a slimmer neck and head, and in the breeding season wears a thin band of white under his brownish throat pouch.

Along the Gulf Coast colonies of olivaceous cormorants nest in trees and bushes. Each pair builds a nest of sticks and grass for the four bluish eggs. Boat-tailed grackles may steal the eggs, and raccoons prey on both eggs and young.

When their nests are disturbed, or when they join in cooperative fishing, olivaceous cormorants break out in a chorus of piglike grunts.

Range: Gulf Coast of Texas and Louisiana to South America. *Characteristics:* blackish body with bluish gloss on head and neck, olive on back and wings; yellowish-brown throat pouch. Young are brownish with pale underparts.

Olivaceous cormorants, length 25"; Thase Daniel

Red-faced cormorants, length 28-30"; Karl W. Kenyon

Red-faced Cormorant
Phalacrocorax urile

THE CLIFFS loom larger, sharply etched against the bright June sky. As your boat plows through the Bering Sea, you can make out the glowing scarlet faces and the dark, snaky necks on narrow ledges that seem inaccessible to all but creatures of the air.

Soon small flocks of inquisitive red-faced cormorants fly out from the ledges and circle the approaching vessel. Metallic tints in their feathers glisten in the sunlight, and the pair of tufts set one behind the other on their heads tells you that these are nesting birds.

If they spot a school of herring and settle down to feed, your boat may knife into the flock before the birds seek safety. Then they dive or scurry sideways with flapping wings and hoarse croaks.

These cliff dwellers fashion nests of seaweed and moss and decorate them with gull feathers. Each nest holds three or four bluish eggs.

Red-faced cormorants have increased in the Aleutians in recent years even though the natives consider them acceptable fare when food runs out in winter. Some hunters throw their hats into the air to draw these inquisitive birds into range of their guns.

Range: N. E. Siberian coast and islands south to the Aleutians; winters to Japan. *Characteristics:* bright red face, blue throat pouch, blackish plumage glossed with purple and bronze. Breeding birds have tandem crests, white flank patch. Young are brownish.

Pelagic Cormorant
Phalacrocorax pelagicus

BOOMING over reefs, the Pacific swells race toward a jagged promontory. Hard by the rocks a flock of small cormorants gently rides the waves, their iridescent coats twinkling green and purple in the sunlight. They plunge again and again for fish; the wildest surf won't deter pelagic cormorants at mealtime.

These fearless fishers dwell along a coastal arc that stretches from southern China to Baja California. In Alaskan waters naturalist Ira N. Gabrielson found pelagics strung around the top of an iceberg "like a glittering black necklace." Their shining plumage inspired Audubon to call them *resplendens*. They have also been called Baird's or violet-green cormorants.

Smaller than other western cormorants, *pelagicus* flies more gracefully and rapidly. Like the red-faced cormorant, he breeds on shelves of cliffs. The three to five bluish eggs rest on a nest of seaweed and grass. Nesting birds utter groans and croaks.

Range: coastal areas from N. Alaska to Baja California, and N. Siberia to S. China; migratory in the north. *Characteristics:* black plumage glossed with green and purple; red throat pouch. Breeding birds have tandem crests, white flank patch. Young are brownish.

Pelagic cormorant, length 25½-30"
Allan Brooks

A REMARKABLE
SPEAR FISHERMAN

The Anhinga
Family Anhingidae

SNAKELIKE NECK *raised like a periscope, anhinga grips his fish dinner. Larger catch (right) he harpooned with his beak. Finding that a turtle had pre-empted his favorite sunning rock (lower), the bird drove off the interloper with a stabbing attack.*

CYPRESS TREES hide the sun. An island of blooms brightens the somber waters, and in the dank air hang sounds that recall the tropics—creaks and rustles and distant calls.

Here, as in many other great swamps of the southeastern United States, lives a bird whose ways seem to hark back to the Age of Reptiles.

His name, anhinga, stems from a language of the Amazonian Indians. Southern fishermen call him snakebird. No wonder. Like a grebe, an anhinga is able to cut down on the air he stores, thus reducing his buoyancy. He sinks until his body disappears and only his small head and long, slender neck show—the latter curved in a serpentine S. When he swims this way he looks startlingly like a snake cutting through the water, head back, poised to strike.

But no snake was ever armed like this, with a spear of horn—long, serrated, sharp as a needle. His use of this weapon gave rise to another of his names: darter. Dipping quietly below the surface (anhingas never dive from the air), the bird prowls slowly, peering from side to side. He sights his prey, the neck tenses, and the beak darts forward. To the surface he comes with the victim—fish, water snake, even a small alligator on occasion—skewered by that deadly lance. The bird flips his catch and gulps it, sometimes first taking it ashore to pound against a rock.

The family Anhingidae includes three other kinds, one each in Africa, Asia, and Australia, in addition to the American species, *Anhinga anhinga*, whose range extends south to Argentina. All are fish eaters and residents of swamplands, generally in tropical or subtropical latitudes. All prefer to hunt in fresh rather than salt water, though they may live near the ocean or around brackish bays.

When the anhinga quits the water to take up his station on a bank or in the top limbs of a tree, he leaves all grace behind. Clinging with yellowish webbed feet to a high perch or holding his soaked wings out to dry in the sun, he seems awkward and ill-fitted for life on land. He perches upright like a cormorant; but no cormorant has so curved a neck or so long a tail. In the air the anhinga becomes beautiful. Whether rising heavily from the water, or easily from a perch on a snag or tree, he quickly proves that he is capable of prolonged flight. Alternately flapping his wings and

sailing, with tail outspread for a rudder and neck thrust forward, he resembles in silhouette an airborne turkey. Some people call him water turkey. Often a flock of anhingas will rise and circle, soaring higher and higher on their big, broad wings until they are almost out of sight, like a group of spiraling hawks. Then the birds may suddenly fold their wings and plummet toward earth, one after another, straight and swift as arrows.

Nesting is the first instinct of a male anhinga in courting season. Without some semblance of a home to offer, he can't attract a female. So he begins to build a nest or hunts up last year's home. The nest is a loose construction of sticks, twigs, and dead leaves couched in a tree. Its height varies. A lining of green leaves or moss renders it habitable.

Standing atop his bulky home, the male darter erects his neck feathers and sometimes his tail. He bends his neck into an S or an inverted U. He spreads and raises first one wing, then the other to flash their silvery patches and attract a passing female. Finally he makes a deep bow. If a

Length 34", William J. Bolte. Opposite: Frank Craighead

female stays to watch, the male steps up the performance. He moves his neck in sweeping arcs, points his bill at her, ruffles his feathers twice as fast as before, and continues bowing. The female, if receptive, bows in return; sometimes both bow in unison. Then they cross necks, rub bills, and preen one another. The male may insert his bill into the female's bill as if to feed her.

Normally anhingas are rather quiet, their most common note being a fast, machinelike clicking or chattering. At the height of display, however, they may utter grunting sounds somewhat like those of a cormorant.

Anhingas often nest in the same general area as herons. Sometimes they can be seen at the edge of large heron rookeries, sometimes in colonies by themselves. The male darter searches for nest materials while the female remains on the site and continues with the construction. Both parents incubate the four pale bluish-green eggs for nearly a month.

Range: S. Oklahoma and E. Texas to E. North Carolina, south to Argentina; migratory in the north. *Characteristics:* long, slender neck, green-tinted black body, silvery wing patches, long tail fan-shaped in flight. Female has buff neck and breast. Young are brownish.

Helen Cruickshank, National Audubon Society

BRIGAND OF
THE SPANISH MAIN

The Magnificent Frigatebird

Family Fregatidae

S O STILL that he seems painted, a huge black bird hangs in the sky, tapered wings spreading a full seven feet. Far below a dolphin breaks water, chasing a flying fish. The great bird closes the twin prongs of his scissor tail, half folds his wings, and wheels. For an instant his orange throat and long gray bill catch the evening sun. Then he hurtles straight down in a silent, streaking dive. Inches above the waves he pulls out, wings extended, beak agape. The flying fish never finishes his last frenzied leap; the pursuing dolphin goes hungry. And the magnificent frigatebird (*Fregata magnificens*) soars back into the evening sky, supper clamped in his hook-tipped bill.

Of the five species of Fregatidae that range the world's tropical seacoasts, only *magnificens* touches North America. He is also called man-o'-war bird, an apt name for a pirate who sails the air with speed and skill to rob other seabirds. If frigatebirds see a booby catch a fish, they may swarm about him, heading off, buffeting, and biting until he drops his prey. Then one corsair seizes the morsel, and the others turn on him until he too must let it go.

The great wings lifting a body of only about three pounds give this buccaneer his marvelous authority in the air. But they can be a liability on water or land. The bird's plumage is not waterproof—immersion can drown him. Entanglement in vines or limbs may starve him. So frigatebirds nest on rock promontories or open treetops, perching on feet that seem too small to hold them. Generally silent on the wing, they exchange harsh chattering calls while on their nests. For six weeks the parents take turns incubating their single chalky egg. The hatchling must be guarded lest a neighboring adult carry it away and eat it.

Range: islands of E. Pacific from Baja California to Ecuador; in the Atlantic from the Bahamas to Brazil and the Cape Verdes. Frequently seen off N. California and from Texas to Florida. *Characteristics:* long bill with hooked tip, black body with green and purple tints, long forked tail. Male has orange throat, crimson when nesting; female has white breast. Young have white head, neck, and underparts.

PUFFED-UP MALE *spends the breeding season with a bright balloon under his beak. He may keep it distended, even in flight (above), until the egg hatches. The female (upper left) lacks this gular pouch.*

94

Magnificent frigatebird, length 37½-41"; Robert I. Bowman (also upper right)

Herons, Egrets, and Bitterns

Family Ardeidae

By ALEXANDER SPRUNT, Jr.

W HEN I WAS A BOY of ten or twelve, my family had a beach house on Sullivans Island, across the harbor from Charleston, in South Carolina's Low Country. I was roaming the upper end of the island alone one day, pushing my way through thickets of wax myrtle, when I came out suddenly on the edge of a salt marsh. As I broke through into the open, a pure white shape rose hurriedly from the marsh. To my startled eyes it looked tremendous as it made off over the grasses, flapping its wide, snowy wings. I saw a bright yellow beak, long, jet-black legs, and a slender neck that settled back between the shoulders as the bird flew off. It seemed almost an animated bit of the immaculate cumulous clouds above.

I stared at the great bird entranced, shivering with excitement, all but rooted to the spot. It was not until later that I found I had seen my first common egret and had thus made the acquaintance of the family Ardeidae. I still think that the sight of one of these lovely creatures floating on wide wings over a quiet lagoon against a backdrop of towering, moss-bannered cypress trees is one of the most appealing sights that nature affords.

Of the world's 64 species of herons, egrets, and bitterns 13 are found in North America. Several of these are more common in the southern states than elsewhere, and local names abound for them. A man must have been raised in heron country to know that a "scoggin" refers to any of the medium-sized herons such as the snowy, little blue, and Louisiana, and that "poor-jo" indicates the great blue heron because he looks emaciated.

The yellow-crowned night heron, reddish egret, Louisiana heron, and snowy egret are largely restricted to the swampy southeastern areas and the Gulf Coast. But two herons, the great blue and the green, range between the Gulf and Canada, and the black-crowned night heron is found across much of the United States save for deserts and high mountains.

The common egret and the immature little blue heron tend to wander after their nesting season is over in late summer. They often fly north as far as New England and southern Ontario. Observers there report sighting the two birds, one large, one small, and both white – since the little blue heron is a white bird until two years old. They remain until autumn's chill sends them southward again for the winter.

The bitterns range widely across the continent. These birds provide striking examples of protective coloration. Time and again I have tried to point one out to bird watchers and couldn't, though the bird sat only a few feet away. When alarmed, a bittern freezes, beak pointing skyward. His long neck then blends so well with his usual habitat of tall, wet grass that he becomes almost invisible.

Herons and egrets are both long-necked, long-legged wading birds with angular body structures but graceful posturings and movements. Some people confuse them

GRACING *a Gulf Coast wilderness, a common egret preens its aigrette* *the filmy plumes of mating season that it wears like a bridal ve* *At feeding time the long, flexible neck and dagger beak strike dou* *at fish while spindly legs keep most of the body high and dr*

96

Frederick Kent Trusl

SOARING HOME *with a token of love, a common egret (left) bears a branch for his mate in Galveston Bay, Texas. There, on an island rookery (above), herons and spoonbills flicker in trees like candles in a dark candelabrum.*

with cranes. Actually, they are very different. In sustained flight, for example, they carry their necks in an S-curve, whereas cranes extend theirs.

Egrets, which could be loosely classed as plume-bearing herons, were nearly wiped out because of their beauty. The demand for the delicate aigrettes for hats and coiffures early in this century dropped the common and snowy egrets to the verge of extinction. Conservation measures barely saved them.

Herons have other enemies besides man. I was once banding little blue and Louisiana herons near Charleston with some staff members of the Charleston Museum when we shot an eight-foot alligator. In his stomach were five bands which we had placed on young herons only two months previously!

Though mortality is high among young herons, those that survive their first year

are long-lived birds. Banding records show that one gray heron in Germany lived more than 24 years! But they have their bad years. One was 1935, when a bird watcher noticed that the number of great white herons in Florida Bay seemed fewer than usual. He reported his concern to the National Audubon Society, which sent me to investigate. The U. S. Coast Guard flew me on dozens of trips from Miami across Florida Bay to the Marquesas Keys. Instead of the 1,200 or so great whites that were supposed to range this area, we could count only 146. Apparently the commercial fishermen who operated there had been killing the squabs for food. The alarming decline in the heron population had been going on for some time.

Then on Labor Day a devastating tropical storm swept across the upper Keys, taking many human lives and further reducing the great white heron population. But the Audubon Society instituted a warden service which carried out patrols. By 1941 the heron population had climbed back to about 800, and since then there has been further improvement. Everglades National Park (map, page 202) was established in 1947, providing more protection for the species. A hurricane in 1960 killed about 40 percent of the great whites, but within four years their numbers increased to 900.

As land development spreads the bulldozer becomes one of the greatest threats to herons. Without wild roosts and rookeries they will disappear.

BRISTLING IN DEFIANCE, *a reddish egret guards its young. If the intruder persists, the bird will extend its wings and charge, stabbing with its bayonet beak.*

Young great white heron (left), panting in the heat, droops wings to let air circulate.

A roost is a place where birds gather in fall and winter. I remember one such roost in a large willow bed beside Tamiami Trail in Florida—a place known as the Blue Shanty. I sat in my car, parked on the shoulder of the road, and watched the birds come in from the surrounding Everglades—herons, more herons, and still more—some low over the grass tops, others a hundred feet up, and many very high, losing altitude like falling leaves. As the birds landed they formed a kaleidoscope of whites, blues, and grays. And their voices! An ever growing clamor of cries, squawks, and guttural croaks continued until dusk and after. Thousands had gathered by then; others were still coming. Even after they had perched and settled down, the vocal din went on, only gradually diminishing in volume.

A rookery is a nesting colony. I have visited heron rookeries from the Carolinas to the Rio Grande Valley of Texas, and when I think of them I linger with pleasure over memories of the oldest known heron-egret rookery in the country. It is a great cypress swamp on the South Santee River in South Carolina. Here the birds have been recorded as nesting for about 140 years.

Nothing but a skiff or dugout should be used to penetrate such a place. These can be propelled without a sound except for the sibilant dipping of a paddle. Silently, then, we enter a realm of tupelo gum, ash, and buttonwood where the age-old calm is scarcely ruffled by a breeze in the treetops, the splash of a fish, or the song of a bird. A wide lagoon stretches before us, with aisles or leads forming passages through the ranks of tree trunks. Sometimes they come to a dead end, sometimes they wind back to the lagoon.

Wide-winged ospreys float overhead. Reptilian anhingas perch on stumps, and an armored back, breaking the surface of the water, gives away the presence of an alligator. A brood of wood ducks threads through the brilliant green carpet of duckweed, and high over the trees a swallow-tailed kite drifts in lazy circles.

All these sights, however, are but an introduction. A smaller lagoon opens to one side, and we turn into it—to see the trees about its rim erupt into an explosion of sound and movement. Birds fill the air, wheeling, flapping, circling with a discordant bedlam of squawks, shrieks, and now and then the gurgling notes of a snowy egret. Hundreds of nests, no more than platforms of sticks, are saddled in the lower growth. A few are low enough so that from our water-level position we can see the eggs—assurance of a new generation of Ardeidae to grace the green marshes and swamplands of our country.

A STRANGER IN THE REEDS prompts a wide-eyed least bittern (right) to stretch high and freeze, using color and pose to blend with them. Forced from its eggs, the bird usually steals away on foot.

Escorting a grazing Florida steer, cattle egrets (below) feast on insects kicked up by the hooves. Originally Old World, the birds spread to South America and by 1952 were established in Florida.

David G. Allen. Right: Arthur A. Allen
Opposite: Frederick Kent Truslow

Great White Heron
Ardea occidentalis

TRACKING the great white takes you into the mangrove country of southern Florida, for this large heron breeds no farther north.

Wading out of the shallow waters of Florida Bay, you crawl carefully through the tangled roots. Your quarry is fishing just out of sight, so the mere crack of a twig may trigger croaks of alarm and a swish of wings. Quietly you part the thick foliage. And there, beyond a marl flat, is a small colony of these beauties.

Sensing something, they stand alert, four feet tall, like alabaster statues against the dark green mangroves. Now they spy you and flap ponderously away on wings that span seven feet, necks drawn in, slim legs streaming aft.

As the tide comes in over the mud flats, the great white heron wades out to feed. He stands dead still in wait for fish or crustaceans or insects to happen by. He has a tremendous appetite—Audubon tells of two captive birds that "swallowed a bucketful of mullets in a few minutes." When the tide reaches up to his full belly, our sated heron heavily takes off.

Great whites usually begin raising a family in late fall or early spring, but they may breed at any time of year. A courting male dances, struts, flies in circles about his mate. In one ritual he stretches his neck low, erects his plumes, and snaps his bill with a loud *bok*.

Great white heron, length 50"; Walter A. Weber, National Geographic staff artist

The flat, bulky nest of dried sticks usually nestles in mangrove branches 12 to 20 feet above the water. The three or four eggs are bluish green or olive.

A hatchling spends most of his first week lying on the floor of the nest, head turned to one side, eyes partially open. Whenever a parent returns, the chick sounds *tick-tick* calls and lunges feebly for the regurgitated food. Later he starts to shuffle about the nest and stretch his wings. And in the style of his elders he scratches the side of his head with one foot.

Hunted by man and reduced by storms, the species was in serious danger in Florida by 1935. But with firm protection the great white has since made a comeback.

Range: S. Florida to Cuba and Yucatán; wanders to N. Florida. *Characteristics:* yellow bill, long neck, large white body, short white plumes on head and back; greenish-yellow legs. Young are dingy white and lack plumes.

 ## Great Blue Heron
Ardea herodias

"On the banks of the fair Ohio, let us pause a while, good Reader, and watch the Heron...."

Thus Audubon writes of the great blue. "He has taken a silent step, and with great care he advances; slowly does he raise his head from his shoulders, and now, what a sudden start! his formidable bill has transfixed a perch, which he beats to death on the ground. See with what difficulty he gulps it down his capacious throat!"

This voracious bird, shown fishing on page 24, frequently catches more than he can swallow. One great blue was found dead with a big fish hung in his throat, its side fins piercing the lining of his gullet.

Not only does the great blue heron stalk his prey, lifting each foot stealthily from the shallows without a ripple, but he also waits motionless. He may stand still as a stump for half an hour until a victim comes by. On rare occasions he lands in deep water, and as he floats he strikes again and again into a school of fish.

The great blue prefers fish. But he also eats frogs, snakes, crustaceans, birds, small mammals, and insects. Sometimes he plunders unprotected fish hatchery pools.

This big blue-gray wader is similar in size to the great white heron but wears longer head plumes. The two birds behave much the same and have been found interbreeding in the Florida Keys. Some authorities believe they are color phases of the same species.

Great blues, nevertheless, range far beyond the northernmost limits of great whites. Five races of *herodias* breed throughout the United States and well into Canada. After nesting the

birds disperse and wander in all directions. Some subspecies of this most widely distributed of our herons migrate south in the fall.

When sunrise pinks a somber forest lake or dusk settles on some remote sandbar or marsh or river canyon, you may see a great blue heron standing in lonely majesty—the finishing stroke of a primitive landscape. Perhaps you try to creep closer. But no! This keen-eyed creature is off in a flurry. His long legs swing to and fro as he beats heavily into the air; then he folds his neck back between his shoulders and trails his feet, rudderlike, as he shifts into a steady, slow-motion flight over the horizon.

This heron—or blue crane, as he's often called—frequently dwells closer to civilization. With long, stately strides he forages in upland meadows, cultivated fields, and even in the pools of suburban backyards.

Migrating great blues flock to the breeding grounds in early spring. Usually they settle on an island or in a secluded patch of woods. Court-

Great blue heron, length 42-52"; Frederick Kent Truslow

GREEN HERON TENSES: *goldfish below. Toehold tight on a log, the hunched bird stabs into a pond in New York State, clamps his prey, flips it around, and straightens up to gulp it down.*

ship rituals often involve scores, even hundreds of the birds. Males strut about defiantly, pecking at rivals and parrying bill thrusts like master swordsmen. Croaking females urge them on. Sometimes groups of herons dance in circles, their big wings flapping up and down. Pairs nibble each other's feathers.

For nest sites they frequently choose the highest treetops, though they may use shrubs or even the ground. Males gather sticks and females work them into place. New nests are small, flat, and flimsy; refurbished ones are bulky. Bird droppings often whitewash the branches and the ground below—a clue to the nest locations.

In these tree homes, silhouetted against the spring sky, the parents take turns incubating the four greenish-blue eggs. Both feed their noisy hatchlings, and at least one remains on duty at the nest at all times to guard the brood against hawks and owls.

The young herons make enjoyable pets. They have been known to perch on a boy's knee and to nibble in friendly fashion at a man's eyeglasses. But an older great blue heron, especially a wounded bird at bay, may attack viciously with his sharp beak.

Range: S. E. Alaska to Nova Scotia, south to S. Mexico and the West Indies; winters to N. South America. Wanders to N. Canada. *Characteristics:* white head with black crown patches and head plumes, whitish plumes on lower neck, front of neck streaked; large bluish-gray body, blackish shoulder patch and legs. Young have black crown, lack head plumes.

Green Heron

Butorides virescens

BY THE SHORE a crow-size bird crouches motionless; from a distance his greenish back feathers look blue. A passing minnow brings the green heron to life. In a flash he spears it. A good swimmer, he may dive in after his next victim.

Smaller than any of our herons except the least bittern, the green heron usually can be found in summer near any brook, pond, or sizable marsh in the eastern half of the United States. A paler form breeds in the Far West and along irrigation ditches of the Southwest. When alarmed, the green heron flicks his tail, stretches his neck, raises his shaggy crest, utters a harsh *skeow*, and flies off across the water. Farm boys know him as "skeow" or "fly-up-the-creek."

A courting male crouches low and snaps his mandibles. Then he thrusts up his head and displays his scapular plumes. He and his mate may nest alone or in a small colony. They build their stick nest 10 to 20 feet high in a tree or, rarely, on the ground. Both parents incubate the four or five greenish-blue eggs; both guard the eggs and young against fish crows and grackles.

Range: W. Washington to central Arizona, N. Texas, Minnesota, and New Brunswick, south to N. South America; migratory in the north. *Characteristics:* small size; glossy blackish-green crown, chestnut neck, white chin and throat stripe; grayish-green back, greenish wings tinged with buff, brownish-gray underparts, yellow or orange legs. Young have streaked necks and breasts.

Little Blue Heron
Florida caerulea

THE SOGGY HEAT of afternoon stills the marsh. A slaty bird with a maroon head inches through the shallows on dark, spindly legs, his keen eyes alert for a stir, a splash, a ripple. In a flash the little blue heron jabs with his black-tipped beak and snaps up a minnow. Where fish abound he may abandon his methodical habits and run through the water, striking time and again until he can hold no more.

Though he is a skilled fisherman, the little blue prefers crustaceans, frogs, and insects. He gathers most of his fare on the borders of streams, lakes, and swamps. Louisianians know him as the "levee walker" for his habit of seeking cray-fish along rice-field levees. He often feeds near estuaries and coastal ponds, but this graceful southerner favors inland waters.

While building their frail nest of twigs, a pair of blue herons may pause to cross their necks and bills and nibble each other's feathers. The nest, set low in a willow or a bush, holds four or five bluish-green eggs. When alarmed, an incubating little blue utters a dry croak.

After breeding season these birds—especially the fledglings—wander as far north as the Dakotas and southeastern Canada. Clad in white until their second summer, the young are often confused with snowy egrets. The herons have greenish legs, the snowy egrets black.

Range: central Oklahoma to central Alabama, and Atlantic coast from Massachusetts south to Peru and Uruguay; migratory in the north. *Characteristics:* black-tipped bill, maroon head and neck, slaty-blue body, dark legs. Young are white with slaty wing tips and greenish legs.

Little blue heron
length 20-29″
Frederick Kent Truslow
Left: adult and white
juvenile, Allan Brooks

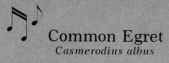

Common Egret
Casmerodius albus

RIVALRY ERUPTS on a Florida sandbar. Two large male egrets stop their gurgling and strutting around a female and square off, long, wispy aigrettes standing erect.

Out darts one bird's yellow beak. The other bird jerks back his head, then strikes. His opponent dodges. When the seesaw flurry subsides they rejoin their black-legged fellows in courtship dances around the females.

The aigrette has been the common egret's bane as well as his beauty spot. Up to 54 of these snowy back feathers form his nuptial train. For this millinery prize plume hunters in the early 1900's received $32 an ounce — nearly double the value of gold at that time. Is it any wonder that "man's greed and woman's vanity," as ornithologist Edward Howe Forbush put it, almost annihilated the common egret in many parts of his range around the world?

But with protection this slender creature has revived in the United States. From the cypresses of South Carolina to the mangroves of Florida, from the willows of Texas to the tules of Oregon, he is a common species. In the United States *albus* is also known as the American egret. He prefers swamp country. Occasionally, however, he nests in dry woodlands.

In a mixed southeastern rookery you'll often find him nesting among other herons, even among anhingas, ibises, and cormorants. His deep, hoarse croak will lead you through a weird world of cypress and moss. Then suddenly, around a bend in the dark water, you see him— ethereally white, perched shyly on a buttresslike

root. Just a glimpse and he's gone, winging slowly and buoyantly to his nest.

Common egrets may build their nest in tules just above the water or in treetops 50 feet high. With sticks and plant stems they weave a flat and flimsy nursery that usually is unlined. Some pairs shore up old nests with new material, providing a bulkier platform for their three or four blue-green eggs.

During incubation the birds perform a nest relief ritual. With a hoarse fanfare the male lands on a nearby branch. Wings raised, he walks along the limb toward his mate. His plumes seem to float on air as he goes. She responds by lifting her head and spreading her plumes. After a few moments in this graceful posture she departs. Now the master of the nest stands over the eggs. Finally he crouches and slowly settles down over them, lowers his plumes, and folds his serpentine neck down between his shoulders.

Nestlings are fed about four times a day—breakfast, brunch, late lunch, and dinner. They stretch their necks and utter *kek-kek-kek* appeals when a parent returns with food. A youngster seizes a parent's bill as if trying to snip it off. The adult bends and regurgitates.

Common egrets flock to the feeding grounds at sunrise. Striking swiftly, they seize fish, frogs, snakes, large insects, and mice.

In recent years these birds have extended their nesting range to Canada and New England. They wander widely after breeding.

Range: S. Saskatchewan and Manitoba; S. Oregon and S. Idaho to central Arizona, N. Texas, S. Minnesota, and N. Ohio; east coast from Massachusetts south to S. South America; migratory in the north. Also found in Europe, Africa, Asia, and Australia. *Characteristics:* yellow bill, large white body, blackish legs and feet. Breeding birds have long white plumes.

COMMON EGRETS *spring, thrust, and swirl in a duel over fishing rights in Everglades National Park, Florida. Victor will occupy a choice rock in a pond.*

Length 37-41"
Frederick Kent Truslow

Snowy Egret
Leucophoyx thula

IN SPRING male snowies sound raspy threats and attack each other with snapping beaks and flailing wings. Then the victor goes a-courting in his glorious nuptial raiment.

Crest up, body bent forward, back plumes streaming out behind in wispy upcurves, he parades about the female. As she displays her airy finery, he spirals up perhaps a hundred yards, then plummets. He tumbles over and over, right-ing himself at the last moment for a graceful landing. His spotless white coat and those waving aigrettes present an unforgettable image of ethereal grace and beauty.

All through the nesting season mated snowy egrets greet each other with raised plumes. They nest near water — a pond, bay, or salt marsh along the Atlantic and Gulf coasts, a tule marsh in the West. In a small tree or bush they build a frail platform of sticks for a clutch of four or five bluish-green eggs. Both sexes incubate, and both gather food for the young.

Snowy egrets, length 20-27"; Walter A. Weber, National Geographic staff artist

A feeding snowy pokes a black leg with a "golden slipper" into the shallows and stirs the bottom. Then the bird rushes about to seize the small fish and crabs it has aroused. Audubon noted that snowy egrets stood on floating logs in the Mississippi and snapped shrimp from the water. They also dine on grasshoppers and other insects.

After breeding, these birds wander as far north as southern Canada. At this time their aigrettes are much shorter and straighter than in spring.

Snowies fly lightly and steadily with a more rapid wingbeat than the common egret. They are much smaller too. So plume hunters, who nearly annihilated these two attractive egrets around the turn of the century, called the snowy the "short white" and the common egret the "long white." With protection the snowy has made a comeback and now breeds farther north than he did before the days of slaughter.

Range: N. California and S. Idaho to Oklahoma, the Gulf Coast, and New Jersey, south to S. South America; migratory in the north. *Characteristics:* white body and plumes (back plumes curve upward during breeding), slender black bill, black legs with yellow feet. Young have yellow stripe on back of legs.

Reddish Egret
Dichromanassa rufescens

SHAGGY NECK OUTTHRUST, the reddish egret lopes swiftly through the shallow water. Suddenly he turns, raises his wings, leaps in the air, stabs his parti-colored bill into a school of fish, and snaps one up. Sometimes he dines in the slow, stately fashion of other herons.

In the United States shortly after the beginning of the 20th century, plume hunters almost wiped out this species. But under warden protection reddish egrets have made a strong recovery amid the Spanish dagger and prickly pear of the Texas coast. Among the mangroves of southern Florida's shores, however, they have increased much more slowly.

They begin to pair in April. Vying for a female, one male frequently chases another on the ground and in graceful zigzagging flights. Courting birds often stand side by side in the shallows and peer down. They also wing in circles about

109

Reddish egrets, length 29"
Right: white phase

the nest area, flinging their heads about and softly calling *crog-crog*.

Both sexes incubate the three or four bluish-green eggs, taking turns on the well-made nest of twigs, stems, and rootlets.

Range: Baja California, the Texas coast, and S. Florida, south to El Salvador and the West Indies; winters to Venezuela. *Characteristics:* flesh-colored, black-tipped bill; chestnut head and neck, slate-gray body, slaty blue-and-brownish back plumes, dark legs. In a rarer color phase plumage is entirely white.

Cattle Egret
Bubulcus ibis

WHY DOES this squat little egret usually tag along beside grazing cattle? Why does he sometimes even ride them piggyback? For food.

Two or three cattle egrets, their short, thick necks swaying in gooselike fashion, often take station near a cow's head. As her plodding hooves flush grasshoppers and other insects, the egrets bolt after them. If one of the birds gets too close to her face, she may shake her horns at him. But the relationship is generally friendly, and if the cow lies down to rest, her entourage of egrets frequently rests too.

These birds also forage near horses and pigs, and – in the Old World – near elephants, camels, and water buffalo. They have even been seen dancing attendance on farm tractors!

Louisiana heron, length 24-28"
Winfield Parks, National Geographic photographer

How these immigrants came to the New World, and when, remains a mystery. They were first reported in northern South America, and one theory has it that they flew across the Atlantic from the bulge of Africa with the help of strong easterly winds. Cattle egrets were discovered breeding in Florida in 1952, and in a remarkable population explosion quickly spread along the Atlantic and Gulf coasts.

At a distance the cattle egret looks like a snowy egret, but it lacks the snowy's slender grace and delicate plumage. In the nuptial season cattle egrets grow buff-colored plumes. Amid much croaking, they settle in colonies in streamside willows or swamp trees. The twiggy nests hold three to five blue eggs.

Range: S. New Jersey to S. Texas, West Indies, and N. South America, spreading steadily; also S. Europe and India to S. Africa and N. Australia. *Characteristics:* white body; during breeding crown, neck, and back plumes are orange-buffy, yellow bill and yellowish legs turn pink. Young have blackish legs.

Cattle egret, length 20"; Roger Tory Peterson

Louisiana Heron
Hydranassa tricolor

STROKING SILENTLY, the graceful Louisiana heron sails past beards of Spanish moss, alights in an oak, and presents his mate with a twig. She carries it about and tries to work it into their nest.

Often these slender birds sit side by side, one resting its head against the other's white flanks. Then they intertwine their long, purplish necks, raise their plumes, and nibble each other's slaty-blue back feathers.

Both share incubation chores. The bird on duty croaks loudly whenever a vulture, fish crow, or boat-tailed grackle threatens the three or four bluish-green eggs. The stick nest may be placed in a tree, on grass, or among weeds.

One of the most abundant herons in the South, the Louisiana heron breeds on oyster-reef islands off Texas, in Louisiana tidal marshes, and on the mangrove and buttonwood islands of Florida. He may settle in a colony of his own kind or join one crammed with other herons.

A flock of thousands of Louisiana herons nearing a colony is a breathtaking sight. They approach at an altitude of 100 or 200 feet, flying with strong, graceful strokes. Suddenly they fold their wings and dive. At the last moment many skid this way and that to soften the landing.

Crouching in shallows, this heron deftly seizes fish, frogs, and crustaceans. "Lady of the Waters," Audubon dubbed the brightly plumed wader. It is also called the tricolored heron.

Range: Baja California, Gulf Coast, and Atlantic coast to Maryland, south to N. South America; wanders to S. California, Arkansas, and New Jersey. *Characteristics:* slaty head, neck, and back, whitish throat stripe, white and purplish head and neck plumes, cinnamon back plumes, white rump and belly. Young have reddish head and neck, brownish-olive back.

Black-crowned Night Heron
Nycticorax nycticorax

A GENERATION AGO a naturalist in quest of blackcrowned night herons would have headed for Cape Cod. Thousands of them bred at the ancient Sandy Neck rookery, one of the most famous in North America. As he plodded the salt meadows, clouds of these dark-backed, gray-and-white birds would swirl squawking into the sky. To the 19th century ornithologist Alexander Wilson the din sounded as if "two or three hundred Indians were choking or throttling each other."

In recent years the great rookery on the Massachusetts coast has been little used. Lumbering and drainage projects have reduced the blackcrown's habitat in many other areas. Yet this squat, short-legged heron is still distributed

Black-crowned night heron and juvenile (left), length 23-28"
Allan Brooks

111

as widely in the New World as in the Old. It is the only bird ever to become a Japanese peer. Legend holds that a tenth century emperor became enchanted with the blackcrown and elevated it to the fifth court rank, or *Go-i*. The blackcrown is still known in Japan as the *goi* heron.

Usually these herons frequent freshwater or salt marshes, but they have been found breeding 160 feet high in the tall firs of Oregon, on western grasslands, and in dense woodlands along the Atlantic coast. Rookeries in city parks, such as the one at the zoo in Washington, D. C., may create a nuisance with bird droppings.

In the crowded rookeries a male usually gathers sticks and weeds and his mate works them into the nest. Mating birds shake their heads, rattle their bills, and nibble each other's plumage. Often they utter soft *wok wok* sounds.

Both parents incubate the three to five bluish-green eggs. Nestlings at first get only regurgitated juices. But soon they tug at the parent's beak for solid food. If a fish is too big to be swallowed whole, its tail sticks out of the bird's mouth until its head is thoroughly digested.

Except when feeding his young, the blackcrown is a nocturnal forager. At dusk or before sunrise he sallies forth with slowly flapping wings. His *quok* call, often heard as he passes overhead in the dark, earned him the nickname "squawk." He stalks frogs and crustaceans, but to catch fish he stands statue-still, then strikes.

After the breeding season blackcrowns roam as far as British Columbia, central Ontario, and Newfoundland. A few winter as far north as Oregon and New England, but most northern breeders head south.

Range: central Washington to S. Saskatchewan and N.E. New Brunswick, south to S. South America; migratory in the north. Also found in Europe, Asia, Africa, and Hawaii. *Characteristics:* greenish-black crown and back, white head plumes, gray wings and rump, whitish underparts; short yellowish legs. Young have streaked brownish-olive back, whitish underparts.

Yellow-crowned Night Heron
Nyctanassa violacea

IN SOUTHERN SWAMPS and bayous, where water moccasins slither and alligators doze, this stocky wader finds a year-round home. Day and night he feasts on crabs and aquatic insects.

When his bulky stick nest is threatened, the shy yellowcrown sounds a rasping *quak* and flies off, neck folded and feet trailing behind the tail. Danger over, the heron circles back to the clutch of three to five blue-green eggs.

The yellowcrown has extended his breeding range northward in recent years. After nesting he wanders even farther north until time to head for winter quarters.

Range: Oklahoma to S. W. Ohio and Atlantic coast from Massachusetts south to Brazil; migratory in the north. *Characteristics:* black head, white head plumes, white crown and cheek patch tinged with yellow; gray body, long orange-yellow legs. Young have speckled brownish upperparts, streaked whitish underparts.

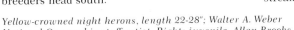

Yellow-crowned night herons, length 22-28"; Walter A. Weber National Geographic staff artist. Right: juvenile, Allan Brooks

Male least bittern, length 11-14"
Helen Cruickshank, National Audubon Society

Least Bittern
Ixobrychus exilis

DISTURBED, the least bittern would rather run than fly. He strides through his marshy domain, grasping reed stems with his toes. He wades when he must or burrows through the cattails like a mouse. Audubon found that one bittern could compress his plumage enough to walk between a pair of books set an inch apart—less than half the bird's apparent breadth.

Our smallest heron, this bittern breeds widely in freshwater marshes or, in the South, in coastal areas. Yet his secretive ways make him hard to find unless his soft courtship cooing or harsh alarm cackles attract attention.

The darker male does most of the nest building. The platform, set on bent stalks, holds four or five bluish or greenish eggs. Both parents feed the nestlings regurgitated fish and crustaceans.

Range: Oregon to S. Ontario and Maine, south to Paraguay; migratory in the north. *Characteristics:* small size; chestnut neck, two whitish back stripes, buffy wing patch, brownish or buffy underparts with dark side patch. Male has greenish-black head and back; female has purplish-brown head and back, streaked throat. Young resemble female but are lighter.

 ## American Bittern
Botaurus lentiginosus

A SPRING EVENING quickens the voices of the marshlands: a swamp sparrow trills, a swallow twitters. Suddenly from deep in the cattails an American bittern joins the chorus.

Amid violent contortions that make him look as if he were about to retch, the bird gulps air, distending his crop and throat. Then he belches forth a guttural croak like the sound of an old wooden pump: *oong-ka-choonk, oong-ka-choonk, oong-ka-choonk.*

Thoreau heard the wild, booming love notes and wrote, "The Bittern pumps in the fen." Many people know this chunky brown heron as the "thunder pumper." Others call him "stake driver." From far off the accented *ka* note sounds like a mallet pounding a stake.

The weird "song" serves to warn a rival as well as entice a mate. And as he courts or threatens, the male displays a ruff of white feathers extending straight out from the shoulders.

When people approach this recluse of the wetlands, he freezes, beak aimed skyward. His body blends with the reeds, even sways with them in a breeze. Thus camouflaged he can still observe intruders in front of him, for his eyes are set low on the sides of his head.

If the intruders get too close, he flaps awkwardly into the air, croaks, and flies to some new retreat. A wounded bittern, however, squats with arched wings, then strikes for the face with a swift thrust of its daggerlike beak.

On a nesting platform of dead cattails or bulrushes the female lays four to six buffy eggs. She incubates them for about 24 days, then feeds the young by regurgitation. The fare includes fish, crustaceans, frogs, mice, and insects.

Range: marshlands of the United States and Canada; winters to Central America. *Characteristics:* brown upperparts, blackish flight feathers, white throat, long neck with black side stripe, streaked whitish underparts.

113

American bittern, length 23-34"; Thase Daniel

FLINT-HEADED WADER
IN SOUTHERN LAGOONS

The Wood Ibis
Family Ciconiidae

By ROBERT PORTER ALLEN

O N WINGS that spanned all of five feet the great birds rose from the southern Florida swamp. They cleared the cypresses with determined strokes and pointed their long necks and heavy bills toward their goal – a shallow pond a few miles away. Returning, they headed for bulky nests high in the tree crowns with food for their young.

Chest-deep in swamp water Fred Truslow and I peered up, aware that we were beholding a rare sight. Wood ibises are really storks – the only storks, out of 17 species of the family Ciconiidae, native to the United States. And they are in danger of extinction here. The birds that swung overhead in easy flight were among the few remaining wood ibises which converge on Florida swamps during the breeding season. Here at Bear Island Rookery they gather from November through April to lay eggs and raise their young. When nesting is over, they scatter throughout the southern states.

The wood ibis (*Mycteria americana*) dwells also in Central and South America. One of the largest wading birds, he stands about 3½ feet tall on stiltlike legs. His flight feathers are black and he is our only wader with a black tail. It contrasts with his white body plumage. Adult birds have a dark, bare pate which explains the nickname "flinthead."

My studies of this bird for the National Audubon Society had brought me to Bear Island with Fred Truslow, nature photographer par excellence. We sought ways to safeguard this species, and Fred's photographs would be invaluable. But now Fred was grumbling that he couldn't take pictures of the storks from down on the ground. "I've got to get up in the air somehow," he said, shading his eyes and looking up.

I saw what he meant. But how could we build a tower without disturbing the birds – possibly even driving them from their nests? "We'll have to make one first," Fred said, "then carry it into the swamp."

So we whacked together an 18-foot tower with a 3-foot-square platform on top for Fred's blind. We carried this monster three-quarters of a mile from our camp to the swamp, at times wading through water up to our belts. We set it up facing a cypress that held four nests. The platform, 14 feet

Length 35-47", Frederick Kent Truslow

WOOD IBIS *reaches with skinny legs for a nest in the Everglades. Parent's wing lining shows the delicate pink flush that appears at nesting time. Two-month-old young are big enough to defend themselves against raids by unmated older ibises.*

Frederick Kent Truslow

SOARING *in formation, wood ibises rise high on thermal currents, then may glide 15 or 20 miles to a feeding pond.*
  To focus on their nests in a cypress, photographer Fred Truslow spent stifling 10-hour days zipped into his lofty blind.

above the water, was still below the level of the nests but high enough to give us a close look at the feeding habits of the nestlings.

The young wood ibises seemed insatiable. We watched the long-legged parents bringing fish, insects, small snakes, and frogs. The birds were so absorbed in their task that they paid little attention to us.

Later I learned firsthand how much food a stork demands. An injured female wood ibis was found near the Bear Island colony. My family took her in and housed her in a chicken pen. We named her Mickey—short for *Mycteria*, the generic name, which comes from the Greek word for "snout."

At first Mickey was weak and frightened. We had to force-feed her. But after a few days of quiet care she began to display an enormous appetite that kept our entire family busy. In fact, we soon discovered that Mickey's tastes were too expensive for us. She disdained frozen shrimp, preferring the more costly live ones. She would dispose of three dozen in short order, then rummage in the water pan for more. We finally persuaded her that we might serve the live shrimp as a special treat—say on off Sundays and Izaak Walton's birthday—but that for her daily fare she would have to make do with frozen mullet, properly

116

defrosted. If the fish were small enough she swallowed them whole, headfirst, a few inches at a time. But the large fish I had to split into sections. She took these readily enough if I tossed them into a pan of water with a hose running in one end to stir things up and make the pieces look alive.

Mickey weighed about six pounds and ate nearly two pounds of fish a day. A more active bird in the wild would eat larger amounts—especially a male, which may weigh ten pounds or more. Obviously these storks require large feeding areas.

In past years they had them. Drought alone affected their numbers, and after drought years the birds always rebuilt their population. But now drainage and development projects are destroying feeding grounds and breeding sites. In the 1950's, during a severe drought, large numbers of wood ibises left their usual haunts for the first time and wandered across the United States as far as New England and Wyoming. Low temperatures and winter gales discouraged nesting attempts in the few remaining colonies. Wood ibis numbers sank to a critical low in 1957. Then, just in time, the normal pattern of rainfall began to restore proper conditions.

When Fred and I visited Cuthbert Lake Rookery (map, page 202) in Everglades National Park in 1959, we found 800 to 900 pairs of these storks well established on the island in the middle of the lake. Here, where big trees had been swept away by hurricanes, the birds were nesting in young ten-foot mangroves.

The two or three grotesque hatchlings in each nest had dome-shaped skulls and yellow bills. Flight feathers began to appear in three weeks, and the chicks hobbled around on bent legs, stretching their stubby wings. In a couple of months, when they were fully grown, they began to make short flights. There is power and dash in the way wood ibises take off, and grace in their slow upward spirals as they ride rising air currents half a mile high.

In the United States the fate of the wood ibis is tied to Florida. Here, in the early 1960's, there were between 8,000 and 10,000 breeding pairs. Though the huge, unspoiled wilderness of a century ago is gone forever, some big areas remain. A few of these serve as feeding grounds. But only three of the regularly used breeding sites—Corkscrew Swamp and two colonies in Everglades National Park—are permanent sanctuaries. Here our lordly stork lives in precarious balance with nature.

Range: Florida and coastal areas of Mexico, Central and South America to Argentina; wanders to S. California, Arizona, and W. Texas, casually northward. *Characteristics:* long curved bill; dark gray bald head and neck, greenish-black flight feathers and tail, white body; long slender legs. Female is smaller than male. Young have feathered head and dingy white body.

NOT SNOWFLAKES *but wood ibises whiten a rookery in Cuthbert Lake, Florida, where hundreds nest.*

Month-old young (upper left) still have downy white necks and crowns. Later they become "flintheads."

Frederick Kent Truslow

Fishing (right), a stork balances,
wings raised and beak open, while
stirring up action with a foot.

Ibises and Spoonbills

Family Threskiornithidae

By ROBERT PORTER ALLEN

ADULT ROSEATE SPOONBIL
wears radiant plume
but the face of a clow
The young (below) are near
white and have not yet lo
the down on their head
Their bills, soft and stubb
at hatching, are taking on th
spatular shape. Here one bathe
its wings in a Florida lagoon whi
the other dodges flying spra

Frederick Kent Truslow

An EXCITED TOURIST, driving along the Overseas Highway between Miami and Key West, pulled into a service station. "Say," he exclaimed to the attendant, "I didn't know there were wild flamingos here in the Florida Keys!"

"Mister," said the attendant with an air of authority, "those pink birds you saw weren't flamingos. They were *rosy-ate* spoonbills!"

In Florida the only people who can't tell a roseate spoonbill from a flamingo are rank outlanders. The locals are proud of their spoonbills. Photographs of the resplendent pink-and-white birds have taken their place alongside bathing beauties, sailfish, and palm trees in Florida Keys brochures. And a local Girl Scout troop chose the roseate spoonbill as its official emblem.

This is the largest North American member of the ibis family – the Threskiornithidae – which numbers 33 species around the world. Among its species is the sacred ibis of Africa, revered by the ancient Egyptians.

In the United States white-faced, glossy, and white ibises may be seen in Florida and along the Gulf Coast. There have even been reported sightings of South America's scarlet ibis. These long-legged species fly with their necks extended. Wading through shallow water, ibises probe for food with their long, downcurved bills, grunting and babbling all the while.

Their big cousin the roseate spoonbill has an unmistakable spatulate bill, which he swings from side to side as he searches the shallows for food. His gorgeous coloration nearly caused his extinction in the United States, for plume hunters gunned down the birds for years. In 1939 only 30 spoonbills remained in Florida. But this is a vigorous species and, with protection, the population increased to more than 400 by the mid-1950's. Since then housing developments have encroached on their nesting areas and once again the Florida spoonbill has declined. In Texas and Louisiana, however, the spoonbill is holding its own.

For years my wife Evelyn and I observed adult spoonbills from a vantage point aboard the National Audubon Society's research boat *Pink Curlew* – a local nickname for the species. Since a heavy cover of red mangrove hides the island rookeries

PINK PINIONS FLASHING, *a flight of spoonbills in Texas takes up formation. All species of the ibis family fly in ragged V's or echelons. Ibises flap, sail, then flap again, while spoonbills generally beat steadily onward.*

in the Keys, young spoonbills are out of sight for the first six weeks of their lives. You can hear their thin, cheeping cries for food, which the parents provide in pre-digested form. But you cannot see the birds unless you go ashore and approach the nests. This the law forbids, for you would panic the closely packed nesting communities. Many young birds would tumble out of their nests and get lost.

We learned the approximate dates of mating, incubation, and hatching. Week after week we watched impatiently for the young to make their debut.

I remember a red-letter day when *Pink Curlew* was anchored near the Cowpens nesting site in Florida Bay (map, page 202). If hatching had taken place on December 15, as we suspected, some of the youngsters would now be six weeks old and should be showing themselves in the treetops. At 9:30 that morning an adult spoonbill glided toward us and landed atop a mangrove tree with a great waving of its bright pink wings.

Then we saw a movement of other wings, paler pink with dark tips. The adult was feeding a young spoonbill while a second youngster begged nearby!

At last the adult flew away, displaying breathtaking colors—pink wings banded in deep carmine and a glowing orange tail. The two nestlings were then emboldened to poke their white heads above the topmost branches. During that morning other youngsters followed suit, raising their heads above the glistening green leaves. To us the birds looked bright and shiny and new, the hope of the species.

Later a peregrine falcon zoomed in with great speed and dash toward the adult spoonbills that were flying in and out of the colony. His passes seemed half in play, for he never actually struck one of them. But the peregrine falcon takes a newly fledged spoonbill now and then, and when this one went after the young, waiting in the treetops for food, he meant business. Starting at one end of the colony, he raked its entire length, sweeping lower each time he approached a young spoonbill.

"Down! Down!" we found ourselves shouting—as if the birds could understand us. "Get your heads down, you young idiots! Take cover!"

Frederick Kent Truslow

After the falcon had made a couple of unsuccessful sweeps, not a white-feathered head could be seen. Abruptly the intruder abandoned the mangroves. Almost immediately the heads of young spoonbills began to reappear out of the tree canopies. They looked like the white blossoms of some exotic plant blooming all at once, as if on signal.

A few days after the young first poked their heads out of the treetops, they started to come up to the shore of the nesting island. There were so many of them together, all vigorously demanding food, that an adult returning from the feeding ground might be pursued by a dozen hungry youngsters at once. As a result, the most persistent ones usually got fed, regardless of their parentage.

Between feedings the young birds probed experimentally for food on their own. Their nestling voices began to change, and although they still bobbed their feathered heads and cried in a high, thin treble, the parent birds reacted differently. A mob of noisy youngsters would scramble around an old bird, wings flapping as each one struggled to get close enough to be fed. But now the adult would pull its head away, mandibles tightly closed. Sometimes it would eventually give in, as if simply for the sake of some peace and quiet, and reluctantly feed the most aggressive.

123

But in a few days even violent entreaties left it unmoved. The young had to learn to fend for themselves.

Taking off, one parent flew in wide circles over the nesting key, followed closely by a bevy of hungry youngsters. Then the old bird peeled off and headed straight for the nearest feeding ground. One or two of the strongest youngsters followed for a short distance, but it was several days before they developed enough confidence to go all the way.

When the young waded in the shallows for the first time, they searched for food exactly as the adults did. Wading forward, they swept their partly opened bills from side to side in a 180-degree arc, feeling for small fish, crustaceans, and insects through a curtain of water and mud. When nerve endings along the inner lining of the bill signal contact, the mandibles clamp shut, trapping the prey.

Even in captivity a young spoonbill will do the same, for this is an instinctive action. Offered live killifish or shrimp in a large basin of water, the bird continues to feel for them blindly, although he can see them perfectly well.

But don't be misled by this behavior—or by the bird's mild and somewhat tomfool expression—into thinking that the spoonbill is

Helen Cruickshank, National Audubon Society. Opposite: Frederick Kent Truslow

a dullard. A friend of mine, after observing these birds at close range, remarked: "You can look 'em between the eyes and tell they haven't got any dern sense!"

So I told him about my experience with spoonbills and painted sticks. Some years before, I had been studying the nesting behavior of black-crowned night herons. To mark the adult birds, I smeared the rims of several nests with red paint. When the birds returned to settle on their eggs, their white breast feathers were stamped with individual patterns of bright red that could be easily recognized. Then, when I was working with roseate spoonbills on the Texas coastal islands, I tried the same technique, using blue paint. At daylight one morning I hastily daubed the rim of a nest, then retreated to my blind.

Soon both nesting birds returned. One, which I took to be the male, stood on a supporting branch and looked intently at the paint. Then he dropped cautiously into the nest and turned the eggs with his bill.

For a few minutes he stared at the paint-smeared twigs at the rim of the nest. Then he reached out with delicate deliberation, spooned up one of the painted sticks by its unpainted end, and dropped it to the ground. Ultimately, he removed every stick and twig that showed the least vestige of paint. Only then, with a satisfied air, did he settle on the eggs. *I* felt like the tomfool!

White-faced ibis, length 19-26"
Frederick Kent Truslow (also right)

Above: juvenile white ibis

White-faced Ibis
Plegadis chihi

AT A DISTANCE this graceful, long-legged hunter appears black. You see him stalking through the shallows of a Texas swamp or perhaps probing the mud of a Utah slough. Suddenly he stabs downward with his sickle-shaped bill and seizes a wriggling tadpole. Next he snaps at a scuttling crayfish. He also dines on insects, fish, earthworms, and small frogs. Hunger satisfied, the white-faced ibis joins a babbling flock and flies to a distant rookery.

These ibises usually nest along shallow freshwater marshes and wet bottomlands. Sometimes they dwell beside tidal flats. They often settle in large colonies with herons, egrets, and other wading birds. Close at hand you can distinguish the glossy sheen of this bird's iridescent plumage — violet, green, or bronze depending on the play of light. Breeding season brings the white facial fringe that explains the name.

The white-faced ibis fashions a nest from dead reeds and twigs, and lines the bulky structure with grass. It usually stands among tall reeds or on a mass of floating vegetation. Both parents incubate the three or four pale blue-green eggs, relieving each other with affectionate billing and guttural cooing. In about three weeks the young emerge, scantily clad in dull blackish down. By late summer they take wing and all the birds then wander far from the breeding site.

Range: E. Oregon to S. Nebraska, south to S. Mexico and S.W. Louisiana; migratory in the north. Also found in South America. *Characteristics:* long curved bill, streaked chestnut head and neck, glossy chestnut-and-green back and wings with purple tints; brownish underparts. Breeding birds have white face.

Glossy ibis, length 22-25"; William J. Bolte

Glossy Ibis
Plegadis falcinellus

THIS DARK-LEGGED WADER closely resembles his western counterpart, the white-faced ibis. He lacks the other's white facial feathers at breeding season; his face is pale and bare. He may add water moccasins to the usual ibis diet. His grunting notes rise in pitch to a bleat. Otherwise he mimics his cousin so exactly that some ornithologists consider the whiteface merely a different race of the glossy ibis.

Range: E. Texas and coastal areas from S. New Jersey to Florida and the West Indies; wanders to Ontario and Nova Scotia. Also found in Europe, Asia, Africa, and Australia. *Characteristics:* like white-faced ibis but lacks white facial ring.

White ibis, length 22-27"; William J. Bolte

 ## White Ibis
Eudocimus albus

SUNSET REDDENS the Florida sky and tints the vast watery wilderness of the Everglades – an ocean of shimmering saw grass interrupted by occasional hammocks of gumbo-limbos and palmettos. Their trunks and the tangle of growth about them gradually darken. Then, from every direction, rank after rank of white ibises come sweeping in.

Over the trees they stream – hundreds, then thousands – in flocks and undulating lines. In unison they beat their wings rapidly, then sail for a spell. Home now from the distant tidal flats where they feed, the birds break formation. Some plummet toward the rookery. Others sideslip and spiral down. As darkness closes in, the trees fill with white ibises.

Our most common ibis, this species gathers in huge roosts in the low country of South Carolina, in the Everglades and the Tampa Bay region of Florida, and around the Gulf Coast. Observers have reported colonies of more than half a million birds. From a distance flocks of white ibises look like great silvery clouds.

Up close, the bird is a striking sight – especially in breeding livery. His plumage glistens pure white except for shiny, blue-black wing tips; and his bill, legs, and the bare flesh around his eyes glow bright red.

White ibises build bulky nests of twigs and leaves six to ten feet up in low trees or bushes and usually over water. In crowded colonies they may place the cradle among mangrove roots or on the ground. They often nest near herons, egrets, and other aquatic birds. At one mixed colony, Audubon counted 47 nests in a single tree.

Both parents incubate the three or four greenish-white eggs speckled with brown. After three weeks the grayish hatchlings appear and the parents begin to feed them fiddler crabs, crayfish, cutworms, and grasshoppers.

The older birds dine on frogs, small fish, and snails. They even gobble young water snakes. Pursuing their prey in marshy shallows, wet fields, or tidal flats, these long-legged waders probe with long slender mandibles. The immense flocks require enormous feeding grounds.

From time to time crows and grackles raid the rookeries. Then the ibises mill overhead, uttering their harsh, nasal alarm: *urnk urnk urnk*. The chicks that survive grow rapidly. Three weeks after birth, decked in mottled brown-and-white plumage, they leave the nest. Two or three weeks later they fly.

Range: coastal areas from Baja California and South Carolina south to N. South America and the West Indies. *Characteristics:* white body, black wing tips; red on face, legs, and long curved bill. Young have gray head and neck, brown back, white underparts.

127

Scarlet ibises, length 23"; Paul A. Zahl, National Geographic staff

Scarlet Ibis
Eudocimus ruber

"JETS OF FLAME!" To William Beebe, explorer and naturalist, no other words seemed to fit the ibises that flashed past him among the Venezuelan mangroves. "Blood red, intensest vermilion, deepest scarlet – all fail to hint of the living color of the bird."

Spectacularly beautiful, the scarlet resembles the white ibis in size, form, and habits. Both have reddish legs, curved bills, and dark glossy wing tips. Here similarity ends: The scarlet's vibrant plumage burns its image upon the memory.

Reports by early observers that the scarlet ibis ranged to southern Florida proved untrue. Only stragglers reach there and the Gulf Coast; most of the birds breed in huge colonies amid the great swamps of northern South America. Naturalist Paul A. Zahl, leading a National Geographic expedition to the Orinoco, observed an "avian Venice" of about 10,000 ibises – mostly scarlets with some whites intermixed. Though Dr. Zahl found no evidence of interbreeding, hybrids have occurred in zoos and some ornithologists believe that scarlets and whites may be color varieties of the same species.

Incubation of the pair of greenish-white eggs splotched with brown takes place during the rainy season. Both parents share the task.

Range: swamps of N. South America; accidental in Texas, Louisiana, and Florida. *Characteristics:* scarlet with black wing tips; long curved bill. Young have gray-brown upperparts and white underparts.

Roseate Spoonbill
Ajaia ajaja

RADIANT IN THE SUN, a roseate spoonbill lands atop a Florida mangrove thicket and teeters precariously. He preens his pink, carmine-patched wings and body and his orange-yellow tail. Then, turning his bald, greenish-gold head, he peers about the island rookery.

Egrets and herons sit on nearby nests, and a stately brown pelican sails in for a landing. Now the spoonbill slowly makes his way toward his mate, croaking *huh huh huh huh huh* as he goes. The female, colorful as he, perches on their bulky stick nest in a mangrove a dozen feet above the water. Bowing and clucking, the male changes places with her, and she takes off for nearby fishing grounds, legs and neck extended.

Of the six species of spoonbills, only *Ajaia ajaja*, the New World representative, wears such bright plumage. The dazzling raiment once made the bird an easy target for hunters and threatened its very existence in this country. The pink feathers were in great demand as fans, which thousands of tourists took north as souvenirs.

This lustrous creature lays two to four white, brown-blotched eggs. The parents take turns on the nest during incubation, which lasts 23 or 24 days. Both gather food for the hatchlings and shield them from pelting rainstorms and the blazing midday sun.

The helpless youngsters, pulsating sacks of pink flesh and sparse white down, in time wax fat and woolly on regurgitated food. At five weeks they clamber about the nest tree, making their way to the ground and back to the nest. At six weeks they poke their heads through the treetops. In a few more days they fly. Soon thereafter they head for the feeding grounds to search for seafood with their broad bills.

The Gulf Coast and Florida form the northern edge of the roseate spoonbill's range. Most of the birds breed in the West Indies and in Central and South America.

Spoonbills that nest in the Florida Keys arrive from the West Indies in September or October. Courtship and nesting begin in November, and the young generally hatch in late December. The old birds display their most brilliant finery during the Christmas season, when the annual flood of tourists begins to crest. After weaning and fledging their young, the spoonbill families disperse in March and April along both coasts of southern Florida. Soon they head back south.

Another wave of spoonbills, few old enough to breed, come to Florida from the West Indies in March. They wing southward again in fall, just about the time the breeding birds begin to arrive.

Texas spoonbills, flying up the coast from Mexico, reach their nesting grounds near Galveston in late winter. They breed in April and May, then disperse and eventually wend their way back to Mexico. Since 1932 the National Audubon Society has guarded the rookery among the salt cedars and mesquites of the Vingt-et-un Islands in Galveston Bay. Recent counts show hundreds of pairs breeding there.

Range: N. W. Mexico, the Gulf Coast from S. Texas to W. Louisiana, and S. Florida, south to Argentina; wanders to California and S. Alabama. *Characteristics:* long broad-ended bill, bald head, white neck, pink body and wings, red shoulders, orange-yellow tail. Young are white.

Roseate spoonbill, length 32"; Frederick Kent Truslow

FRESH FROM THE BATH, *an American flamingo preens her pink plumage, source of her family name. Phoenicopteridae derives from a word meaning "red-feathered" that ancient Greeks applied to her Old World relatives.*

SLENDER BEAUTY OF THE TROPICS

The American Flamingo

Family Phoenicopteridae

By PAUL A. ZAHL

Before World War II a breathtaking sight awaited naturalists visiting sunbaked, desolate Andros Island, largest of the Bahamas. Along the shores of the shallow lakes that dot the island's interior stretched a strange line of pink, bright against the dark green background of mangroves. As the visitors drew near they heard a loud, gooselike honking and suddenly the pink line came alive. Thousands of wild flamingos raced across the shoals, long legs sending the spray flying, wings beating furiously. For a moment the lake seemed swept by a shimmering sheet of fire. Then the birds boiled into the sky and, with long necks outstretched and legs penciling aft, dipped over the horizon.

On Andros the shy, fragile-looking American flamingo (*Phoenicopterus ruber*) found a haven from civilization and a supply of the small mollusks and organic-rich mud so important to his diet. Each spring vast bird cities came to life, brightening the drab landscape. Wing-fluttering courtship dances occurred along the shoals. Webbed feet heaped up mud and crooked beaks shaped it into cylindrical nest mounds rising above the water. Soon a single chalk-white egg lay in each mound and both parents began the month-long incubation, taking turns on the nest, their stiltlike legs folded underneath and sticking out behind.

In the early 1940's warplanes on training flights roared above the Bahamas. Young pilots were intrigued by the sight of immense vermilion patches on Andros Island. Occasionally some of the men, bored with routine flying, dived to investigate. As the planes swept low and fast toward one or another of the flamingo cities, the birds began to stir. Those that were nesting rose uneasily. Thousands of ungainly heads periscoped toward the approaching noise. Honks of fear welled up.

Suddenly panic took over. All the flamingos began to run, legs slashing through the shallow water and across the nest mounds. I have seen the sad results of such stampeding takeoffs: the devastation of broken eggs spilling their embryonic contents down the walls of the mounds. Soon lizards and vultures arrived to feast on the ruins. Many of the adult flamingos did not even return to the rookeries.

At the end of 1945 the warplanes left and large groups of flamingos started coming back. In June of 1946 I found numerous new mounds in one of the old rookeries. Impatient females began to set and white eggs appeared. All seemed well.

One day a dinghy with a white butterfly sail arrived from another part of Andros. The two natives aboard knew that the law protecting flamingos was seldom enforced. To them flamingo meat was tastier than chicken and flamingo eggs were a delicacy. As the dinghy sailed closer, sentinel birds in the rookery began to squawk. When the men leaped from their beached boat, baskets in hand, the flamingos streamed into the sky, and the nest robbers filled their boat with eggs and left.

When the flock returned, a few parents found eggs. They resumed incubating. The others replastered their mounds and a week or two later had new eggs. By mid-August there were shell tappings. The frail chicks struggled hard to get free of the tough shells. If left alone they would have fledged in a couple of months. They would have learned to take off and, after a number of flip-flops in the water, to land. They would have followed the adults to remote bights to learn the art of feeding in the shallows: plunge the open beak upside down into shallow water, shake the head to strain out sand and water, swallow whatever is nutritious in the mud.

But these young were not left alone. The dinghy with the white sail returned, this time with three poachers. Again the parent birds flew off in terror, and the men went after the nestlings. Many chicks fled along the shore or tried to swim out into deep water. The older ones flapped their wings violently in a vain effort to fly.

At first the poachers threw stones. It was difficult to miss. A stone landing in a group of flightless birds usually left one dead. This wasn't efficient enough. So the men drove the nestlings out of the water and onto a beach. One poacher stayed on the inland side of the birds to discourage their getaway. The other two unwound a

132

IN SERPENTINE FLIGHT *formations of flamingos undulate across the sky. Spanish explorers saw them as flying crosses and piously protected the eggs. At a muddy rookery (below) on Great Inagua Island in the Bahamas, the birds brood upon their mounds of marl, stretching their necks and swiveling their heads to gawk at an intruder.*

ball of twine. Fifty feet apart, holding the line taut and low, the two men ran, drawing the line around the young birds. Some chicks vaulted over or darted under; some escaped into the brush. Others, especially the older birds with long legs, were caught at knee level. They fell, legs fractured.

Afterward a score or so of disabled nestlings lay on the sand or floated on the water. The men picked up these fluttering birds by their broken legs and tossed them into the dinghy.

When the boat left, the adult birds landed again. Surviving young crept back to their parents; to many others none returned and in a few days the old birds left the rookery. There was no use trying to lay new eggs, for the hurricane season, a period of grave danger for birds, was imminent.

Episodes like this drove flamingos from Andros. But the birds survive on other islands, thanks in part to the Society for the Protection of the Flamingo in the Bahamas.

A generation ago birds from the Bahamas colonies wandered to Florida in fair numbers. Today any flamingos seen in the wild in Florida are more than likely escapees from the captive flock at Hialeah Park in Miami. Captive flamingos entertain visitors at Ardastra Gardens in Nassau and at many zoos and bird parks.

But the American flamingo is too highly specialized to adapt to the 20th century. Without vigilant protection it will vanish. Four other species in the family are found in South America, southern Eurasia, and Africa.

Range: S. E. Mexico, Cuba, Bahamas, islands off Venezuela, and the Galapagos Islands; wanders to S. Florida, Hispaniola, and N. E. South America. *Characteristics:* "Roman nose," long neck, slender rose-pink body, scarlet wings, black flight feathers, long reddish legs. Young are gray with pinkish underparts and wings.

HIGH-STEPPING FLAMINGO *drill team, 50 strong, parades through Nassau's Ardastra Gardens. At their trainer's commands, the great birds*

B. Anthony Stewart, National Geographic photographer

about face, mark time, and march.
Halted midst jasmine and orchids, they
pose like prima donnas for close-ups.

Such captive birds, pinioned from youth,
are paler — and bolder by far —
than their wild and secluded brothers.

135

LONG-NECKED HONKERS AND BUGLERS

Swans and Geese
Family Anatidae, Part 1

By S. DILLON RIPLEY

CHESAPEAKE BAY is one of the traditional places to meet members of the family Anatidae—the swans, geese, and ducks. Here, on the Atlantic flyway, they come swinging over in long, wavering lines while gunners hurry to get their decoys set and start the season. And here, sailing down the bay on a mild, fogbound day, I got my first view of whistling swans.

The fog had begun to clear, revealing patches of blue sky, when I heard a *tirra-lirra* rising and falling, the notes jumbled as though an untrained boys' band were tuning up on tin horns. It was a rollicking noise, yet sometimes mournful too. Then a long string of whistling swans flew over, their wings hardly seeming to move but

HUNTERS *set out Canada goose decoys in a Maryland river near Chesapeake Bay as waterfowl stream overhead.*
Bates Littlehales, National Geographic photographer

conveying a feeling of surging power. When the fog rolled away I saw another group on a marshy point. Their long, straight necks were erect—the telltale field mark of the species. Through glasses I could see the black bills, each with that faint yellow streak dropping like a tear below the eye.

The whistler is one of some 144 members of the Anatidae. All have webbed feet and bills with minute toothlike biting edges called lamellae. All share habits of display, pairing, nesting, and feeding. Swans and geese are generally larger than ducks, described in chapters beginning on pages 154 and 172.

To me the far-ranging whistler has always seemed a perfect symbol of the wilderness. The birds come and go on their own, without let or hindrance. They can be killed only illegally, and to what purpose? Swans are fortunately unpopular as table fare, and the trade in swanskins and swansdown has passed into history. I feel that only a fool would kill a swan, for to do so is to impinge on your birthright, to sully your natural surroundings, to scar your soul a little.

The trumpeter swan, big brother of the whistler, may weigh over 30 pounds and is known to live more than 30 years in captivity. Say *ko-hoh* aloud to yourself in a guttural, rasping voice and it will convey in faint measure the call that rings like a trumpet over the lakes and sloughs of Montana, echoing back from sheltering mountain slopes. For the most part these are gentle birds—their aggressiveness in breeding season is largely bluff. But lift a trumpeter as I did once in Manitoba, with its four-foot wings thrashing your arms and legs, and you wonder momentarily if you *can* subdue such a creature, even long enough to get a band on its leg.

Our third swan is the mute, a species from Europe which has been kept on ornamental ponds and lagoons since colonial times. I have been in close touch with mute swans since I was 15. At my New England school we wintered a pair in a barn and each spring I carried them down to a lake, one at a time, my arms aching with the strain. It was a point of pride for me to do this, for my schoolmates were impressed with my careless air of expertise as I grappled with the great birds.

It is the mute swan, according to legend, that sets its wings when mortally wounded and glides to the water singing a strange and haunting "swan song." This story perhaps arose from the reaction of some hunter who, killing the swan, was elated yet felt he had destroyed something nobler than himself.

O F ALL OUR GEESE the most thrilling to me are the elusive, beautiful snow geese. As a boy in Litchfield, Connecticut, I always hoped to see some exotic waterfowl. Our local geese are Canadas—large honkers, brown with black necks and white cheeks, which nest in small numbers on surrounding ponds and in the fall fly up and down our valley in tight V's, making high distinct *uh-uck* noises.

I thought I'd never be lucky enough to see the greater snow goose, the almost legendary white species with black wing tips which migrates up the Hudson to the Far North. A little group of them veer east and fly across western Connecticut and central Massachusetts, presumably to rejoin the main flight in Quebec. Why? Perhaps the habit dates back to the Ice Age when the river valleys were different.

By luck I have seen this flock three times, once on March 25 in the 1930's, once on April 6 in 1945, once with my family in 1961, on March 24. That last was a day of scudding clouds and beating rain. We stood in a meadow and watched a ragged line of geese looping in from the southwest, just above the trees. Their irregular cadence of one-syllable honks immediately distinguished them from the Canadas, which have a double-syllable call. So did their manner of flight. The whole group waved across the sky like a white ribbon eddying in a playful breeze. Brushing the rain out of my eyes I tried to count in units of ten. There were over 200 geese, maybe 225.

And to our amazement a single straggler sank toward the earth and came to rest right on our pond, making all our own geese cry out with excitement. He was a young male, dull brownish-gray with black wing

Frederick Kent Truslow

COMING IN FAST, *a Canada goose braces for a landing at Gaddy's Wild Goose Refuge in North Carolina. Keeping balance with outstretched neck, he brakes with his fanned tail and flails his wings to kill speed. Feet and tail furrow the water (opposite) and he sets his wings in gliding position to stabilize his body. The head rises to its normal pose as his weight settles amid the spray.*

A quick run, sometimes only a leap, is all he needs to take off again. At cruising speed the Canada goose flies about 45 miles per hour.

tips. What a thrill he gave us! We watched in fascination as our tame flock greeted him, gabbling and tooting their astonishment.

The wayfarer stayed 20 days, sometimes flying from pond to pond with our geese. He seemed about to become a fixture. I even inquired if I could buy a female snow goose from a bird dealer. Then on April 13 he rose on a southwest breeze and flew out, strong and purposeful. Something told me he was going for good. "Wave good-bye to him, girls," I called to my children. "He's on his way."

We never saw him again. I hope he made it safely to his goal, Greenland perhaps.

GREAT WINGS *thrust and drive as trumpeter swans gain altitude in the Montana skies. These mighty waterfowl retract their legs astern except in bitter cold. Then they may fold them forward to snuggle their feet in warm, thick breast feathers. To become airborne, the 30-pound birds must race across the water 100 feet or so, their big webbed feet kicking up a wake of spray ten feet high. A smaller whistling swan (opposite, lower) makes such a takeoff in the Canadian Arctic.*

CANADA GOOSE, *artfully carved, ruffles its wooden plumage in the shop of Lemuel and Stephen Ward, decoy makers of Crisfield on Maryland's Eastern Shore. Some 2,000 years ago Indians fashioned lures of bound bulrush stems to attract ducks. Hunters still use decoys to entice wildfowl close enough for a shot. Their paint must not gleam; they must be skillfully weighted to ride the waves without bobbing. Though plastic models work well, handmade decoys are hard to beat.*

Bates Littlehales, National Geographic photographer

140

One great concentration of geese winters on the marshy flats of western Louisiana, near the Gulf of Mexico. At dawn and dusk the air pulsates with wingbeats as snows, blues, and Canadas pass overhead to feed on inland fields and marshes. The moon is almost obscured by the flocks as though by a cloud. And the noise! At times it fills and possesses you to the exclusion of all else. Another great spectacle occurs in the interior valleys of California, where the sparkle of wings dazzles you as Canadas, snows, and whitefronts rise from a marsh or grainfield.

A distant cousin of the Canada is the nene, or Hawaiian goose, the state bird of Hawaii. The species dwindled until by the 1940's probably fewer than a dozen wild nene remained. But state authorities joined forces with the Severn Wildfowl Trust of England, Herbert Shipman, a Hawaiian rancher with a captive flock, and myself. We moved part of the captive stock to a breeding refuge in England and, later, some to my pond in Litchfield. More than 200 nene reared in captivity have been set free to reoccupy their old habitat (page 205).

What an experience! This was one of the few times that a species has been saved by man, despite man's own folly in allowing it to come close to extinction.

C. G. Hampson. Upper: Frederick Kent Truslow

Trumpeter Swan
Olor buccinator

ALONG THE INDIAN TRAILS of tidewater Carolina in 1700 the English adventurer John Lawson found great flocks of wintering swans which, he wrote, "we call trompeters because of a sort of Trompeting Noise they make."

Some 70 years later Samuel Hearne, trekking across northern Canada, heard them "in serene evenings after sunset, make a noise not very unlike that of a French horn, but entirely divested of every note that constituted melody...."

Other explorers met Indians who cherished the plumage of these magnificent white birds as symbols and for decoration. And the remains of prehistoric villages in Ohio and Illinois show that the bones of trumpeter swans were used as tools and were cut up for beads.

Clearly, the largest of our waterfowl was abundant and widespread in the wildlife paradise that once was America. Trumpeters bred across northern Alaska and Canada east to Hudson Bay and as far south as Iowa and Missouri. They wintered along the Atlantic seaboard to the Carolinas, in the Mississippi Valley, along the Gulf Coast, and westward to the Pacific.

But as the white man settled the wilderness, the swans paid dearly, for their beauty and size made them tempting targets. By Audubon's day the trumpeters were scarce in the East. The great bird artist, incidentally, preferred trumpeter quills for drawing fine detail. The quills, he wrote, "were so hard, and yet so elastic, that the best steel-pen of the present day might have blushed, if it could, to be compared with them."

Between 1853 and 1877 the Hudson's Bay Company handled some 17,000 swanskins, many of them from trumpeters. The beautiful plumage was sold on the London market for adornment and to make powder puffs and down coverings.

By 1900 the trumpeter was nearly extinct. In 1918 the Migratory Bird Treaty Act outlawed the hunting of trumpeters. But it was almost too late. In 1933 only 66 of these great swans were reported in the United States!

Four years later came a turning point in the trumpeter's struggle for survival: The Red Rock Lakes National Wildlife Refuge was created in the isolated Centennial Valley of southwest Montana. Here under the rim of the Continental Divide the fragile nucleus grew. Today several hundred trumpeters nest in the sloughs, marshes, and sedge meadows of this mountain region.

As the swan population slowly increased, some of the birds were captured and transported to start breeding colonies in Oregon, Nevada, and Wyoming. In 1963 four cygnets were hatched at the Lacreek National Wildlife Refuge in South Dakota. They were the first wild trumpeter swans raised east of the Rockies in the United States in more than half a century!

Perhaps 1,000 or 1,500 trumpeters live in Alaska. Another 100 or so dwell in western Alberta, and scattered pairs are seen in southern Alberta and in Saskatchewan. In winter about half the population of this species retires to the lakes, rivers, and estuaries of British Columbia.

The trumpeters of Centennial Valley do not migrate despite winter temperatures as low as 40° below zero, for the valley's spring-fed waters are warmed by the same subterranean heat that makes Old Faithful boil up in Yellowstone National Park. To tide the birds through the bitter months, the U. S. Fish and Wildlife Service puts out about 1,000 bushels of grain each year.

Feeding themselves, the swans tread the shallows rapidly to churn aquatic plants free from

Trumpeter swan, length 58½-72", in Red Rock Lakes National Wildlife Refuge, Montana; Frederick Kent Truslow

the bottom. Then they turn bottoms up to gather the loosened vegetation.

When disturbed these 30-pound birds take off like bombers under full throttle. They splash through the water for about a hundred feet, then lift off and retract their large feet up under the tail. Powerful wings that span eight feet thrust at the air; long necks undulate slightly. If they pass close by, you can hear the clatter of flight quills. Even at a distance the birds' resonant bugling reaches your ears. It helps distinguish the trumpeter from the smaller whistling swan.

At about three years of age trumpeters pair off, but they don't begin breeding until they reach five. They probably mate for life. On quivering wings a cob and pen, as the male and female are called, tread toward each other on the water in courtship display. Often they nest atop a muskrat lodge. Like steam shovels, the birds grab billfuls of vegetation, pivot, and drop the loads on the site. The finished home may measure five feet across.

The pen incubates her three to seven dull white eggs about five weeks. She spends much time preening her beautiful feathers – pure white except for rust stains on head and neck acquired from dipping into iron-rich water. Her black bill may be brightened by a red streak on the lower mandible, called a "grin line."

Newly hatched cygnets wear either gray or white down. They grow rapidly and by October are usually ready to take to the air.

Range: central Alaska to W. Alberta, south to N. E. Nevada and South Dakota; migratory in the north. *Characteristics:* large white body, black bill; deep voice. Young are pale grayish with yellowish feet and pinkish bills.

143

♪♪ Whistling Swan
Olor columbianus

AUTUMN'S BREATH stains the tundra in gaudy patterns of red and gold. Over a vast stretch of lakes, ponds, and islands in Alaska and northern Canada companies of whistling swans practice formation flying. Then one day the flocks point south and the grueling journey begins.

A strong old cob leads each wedge or ribbon. The dusky cygnets, placed between snowy veterans, are sucked along by the air turbulence stirred up by the stronger bird ahead. Necks stretched, wings beating slowly and regularly, the whistlers climb until they are nearly invisible from the ground. When storms or mountains force them higher, ice crystals swirl from their wing tips. High-pitched hooting notes—*wou-wou-ou*—drift downward, punctuated by the piping of the youngsters. Often you can hear the babble of a flock long before you can make out the specks against the sky. It was a whistler at 6,000 feet that struck and crippled the tail of an airliner in 1962, causing the plane to crash.

Migrating whistlers frequently visit large inland bodies of water en route to coastal winter resorts. The Bear River Migratory Bird Refuge in northern Utah plays host in the latter part of November to one of the largest single concentrations of whistlers. Here the birds feast on sago pondweed. If the weather isn't too severe, many spend the winter. Others continue west.

Along the Atlantic coast whistlers join Canada geese on inlets from Maryland to North Carolina. On the shallow estuaries of Chesapeake Bay the whistlers sample wild celery, widgeon grass, and thin-shelled mollusks, turning tails up to root out submerged plants. Leftovers provide floating forage for other waterfowl.

The law protects the whistlers in their winter homes. Their own wariness and the remoteness of their summer homes add to their safety. Much more abundant than the trumpeters, they are in no danger of extinction.

Paired whistlers heap up a massive nest of grass, moss, and roots close to water. Cradled in swansdown, the four or five creamy-white eggs hatch in about 40 days.

An Old World relative, the mute swan (*Cygnus olor*), was introduced here and has long been familiar in our parks. This royal bird of England also lives in the wild on Long Island and in the lower Hudson Valley of New York. It has an orange bill with a black knob at the base and is larger and more graceful than the whistler.

Range: W. Alaska to Baffin Island; winters to N. Baja California and North Carolina, occasionally to Florida and the Gulf Coast. *Characteristics:* white body, long neck, black bill usually with yellow spot at base. Young are ash gray with pinkish bills.

Mute swan, length 58"; C. G. Hampson

Barnacle goose, length 26"; Russ Kinne, Photo Researchers

Barnacle Goose
Branta leucopsis

YELPING LIKE A PACK of terriers, the strikingly marked geese circle the lonely coast of western Scotland, then head out to sea. With the formation well on its way, the lead bird drops out and returns to shore to pick up another detachment. Soon the great flock is gone and the coastal flats lie silent under the late April sun.

Many of these barnacle geese find a summer home in northeastern Greenland. Others, departing from wintering grounds elsewhere in northern Europe, make for nest sites on Arctic islands of the Old World. There on ledges and cliffs each pair lines a hollow with down. While the female incubates the four or five grayish eggs, the gander guards against Arctic foxes.

The young hatch in about 24 days. Norsemen believed they came from barnacles attached to driftwood at sea—hence their name.

Buoyed by strong updrafts, the goslings scramble down the cliffs to the nearest lake or bay. Parents sometimes carry the youngsters in their bills. One adult was seen flying down to the water with a gosling on its back!

These handsome geese go ashore to feed on grass, leaves, and moss but never wander far from the coast. In the fall a few barnacle geese occasionally straggle to the eastern United States and Canada. For the bird watcher who sights them it's a banner day.

Range: E. Greenland, Spitsbergen, and Novaya Zemlya; winters in Europe. *Characteristics:* white forehead and face, black line from eye to bill; black crown, neck, and breast, barred gray back, white belly. Young have dusky face, barred brown back.

145

Canada Goose
Branta canadensis

THE DAYS SHORTEN, the fields turn brown, the leaves begin to glow. Then one day a faint honking drifts over the countryside. Men pause at their labor and scan the northern sky. The honking grows louder; finally the great flying wedge comes into view. The wild geese are back and you wonder where the summer has gone.

To most of us "the wild geese" are Canadas, the most widely distributed of our geese. Boldly patterned, heavy-bodied, with powerful wings spanning up to six feet, these splendid waterfowl stream south in strung-out V's that give each bird an unobstructed view forward. Wise old ganders lead the flocks over the Pacific, central, Mississippi, and Atlantic flyways.

Hunters lying in wait along the ancestral routes quickly learn to appreciate naturalist Francis H. Kortright's tribute: "Sagacity, wariness, strength, and fidelity are characteristics of the Canada goose which, collectively, are possessed in the same degree by no other bird. The Canada in many respects can serve as a model for man."

When the weary migrants glide down on set wings to a feeding ground, one or more birds stand sentinel as the others feed. A warning call from the sentries brings all heads to the alert. The birds crane toward the source of danger, ready in an instant to take wing. Paired birds are so devoted that when one is shot, the other often stays behind to risk the same fate.

Night and day these migrants persevere on a journey that may stretch 4,000 miles. They find winter haven in eastern coastal waters, in Mexican lagoons, in interior valleys of California, even in Alaska. Many settle in wildlife refuges.

Through the cold months the honkers follow regular habits. Around sunrise and again before sunset they scatter to graze. They dine on waste grain and on the tender shoots of new crops. They may dip underwater to nibble the roots of aquatic plants. Between feedings they rest on open water or sandbars.

When the days lengthen, the pattern changes. The multitudes become restless, the gabbling increases, and there is much preening and oiling of feathers. Then one morning a group breaks off from the main body and heads north in the familiar V formation. *Ka-runk*, calls the lead gander. *Ka-runk, ha-lunk*, reply his followers. Spring migration has begun.

Canada geese set course for the breeding grounds where they hatched. For some birds already in Alaska and in western marshlands, the flight is short. Others travel from Mexico to the Far North. There two-year-old ganders engage in savage battles over females, each conqueror winning a mate for life.

Because they are clannish, Canada geese tend to inbreed. This often develops distinct characteristics in the various nesting colonies. The ten races of *canadensis* include the largest and smallest of all American geese. The small cackling goose, which breeds in Alaska and winters in the Central Valley of California, is hardly bigger than a mallard and weighs no more than five pounds. Its high-pitched yelps contrast sharply with the deep-throated honking of its larger relatives. The giant Canada goose, a midwesterner once thought to be extinct but recently rediscovered, may tip the scales at 18 pounds.

The larger races breed farthest south in forest or prairie regions near a marsh or river. Nesters heap grass and sticks on an islet or atop a beaver lodge. In the northwest they may breed on a cliff ledge. Or they may move into an osprey nest before the owners return from winter quarters. In the Far North the smaller subspecies breed on

islets in the tundra: a hollow lined with grass and down serves for nesting.

The goose incubates the five or six creamy eggs 28 to 30 days. The gander constantly guards her, and never is his strength and fidelity more in evidence. Visiting a nest in Kentucky, Audubon was whacked by a gander's wing and thought his right arm was broken. In 1941 a horseman accidentally trod on a nest in Ontario. Two Canadas dived at him. One hit him and knocked him from the saddle. The impact killed the bird.

Within 48 hours of hatching, the greenish-yellow goslings follow their father to the water to feed, mother bringing up the rear. The babies double their weight in a week but cannot fly until they grow wing feathers. After nesting the adults molt their flight feathers and the whole family is earthbound for nearly a month.

Adult birds show a remarkable concern for the young, even for those of other parents. One gosling left its broodmates to follow the rubber raft of naturalists John and Frank Craighead down the fast-moving Snake River of Wyoming. The little bird bobbed along for several miles until a pair of nesting Canadas spotted it.

"The gander raced across the current, feigning a broken wing to draw us off," the brothers wrote in *National Geographic*. "The female . . . called urgently. The gosling responded, and, as we drifted past, the goose slipped between raft and orphan to herd the young adventurer ashore.

"It was a clear-cut case of kidnaping – for protective custody."

Range: W. Alaska to Baffin Island, south to N. California, Utah, N. E. Texas, and Maryland; winters to central Mexico. Introduced in Iceland, Britain, and New Zealand. *Characteristics:* black head and neck, white "chin strap," tail coverts, and belly, black feet; back is grayish brown to dark brown, breast gray to brown.

Canada geese, length 22-43"; Walter A. Weber, National Geographic staff artist

Brant

Branta bernicla

UNMASKED BY AN EBBING TIDE, beds of eelgrass glisten on the mud flats of a bay in late winter. Eastward, beyond a salt marsh, the dunes of a barrier isle ward off the pounding Atlantic surf.

Soon wavy lines of small black-and-white geese fly in on long, rapidly beating wings. The flocks thicken until a great raft of brant spreads over the shallows. The graceful saltwater geese ride buoyantly, white sterns contrasting with dark foreparts and pale sides. A mounting din of grunts and gabbling envelops the cove.

The hungry brant tip up like barnyard ducks as their heads dip down for the succulent white lower stems and roots of the eelgrass. They pivot quickly to snap up plant morsels and roll the food into neat balls before swallowing. When the incoming tide floods the plants, the brant dine on severed fronds that float on the surface. Then they gather on sandbars and swallow grit, which helps digest their meal. With nightfall they head east to rest on the sea.

Beginning about 1931 on the East Coast, a blight devastated the eelgrass, and the brant population sharply declined. Some birds survived by eating a type of alga called sea lettuce and the roots of marsh sedges. The eelgrass gradually recovered. So did *bernicla*, but never to its former abundance. The U. S. Fish and Wildlife Service reports that some 183,000 brant now winter along the Atlantic coast, and a much smaller number on the West Coast.

By the end of April most brant are headed for their nesting grounds, flying low over the water in line abreast. They breed farther north than any other goose, as far as northern Greenland. On a coastal islet or near a shallow pond the gander stands guard while his mate incubates three to five creamy eggs in a hollow lined with moss and a luxuriant blanket of down. An extended period of harsh weather on the breeding grounds may destroy the nests and kill off most of the young birds. In such years flocks that wing south are mainly adults.

Widely distributed over the northern hemisphere, the brant (or brent in the British Isles) has long been relished by gourmets. "I can not think of any more delicious bird," wrote ornithologist Arthur Cleveland Bent in the 1920's, "than a fat, young brant, roasted just right and served hot, with a bottle of good Burgundy."

Range: arctic regions of E. North America and Eurasia; winters along the coasts from Massachusetts to North Carolina, from British Columbia to California, and in the Old World to N. Africa and Japan. *Characteristics:* black head, neck, and breast; white neck patch and undertail coverts, whitish sides, pale gray belly.

Black Brant

Branta nigricans

SUMMER CLOTHES the bleak coastal tundra of Alaska with bright green grass and patches of reeds and pink lousewort. In the moist turf small colonies of black brant tend their nest hollows.

For four weeks each goose incubates her four to eight buffy eggs on a bed of grass and down. When a sitting bird leaves the nest, she carefully pulls the down over her clutch. Soon after they

Black brant, length 23-26"

Brant, length 22-30"; Walter A. Weber, National Geographic staff artist

hatch, the downy chicks hurry to the sea, for these are birds of the littoral.

As the short summer wanes, families gather in flocks at favorite feeding spots. Here Eskimos wait behind turf blinds. When the mass of birds grows sufficiently large, the shoot begins. Black brant stored in ice cellars provide meat through the long winter.

Strung out like rippling pennants, the survivors migrate to the salt bays, estuaries, and lakes of the western states. Like their more widely distributed relatives, these brant dine mainly on eelgrass in sheltered shallows.

Habits of the two species are much the same. In plumage, *nigricans* differs in having darker underparts and an unbroken collar of white.

Range: arctic regions of W. North America and E. Asia; winters on West Coast from British Columbia to Baja California, inland to Nevada; also in Siberia and China. *Characteristics:* black head, neck, and breast; dark belly, white neckband and undertail coverts, whitish sides.

White-fronted goose, length 26-34"; Thase Daniel

White-fronted Goose
Anser albifrons

THEY LEAVE the Far North as early as any other goose that breeds in the Arctic. By the first week in September the whitefronts reach British Columbia. Their neat V formations, led by old ganders, pass so high overhead that the birds seem barely to move. Yet they are among the speediest and most agile of geese.

High up, these dots against the sky resemble formations of Canada geese. When the birds break ranks and dive and tumble down to a field or lake, certain distinctive traits stand out: the white face patch around the base of the bill, the white bellies splashed with black, and the clanging, chuckling *kah-lah-a-luck* calls. Lacking the face patch, the young whitefronts look like blue geese but have yellow rather than dark feet.

From southern Canada the "specklebellies" or "laughing geese," as the whitefronts are called, sweep down to that great funnel of the Pacific flyway, the Tule Lake and Lower Klamath region of northern California. Here each fall the breathtaking congregations of waterfowl may total several million birds. Some whitefronts stay for the winter. Others spread south into California and Mexico, where they feed in stubble fields and rest on ponds. Still other flocks move south from Canada through the plains to the Gulf Coast. A few whitefronts that breed in Greenland sometimes visit the East Coast.

Mystery surrounds one race. Known as the tule goose, this large dark bird winters in the Sacramento Valley of California. Its breeding grounds are unknown though at least two major expeditions have searched northern Canada for them.

Two other races breed on shores around most of the Arctic. Each grass nest holds five or six buffy eggs. The goslings are beautiful creatures in their downy coats colored in shades of olive.

Range: arctic tundra except N. E. Canada; winters from British Columbia to Illinois, south to S. Mexico. In the Old World winters to Africa, India, and Japan. *Characteristics:* white muzzle, pink bill, gray-brown upperparts, whitish belly irregularly marked with black; yellow feet. Young have dark face and body, whitish belly.

Snow Goose
Chen hyperborea

LOW CLOUDS scud across the tundra in tattered ranks. The raw September gusts that drive them harden the pack ice on the sea and glaze the ponds inland. The snow geese have been stirring for days. Now it's time.

From the arctic shores of Alaska and Canada the lesser snow geese, smaller of two races, swing south in broad V's and ragged, sweeping curves — a beautiful spectacle of gleaming white bodies

Blue goose length 25-30"

and black-tipped wings. They announce their coming with a resonant, melodious honking.

Many resort to the Puget Sound region and to the Central Valley of California. Others aim for the headwaters of the Mississippi, then sweep down the valley to winter along the Gulf Coast.

The migratory hordes no longer whiten western fields like a premature blizzard, but the lesser snow goose – called "wavey" in Canada from the Indian word for goose – remains one of the most abundant of our geese.

Bigger, chunkier, but much less numerous, the greater snow geese fly south from Greenland and northeastern Canada. Virtually the entire population calls at St. Joachim on the St. Lawrence River. Thence the flocks proceed to winter quarters on coastal salt marshes. Feeding in the shallows, these geese literally mow marsh grass that stands "belly deep to a cow."

Sitting on the water with its wing tips hidden, a snow goose may be confused with a swan. But the goose's neck is distinctly shorter. And only the snow and blue geese wear a black "grinning patch," a broad band along the mandibles that seems to give the birds a leering expression.

Their scientific name hints at where snow geese breed – *hyperborea*, "beyond the north wind." There, on the desolate, soggy tundra each goose incubates four to eight dull white eggs in a depression lined with moss and down.

Range: arctic coasts from N. E. Siberia to Greenland; winters from S. British Columbia to N. Illinois, south to central Mexico and W. Florida, and along the East Coast from New Jersey to North Carolina. Winters in the Old World to Japan. *Characteristics:* white with black-tipped wings, pink bill and feet; head often rust stained. Young are dusky with dark bill.

Juvenile blue goose

Blue Goose
Chen caerulescens

FOR SIX WEARY YEARS Canadian naturalist J. Dewey Soper scoured the northern wastes for the nest of the blue goose. Everywhere he went Eskimo tribes helped in the quest. Finally he learned that the birds nested on the tundra near Foxe Basin. Kavivau, a hunter of Cape Dorset, had seen many while tracking caribou.

In the spring of 1929 the Eskimo and the naturalist got together. They sledged across the Foxe Peninsula of Baffin Island and on the shores of

Snow geese, length 23-38"
Walter A. Weber
National Geographic
staff artist

151

Foxe Basin set up Camp Kungovik – the name Kavivau's people used for the dark-bodied goose.

On June 2 a couple of blues and 11 lesser snow geese flew over, honking noisily. By mid-June thousands of both kinds were overhead, breasting a howling northwester in varying formations – line abreast, Indian file, bunches, and a few V's. They settled close by, and when the sun sank near midnight in a glow of red and gold, the massed geese looked like great snowbanks against the dark tundra.

On June 20 Soper's aides found a blue goose nest with a single egg punctured and emptied, apparently by a parasitic jaeger. Later many more nests were found. Built of moss, grass, and down, they each held three to five white eggs.

Soper had traveled 30,000 miles in quest of the blue goose nest. He found it, as he wrote in his treatise *The Blue Goose*, in "a polar panorama of far-reaching desolation; of vast, sodden marsh-lands bounded by the reeking mud flats and the everlasting ice of Foxe basin; of a gloomy land, haunted by leaden skies and harassed by chilling gales of rain and snow."

But what of those lesser snow geese that traveled with the blues? Scientists have learned that while the two types may nest separately, they also breed in mixed colonies. In such groups snow and blue geese interbreed and produce both dark-bodied and white offspring. In recent years the blues have become more abundant and have spread westward. As ornithologists learn more about them, many believe that the two kinds may prove to be color phases of one species.

Migrating in fall, blue and snow geese pause at James Bay, then fly south – sometimes nonstop – to the Louisiana and Texas coastal marshes. There they feast on the marsh plants.

The spring migration follows a more leisurely pace up the Mississippi Valley. Wave upon wave of blue and other geese arrive in Manitoba in April. They rest for a few weeks, then, flock by flock, disperse to the Far North.

Range: Perry River and Eskimo Point areas, and Banks, Southampton, and Baffin Islands in Canada's Northwest Territories; winters on Gulf Coast from Louisiana to E. Mexico, occasionally on Atlantic coast from Maine to Georgia. *Characteristics:* white head (often rust stained) and neck, grayish-brown body, bluish gray and black on wings. Young have dusky head and neck.

Ross' Goose
Chen rossii

SEARCHING for a Northwest Passage in the late 18th century, Samuel Hearne of the Hudson's Bay Company found flocks of white geese west of the bay. "They are so small," he reported, "that ... I eat two of them one night for supper."

Ross' goose, length 21-25½"

Hearne's "delicate and diminutive species" was scientifically described in 1861 and named for Bernard Ross, chief factor of the Hudson's Bay Company, who had collected some specimens. Thereafter for 77 years naturalists knew *rossii* as a mysterious migrant that summered somewhere in the immense wilderness of the Canadian Arctic. The stubby-billed bird showed up in the fall on Great Slave Lake, then headed southwest over the Rockies and Sierras to California's Central Valley, where it was often seen with the larger, more abundant snow goose.

The breeding grounds remained a mystery until 1938 when, appropriately enough, a Hudson's Bay Company official found a nesting colony in the Perry River region. Built of willow twigs and lined with grass and down, the nests each cradled three to six white eggs.

Today the species numbers about 30,000 birds. Strictly protected, they winter in California's interior valleys, gleaning grass shoots and waste grain. Their *kug* calls sound like grunts.

Range: Perry River and McConnell River areas, and Banks and Southampton Islands in Canada's Northwest Territories; winters in California. *Characteristics:* small size; white with black-tipped wings, reddish bill with warty base.

Emperor Goose
Philacte canagica

THE FEEDING FLOCKS of chunky, short-necked geese fly low, wings almost brushing the ground. *Kla-ha, kla-ha*, their strident calls ring out as they settle on the marshy tundra to feed on berries. Some move on to pry shellfish from the mud flats; others feast on kelp snagged by rocks as the Bering Sea ebbs. These are emperor geese, aptly described by their generic name, *Philacte*. Derived from Greek, the name means "lover of the seashore."

The emperor wears a blue-gray coat marked with crescents of black and white that look like scales. This hardy northerner is one of the handsomest of our geese and one of the least known. In winter a few wanderers may straggle as far south as the bays of northern California, where they thrive on eelgrass with flocks of black brant. Some have even been observed wintering on fresh water in the Sacramento and San Joaquin valleys. But most emperor geese in the New World spend the cold months in the Aleutians and on the Alaska Peninsula.

The short journey to their breeding grounds begins in March or April. In migration they fly high in line abreast. When they arrive on Alaska's northwest coast, ice still chokes the deltas and salt lagoons. Often the flocks rest on ice floes.

The groups soon pair off. Each gander strides around his mate, swinging his head and sounding low notes. He quickly drives off any rival and stands guard while his mate feeds.

Using grass, moss, and down plucked from her breast, the goose prepares her nursery near the water on a tundra islet, in a salt marsh, or on a pile of driftwood that marks high tide. While the gander combs the beach for food, she incubates the five or six creamy eggs. If an intruder approaches, she flattens on the nest, her white neck stretched on the ground. Once hatched, the young of the emperor, one of the most aquatic of Alaskan geese, quickly take to the water.

Some observers have noted that the flesh of emperor geese is rank and scarcely fit to eat. Nevertheless, for the Eskimos this bird is an important food source. Villagers near the nesting grounds gather the eggs and drive the flightless molting geese into enclosures where they are clubbed or speared to death, sometimes by the thousands. And gulls, jaegers, and owls take heavy toll of the pearl-gray goslings.

Survivors roam the coast until the wing feathers of young and old are grown and the turning of the season summons them southward.

Range: Arctic and Bering coasts of Alaska and Siberia; winters in Aleutian Islands and Alaska Peninsula, also E. Siberia. *Characteristics:* white head, hindneck, and tail; black throat; blue-gray body barred with black and white. Young have dusky heads.

Emperor goose, length 26-28"; Karl W. Kenyon. Opposite: Russ Kinne. Photo Researchers

Surface-feeding Ducks and Tree Ducks

Family Anatidae, Part 2

By S. DILLON RIPLEY

BLACK DUCKS *rise from a Maryland marsh on a misty November morn.*

Painting by John W. Taylor
Courtesy C. A. Porter Hopkins

F ROM A BLIND on the Maryland Eastern Shore I have often watched the black
ducks come in. The white undersides of their wings shine in the pale winter sunrise as they bank and swerve to make a landing. And then often, for no apparent
reason, they abruptly veer away, safely out of gunshot. What scares them off? Many
an old-time gunner will tell you that a black duck is so keen of perception it can even
sniff danger—so woe betide you if you light your pipe in the blind and expect to
"stool" or lure the birds in to the rig of decoys.

The elusive, chocolate-hued black ducks are the commonest of their tribe in the
eastern United States. Their close relatives, the mallards, have been introduced
in the East so often that they now have established themselves virtually throughout
the range of the blacks. The two species hybridize, but the blacks have not been
swamped by interbreeding with mallards. Hardy and persistent, the blacks have
hung on in the face of drained marshes and advancing civilization.

Blacks and mallards are probably the best known of the 13 surface-feeding ducks
that range in North America north of Mexico. These pond and marsh dabblers feed
on weeds in fresh or brackish water and sometimes on grain in fields. Most of them
have a distinct speculum or "beauty spot" of bright color on the rear edge of each
wing. They generally have smaller feet than the diving ducks and their hind toes
lack the characteristic wide lobe of the divers (page 21). In our climate the male
surface feeders usually wear brighter plumage than the females.

During the summer weeks that follow breeding season, males in the northern
hemisphere molt out of their gay winter garb into a somber dress resembling that of
the females. This eclipse plumage, produced by hormones, probably helps conceal

the drakes when their wing molt renders them flightless (page 29). Without this drab protective coloration they might fall prey to hawks or other predators.

My favorite among the surface feeders is the wood duck – the brightest-hued North American duck and one of the most beautiful birds in the world. The male's back and crest shimmer with rich iridescent shades of metallic green and purple. The female wood duck is also pretty – demurely so, like a Quaker lady. Her iridescence is grayish, and she has a white patch around her eye and a white throat.

Sometimes in the late afternoon I sit by my pond in Connecticut and watch the female wood ducks on the bank. One may stretch her neck toward another, and open and close her bill a few times as a threatening gesture. She makes a faint noise, and I hope she will not sound her penetrating *whoo-eek* call. Should she do that all the other ducks would move away, alarmed and restless. I know of no more effective alarm call.

As the sun sets, the swimming wood ducks mottle the water, breaking it into fragments of reflected color – pink and orange-yellow. Then from across the pond comes a whisper, a whistling of quick wingbeats. For a moment flying shapes are silhouetted against the bright western sky; then they drop toward the pond, sideslipping, each to land with a creaming plash and a riffle of spray. These are male wood ducks. Crests erect, they swim in a half circle, arranging their feathers to show off their colors to best advantage. One of them calls – an ascending whistle – and a female answers with her *whoo-eek*. And at that, all the birds move off toward the shadow of the farther bank. The ballet has ended. But in the gathering darkness its spell lingers, and it is hard to leave the pond and walk away.

Pintails are another of my favorite species. They are gray and white, the males with long, pointed tails and iridescent brown heads. I love to watch pintails fly in to a pond. They circle swiftly, circle again, and finally drop straight in, standing upright in the air, thrashing their wings in front of them to cut speed.

I always feel that I can tell pintails at a distance. They fly fast and have an angular outline as they gain altitude. But these ducks can surely see me first. H. Albert Hochbaum, the ornithologist, tells of a male pintail that sighted his mate 200 yards away on a sandbar, following her when she flew off. That's like a man being able to distinguish his wife four-fifths of a mile away!

Most of our surface feeders form flocks, but in the southern and southwestern states mottled and Mexican ducks keep to single pairs or small family groups and so do not fall before hunters as easily as birds in big wintering formations. I have watched pairs of mottled ducks on Avery Island, Louisiana, and in the cattle country of the Texas coast. These elusive birds stayed by themselves, apart from the crowds of pintails, mallards, gadwalls, and shovelers.

The soberly garbed gadwall of the West, the big-billed shoveler, and the European and American widgeon are small but handsome ducks. On a crisp morning in a duck marsh the shrill whistle of the American widgeon, or baldpate, has a cheery sound. Closely related to the shoveler are the cinnamon and blue-winged teal. Rust-red in his winter breeding plumage, the cinnamon teal of the West wears a blue patch on his wings identical to the mark of the bluewing. Bluewings now range locally in Connecticut, and a few come to our pond in August, the youngsters flying awkwardly. The third species of North American teal, the greenwing of the prairies, flies as fast as any of the larger ducks.

MALLARD IN MOUTH, *a Chesapeake Bay retriever sloshes ashore, gent carrying the bird to his master. Here a tame, trussed duck, patiently endurir*
156 *its undignified role, helps teach a new dog the old trick of retrievir*

Bates Littlehales, National Geographic photograph

In the southern states occur two species of tree ducks, both little known to hunters. The fulvous tree duck nests inconspicuously in marshy fields of coastal Texas and Louisiana, and occasionally wanders north and eastward. His cousin, the black-bellied tree duck, crosses the border from Mexico into Texas. Tree ducks, classed separately from the surface feeders, are almost gooselike with their long necks and legs, and they would rather wade than swim. They fly rather slowly, legs often dangling behind, and their high whistling calls differ from all other duck calls.

I have sometimes seen more than a hundred tree ducks circling over a pond, whistling together, rising on the air currents like a flock of miniature vultures. All that shrill noise made it seem as though the birds were undecided, some wanting to fly away, some to return to the pond, and some merely crying out because they enjoyed the exercise and excitement. Finally the flock swung off and headed for a distant grainfield. Tree ducks love to feed on stubble fields, just as do their big cousins, the geese.

In spring and fall most of the surface-feeding ducks tend to follow well-defined migratory paths. The Atlantic flyway is one, a coastal route that the blacks and mallards take from Labrador and the Maritime Provinces of Canada to the bays of Virginia and the Carolinas. A spur from the eastern Great Lakes follows either the Hudson River or the Delaware and meets the Atlantic flyway. Other major flyways sweep down the continent, some reaching as far as northern South America. Teal hatched in Alaska sometimes get caught in fishing nets on the Caribbean coast of Colombia. Over the years each species of waterfowl tends to follow the same pathway. To me nothing can be more thrilling than the whistling of wings, the sight of flocks against the sky, the knowledge that this ordered progression has begun again.

David G. Allen. Opposite: Arthur A. Allen. Below: Karl Maslowski, National Audubon Society

"DUCKS ARE A-DABBLING, UP TAILS ALL!"
*Kenneth Grahame must have watched the
surface feeders in action to write
this line in* The Wind in the Willows.
*Browsing stern high, a male mallard
(above) shows how it's done.*

*Mallards are just as avid
out of water. Swarming over
a feeding log (left) at
Cornell University's
Sapsucker Woods
bird sanctuary at
Ithaca, New York,
they gang up on
Canada geese until
pecked out of the way.
Mallards eat everything
from willow seeds to larvae.*

*Like a ship's figurehead,
a female wood duck (right)
juts from her nest hole in a
hollow tree in an Ohio forest.
A creature of habit, the wood duck
may return to the same nest year
after year and it's frequently near
the hole where the bird was hatched.*

Black-bellied tree ducks, length 20-22"; Paul Schwartz
Fulvous tree ducks, length 18-21"; Paul A. Johnsgard, National Audubon Society

Black-bellied Tree Duck
Dendrocygna autumnalis

NEARLY INVISIBLE in their leafy cover, they perch straight and still. Then suddenly they explode, wings a-flutter, filling the air with loud, clear whistles: *pe-che-che-ne.*

Seen from below, their unusually large wings match in color the black bellies that give these tree ducks their name. On the upper surface white covers most of the wing's central area.

Over a feeding place—a marsh or shallow pond—the birds brake for a landing, gangling necks and long legs angled toward the water. No great swimmers, these ducks wade in the shallows to snip weed and grass seeds.

In Mexico, where the blackbelly abounds and reputedly destroys much grain, he is known as *pato maizal*, cornfield duck.

He crosses the border to breed in the brush country of south Texas, but much of his habitat there has been destroyed. You can still find him in the thickets of the Santa Ana National Wildlife Refuge along the banks of the Rio Grande and occasionally in Arizona and California.

Mated birds incubate their 12 to 16 white eggs in a tree cavity. The downy ducklings tumble to the ground and follow their parents to water.

Range: S. Texas to Argentina; migratory in the north. *Characteristics:* coral bill, gray face, cinnamon-brown crown, neck, back, and breast; black belly, black wings with white patch, long pink legs. Young have grayish-buff underparts.

Fulvous Tree Duck
Dendrocygna bicolor

OUT OF THE SOFT APRIL NIGHT the tawny raiders sweep down on a newly sown rice field in the Cajun country of Louisiana. Through the dark hours their flat, serrated bills sift the mud for germinating seeds. At dawn they return to the coastal marshes to roost.

When the rice is tall enough for cover, these long-legged, gooselike birds stop commuting. Now the fulvous tree ducks weave baskets of straw among the growing shoots, sometimes with a ramp leading from the rim to the ground. Usually each nest holds 12 to 14 white eggs, but on occasion two or more females may lay 30 eggs in a single basket. The eggs in these "dump nests" may go untended.

Some farmers regard fulvous tree ducks as pests and destroy every egg they find. Others gather the eggs and place them under barnyard hens. The ducklings adapt to captivity quite well.

In the Central Valley of California these ducks often nest in marshes bordering farmlands. A few choose tree cavities, but as a rule they seldom alight in trees, despite their name.

Variously known as whistling duck, fiddler duck, or squealer, the fulvous tree duck has a curious range: He is found in five widely separated regions in the New and Old Worlds. In the United States he has wandered far from his usual haunts in recent years. His whistles pierce the night stillness along the Atlantic coast as far north as New Jersey. In the west he occasionally visits Washington and British Columbia.

Range: central California to S. W. Louisiana, south to central Mexico; winters to S. Mexico. Also found in South America, E. Africa, and India. *Characteristics:* tawny head and underparts, blackish back, creamy side stripe, white rump patch, long neck and legs.

Mallard
Anas platyrhynchos
(Picture on following pages)

THE PINTAILS started south under the benign sun of August. The teal and canvasbacks are gone too. But many of the mallards hang on through the nippy days of early autumn. They loaf and preen in the shallows, and when they take wing they spring straight up into the air in the telltale style of pond ducks.

Then one day in November a stiff wind from the northwest churns up whitecaps on the lakes of central Canada. The barometer rises and the temperature drops below freezing—and stays there. Now even the hardy mallards move on. They can live with cold, but they must have open water. Near brackish estuaries in southeastern Alaska mallards stay all winter.

Best known of all ducks, the mallard ranges over much of the northern hemisphere. Progenitor of most of our domestic breeds, this bird has provided an important source of food for man for thousands of years. In North America it is the most abundant waterfowl, the most heavily hunted, and the most intensively studied.

Mallards begin their fall migration in clear skies. Along the routes hunters crouching in camouflaged stake blinds hope for squally weather. Then the ducks fly low where they may be attracted by the decoys.

Gunners await these succulent birds on the marshes of Manitoba and along the lakeshores of Minnesota. Some hunters head for Bear River in Utah. Other patient nimrods brave the damp chills in Illinois cornfields, Arkansas swamps, South Carolina bottomlands, and on farm ponds scattered across the continent.

Wintering mallards concentrate most heavily along the Gulf Coast and in the Mississippi Valley south of the line of frozen ponds. Hundreds of thousands throng the White River National Wildlife Refuge in Arkansas. By then the males have shed their drab summer garb, and their fresh finery of rich chestnut and green contrasts sharply with the brown dress of the females.

The sexes also differ in voice. The females utter a resounding *quack*, louder than the soft, reedy *kwek* of the drakes. The flocks become especially vociferous at mealtime as they gather their fill of seeds, aquatic plants, and grain.

When winter retreats, the mallards push north with slow wingbeats that rarely dip below the level of their bodies.

Over thawing marshes groups of drakes pursue single ducks in courtship. The female usually terminates the chase by turning to touch the favored suitor with her bill. Then the couple flies off. She selects the nesting territory; he defends it against intruding pairs. The duck usually builds her nest of grass and down among concealing reeds. But she may choose a pile of brush or an unused hawk's nest in a tree.

Soon after she begins to incubate her 8 to 12 buffy or whitish eggs, the male deserts her, molts into eclipse plumage, and whiles away the summer in the seclusion of the sloughs. Clad in shades of sepia and yellow, the downy young-sters follow their mother to water as soon as they are strong enough to walk. Courageous, ever watchful, she sends the little ones scattering at the first sign of danger.

Wildlife artist Allan Brooks surprised one family in a shallow pool. At the mother's warning *quack* the ducklings dived and sat on the bottom "with heads up, their wide-open beady eyes regarding me through the limpid water."

*Male mallards (green heads) and female (upper), length 20-28".
Swimming and far right: male pintails (white throats),
length 25-30", and females,
length 20½-22½". Walter A. Weber,
National Geographic staff artist*

162

"I waded in," Brooks continued, "and touched each little form in turn. Instantly they rose buoyantly to the surface and pattered away to join the anxious mother."

In former times nesting mallards were uncommon in eastern North America where their close relatives, the black ducks, held sway. But mallards breed well in captivity, and many have been released in eastern areas. They interbreed with black ducks, pintails, and other species.

Range: N. W. Alaska to S. Ontario, south to Baja California, S. Texas, Illinois, and Virginia; winters to central Mexico. Also found in Europe, Asia, and Africa. *Characteristics:* violet speculum or wing patch bordered with black and white; white wing lining. Male has green head, white collar and outer tail feathers; brown back, black rump, chestnut breast, grayish belly. Female is mottled brown, paler on underparts.

Pintail
Anas acuta

THEY LEFT the north country earlier than most of their relatives, and they seem in a hurry to get back. As soon as the pond ice cracks you can expect the vanguard flocks of pintails.

Slender, streamlined, they fly swiftly and gracefully. The male is especially easy to recognize with his snowy breast and long needle of a tail. Pintail describes it well; so does *acuta*.

Sighting a thawing pool, the flock circles and sweeps sharply down in a zigzagging dive. Near the surface the birds level off and drop in. They sit high on the water, tails angled upward. The drakes sound a mellow whistle, the females a low quack. When feeding on aquatic vegetation and insects, they don't upend as often as other surface-feeding ducks, for their long necks

Black ducks

enable them to reach down deeper. If an intruder approaches, the mobile necks shoot straight up and the birds scan their surroundings.

These trim greyhounds of the duck family breed more commonly in western North America than in the east. Nevertheless they have the widest breeding range of all our ducks.

They nest on the shores of California and about tundra pools on the fringes of the polar sea. On the prairies of the Dakotas and southern Canada a farmer, preparing his field for a crop of spring wheat, sometimes flushes an incubating female. Clods of earth from the passing harrow may bend the stubble over her nest before she moves, for pintails are close sitters.

Lined with straw and down, the nest hollow holds six to ten greenish or buffy eggs. Soon after hatching, the ducklings follow their mother to the nearest water. On the prairie this may be a mile from the nursery. She broods them alone and defends them against marauders with remarkable courage. By July the young birds are on the wing. A month later adult males, beginning to change now from dull summer to natty winter plumage, assemble on the lakeshores. They lead the southward migration, followed by the fledglings and the adult females.

Each fall more than a million pintails convene at the Sacramento National Wildlife Refuge in California. Other pintails resort to freshwater marshes of the interior and to brackish coastal marshes. Some cross the Pacific to Hawaii. In 1942 one weary flock turned up on Palmyra Island, more than a thousand miles south of Hawaii. One bird had been banded 82 days earlier in Utah, after being cured of botulism.

Range: Arctic and subarctic regions of the northern hemisphere south to S. California, N. W. Pennsylvania, S. Europe, and Siberia; winters to Colombia, Africa, India, and Hawaii. *Characteristics:* greenish-bronze speculum or wing patch with one white border. Male has brown head, white throat, white breast and neck stripes, grayish back, long thin tail. Female is mottled brown with short pointed tail.

Black Duck
Anas rubripes

AN EAST WIND and a high tide – this is the litany of the hunter on the Atlantic flyway. For when onshore gusts ruffle the estuaries and the surge of the sea whispers through the salt marshes in the gray dawn, the black ducks come. They sweep in, soot-dark shapes flashing their white wing linings, and as they pass over the duck blinds they seem to mock the gunners concealed below: "We are your target – hit us if you can!"

The black duck winters in coastal marshes and wooded swamps. Often he finds sanctuary by settling amid densely populated regions. Many of his kind inhabit the Mississippi and Great Lakes drainages. And the species is increasing in the West.

Wintering ducks probe for blue mussels, periwinkles, and limpets. Flocks form rafts in open water during the day, then come in to salt marshes to feed at dawn and dusk. Spring sends many north; others move inland to find nesting sites near a stream or freshwater pond.

Courting drakes pursue prospective mates from one end of a pond to the other and the woods resound with the low, husky notes of the males and the quacks of the females. Neat, well-concealed nests fashioned in a tangle of grass or underbrush hold 6 to 12 greenish-buff eggs.

The females take over the care of the downy youngsters. Following their mothers to alder-lined streams, the ducklings gorge on insects for a couple of weeks. By the age of eight weeks they are deserted and they join wandering bands of adult drakes. Then as ice closes the freshwater feeding grounds, the birds return to their coastal haunts, again to run the gauntlet of guns.

Range: N. Manitoba to Newfoundland, south to North Dakota and E. North Carolina; winters to S. E. Texas and Florida. *Characteristics:* yellowish or olive bill, dusky crown, streaked light brown head and neck, mottled dark brown body; black-bordered violet wing patch, white wing lining, brownish or reddish feet.

Mexican Duck
Anas diazi

NEVER ABUNDANT, even in frontier days, the Mexican duck declined in the United States until its future seemed all but hopeless.

Called New Mexican duck north of the border, this brown dabbler bred in the swampy thickets of the upper Rio Grande Valley and in the marshes of the state's southwestern corner. But drainage operations destroyed much of this nesting habitat, and by the 1950's only about 150 Mexican ducks remained in the state.

Alarmed at the trend, wildlife biologists of the New Mexico Department of Game and Fish set about to reverse it. They rehabilitated remnants of the old nesting areas and developed new ones. Then in 1959 they established a captive flock. From this nucleus 25 hatchlings grew to maturity two years later. Conservationists hope that release of the captive birds in preserved habitat will ensure the Mexican duck's survival among the fauna of the Southwest.

Below the border *diazi* faces an uncertain future, though the population numbers about 20,000. Here too drainage has wiped out homesites, and hunters take a toll of nesting birds.

Both sexes look much like the female mallard. The two species frequently interbreed, and their voices are similar.

The female Mexican duck incubates her five to nine greenish eggs in an arched nest set in dense sedge or rushes. Strangely enough, one female was seen carrying an egg away in her bill after she was disturbed on the nest.

Range: N. New Mexico to central Mexico. *Characteristics:* mottled brown body, purplish speculum bordered with black and white. Male has yellowish-green bill. Female has orange bill.

Mottled Duck
Anas fulvigula

WHEN THE BLACK DUCKS leave the Gulf Coast marshes in spring, this pale copy remains. French-speaking Louisianians call it *canard noir d'été* – summer black duck. Ornithologist George H. Lowery, Jr., says it is so typical of the coastal parishes that it "would surely speak a special brand of Cajun, if ducks could talk."

More carnivorous than many of its surface-feeding kin, the mottled duck dines on mollusks, insects, and fish as well as on seeds and aquatic plants. Set in a salt or brackish marsh, the down-lined nest holds 8 to 11 greenish eggs. A subspecies, dwelling in Florida and named for the state, often hides its nest under palmettos.

Range: coastal Texas and Louisiana and the Florida peninsula. *Characteristics:* yellow or orange bill, brownish cap, buffy face and throat, mottled brown body, black-bordered purplish speculum, white wing lining.

Black duck

Walter A. Weber, National Geographic staff artist

Mottled duck length 20"

Black duck length 21-25"

Mexican duck length 20-22"

Blue-winged teal
males (white face crescent)
and females, length 14½-16"

Green-winged teal
males (green head patc[h]
and females
length 12½-15½

Cinnamon teal
male (right) and females
length 14½-17"

Walter A. Weber
National Geographic staff artist

Green-winged Teal
Anas carolinensis

BOTTOMS UP, feet kicking for balance, green-winged teal probe the mud of ponds and sloughs for the seeds of pondweed and sedge.

When disturbed, these smallest of our puddle ducks leap straight up, then level off in tight formation. Like feathered minnows, the greenwings twist, turn, and dive in perfect unison. Observers marvel at such speed and precision.

Most greenwings winter in the Gulf states and in Mexico. The first sign of spring draws them north to the nesting grounds, mainly in the Canadian prairie provinces and Alaska. In a grassy hollow near water each female deposits 10 to 12 whitish eggs. The drake replies to her quacking calls with a short whistle.

A relative, the common teal of Eurasia (*Anas crecca*), resides in the Aleutians and appears as a stray along our Atlantic and Pacific coasts. The male lacks the greenwing's vertical white bar on the front of the wing. The females of both species have similar plumage patterns.

Range: N. Alaska to Newfoundland, south to S. California, N. New Mexico, S. Minnesota, N. Ohio, and Massachusetts; winters to Central America and the West Indies. *Characteristics:* small size, green-and-black speculum or wing patch with buffy border; whitish belly. Male has slightly crested chestnut head with green patch; grayish-brown back, white bar on front of wing. Female has brownish upperparts.

Blue-winged Teal
Anas discors

To A MIDWESTERN farm boy, summer means cornfields drowsing under fleecy clouds, ponds full of hungry sunfish, and wild ducks – usually blue-winged teal – in the reeds.

Unsuspicious and adaptable, the bluewings hung on in the upper Mississippi Valley after drainage and cultivation drove out many other waterfowl. Hardly a pothole or creek lacks some blue-winged tenants during the breeding season.

Though their breeding range spans the continent, these ducks concentrate in the prairie country of the United States and Canada.

Nesting birds often hide their nests in tall grass. A cavity in a muskrat house will sometimes serve, and one duck with penthouse tastes settled atop a 25-foot haystack. The cradle of down and grass holds 8 to 10 creamy-white eggs.

Flooding, mowing machines, and prowling mink imperil the incubating bird. If she survives these hazards, the clutch hatches in about 22 days; a few hours later she escorts her downy brood to water. The youngsters grow rapidly and can fly at six weeks.

As summer wanes many potholes dry up, forcing the family groups to gather at the larger marshes. During these pre-migration get-togethers mix-ups occur. Some youngsters lose their mothers and "adopt" a foster parent. One harried duck was seen leading 42 ducklings.

Bluewings start south while summer still bakes the prairies. Like the greenwings, these birds are swift and agile flyers. In the southbound flocks male and female bluewings look alike, for the drakes wear the eclipse plumage of summertime until the onset of winter. Their twitters and peeping whistles, however, differ from the faint quacking of the females.

The migrants pause at shallow ponds to eat their fill of seeds, aquatic plants, snails, and insects. They can be decoyed and make relatively easy targets, but most of them head south before the northern hunting season begins.

While a few bluewings find winter haven in marshes of the southern United States, an estimated 95 percent of the population spends the cold months south of the border.

A vanguard of restless bluewings begins the reverse migration as early as January. During the leisurely trip north courtship begins. Usually no more than two males vie for a female, but one observer counted 24 amorous drakes swimming around a single duck, all bowing continually to gain her favor.

Range: central British Columbia and N. Saskatchewan to Nova Scotia, south to S. California and N. North Carolina; winters to Brazil. *Characteristics:* blue patch on forewing, green speculum with one whitish edge. Male has slate-gray head, white face crescent, brownish back, spotted paler underparts, white flank patch. Female is mottled brown with whitish belly.

Cinnamon Teal
Anas cyanoptera

ON SHALLOW STREAMS and tule-rimmed ponds this friendly westerner paddles quietly about, sampling seeds. At times small flocks chase each other playfully over the water. If you break in on their romp, the cinnamon teal may fly off – but not very far. At most you'll hear a low chatter from the males, a weak quack from the females.

Hidden in reeds, their down-lined nests each hold 6 to 12 whitish or buffy eggs.

This species behaves much like the bluewing, and the females can hardly be told apart.

Range: S. British Columbia to S. W. Saskatchewan, south to central Mexico; winters to Panama and Colombia. Also found in central and S. South America. *Characteristics:* blue patch on forewing, green speculum with one white edge, whitish wing lining. Male is cinnamon-red; female is mottled brown.

167

Gadwall
Anas strepera

NO STRIKING COLORS mark the male gadwall. Yet he is a handsome dabbler, clad in a pleasing blend of soft gray, brown, white, and black.

Some people find him hard to identify in a mixed flock that includes American widgeon and pintails. On the water the "gray duck," as the gadwall is often called, sits low and his black stern shows noticeably. In flight he displays a white patch on the rear edge of each wing.

In North America the gadwall, one of the most widely distributed of the ducks, summers mainly in the prairie regions. Recent records of gadwalls nesting in salt meadows along the Atlantic coast suggest that the species has begun to occupy a separate range in the East.

Good walkers, gadwalls search woodlands and fields for acorns and grain. They also dine on aquatic plants. For nesting they often choose a grassy islet. Hidden among tall reeds, the down-lined scrape holds 10 to 12 white eggs.

Range: S. Alaska to central Manitoba and E. Quebec, south to S. California, N. Texas, S. Wisconsin, N. W. Pennsylvania, and E. North Carolina; winters to S. Mexico and N. Florida. Also found in Europe, Africa, and Asia. *Characteristics:* chestnut forewing, white rear wing patch, whitish belly and wing lining, yellow feet. Male has brown head, gray back and sides, black rump. Female is mottled brown.

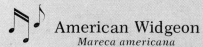 # American Widgeon
Mareca americana

RAFTS OF DIVING DUCKS — canvasbacks, scaups, and redheads — collect each fall where rivers empty into bays. Here they feast on beds of wild celery. Here too come winged pirates — American widgeon — maneuvering in tight flocks with the grace of swallows.

Unadapted for diving, the surface-feeding widgeon wait for the divers to bring up the succulent celery, then snatch it away and swim off, chest low and tail high. If an intruder interrupts their poaching, the widgeon are quick to flush.

Among the wariest of ducks, widgeon often spend their days far offshore, returning to the coast in the evening. On land they trot about like pigeons and graze like little geese. In California they swarm over fields of alfalfa and visit the fairways of golf courses. The drakes, set off by a snowy crown that inspires the name baldpate, sound little musical whistles. The ducks utter harsh croaks.

On a weed-choked islet in a lake or on open grassland far from water, the nesting duck lines a hollow with leaves and down and lays nine or ten creamy-white eggs.

Range: W. Alaska to Manitoba, south to N. E. California, N. Arizona, and Nebraska, rarely to W. Pennsylvania; winters to Central America and the West Indies. *Characteristics:* grayish neck, small bluish bill, white patch on forewing, green-and-black speculum, whitish belly. Male has white crown and flank patch, glossy green head patch, pinkish-brown body. Female has gray head, brown body.

European Widgeon
Mareca penelope

EVERY SO OFTEN an ornithologist ticks off the evidence about the European widgeon and reiterates a theory from the 19th century — that some birds of this species nest in the New World.

A few European widgeon move south along our east and west coasts in fall. There is a corresponding movement through the Mississippi Valley in spring. Some specimens have been taken in Canada at times when the birds should be near their breeding grounds. Hence, the theory goes, they must nest in North America, perhaps in northeastern Canada or Greenland.

But where? No European widgeon has ever been recorded laying its eggs in the New World.

Across northern Europe and Asia *penelope* breeds on farmlands and tundra and in woodlands. The nest of down and grass holds seven or eight creamy-white eggs. In winter the European may join his American cousin in feeding on pondweed and widgeon grass. The Old World drake has a darker crown than *americana*.

Range: Iceland, Europe, and Asia; winters in central Africa, S. India, the Philippines, and a few in Canada and U. S. *Characteristics:* white patch on forewing. Male has buff crown, chestnut head and neck, gray back. Female is like American widgeon but has duskier wing lining.

European widgeon, males (buff crown)
and female, length 16½-20"
Walter A. Weber, *National Geographic staff artist*

Gadwalls, males (gray back)
and females, length 18½-23"

American widgeon
males (white crown)
and females
length 18-23"

169

Wood ducks, male (center) and female
length 17-20", Walter A. Weber
National Geographic staff artist

Female shoveler
William J. Bolte (also opposite)

Wood Duck
Aix sponsa

THE MOST EXQUISITE of American ducks displays the rainbow in his plumage and a touch of poetry in his scientific name, *Aix sponsa*. A hybrid of Greek and Latin, the phrase signifies "waterfowl in wedding raiment."

From crest to tail the male wood duck glows with iridescent hues set off by natty white stripings. What a thrill it must have been to meet him in the primeval setting described by ornithologist Edward Howe Forbush: "Deep flooded swamps where ancient mossy trees overhang the dark still waters, secluded pools amid the scattered pines where water-lilies lift their snowy heads and turtles bask in the sun, purling brooks flowing through dense woodlands where light and shade fleck the splashing waters, slow flowing creeks and marshy ponds—these are the haunts of the Wood Duck."

We have lost much of the setting, and early in the 20th century we nearly lost the duck. Drainage and logging eliminated many woodland swamps and with them the big hollow tree trunks used by wood ducks for nesting. Commercial gunners took heavy toll; stuffed wood ducks were handsome adornments in the home and the bird's feathers made dandy artificial trout flies.

Enacted barely in time, a 1918 law placed the species under protection and the wood duck gradually recovered under wise conservation measures. By 1941 *sponsa* had once more become a commonly seen bird.

Able to survive close to human settlements, the wood ducks have been greatly helped by a widespread program of nest box building. For those who wish to build a home for a pair of these charming tenants, the U.S. Fish and Wildlife Service in Washington, D.C., provides plans for a number of successful nest structures.

Wood ducks pair off on their wintering grounds. Then the female leads the drake back to the region where she was hatched or to the area where she nested the year before. In a tree hollow or a large woodpecker hole as high as 50 feet she lays 10 to 15 white eggs.

On the water, wood ducks feed on insects and duckweed. They also explore the forest floor for acorns. They squeal and chatter when dining. When alarmed they call *whoo-eek*.

Range: S. British Columbia to N.W. Montana and central California, and from S. Manitoba to Nova Scotia south to S.E. Texas and Cuba; winters to central Mexico. *Characteristics:* crested; white throat and belly. Male has white-striped face, iridescent green, bronze, and purple head and back; white bar in front of wing, spotted chestnut breast. Female has grayish-brown back, buffy flanks, white patch around eye.

Shoveler
Spatula clypeata

CHURNING ABOUT in tight circles, the little ducks scoop up pond water and ooze with their broad-ended bills. Then, like prospectors panning for gold, the shovelers sift the mouthfuls. Water and muck sluice out through comblike "teeth" or lamellae that fringe the mandibles. The "nuggets" remain—seeds, insects, minnows, mollusks, and tadpoles.

Except for the oversized bill, the shoveler resembles the blue-winged teal and flies the same way. As both spring up from the water and alight the rattle of their wings is similar.

With mild weather shovelers head for prairie breeding sites. Hidden in tall grass and cushioned with down, the nest holds 10 to 12 buffy or grayish eggs. Hatchlings show no sign of the spatula bill, but within two weeks there is no mistaking it. At the first sign of frost these warm-weather birds depart. Some cross more than 2,000 miles of ocean to winter in Hawaii.

Range: W. Alaska to Hudson Bay, south to S. California, New Mexico, Nebraska, N. Alabama, and Delaware; winters to Hawaii, Central America, and the West Indies. Also found in Europe, Asia, and Africa. *Characteristics:* huge bill, blue wing patch, white-bordered green speculum, white wing lining, orange legs. Male has blackish-green head and rump; white chest, upper back, and flank patch; chestnut belly and sides. Female is mottled brown.

Male shoveler, length 17-20"

DEEP UNDERWATER FEEDERS
OF LAKES AND BAYS

Diving Ducks, Mergansers, and Ruddy Ducks

Family Anatidae, Part 3

By S. DILLON RIPLEY

AMONG THE FIRST DUCKS that I kept in my youth were redheads. Connecticut lies east of their normal range, but this pair took to my pond readily when I released them. They swam straight to the center, preened, then bathed, dunking their heads and lifting them to let the water run over their backs. At feeding time they would dive for pondweed, and I could see them turning and twisting, their bodies encased in a silvery sheen of bubbles.

Such diving ducks as these form our third division of the Anatidae. All have pronounced lobes on their hind toes (page 21). All have shorter and broader bills than the surface-feeding ducks. Their legs are set back on their bodies, giving them a waddling gait on land. To fly they must patter along the surface for some distance instead of merely jumping into the air. These ducks spend much of their lives at sea or on large bays or lakes. They obtain their food by diving, commonly to depths of 40 feet, rather than tipping up like the surface feeders.

Redheads and canvasbacks, so familiar to North American sportsmen, together with ringnecks and scaups make up one grouping of short, tubby-bodied divers called the pochards. Of the pochards I knew as a boy, my favorite was the redhead. I loved to watch the male display, thrusting his head forward and sometimes back onto his shoulders, inflating his neck, and sounding a loud *quirrr*. The female laid eggs in a variety of places, some in her own nest, some in the nest of my black duck. I dug a burrow in the bank of the pond for my wood duck to use, and a contest for its possession developed between the wood duck and the mother redhead. The wood duck won, rolling two redhead eggs out of the hole—one clear into the water. I rescued the other and put it under a bantam hen, where it hatched successfully.

I knew that redheads used the nests of other species on their breeding grounds in the sloughs and potholes of the Dakotas and Manitoba. I wondered then, as I wonder now, how the young knew they were redheads and not coots or mallards or whatever their foster parents might be. I think the young have an inherent response to the "assembly" call of their rightful mother.

Like migrating surface-feeding ducks, pochards in autumn follow flyways south from their cold lakes and marshy ponds. All may appear on coastal bays and sounds

172

at this time. But it is the second grouping of diving ducks—the goldeneyes, eiders, scoters, and the bufflehead, oldsquaw, and harlequin—that people more generally associate with salt water. I was eager to get some sea ducks for my pond, and with a friend I set out to acquire eider eggs. Armed with a permit, we drove to Maine and early one morning chugged out to sea in a fishing boat while gulls dipped over us. A gray wall of fog loomed ahead. We plowed into it, then slackened pace as a foghorn brayed nearby. Suddenly a pile of rocks appeared dead ahead—and beside it, to our delight, a group of eiders swam through the surf, heads held high.

We collected the eggs with little trouble, packed them in a cotton-lined box, and headed home. There we slipped the eggs under three setting hens. Five baby eiders hatched—shapeless balls of brownish-gray down. They soon came running at the sight of an earthworm. When I went to feed them they would rush under my feet and work me over with insistent pecks, grabbing at my shoelaces (which seemed like worms), and sometimes nuzzling into my coat pockets. I would toss a piece of worm into the pond, and they would turn turtle and dive after it, trapped air streaming away from their down. They looked like silver rockets.

Sometimes they would sit out on the pond in a little flotilla. Then one or two would drift away and set up a great noise, *qua-qua-qua, wheep-u-wee.* The others would dash through the water to join them and, reunited, all would lift their heads and sing a wild chorus.

I tried keeping scoters—odd-looking sea ducks with bright-colored bills—and found them uniformly difficult, if not impossible. They snap and hiss, positively skipping up and down in their eagerness to bite the hand that is about to feed them. They seem so different from eiders or oldsquaws that I feel they belong to a very different branch of the waterfowl clan.

Distant cousins of the diving ducks are the mergansers, handsome fish-eating birds whose narrow, cylindrical bills have serrated edges for grasping prey. Primarily

KICKING HARD, *canvasbacks dive for the wild celery that makes them an epicure's delight. Mollusk-eating common goldeneye (opposite) is less tasty, less hunted.*

David G. Allen. Opposite: C. G. Hampson

freshwater birds, mergansers dive quickly and swim like a flash. During migration a few would drop in at my pond and stay for a day or two, adding a touch of color and a sense of mystery and wildness to the scene.

A final relative, included with the diving ducks, is the little ruddy duck with stubby bill and spiky tail feathers that often cock straight up as it rests in the water. I succeeded in getting four ruddies to live on the pond. They are wonderful to watch in spring when the males display. Crests erect, they bob and pump their heads at high speed. They are so small and move so fast as they perform that they seem almost like insects. Sometimes a little drake kicks water up and back with both feet; sometimes, breast high, he skims over the surface, ticking and quacking. This may or may not impress the female. But if another male tries to cut in, she is apt to get involved in a three-ring circus—fighting in, under, and over the water.

Ruddy ducks commonly raise their young with foster mothers, probably because several females may lay in a single nest. Often one or two ducks mother a swarm of 30 or 40 puffball ducklings, who apparently need little more than general shepherding among the reedy pools of a prairie lake.

Father ruddy may help with the young, unlike many other male ducks who tend to join bachelor clubs once nesting begins in earnest. Young ruddy ducks usually go off after three weeks, often in large packs.

What a pleasing sight the diving ducks make when settled on the water! They turn and twist at their ease, now diving for food, now

LANDING, *a redhead plops into the water with forward-fanning wings. To take off, the ducks must sprint across the surface (opposite, upper).*

preening an errant feather, now at last asleep, heads tucked under their wings. Such a sight, as I stand beside my pond in the evening, casts an almost hypnotic spell.

Welling up from the silence come distant calls—the *qua qua* of eiders at the other end of the pond, the faint, flat *quek* of a female Barrow's goldeneye. They die away at last and all is silent again. And then, as I turn away, I hear the whisper of pinions as three ducks—I cannot tell what they are against the darkness of the trees—rise and circle. They will feed tonight on a distant marsh. I hear them go and feel a sense of peace, of oneness with the world of nature.

Arthur A. Allen. Opposite: Thase Daniel

AS A COMMON EIDER *lays her eggs she plucks down from her breast to place around them (left). Leaving the nest to feed, she draws the protective quilt over the clutch (lower).*

Canadians, Icelanders, and other northland dwellers have made an industry of harvesting the eider's down, a material used in lightweight arctic clothing and sleeping bags. Farmers protect the nesting sites to encourage the ducks to return each year, then gather the down from the nests. Collections from 35 to 40 nests equal a pound of commercial down. When the duck has no more down she covers her eggs with leaves and dead grass.

Walter A. Weber
National Geographic staff artist

 Canvasback

Aythya valisineria

AUTUMN GUSTS chill the canvasback hunter on Chesapeake Bay. Patiently he waits and watches while his decoys bob well out from shore and wavelets lap at the pilings of his pine-thatched blind. At last the wary "cans" slant in for a landing, wings roaring above the wind song.

The hunter rises and puts his shotgun to his shoulder. Startled, the cans veer off and drive for altitude. The hunter fires. If his aim is true his reward for enduring hours of cramps and cold will be an epicure's delight.

Sportsmen rate the canvasback as one of the most succulent ducks—if it eats the right food.

On the Susquehanna Flats in Maryland it probably owes its famous flavor to a winter diet of wild celery, *Vallisneria*, from which the bird derives its specific name *valisineria*.

Exclusively North American, canvasbacks breed from Alaska to the Great Basin but nest in greatest numbers on the prairies of central Canada. Before the first freeze-up the wedge-shaped flocks fan out, some winging over the Great Lakes to the Middle Atlantic seaboard, some swinging down the Mississippi Valley to the Gulf of Mexico, some migrating along the Columbia River to the Pacific coast.

Wintering canvasbacks gather in large rafts on bays and estuaries. At a distance the drakes, sitting low in the water, appear mostly white. The

Canvasbacks (males with black breasts), length 19½-24"; Walter A. Weber, courtesy Joseph W. Brooks, Jr.

sloping profile of the bird's dark head inspired the Cajun name *canard cheval* – horse duck.

At feeding time canvasbacks move in closer to shore, where they may dive as deep as 30 feet for aquatic plants. Western canvasbacks favor wapatoo and pondweed, and these birds may make as delicious table fare as the eastern migrants. But when *valisineria* feeds on shellfish and rotting salmon in the Pacific Northwest, its flesh becomes unpalatable.

After the thaws of spring, canvasbacks reach their breeding grounds. Here the drake, usually given to hoots, courts the female with *ick ick cooo* notes. She answers *kuk kuk*. Pairs select a slough or pond as their nesting territory, generally near a large lake. In a bed of cattails or rushes

the female weaves a platform of plant material. Here she incubates seven to nine greenish-gray eggs, while her mate joins other drakes in open water and molts into eclipse plumage.

When droughts shrink the prairie potholes, canvasbacks in the region fail to breed. Closed seasons then protect the species until the rains come and the birds resume breeding.

Range: central Alaska to S. E. Manitoba, south to N. California, central Utah, and N. Minnesota; winters from S. British Columbia to N. Tennessee, Lake Erie, and Massachusetts, south to central Mexico. *Characteristics:* long sloping head, long dark bill. Male has rusty-red head and neck, black breast, whitish body. Female has brown head, neck, and breast, grayish body.

Redhead
Aythya americana

CONCEALED in a jungle of bulrushes, a canvasback settles on her nest to begin incubation. Another brownish duck—a redhead—swims up a narrow access channel to the nest and forces herself in beside the owner. The canvasback pecks savagely at the intruder, but the redhead closes her eyes and refuses to budge. After a few minutes the redhead rises and goes her way, leaving behind a creamy egg.

Some nests of canvasbacks and other species contain as many as 20 eggs laid by *americana*. Two or more redheads may also lay a similar number in a communal "dump nest."

Each female, however, normally builds her own nest of matted vegetation. The 10 to 15 eggs hatch in 22 to 24 days. The redheads feed and loaf in a nearby area of open water cleared by muskrats. Here the ducks find room to take off, rising with a loud quack quite unlike the *meow* or *keyair* of the chestnut-headed drakes.

Over the years droughts and overshooting have caused temporary declines in this once common species. But a permanent decline has resulted from drainage of nesting areas. Many redheads nest on western wildlife refuges, but the majority still breed among the potholes and sloughs of undrained northern prairies.

Leading her youngsters overland to a big lake, the duck shows them how to rush at surface insects and, later, to dive for pondweed. Redheads also eat wild celery, muskgrass, and shoalgrass. Though they can dive ten feet, they sometimes dabble in shoals with river ducks.

They migrate in fast-moving V's, mainly along the Pacific and Central flyways. The largest winter concentrations are on the south Texas coast.
Range: W. Canada to N. W. Minnesota, south to S. California, S. Wisconsin, and N. W. Pennsylvania; winters from S. British Columbia, Nevada, N. Arkansas, and E. Maryland to S. Mexico.

*Redheads
male and (left) females
length 18-22"
Walter A. Weber
National Geographic staff artist*

Characteristics: black-tipped blue bill, pearly speculum or wing patch. Male has red-brown head and neck, black chest, rump, and tail; gray back, whitish underparts. Female is brownish with light patch on face near bill.

Ring-necked Duck
Aythya collaris

HUNTERS OFTEN CALL this tasty dark-backed duck "ringbill." They can spot the chestnut band about the drake's neck only up close. But they can easily make out the light rings on the bluish bill —one behind the black tip and another around the base. These appear in both sexes.

Most ringnecks breed in the reedy borders of bogs and ponds north of the prairies in western Canada, though isolated colonies now reach the Maritime Provinces and Maine. These late spring migrants arrive at their nest sites in loose flocks. The male erects his crest and whistles; the female responds with a *cherr*. Red-winged blackbirds in the area often drive off the crows and ravens, leaving the duck to incubate peacefully the 8 to 12 olive-buff eggs in her grassy cradle.

Ringnecks can dive 40 feet but frequently dabble in the shallows for pondweed seeds and bulrush tubers.

Range: N. British Columbia to Newfoundland, south to E. California, E. Arizona, N. Nebraska, and Nova Scotia; winters from S. British Columbia, New Mexico, N. E. Arkansas, and Massachusetts south to Panama. *Characteristics:* peaked crown, two whitish rings around bill; light gray speculum. Male has black head, back, and chest; chestnut neck ring, white wedge on sides; dark wings, belly, and tail. Female has white eye rings, brownish upperparts, pale underparts.

Greater scaup
male

Lesser scaup
male

Greater Scaup
Aythya marila

IN HIGH, FAST FLOCKS greater scaups arrive with cold weather on estuaries and bays. Here they assemble in huge rafts, some containing more than 50,000 birds. The black-and-white drakes catch the eye as they ride easily on choppy waters. Normally quiet, greater scaups raise a din of *scaup, scaup* calls when alarmed.

Sometimes an entire flock dives at once, remaining under for a full minute. They eat wild celery and widgeon grass along the shores, and glean shellfish outside the line of breakers.

These circumpolar "big bluebills" nest mainly in hollows in the tundra near ponds. The female incubates seven to ten olive-buff eggs.

Range: N. Alaska to central Quebec, south to N. W. British Columbia and S. E. Michigan; winters mainly along coasts south to Mexico. Also found in Europe, Asia, and N. Africa. *Characteristics:* blue bill, white breast, long white stripe on wing. Male has black head and neck with greenish gloss; whitish back and sides, black chest and tail. Female has brown upperparts and chest, white face and belly.

Lesser Scaup
Aythya affinis

WINTER TOURISTS in California and Florida delight in feeding "little bluebills" along lakefronts in city parks. These lesser scaups also migrate to streams, ponds, and salt bays. They are the most abundant diving duck along the Mississippi flyway.

Though closely resembling the greater scaup, the exclusively American *affinis* has a more spatulate bill and a purplish head. It nests farther south, concentrating in Canadian prairie sloughs, and winters more often on inland waters.

A dimple in the ground, lined with grass and down, cradles the 9 to 12 olive-buff eggs. Usually near water, the nest often has quick access to a muskrat canal. An expert diver, this scaup feeds on pondweed, snails, and aquatic insects.

Range: central Alaska to N. Manitoba, south to N. E. Colorado and N. E. Iowa; winters from S. British Columbia, N. Arkansas, E. Maryland, and Connecticut south to N. South America and West Indies. *Characteristics:* like greater scaup but smaller with less white on wing. Male has grayer sides, purplish gloss on head.

Male greater scaup
length 15½-20"

Female
er scaup

Male lesser scaup
length 15-18½"

Ring-necked ducks
females (brown) and males
length 14½-18"

Common Goldeneye
Bucephala clangula

A MARCH SNOWSTORM drops a blanket of white across a New England estuary. Ice cakes litter the surface, but the bleak setting fails to dampen the fervid courting by goldeneye drakes. They swim in restive flotillas about the drab ducks. Suddenly a drake throws his puffed-up greenish head forward, jerks it back to his rump, utters a nasal *spee-ick*, then kicks a jet of water to the rear, exposing his bright orange feet.

A female responds. Stretching her neck on the water, she drifts as though dead, then comes alert and dives. The drake dives with her.

While searching for nest sites, goldeneyes scatter across the vast evergreen forests stretching from Alaska to Newfoundland. They appear early on the breeding grounds, occupying openings in the ice of lakes or streams. The whirring of their wings gives them the nickname "whistler."

A cavity in a rotten hardwood by a marsh-fringed lake commonly serves as a nest. As incubation proceeds the female wraps her 8 to 12 greenish eggs in a blanket of down.

In fresh water the whistler overturns loose stones for crayfish and caddis fly larvae. On coastal bays and inlets, where the species normally winters, this skillful diver harvests mud crabs and mussels. At sunset, rafts of the birds form on the open sea to rest.

Where ponds stay ice-free, many goldeneyes never migrate. In Yellowstone National Park flocks of them winter on stretches of river kept open by hot springs and geysers.

Range: W. Alaska to N. Quebec and Newfoundland, south to S. British Columbia and Maine; winters from S. E. Alaska, central Nebraska, Minnesota, and Newfoundland to S. California and the Gulf Coast. Also found in Europe and Asia. *Characteristics:* white wing patches. Male has green-black head, high crown, white facial spot and underparts, black back. Female has brown head, white collar, grayish body.

Common goldeneyes (males with face patch), length 16-20

Barrow's Goldeneye
Bucephala islandica

SIR JOHN BARROW, a founder of the Royal Geographical Society in 1830, vigorously promoted Arctic exploration. Fittingly, the duck bearing his name is a hardy northerner that endures savage winters by shifting to ice-free coves and inlets along the coasts.

Barrow's goldeneye breeds in two widely separated ranges. One group nests from Labrador to Iceland. But the larger population summers in the western mountains. Here these birds shoot

Male Barrow's goldeneye, length 16½-20"
Arthur W. Ambler, National Audubon Society

Walter A. Weber, National Geographic staff artist, courtesy Walter Masterson

the rapids like daredevil canoeists, sometimes riding over a small waterfall to apparent death only to emerge intact from the foam and spray.

During mating season the mewing calls of the purplish-headed drake sound frequently around wilderness lakes in the Northwest. A whole flock may suddenly take off on whistling wings and circle the area a couple of times before splashing down to resume their courting.

Cavities in decaying trees near a pond or lake usually provide the nest sites. In sparsely wooded Iceland, however, *islandica* lays its 6 to 15 pale green eggs in a rocky crevice, a hole in a stream bank, or the peat wall of a sheep shelter.

This species feeds in fresh water on pondweed, aquatic insects, and crustaceans, especially crayfish. The ducks bob for these, probing under stones near the shore. In salt water the Barrow's eats crabs, periwinkles, and sea lettuce.

Range: S. Alaska and N. W. Canada south to central California and Colorado; also N. Labrador, S. W. Greenland, and Iceland. Winters along coasts to central California and New York. *Characteristics:* like common goldeneye but male has white facial crescent, purple gloss on black head, lower crown.

181

Buffleheads, males and (center) female, length 13-15½"; Walter A. Weber, National Geographic staff artist

Bufflehead
Bucephala albeola

SWIMMING SPRIGHTLY, the tiny bufflehead rises directly from the water, taking off more steeply than other, larger diving ducks. Often this bird bursts into the air from below the surface, like a feathered Polaris missile.

Silent much of the time, the squeaking drakes and their quacking mates breed mostly in the woods of northwestern Canada. A lakeside aspen makes an ideal nest site. Flickers dig the chamber. When they desert it the duck moves in, squeezing into an entrance perhaps three inches wide. She lays 10 to 12 ivory eggs on a bed of wood dust, flicker feathers, and down.

The broods eat caddis fly larvae and dragonfly nymphs. In the fall most buffleheads fly to coastlines south of British Columbia and New England, where they pursue small fish and dive for shrimp and mussels.

During migration small flocks of juveniles, females, and a couple of old drakes break the journey by resting on reservoirs and lakes. At long range the drakes seem white. But binoculars reveal a black-and-white pattern – also the outsize head that inspired the name "buffalo-headed." This was shortened to the present name.

Range: central Alaska to N. Ontario, south to S. British Columbia and N. Montana; also in the mountains of W. Oregon and N. E. California. Winters from Commander Islands, S. Alaska, Great Lakes, and New Brunswick, south to central Mexico. *Characteristics:* small size, big head, white wing patch. Male has black iridescent head with large white crown; black back, white underparts. Female has grayish upperparts, white cheeks, pale breast.

Oldsquaw
Clangula hyemalis

LONG SHADOWS stripe the tundra in the slanting light of the midnight sun. From every lakelet comes a sound like the baying of distant hounds. With the thawing of inland waters, courting oldsquaws are returning to their breeding grounds.

Their incessant yet melodious chatter gave rise to the name "oldsquaw" among northern fur traders and Indians. Other names include "granny," "jack-owly," and "ha-ha-way." Science, taking note of the clangor, dubbed the bird *Clangula hyemalis*, signifying noisy winter duck.

The most abundant of arctic ducks, *hyemalis* breeds north of the tree line around the globe. Their brown-and-white plumage darkened for mating season, the drakes patrol ponds and the females look for nest sites. Usually the five to seven olive-buff eggs rest in a depression among rocks or at the base of a clump of dwarf willows. Some oldsquaws nest on low maritime islands with eiders and terns. Constantly harassed by gulls and skuas, females may combine their broods in a protective convoy system. The young learn to seize aquatic insects and snip pondweed and grasses. When half-grown they go to sea.

At winter's approach many oldsquaws head for seacoasts to the south. They also throng to the Great Lakes – fishermen there took 27,000 in their gill nets one season. Skillful divers, oldsquaws have been trapped at a depth of 200 feet!

These birds flock to tidal rips and offshore shoals to feed on mollusks and crustaceans. Piebald in their winter garb, the chubby drakes with long, pointed tails ride the swells easily.

Oldsquaws frolic in tempestuous weather. Arthur Cleveland Bent watched them on the New

England coast where, "driven like snowflakes ahead of a howling norther, flock after flock of these hardy little sea fowl sweep and whirl over the cold gray waves; or high in the air they twist and turn, twinkling like black and white stars against the leaden sky."

Range: N. W. Alaska to N. Greenland, south to the Aleutians and S. E. Labrador; winters to Washington and South Carolina. Also found in Europe and Asia. *Characteristics:* male is brownish black with white eye patches, flanks, and belly: has long needle-pointed tail. Female has dark crown, face patch, and back, whitish head and underparts; paler in winter. Winter male has white head, neck, and shoulders; dark face patch, back, and breast.

Oldsquaws in winter plumage and (flying) in summer; males (long tails) 19-22½", females 15-17"

Harlequin Duck
Histrionicus histrionicus

REVELING IN WINTRY STORMS, harlequin ducks haunt sea-bashed headlands north of Long Island and California's Monterey Bay. From afar all the drakes look dark. Close up they show a startling pattern of chestnut, black, and slaty blue, spangled with white. It suggests the parti-colored costume of Harlequin, Columbine's buffoonlike lover in 18th century Italian comedy.

Grouped in line or abreast, the ducks paddle with impunity on the turbulent waters. They search kelp-covered boulders and dive through the breakers for crustaceans and mollusks.

Often called "lords and ladies," the hoarse drakes and their shrill mates move inland to breed. They fly fast, following mountain streams until these become glacial torrents. Ideal nest sites for the six or seven buffy eggs include hollow stumps and rock cavities, all near water.

Walking on the stream bottom, *histrionicus* probes for the larvae of stone flies and caddis flies. When the females begin incubation the drakes return to the coasts for the eclipse molt.

Range: central Alaska and N. W. Canada to central California and Colorado; also from S. E. Baffin Island and S. Greenland to central Labrador; winters along coasts to central California and Massachusetts. Also found in Europe and Asia. *Characteristics:* male is grayish-blue with black crown, reddish-brown sides, and white patches throughout. Female is dusky brown with three white patches on side of head.

Harlequin ducks, males and (left) female, length 14½-21"

Steller's Eider
Polysticta stelleri

IN NOVEMBER, 1741, a Russian ship exploring the seas beyond Siberia was wrecked by a storm in the Commander Islands. Among the castaways was Georg Wilhelm Steller, a German zoologist. His description of the islands mentioned a colorful little duck, later to bear his name.

Steller's eiders still throng on the Bering Sea, often far from land. Near shore they favor deep waters, where they dive with half-opened wings for mollusks. Winter storms may drive some birds to shelter in Aleutian coves, but most remain as far north as the pack ice allows.

Pointed wings whistling, *stelleri* flies north in spring to nest on the tundra along Bering Strait. The black-and-white males don't incubate the six to ten greenish eggs but stand guard at nearby ponds, warning their mates of danger with a puppylike bark. On fresh water Steller's eiders tip up like mallards to gather aquatic grasses.

Range: Arctic coasts of Siberia and Alaska south to St. Lawrence Island and W. Alaska; winters to the Kuril Islands, the Aleutians, and S. Alaska. Also found in Europe. *Characteristics:* small size; purplish speculum or wing patch. Male has white head with green bump; black throat and back, reddish underparts. Female is mottled brown with white wing lining.

Spectacled eiders, female (left) and male, length 20½-22½"; Allan Brooks

Steller's eiders, female (left) and male, length 17-18½"

Common eiders, male (left) and female, length 23-2

King eiders, female and (below) male, length 18½-25"

Russ Kinne, Photo Researchers

Common Eider
Somateria mollissima

ST. CUTHBERT, a seventh century ascetic, created one of the earliest known bird sanctuaries: He made Britain's Farne Islands a haven for nesting common eiders. No one knows why he held the birds in such esteem, but a tradition that eiders are sacrosanct survives there.

For practical reasons Iceland, Norway, and Denmark later extended protection to these oceanic birds. The dull gray eiderdown, which the nesting duck plucks from her breast to cradle her eggs, is unsurpassed as an insulator for cold-weather gear and fine bedding. It has supported a lucrative trade for centuries. Icelanders try to entice the birds to refuges by ringing bells and hanging up colored ornaments. The eiders occupy artificial nest sites — shallow pits in the ground and recesses in stone walls. Some move into farmhouses and live with the family.

In North America Eskimos once made superb blankets from the breast skin and down of the common eider. Still prized by them for the eggs and the fishy-tasting meat, *mollissima* has been severely reduced by over-hunting. But the duck has made a gradual comeback since 1939, when the Hudson's Bay Company set up eider farms to harvest the down from the nests (page 175).

The cooing drakes and their quacking mates normally breed in dense colonies on flat coastal islands. Clumps of grasses growing on stony shores shelter the nest. Shaped of plant material, and luxuriously lined with the soft down, it holds four to six olive eggs. During the first days of incubation the drake often squats solicitously beside his mate.

Hatchlings go immediately to sea, where several broods often combine under the eye of a "baby-sitter," an unmated or immature duck. Gulls and skuas nevertheless take a cruel toll of the youngsters. Adults fall prey to seals, killer whales, and sharks.

Largest of the diving ducks, *mollissima* is the only one to fly with alternate flapping and sailing. The bulky, thick-necked ducks travel sluggishly in long lines low over the water. Four of the six races range North American waters, often spending the year close to pack ice. The hardy divers haunt reefs and shoals, feeding on crabs, sea urchins, and mollusks. Shellfish two inches long are swallowed whole and their shells ground to pulp by the bird's powerful stomach muscles. One eider's stomach held 185 mussels!

Range: Arctic coasts from Alaska to Greenland, south to the Aleutians and Maine; winters to Washington and Long Island. Also found in Europe and Asia. *Characteristics:* large size. Male has white head and back, black crown and belly. Female is rich brown, heavily barred.

King Eider
Somateria spectabilis

WHITE IN FRONT, black behind — this pattern identifies male king eiders at a distance on the sea, where the species spends most of the year.

Up close, breeding drakes display a prominent orange knob at the base of the bill. Ornithologist George Miksch Sutton believes the common name of this circumpolar eider is a contraction of *kingalik*, an Eskimo word meaning "he has a nose." When an Eskimo shoots a fast-flying drake, he immediately bites off this knob and devours the tough, greasy morsel.

In winter king eiders appear as far south as the Aleutians, New England, and occasionally the Great Lakes. Most of them, however, stay close to pack ice, usually not far offshore. Over reefs *spectabilis* dives for crabs, shrimp, and sea urchins, rarely venturing into sheltered bays.

The cooing drakes and the croaking females nest in isolated pairs on mossy tundra well back of the shoreline. Pond edges and stream banks are favored localities for the down-lined nest containing four to seven olive-buff eggs. The young eat gnat larvae and plants.

Range: Arctic coasts from Alaska to Greenland; winters from edge of Bering Sea ice to the Aleutians and from S. Greenland to New Jersey. Also found in Europe, Asia. *Characteristics:* male has orange bill and forehead shield, pearly crown, greenish cheeks, whitish neck and breast, black back and belly. Female is brown, heavily barred with black. Young are grayish brown.

Spectacled Eider
Lampronetta fischeri

VIVID against his pale green head, white "spectacles" distinguish the drake of this eider and make him a prize target. Eskimo gunners coveting the velvety patches as ornaments have severely reduced the spectacled eider's numbers along the northwestern coast of Alaska.

These quiet birds breed on the tundra of river deltas, where they feed on insects, pondweed, cranberries, and sedges. In scattered colonies never more than two miles inland, each duck scrapes out a hollow in a tussock and lays five to nine olive-buff eggs on a lining of plant material and breast down. After incubation begins drakes desert their mates and fly to their winter territory, mainly on the open waters of the Bering Sea. There they dive for mollusks.

Range: Arctic coasts of Siberia and Alaska south to St. Lawrence Island and S. W. Alaska; winters to the Pribilofs, Aleutians, and Kodiak Island. *Characteristics:* male has green head, white eye patch, neck, and back; black underparts. Female is barred brown; pale eye patch.

White-winged Scoter
Melanitta deglandi

IN MAY, after most migrants have gone north, strings of white-winged scoters head west on Long Island Sound, flying fast on whistling wings. They are bound for breeding grounds in the Canadian interior by way of the Great Lakes.

From Pacific shores other wavering lines cross the Rockies to the same area. En route thousands of these chunky dark birds may bed down on a single lake, burying their bills in their feathers.

Sustained by aquatic insects and pondweed, these scoters nest near prairie ponds and forest lakes, or on the tundra. Under shrubbery the whitewing conceals 9 to 14 pinkish buff eggs in a scrape lined with leaves and twigs.

The males leave the breeding grounds as early as July, the females and young following about three months later. Some Atlantic birds arc through Labrador before heading south across the Gulf of St. Lawrence. Forming in rafts on bays and sounds and offshore shoals, these "sea coots" dive to 40 feet in search of mussels. A few whitewings winter on inland waters.

Range: N. W. Alaska to N. W. Ontario, south to N. E. Washington and central North Dakota; winters to Baja California, Colorado, Nebraska, Louisiana, Tennessee, and South Carolina. *Characteristics:* large size, thick neck, white wing patch, reddish feet. Male is blackish with white eye patch. Female and young are dusky brown with two pale face patches.

Surf Scoter
Melanitta perspicillata

JUST BEYOND the breaking waves, low-flying surf scoters skim to a landing. They hold their whistling wings erect like sails and plow to a standstill. Lifted to the crest of a swell, the drakes show the white head patches that gave rise to the nickname "skunkhead coot." These scoters plunge in the combers for shellfish and assemble over mussel beds in bays.

Spring migrants flock to the tundra and muskeg country. Occasionally whistling or croaking, the taciturn scoters nest near ponds and lakes, where they feed on insects and pondweed. A grass- and down-lined depression hidden amid bushes cups the five to nine buffy eggs.

Range: W. Alaska to N. W. Canada, south to N. British Columbia, and in James Bay and central Labrador; winters along coasts to the Gulf of California and from Nova Scotia to Florida, also on the Great Lakes. *Characteristics:* like whitewing but slightly smaller and lacking white wing patch. Male has white patches on forehead and nape, red and black patches on heavy white bill.

Common Scoter
Oidemia nigra

EGG-HUNGRY ESKIMOS know exactly where to find nests of this bird. The hunters scan the sand dunes behind Bering Sea beaches, noting the tallest clumps of grass. Under these canopies the common scoter lines a hollow with plant material, then lays six to ten light buff eggs.

Like some of the whitewings, non-breeding common scoters appear in summer as far east as Newfoundland. The species migrates to a winter range on the open seas off both the Atlantic and Pacific coasts. Rarest of the three scoters, *nigra* nevertheless gathers in considerable numbers off Martha's Vineyard and Nantucket.

These "black coots" rise more quickly from the water than other scoters, their silvery underwings winking. They patrol the ocean in flocks, the black drakes calling in bell-like whistles. The brownish females utter only a harsh croak.

Common scoters feed over reefs, where they dive for mussels, barnacles, and limpets. They occasionally inflict damage on commercial oyster and scallop beds.

Range: N. Alaska to the Aleutians and S. Alaska; winters on coasts to S. California and from Newfoundland to South Carolina, and on the Great Lakes. Also found in Europe and Asia. *Characteristics:* like surf scoter but has silvery wing linings, dark feet. Male is wholly black except for yellowish bump on bill. Female has dark crown, grayish cheeks and throat.

Ruddy Duck
Oxyura jamaicensis

LATE SPRING on a prairie slough blends sky and water behind a veil of haze. Reaching for the sun, new growths of reeds and bulrushes form a backdrop for the courtship of ruddy ducks.

Each dumpy drake swims round a female, his fan-shaped tail cocked at a jaunty angle. He slaps his bill against his puffed-up chest, chokes out a rattling *ip-ip-ip-ip-u-cluck, cluck,* then scoots over the surface or kicks a jet of water backwards. If the duck approves, she stretches forth her neck with bill wide open.

Like the redhead, some ruddy ducks lay their

Ruddy ducks, male (left) and female, length 14½-16", Allan Brooks

Common scoters
male (right) and female
length 17-20½"

Juvenile whitewing

Surf scoters, male and
(left) female, length 17-21"

White-winged scoters
male (left) and female
length 19-23½"

first eggs in the nests of other species. Some weave loose nests but abandon the clutches placed in them. Sooner or later the female interlaces a platform of vegetation, attaching it to upright stems several inches above shallow water. The eggs in this nest—six to ten is the usual number—she incubates for 21 days.

Rough-grained and white, the outsize eggs of the ruddy duck qualify as wonders of the bird world. They are larger than those of the canvasback, which weighs more than twice as much as *jamaicensis*. In fact, a one-pound ruddy female may lay a clutch weighing three pounds!

When danger threatens a family of ruddies, the youngsters sail off in a tight body; their parents, accomplished submariners, sink slowly out of sight. Throughout the summer the species probes the bottoms of sloughs and muddy creeks for pondweed seeds and stems.

Flight does not come easily to ruddies. Pattering furiously into the wind, they labor with stubby wings to get airborne. Their buzzy, erratic passage takes them southward at night to shallow, brackish bays and large inland lakes. Behind them they occasionally leave flightless young, hatched too late to escape the ice.

Wintering ruddy ducks dive for wild celery and mollusks; while resting on the surface the birds often seek the company of coots. The lively, frolicsome ruddy is sometimes called the "booby coot" or "widgeon coot," only two of its more than 60 nicknames. Others are "stifftail," "blatherskite," and "fool duck."

A tropical cousin, the masked duck (*Oxyura dominica*), sometimes crosses the lower Rio Grande into the United States. White wing patches help distinguish it from *jamaicensis*.

Range: central British Columbia to N. Manitoba, south to Guatemala, central Arizona, and Pennsylvania; winters to Costa Rica, the Bahamas, and Massachusetts. *Characteristics:* small size, white cheeks. Male is rusty red with black crown, blue bill; in winter, grayish. Female is like winter male with dark stripe on cheeks.

Hooded Merganser
Lophodytes cucullatus

LEFT BY MARCH FLOODWATERS, a lagoon mirrors half-submerged woodlands on a midwestern river plain. While red-bellied woodpeckers frolic through the treetops, hooded mergansers float quietly on their reflections.

Suddenly the black-and-white drakes grunt and break into a colorful courtship ritual, recorded by ornithologist Edward Howe Forbush. "Gallantly they dash back and forth, rippling the dark waters, expanding and contracting their flashing fan-shaped crests, now proudly rising erect on the water with bill pointed downward and head drawn back, now speeding in rapid rushes to and fro. The ardent males chase the females . . . even following them under water."

The only merganser restricted to North America, *cucullatus* breeds mainly in low, wet woods across the middle of the continent. Wood ducks often battle this species for possession of tree cavities and hollow snags overlooking a pond or slow-running stream. Sometimes the claimants end up sharing the same chamber, incubating their clutches in shifts. One ornithologist found a communal nest containing 30 wood duck eggs and five of the hooded merganser!

Essentially a bird of woodland waterways, the hooded merganser occasionally turns up on a prairie slough. In the absence of nesting trees the duck chooses a recess under an overhanging bank or a shoreline stump. Usually glossy, the 6 to 18 eggs call to mind white billiard balls.

The fluffy young hatch in a month and flutter to the ground, sometimes from as high as 75 feet. They form on water in a tight group resembling a swimming muskrat. This may deceive roving predators like the sharp-shinned hawk.

Commonly seen in pairs during winter as far south as the Gulf of Mexico, male and female dive for insects and small fish. Hunters call this and other mergansers "fish ducks."

Hooded mergansers perch readily on drowned snags and take off with agility and speed from the water. Wings ablur, heads extended like long, slender sticks, the birds fly with a deftness and an abrupt change of direction reminiscent of the green-winged teal.

Range: S. E. Alaska to New Brunswick, south to S. W. Oregon, Iowa, and E. Arkansas; winters to central Mexico. *Characteristics:* male has black-bordered white crest, black face and neck, white breast with two black bars in front of wing; brownish sides. Female is brownish gray with buffy crest and white breast.

Hooded mergansers
male (left) and female
length 16-19"

Red-breasted mergansers
males (wide white collar)
and female, length 19½-26"

Common mergansers
male (left) and female
length 22-27"

Allan Brook

BOWING STIFFLY, *a rocking redbreast croaks a courting song. Nuptial antics begin in late winter.*

Common Merganser
Mergus merganser

RAKISH AND LONG-BODIED, common mergansers resemble avian submarines, especially when the birds settle low in the water and disappear without a ripple. They also crash-dive, leaping forward in graceful arcs.

When freezing inland waters force common mergansers south, they fly in swift lines for open rivers across the northern United States. There these birds, largest of mergansers, pursue prey for which their streamlining designs them—the fingerlings and fry of freshwater fish. Mostly they feed on trash species like minnows, chubs, and suckers, taken in slow waters.

The purring, black-and-white drakes and their grayish mates breed in northern evergreen forests. Close to brooks and lakes they select a tree cavity, sometimes 100 feet above the ground, for the 9 to 12 pale buff eggs. The brown-and-white ducklings make a fetching sight drifting downstream, particularly when two or three perch on the back of their mother.

Range: S. Alaska to Newfoundland, south in the mountains to California and N. Mexico, and to S. W. South Dakota, New York, and Nova Scotia; winters to N. W. Mexico, Texas, and Florida. Also found in Europe, N. Africa, and Asia. *Characteristics:* salmon-pink breast. Male has greenish-black head, black back, whitish wing patches. Female is gray with crested reddish head, white throat and wing patch.

Red-breasted Merganser
Mergus serrator

WHEELING AND DIPPING, gulls pinpoint a school of herring on its spring spawning run up an East Coast river. Red-breasted mergansers flock in to partake of the feast. Swimming on an extended front, one group of ducks drives its prey into a shallow cove. The fish double back, but few escape the darting serrated bills that have earned all mergansers the nickname "sawbill."

Unlike the common merganser, which favors freshwater lakes and streams, *serrator* spends much of its life on salt water. Also more gregarious, the redbreasts assemble in hundreds around river mouths, in the channels of salt marshes, and beyond the breakers off sandy shores.

In late winter frenzied courtship begins along the southerly coastlines of the United States. Bill wide open, each drake kicks up jets of water with bright red feet and teeters stiffly, immersing his breast with repeated bows.

To breed, the birds fly to northern forests and tundra edges. Tucked under a log or the canopy of a dwarf evergreen, usually near salt water, the nest holds eight to ten olive-buff eggs.

Range: N. Alaska to Greenland, south to the Aleutians, central Michigan, and Newfoundland; winters to Baja California and Florida. Also found in Europe, N. Africa, Asia. *Characteristics:* crested; white wing patches. Male has green-and-black head, black back, reddish breast, white collar. Female is gray with reddish head.

189

MYRIAD WINGS *and nature's wild music fill the air as waterfowl rise, wheel, and sett* *at Tule Lake, California, where Mount Shasta looms. Bird watchers in Oregon* 190 *have a field day at Malheur (right), once desert and now another teeming refuge.*

The Battle Against Extinction

By ROBERT M. McCLUNG

W E STOPPED by a canal to inspect a beaver dam. Pintails and mallards gabbled in the reeds, and a great blue heron stalked through the shallows.

I heard a dull, roaring sound in the distance—like far-off surf or summer thunder. "What's that noise?" I asked my companion, manager of the Swan Lake National Wildlife Refuge in Missouri.

"Come—I'll show you," he answered.

Our pickup truck jounced across a green field of winter wheat. A huge flock of Canada geese took off ahead of us, thousands of broad wings beating a noisy tattoo against the crisp October air. Reaching the lake, we found its silver surface almost entirely covered with geese. Flying V's and long, wavering lines wheeled overhead. As the geese came in, the tumult of beating wings and raucous calls blended into a mighty symphony.

I gazed in fascination at the spectacle. "Any idea how many?" I asked.

"About 100,000 at last count. Some years we've had up to 130,000."

"How many used to come in before the refuge was established?"

"About four or five thousand," he said.

"Winter sports in northern Louisiana: shooting wild pigeons." From Illustrated Sporting and Dramatic News, *July 3, 1875*

PASSENGER PIGEONS *once darkened North America's skies. In 1810 in Kentucky, ornithologist Alexander Wilson estimated more than two billion of the long-tailed birds in a mile-wide flock stretching 240 miles. A century later, through wanton slaughter, the species became extinct. Denver Museum preserves this mounted specimen.*

When Edwardian fashion smiled on plumes (opposite), snowy egrets (upper) barely survived.

A small shield-shaped sign stood nearby, marking the refuge boundary. Across its center, in dark blue paint, was stenciled the emblem of the United States Fish and Wildlife Service—a silhouette of a flying Canada goose. I had seen a lot of that marker, but never before had it seemed so appropriate.

Touring our national wildlife refuges, I had seen that sign in marshes, deserts, and cypress swamps, on mountaintops and plains. I had seen squadrons of white pelicans soar in perfect formation above a lake in Oregon; clouds of herons, egrets, and ibises settle on a Florida rookery; a flock of whistling swans in majestic flight

iot Porter. Below: Seidman

over North Dakota. I had seen a great deal of a refuge system that totals more than 28 million acres and extends from the Aleutian Islands to Maine, and from Laysan Island in the Pacific to the Florida Keys and Puerto Rico.

WHEN the first white settlers arrived, North America was one big refuge for birds and other animals. Kept in balance by nature, they flourished, a seemingly inexhaustible resource. But the colonists hewed farms out of the wilderness, built cities and roads. Everywhere they went they slaughtered the wildlife.

Passenger pigeons, one of the widely abundant land birds then, nested in vast colonies, where they were slaughtered for food and feathers, even for hog feed. "The passenger pigeon needs no protection," the Ohio Senate asserted in 1857, rejecting a conservation bill.

In 1878 the last great concentration of passenger pigeons nested near Petoskey, Michigan — some 136 million birds in an area 15 miles wide by 75 miles long. They were killed by the millions and sold at 15 to 25 cents a dozen. In 1914 a lone bird died in the Cincinnati Zoo, and the passenger pigeon followed the great auk, the Carolina parakeet, and the Labrador duck into extinction.

The heath hen, once abundant from New England to Virginia, was hunted so eagerly in New York that in 1791 the state passed a law protecting the species from April 1 to October 5 of each year — one of our earliest conservation laws. By the 20th century heath hens lived only on the island of Martha's Vineyard, where they were rigidly protected. But fires, predators, inbreeding, and epizootics took their toll. The single survivor was last seen on March 11, 1932.

Thanks to a few farsighted individuals and conservation groups, our first national wildlife refuge was established in 1903. Pelican Island in Florida's Indian River was set aside "as a preserve and breeding ground for native birds."

These native birds were brown pelicans which nested, thousands strong, on the three-acre island near the little coastal town of Sebastian. Commercial fishermen, mindful of the pelicans' fondness for fish, frequently raided, killing the birds and scattering their nests. A group of ornithologists, the infant American Ornithologists Union, protested, and President Theodore Roosevelt proclaimed the place a refuge.

I visited Pelican Island in a Fish and Wildlife Service floatplane and looked down on a patch of white sand fringed by mangroves. Sand and trees were alive with brown-and-tan birds. Pilot Tom Wood landed and taxied close. We waded up a spongy beach, white with droppings, and saw a nest with a parent bird guarding two newly hatched young, grotesque in their nakedness. "No closer," warned Tom. "If we scare the old bird away, those young won't stand the hot sun for long."

A quick census showed 2,500 pelicans on the island and 1,200 nests. We also counted cormorants, egrets, herons, anhingas, and a few wood ibises.

In 1916 the Migratory Bird Treaty gave the United States and Canada a solid basis for safeguarding waterfowl. Yet their numbers dwindled. Drought, hunting pressure, and drainage of wetlands all cut back the populations. In 1934, while dust storms howled through the West, waterfowl reached a low point.

President Franklin D. Roosevelt appointed a Duck Committee. Advice poured in: "incubate millions of eggs artificially"; "try artificial insemination"; "restore the drained marshlands." The last suggestion made sense. To raise the purchase price for these acres a stamp was required of all duck and goose hunters. It still is.

Chains of new refuges began to spot the principal migration routes. Today, along each of the major flyways – the Atlantic, Mississippi, Central, and Pacific – the birds can find safe breeding areas in the north, suitable wintering grounds in the south, and sanctuaries in between where they can feed and rest during migration.

O N A BRIGHT FALL DAY a flock of whistling swans in a marsh heralded my arrival at Lower Souris refuge in North Dakota. "We get about 5,000 swans at the height of migration," the manager told me. "Besides being a prime breeding ground for ducks and geese, Lower Souris is a resting place for birds coming down from Canada."

Driving along one of the great dikes that control these restored marshlands, I saw flocks of blue and snow geese on one side, grazing in the stubble of a grainfield, while on the other side a flight of mallards and pintails whistled in to land on the marsh. We passed deep ditches that add miles of shoreline for nesting birds. And crossing a field we skirted a number of small ponds. "Artificial potholes," the manager explained. "We scooped them out with bulldozers. Some go dry by July – but that's long enough for ducks to hatch their young and lead them to the marsh."

We stopped to watch a porcupine waddle across the road, and just then a short-eared owl flew by. My companion squeaked into his cupped hands and in a few minutes four owls swooped nearby in ghostly flight. "They keep the rodents in check," he said, "saving the grain for the waterfowl." Farmers lease much of the higher land, harvesting 60 percent of the crops and leaving the rest for the birds. In addition, the refuge staff puts out 15 to 20 thousand bushels of grain each fall.

Some of the well-fed waterfowl from Souris head southward through the Great Plains into Mexico and Central America. Others set their course for the Mississippi – a watery superhighway leading straight to choice wintering grounds along the Gulf of Mexico. To safeguard them on their long journey, two refuges, the Upper Mississippi and the Mark Twain, stretch along more than 500 miles of river from

UT OF LIMBO *flies the trumpeter swan, escaping the mists of extinction and the ghostly company of Labrador ducks (upper left), passenger pigeons (upper right), Carolina parakeets (center), and flightless great auks (lower) – North American species as dead as the dodo of Mauritius, exterminated by man in 1681.*   195

Walter A. Weber, courtesy National Park Service

Alaska

From alpine glen to tropic marsh
U.S. migratory bird refuges
offer haven to hard-pressed species

Robert M. McClung. Left: Frederick Kent Truslow

Canada goose family closes ranks
for defense near grassy banks
in Bear River refuge, Utah.

Geese swarm skyward at Swan Lake
refuge, Missouri, where 100,000
may gather during migration.

CANADA

Washington
Oregon
Montana
N. Dak.
Minn.
Wis.
Mich.
Vt. Maine
NH.
New York Mass.
Conn. R.I.
Idaho
Wyoming
S. Dak.
Nebraska
Iowa
Ill.
Ind.
Ohio
Pa.
N.J.
Nevada
Utah
Colorado
UNITED STATES
Mo.
Kentucky
Virginia
Md. Del
W. Va.
California
Kansas
Tenn.
N.C.
Arizona
New Mexico
Oklahoma
Ark.
Miss.
Ala.
Georgia
S.C.
MEXICO
Texas
La.
Florida

Richard Tenaza. Right: Robert C. Hermes

National Geographic map by Isaac Ortiz, research by John D. Garst

Pelicans still crowd Pelican
Island, Florida, first of the
U.S. national wildlife refuges.

Brandt's cormorants perch above
boiling seas on the Farallon Islands
off California's Golden Gate.

Wabasha, Minnesota, to near St. Louis, Missouri. From a red Cessna stenciled with the wild-goose emblem I had a duck's-eye view of the Upper Mississippi refuge: rich bottomlands, wooded islands, dams, locks, and marshes swarming with ducks.

Along the Atlantic flyway, migrating waterfowl rest and feed at coastal refuges from Maine to the Florida Keys. A large segment of the Atlantic brant population often spends much of the winter at Brigantine refuge in New Jersey. Greater snow geese concentrate at Back Bay, Virginia, and Mackay Island in North Carolina.

On a winter day, cold but sunny, I explored Chincoteague refuge on Assateague Island, Virginia. Four of us filled a jeep, all carrying binoculars and bird lists, for we were participating in the regular Christmas Bird Count of the National Audubon Society and the Fish and Wildlife Service. Hundreds of similar groups were doing the same thing from Alaska and Hawaii to Key West. Heading south on the smooth white sand, we ticked off various shorebirds. Offshore, scoters, goldeneyes, mergansers, and one oldsquaw bobbed in the waves that rolled toward us in gray-green breakers and sometimes showered us with icy spray. Then we drove through a pinewood and counted meadowlarks, flickers, and other land birds. We recorded nearly 10,000 birds of 57 species. Chincoteague serves as a haven for them all.

Three of the West's greatest refuge areas, Bear River in Utah, Tule Lake-Lower Klamath in California and Oregon, and Malheur in Oregon, count their ups and downs as their waters rise and fall. In 1824 mountain man Jim Bridger took his buffalo-hide canoe down the Bear River and reported "millions of ducks and geese." But as Utah became settled, market hunters shot as many as 200,000 waterfowl a year, while irrigation funneled off water. By 1900 the marshes were drying up. Then "duck sickness"—botulism—struck, killing birds by the hundreds of thousands. By the 1920's most of the waterfowl were gone.

Bear River Migratory Bird Refuge, established in 1928, set out to re-create past conditions. And it did! As I drove toward it through Brigham City, I saw a huge sign spanning the main street: "Gateway to the World's Greatest Waterfowl Refuge."

Along its 350-mile course the Bear River is now one of the world's most completely utilized rivers. Most of it still goes for irrigation during the growing season. After harvest the refuge gets a larger share of the water. Five diked impoundments, each covering some 5,000 acres, fill up in

National Audubon Society

Puerto Rico •

"WHEN I HEAR of the destruction of a species I feel just as if all the works of some great writer had perished." So wrote Theodore Roosevelt in 1899. Four years later, as President, he established the first unit in a national wildlife refuge system that now extends its nearly 300 reserves from Hawaii to Puerto Rico. Here in 1915 "T.R." inspects a royal tern colony at an Audubon sanctuary off the Louisiana coast.

IMPROVING ON NATURE, *dikes and ditches control water levels at Tule Lake refuge.*

winter. Canals and spillways permit raising or lowering of water in any unit. Once again hordes of waterfowl flock to the area, almost as in the old days.

The fall concentration of migrants, sometimes close to a million, had not come in when I visited the refuge in August. Nevertheless the whole area seemed alive with birds, for some 60 species nest here. Everywhere I looked were grebes and coots. Common egrets rose as I drove down a dike road, and a squadron of white pelicans sailed overhead. Thousands of mallards, pintails, and teal fed in the marshes; flocks of black-necked stilts, avocets, and willets waded in the shallows.

Another great waterfowl nesting area, Malheur National Wildlife Refuge, lies amid sagebrush desert and red-brown volcanic mountains some 40 miles south of the old cattle town of Burns, Oregon. A wide, verdant valley with numerous lakes

Edwin G. Huffman and (top left)
Robert M. McClung

ALL IN A DAY'S WORK, *a biologist at Bombay Hook refuge, Delaware, patrols by canoe. He washes crude oil from a duck (left), then pens it until natural oil returns to waterproof its feathers. He force-feeds a sick duck, frees an outpatient, and adjusts stop logs (upper) to control water level. Refuge manager checks water salinity (right).*

and marshes, Malheur is watered by two rivers, the Silvies and the Donner und Blitzen.

Peter French, a feudal-style cattle baron, settled at Malheur about a century ago, and his famous "P" ranch covered much of the southern end of the valley. In 1908 the Government declared the northern end a bird reservation but failed to get control of the streams. Malheur turned to dust, its lakes empty, its marshes dry, its alkali flats cracked and lifeless. Its wildlife disappeared.

In 1934 the Government used emergency duck funds to buy the "P" ranch and water rights of the Donner und Blitzen, broke the dam that diverted the river, and let the marshes fill again. As I drove from headquarters to the old ranch I passed ducks and geese gabbling in the shallows, sandhill cranes feeding in a field, and flocks of glossy ibises and white pelicans rising.

Just 170 miles southwest of Malheur lies perhaps our most famous waterfowl area—the Tule Lake-Klamath marshes, situated at a strategic crossroads on the Pacific flyway. Each fall millions of ducks and geese, funneling down from Alaska and western Canada, rest here before moving on to Mexico. In spring some nest here.

As at Bear River and Malheur, the Lower Klamath marshes were drained for farming during the 1920's and early 1930's. Much of the alkali soil would not grow crops, but the damage was done. Migrant waterfowl, with no place to rest, had a hard time of it until the lands were reflooded.

Some refuges were set aside for colonial nesting birds. Such are the famous island refuges in the Aleutians and Pribilofs, where hundreds of thousands of auks and murres breed. Such is Three Arch Rocks off the Oregon coast, the base for the largest murre colony this side of Alaska as well as for a herd of Steller's sea lions.

Okefenokee Swamp became a Georgia state game reserve in 1919, a national wildlife refuge in 1937. The great swamp remains a unique section of primitive America; its very name connotes mystery and romance. In this vast watery wilder-

ness of moss-draped cypress forests and jungles of sweet gum and bay trees, bull alligators roar in spring and black bears pad through gloomy woods. Water lilies festoon flooded prairies. And here the Fish and Wildlife Service forgets about "management" and settles for preserving this lost world in all its primitive beauty.

With Okefenokee's manager and the refuge biologist, I drove to Camp Cornelia, the rustic subheadquarters on the eastern side of the swamp. Switching to a flat-bottomed boat, we put-putted up "Jackson's Folly," the 14-mile canal dug in 1889 in a vain attempt to drain the swamp so that its cypress timber could be taken out.

Okefenokee occupies a shallow saucer of land some 100 feet or more above sea level. Fed by myriad springs, the blackish waters constantly move. Two rivers, the St. Marys and the Suwannee, drain the area. "Try a drink of Okefenokee water," the refuge manager urged. I did, and found it clear and sweet.

We passed under tangled vegetation that enveloped the canal. Great black-and-yellow swallowtail butterflies flitted about. Turtles and gators slithered off logs.

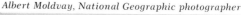

BANG! *A flock of Canada geese is trapped at Blackwater refuge, Maryland. Cannon nets such as this capture birds for banding so biologists can study their movements.*

Developed at Swan Lake refuge, Missouri, the light net is fired from bazookalike tubes by cartridges of gunpowder. When waterfowl flock to an area baited with corn, a man in a distant blind sets off the charge by remote control. The net, more than 100 feet long, sails over the birds (below) and settles gently upon them (left).

Netted birds are banded and released. Young birds may be shipped to another refuge in an effort to reestablish a species in a region where it once nested. Sometimes wild-goose eggs are hatched in incubators and the goslings raised on the refuge, which then becomes home.

Albert Moldvay, National Geographic photographer

The Everglades map

Everglades
Tamiami Trail *The*
Mia
Bea
MIAMI
Tamiami Canal
Coral Gables

E v e r g l a d e s
Shark Valley
Observation Tower

EVERGLADES
NATIONAL PARK

Pineland
Trail
Pa-Hay-Okee
Overlook
Homestead
Florida City
Park Headquarters
Mahogany
Hammock
Royal Palm
Station
Anhinga and
Gumbo Limbo Trails
Whitewater
Bay
Cuthbert Lake
Rookery
JOHN PENNEKAM
CORAL REE
STATE PAR
Cape Sable
Mangrove Trail
Flamingo
Key Largo

F l o r i d a   B a y
Tavernier
Cowpens Nesting Site
Islamorada
STATUTE MILES
▲ *Points of Intere*

Frederick Kent Truslow

National Geographic map by Isaac Ort
Below: Winfield Parks (left) and James P. Bla
National Geographic photographe

Marquesas
Keys
Key West

Marathon. *Overseas* Highway *Keys*
F l o r i d a

PARADISE FOR BIRDLIFE, *Florida's vast Everglades include the national park, largest subtropical wilderness remaining in the United States. Here nature-hikers get a briefing (below) before touring a sun-dappled jungle trail (right).*

202

Herons, egrets, and wood ducks took off at our approach. We passed boats—families enjoying the balm of the wilderness as much as the fishing.

I learned that a layer of peat, in places 15 feet thick, underlies the whole swamp. Parts of this layer break off, float to the surface, and shrubs and trees grow on them. The naturalist touched one of these floating islands with an oar and it swayed. I began to understand the name Okefenokee, Indian for "trembling earth."

Loxahatchee, a wildlife refuge west of Delray Beach, Florida, includes some 145,000 acres of the Everglades. It is a fisherman's paradise and home to the rare Everglade kite and thousands of aquatic birds. I watched great flocks of white ibises coming in to one of the rookeries at sunset one March evening. They flew straight and true until close to the roost, then peeled off and dispersed into the trees like bits of paper in a ticker tape parade. The next day, perched on the high seat of an airboat, I zigzagged across flooded meadows where no conventional boats could go.

C RAB ORCHARD in southern Illinois demonstrates how a refuge can serve in many ways. During the depression of the 1930's this was a poverty-stricken area where Crab Orchard Creek overran its banks every spring and swamped farms. Engineers built a flood-control dam which by 1941 had formed a 7,000-acre lake. Beside it the War Department put up an ordnance plant complete with roads, sewage and water systems, even a railroad. After World War II the entire Crab Orchard project was slated as a multiple-use refuge to be developed for wildlife conservation, recreation, and industry. The Fish and Wildlife Service split the refuge into three sections.

Toby Massey. Inset: Melville Bell Grosvenor
AIRBOAT SKIMS *over Everglades marshes and sawgrass flats on a poacher patrol. Anhinga awaits that "ample natural food."*

IT IS MISTAKEN KINDNESS TO FE... WILDLIFE HERE, AND IT IS PROHIBITE... DO SO, BECAUSE THERE IS. AMPLE... FOOD. ARTIFICIAL FEEDING ENCOUR... VULNERABILITY TO DISEASES, DEPE... UPON MAN, AND AN UNNATURAL...

At one of these – the area at the west end of the lake – I saw boating, fishing, and swimming. The refuge manager told me that hunting is allowed in the fall, and that field trials for hunting dogs take place here.

We progressed to the second area, east of the lake, where the ordnance plant had operated. Private industries now lease its installations. The refuge manager supervises industrial activities so that the great flocks of geese won't be disturbed.

Wildlife receives the third and largest section. Here are marshes and lake areas, also fields whose crops help feed the waterfowl in fall and winter. We passed a cornfield where four rows still stood for every eight that had been harvested. Hundreds of Canada geese were feeding there.

C AN THESE REFUGES assure a future for our wildlife? A thoughtful person would have to say "No." The problem, of course, is people – and more people. By the year 2000 our population may be 350 million or more. The pressure of people and the commerce needed to support them inevitably will tend to squeeze out wildlife.

Most of our extinct birds would still be with us had they received adequate protection in time. In most cases they died out because of hunting excesses and the destruction of their habitat. And despite our best efforts a few species such as the whooping crane have almost passed the point of no return. At their wintering grounds at Aransas, on the Texas coast, these great white birds are rigidly protected; at their nesting area in Canada's Wood Buffalo National Park they also find sanctuary. But on their migration route they face many hazards. Moreover, their Texas quarters are cramped. Yet more land is hard to get, for Gulf Coast industry is expanding.

More encouraging is the astonishing comeback of the trumpeter swan. In 1933 only some 60 remained in the United States. Now there are about 800, not counting those in Alaska. Red Rock Lakes refuge in Montana is largely responsible for the increase. Birds transported from there have done

Hawaiian goose, the nene, says "nay" to extinction

HIGH ON THE MOUNTAIN SLOPES of Hawaii, you may hear the thin *uck-uck* calls of the nene, world's rarest goose. Five or six birds circle overhead, land, and begin shouldering each other for the best view of the visitor. For the "nay-nay," as Hawaiians pronounce it, has a curiosity and a gentle, trusting nature that made it all too easy to kill.

Wild nene dwell only on the islands of Hawaii and Maui. They do not migrate except from breeding place to grazing area. They fly with easy strokes, and on the ground they stand erect, holding high their ruffle-feathered necks and uttering low conversational moans.

Lacking plumes, they were not highly regarded by the Polynesians, for they could contribute nothing to the feather cloaks of chieftains. Villagers hunted them for food or tamed them as pets.

Western settlement of the Sandwich Islands, as Captain Cook named Hawaii, nearly spelled the end of *Branta sandvicensis*. Goose meat proved a delicious change from salt pork, fish, and tubers. Reportedly, thousands were slaughtered, salted down, and shipped to California in clippers to feed the forty-niners. By 1911, when hunting was finally banned, hardly a nene remained.

In 1918 Herbert C. Shipman, recalling stories of nene flocks on his home island of Hawaii, set out to save the goose from extinction. He accepted a pair from a friend. They multiplied. In nine years he had a small flock and could give a few pairs to a game farm on Oahu. Here 37 geese were raised.

Enthusiastic legislators and ranchers shipped pairs off to islands where the nene had never lived in the wild—Kauai, Lanai, Molokai. There they failed. But a few wild birds lived on the high saddle between Mauna Loa and Mauna Kea on Hawaii. The long struggle had not ended after all. The birds were still breeding.

Derek Bayes, Black Star. Upper: Jerry Chong

In 1950 Peter Scott, Director of the Severn Wildfowl Trust in England, sent the curator of the trust, John Yealland, to study the rearing of nene goslings. Herbert Shipman sent two of his precious birds back to England with Yealland. To the consternation of all, both turned out to be females.

A proven gander was sent to England, mated with both females, and nine goslings got the colony off to a fine start. More than 100 descendants have gone to breeders in Europe—and to the Connecticut pond of Dr. S. Dillon Ripley, author of our chapters on swans, geese, and ducks.

In England nene are raised with other wildfowl (upper left), banded, and crated for shipment. Greeted at Honolulu with a snack (lower), they are backpacked by boy scouts into their new home, Haleakala Crater on Maui (above).

The birds reared by Scott and Ripley, plus those raised by fish and game officials in Hawaii, have brought Hawaii's state bird back from the brink of extinction. On their ancestral islands the nene now number more than 200. The world population totals perhaps 500.

SEABIRDS WHEEL *above their remote island nesting ground. Here, free of man's irresistible pressures, frigatebirds and terns breed and prosper and die, their numbers ever in harmony with the laws of nature.*

well in other areas, such as the National Elk Refuge at Jackson Hole, Wyoming, where I saw several trumpeters and their young.

Other threatened species are not so fortunate. Some 40 California condors keep a precarious toehold on the edge of survival in the Sespe Wildlife Area in California. The ivory-billed woodpecker's doom has been sealed by the cutting of the great virgin forests of the South. The Eskimo curlew is probably too far gone to be saved. Once abundant, the species has not been reported for years except for lone sightings on Galveston Island, Texas.

Even with our splendid refuge system birds and other wildlife still face many threats. Year after year men drain swamps or flood them by damming streams. They cut down forests for timber and plow prairies for crops. Month after month they build more superhighways, more airfields, and more sprawling suburbs. All these take land away from wildlife.

The increasing use of chemical insecticides and herbicides may prove the most serious threat yet to wildlife. Poisonous hydrocarbons pass from leaves and soil into insects, fish, and earthworms, and thence into the bodies of birds. Dr. George Wallace, a pioneer in the study of the effect of DDT on songbirds, predicted that unless we call a halt, "we shall have been witnesses, within a single decade, to a greater extermination of animal life than in all the previous years of man's history on earth."

In New York's Bronx Zoo a sign warns: "You are looking at the most dangerous animal in the world. It alone of all the animals that ever lived can exterminate (and *has*) entire species of animals." The sign is under a mirror.

Yet if we must blame ourselves for wiping out great segments of wildlife in the past, we also may take credit now for trying to save what we can for tomorrow. Around the turn of the century plume hunters slaughtered thousands of birds in their rookeries to

Photographed at St. Brandon Islands in the Indian Ocean by David Larcher

sell the feathers to milliners. When the early Audubon societies tried to fight this massacre, two of the wardens were shot and killed by poachers. Today National Audubon Society wardens teach thousands of schoolchildren the intricate wonders of nature and lead parties of visitors through the society's many sanctuaries.

Wild birds rising skyward on sweeping wings are no longer considered solely as targets for guns. We find other values in such displays of grace and purpose—a fresh understanding of nature's patterns, the joy of a truly beautiful sight.

To guarantee a future for North America's wildlife we must set aside additional havens of natural habitat while the opportunity still exists. We all have a stake in building up the refuge system, for our irreplaceable wildlife belongs, not just to the sportsman and the nature lover, but to all the people.

MASTER SOARERS
AND GLIDERS

Condors and
Vultures
Family Cathartidae

By ALDEN H. MILLER

SAILING GLORIOUSLY *on thermals that rise above
its wild and vanishing domain, a California condor
opens its wing-tip slots, tilts its tail,
and cocks a wary eye at its only enemy: man.*
Frederick Kent Truslow

A MAJESTIC BIRD sailed over the crest of a ridge in southern California. As this largest of North American soaring land birds passed above my head in superbly controlled flight, I looked up at wings spanning nine feet and heard the musical whine of air moving through their tips. Then the sound receded; the great bird swept past the ridge and circled the far slope, scanning the tangled chaparral with sharp eyes. Thus, while climbing the rugged north side of Mount Pinos, did I first meet the California condor.

That was in 1922. Today, fortunately, a few of the huge birds still soar over this rough mountainous country northwest of Los Angeles. Here steep slopes, inaccessible cliffs, and dense tangles of brush form a wilderness which man has not yet fully penetrated. And here, relatively free from man's wanton persecution and steady encroachment, the condors can nest, roost, and raise their young.

I have studied some of their nesting sites—flat spots in potholes, caves, and dens formed by tumbled boulders. Always the sites were fairly clean though sometimes still in use. Always they were large enough to accommodate the single huge youngster and at least one parent. In some cavities I could stand upright.

Visits to such sites may cause the birds to abandon their nests. We have learned that though a condor may fly over you or perch above your head in a big-cone spruce without showing fear, the bird retreats from places that people frequent.

The California condor is one of six species of the family Cathartidae, the New World vultures. The Andean condor is a bit larger than the California species and the two differ in habits, structure, and markings. The brilliantly colored king vulture inhabits tropical America; the yellow-headed vulture ranges from southern Mexico to central South America. The black vulture and the turkey vulture also breed in both North and South America.

With wingspans from five to ten feet, all members of the family soar—that is, glide gradually downward within a mass of air that rises faster than they descend. All can quickly find such upward-moving air masses and circle effortlessly within them. All have broad wings with slotted tips to lend stability. All manipulate marvelously the size of the slots, the position of the feather tips, and the bending and the angle of the wings. Our vultures lack grasping talons and tearing beaks. Their feet serve only for walking, perching, and sometimes bracing when they tug at food. Their specialized bills quickly snip away meat, hide, and tendons of dead animals. Their bald heads and bare necks minimize soiling as they feed; a bare surface is easier to clean than a mat of feathers.

The black vulture carries more weight in proportion to its wing area than the other North American species. Because of this heavier wing loading, the black vulture soars the poorest but maneuvers best. The turkey vulture, lightest on the wing, rocks unsteadily in rough air but can stay aloft with the least effort in a calm. The California condor has the most trouble getting airborne. Usually the great bird can launch itself from a high place, but sometimes it must gallop along the ground or jump up, wings flapping. Once in the air it flies with amazing steadiness, making long traverses and wide circles with grace and deliberation—a highly tuned sailplane with reflexes instead of instruments and tendons instead of control cables.

To help save this magnificent species from extinction an investigation of condors began in 1963. Sponsored jointly by the National Audubon and National Geographic Societies, the program was carried out by the University of California's Museum of Vertebrate Zoology, of which I am director. As our field research team we named Ian and Eben McMillan, central California ranchers and experienced ecologists and conservationists. They knew condors from old, having worked with Dr. Carl B.

Koford during his exhaustive study of the species in the 1940's. For a year and a half the McMillans stayed almost constantly in the field, recording the numbers of condors, noting their food supply, and interviewing local people to learn the causes of condor deaths. Several different estimates of the condor population led us to a sad conclusion: The birds are scarcer than ever. Their number dropped from about 60 in the 1940's to about 40 in the 1960's. Yet the McMillans found the birds were still producing young at their natural rate—which is very slow. They don't breed until their sixth year, then produce only one youngster every other year.

Their regular raising of young shows that the species can survive; their loss of population indicates that probably three or four condors are shot every year. We discovered nine instances of people firing at the birds in four years. At least five of these illegal shootings killed or injured a bird. And this must represent only a fraction of the violations, for as the condors soar over Los Padres National Forest they make tempting targets for uninformed and unsympathetic hunters.

Poison, too, probably kills some birds. Condors generally make a swing into the southern San Joaquin Valley to feed. Here they may pick up poisoned rodents. A final factor: Human disturbances in the condor refuges and adjoining buffer areas continue to threaten the successful nesting of the birds.

Now that our project is finished, I believe that by educating the public, enforcing laws, and maintaining, indeed adding to, the present refuges we can save the California condor, a glorious natural monument for North America and the world.

CONDOR-WATCHING BROTHERS, *Ian (with binoculars) and Eben McMillan, perch high above the Cholame Flats, a favorite feeding ground for the great birds in their mountainous southern California range.*

Carefully spying on the shy birds, the McMillans counted heads and checked habits in a survey directed by the author and sponsored by the National Audubon and National Geographic Societies. Sad findings: uninformed gunners kill condors faster than they can reproduce.

Majestic pinions spread, a condor (right) balances on a cliff ledge near the entry to its nesting cavity.

BLACK VULTURES *crowd and shuffle about the carcass of a donkey at a roadside near the Mexican border. These ruffians of the vulture tribe occasionally kill small birds and animals but live mainly on dead flesh. By scavenging they help reduce disease.*

Arthur A. Allen. Above: Carl B. Koford. Opposite: Gladys McMillan

Turkey vultures, length 26-32"; David G. Allen

Turkey Vulture
Cathartes aura

FRIGHTEN a turkey vulture from its prey at the side of the road, and with a few labored flaps it takes off. As it starts its graceful soaring you see the full six-foot span of the wings. They tilt to form a dihedral angle that stabilizes the bird in turbulent air. The fingerlike tips curve upward as the bird rocks gently from side to side.

Hanging thus on an updraft, the turkey vulture is a common sight over much of the United States and southern Canada. Its head constantly turns as it scans the ground: Is that object good to eat? Is it dead? Is it safe to descend and feed?

Unlike condors and black vultures, turkey vultures use their sense of smell as well as sight to find food. Even though they can see their meal below them, the birds usually seem to test it before coming in to eat. Experimenters have found that well-hidden food still attracts the birds if it is odoriferous enough. Releasing gas that simulates the smell of decaying meat brings turkey vultures in close.

These birds can thrive in a variety of habitats, partly because they feed on many different kinds of animals. They devour the carcasses of cattle, horses, rodents, snakes, and fish. Sometimes they eat vegetable matter.

Turkey vultures use caves, hollow stumps, and thickets for nest sites, laying the two brown-blotched eggs on bare ground or on a mat of decayed wood or leaves. If you approach a nest containing eggs, the incubating parent may fly when you are some distance away. But when the downy white young have hatched, the adult stays beside them, even allowing you to touch it.

The nest at first is clean, but when the parents are feeding the young by regurgitation, the stench of carrion soon discourages human visitors. The chicks grow fairly rapidly, gain dark plumage similar to their parents', and 62 to 65 days after hatching they can fly.

Many turkey vultures migrate, leaving the northern part of their range and flying south in loose flocks of 20 to 30 or so. Since they are soaring birds, they seldom travel far in straight lines but must circle frequently to gain altitude before resuming their gliding path.

Range: S. Canada to S. South America. *Characteristics:* dark brown or blackish with gray on underside of wings; adult has bare red head.

Black Vulture
Coragyps atratus

IN HOT, HUMID REGIONS where no sanitary engineer removes dead animals and other organic wastes, black vultures are a common sight. Hunting in groups, they scout butchering grounds, dumps, sewage outlets, and roadways. When one finds food the others react quickly. If the carcass is large enough dozens of the birds assemble on it, shouldering one another, hissing, tugging in their fight for flesh. Men may shudder at the sight yet admire the boldness and competence of *atratus*. No vulture cleans up carrion more efficiently.

Though they soar readily, black vultures are heavy on the wing and often make short, hurried wingbeats to keep aloft, to maneuver about their roosts, or when coming in to food. They build no nest but lay their eggs in dark protected places – under dense vegetation, perhaps, or in shallow caves. They commonly use a hollow tree trunk, sometimes entering from above and descending several feet to a secluded chamber.

Both parents share in incubating the two eggs, richly splotched with dark brown and chestnut. Both feed the young by regurgitation. Though carrion is the usual fare, black vultures will sometimes kill piglets, kids, or small chickens. They may also take young from the nests of herons. But the benefits of these scavengers far outweigh what little damage they do.

Range: S. Arizona to Maryland, south to S. South America. *Characteristics:* bare black head, black plumage except for whitish patch near wing tip; short square tail.

Black vultures, length 23-27"; Frederick Kent Truslow

California Condor
Gymnogyps californianus

ONLY IN THE JUMBLE OF MOUNTAINS rising northwest of Los Angeles does the California condor still nest. Here in the great bird's last retreat air currents playing over the slopes provide lift for its mighty wings.

As the morning warms up and thermals start to rise, the condors take off. They cruise along Frazier Mountain and Mount Pinos toward their chief foraging ground, the more open country to the north. Though they may find carrion high in the mountain pastures the birds mainly search, as they always have, the lower foothills and plateaus, sparsely dotted or lined with oaks.

They range northward in the hills on both sides of the San Joaquin Valley, their paths describing a U round the valley's southern end. The northern part of this range lies more than 100 miles from the condors' principal refuge, Sespe Wildlife Area—too far for these birds to make daily trips back and forth. But since they easily glide at 30 miles an hour they can regularly search the great cattle holdings in the southern part of the valley for food.

As they soar along the ranges the adults can be distinguished by the long white patches on the undersides of their wings and by their yellow-orange heads. The young, just as big by the time they can fly, have black heads and lack the white wing marking. Except for occasional grunts and hisses California condors are voiceless.

These great birds take a long time to mature. Not until their sixth year do they nest; then raising the single chick occupies the parents from hatching time in May until the next spring. New nestings, therefore, take place every other year.

The pale green or blue egg is a little over four inches long—about the size of a swan's egg. From hatching until October the chick stays in the nest cavity. It then begins to venture forth, and in a few weeks it can fly after the adults for short distances. The parents may feed it by regurgitation even when it is 15 months old.

Condors used to feed mainly on dead elk, antelope, deer, and rabbits. Since elk and antelope have disappeared from the birds' range, they now depend on the carcasses of cattle, sheep, and deer, and at times they take those of rabbits, dogs, and squirrels. The few remaining condors find plenty of food. They compete successfully with turkey vultures and ravens—when these smaller species face a huge condor there is no question who gets the first meal!

Range: southern Coast Ranges, Tehachapi Mountains, and western foothills of the Sierra Nevada in S. California. *Characteristics:* great size, black plumage; adult has yellow-orange head and long white patch on underwing.

STILL GROUNDED *by the chill of night, two condors preen and bask in the morning sun. They have lowered the ruffs that warm their bare necks; now they wait on their cliffside perch for the canyon air to rise so they can ride a thermal into the sky.*

Length 45-55", Frederick Kent Truslow

H. A. Thornhill, National Audubon Society

WORLD'S KEENEST EYE *enables hawks like this redtail to spy and strike furtive prey.*

By DEAN AMADON

SHARP-EYED RAIDERS OF THE SKY The Hawks

Family Accipitridae, Part 1

I STILL REMEMBER climbing to my first hawk's nest. My family was living in the rolling, woods-patched country of western New York and a pair of red-tailed hawks had built their nest in the tallest tree in our neighbor's sugar maple grove. It was a difficult climb for a boy of 12. The first time I tried it, my knees knocked so from fright and exhaustion that no more than halfway to the nest I had to give up.

Next day I tackled it again and at last, clinging nearly 70 feet above the ground, I looked into the great nest—the end product of many seasons of use. As I studied the three brown-spotted eggs cradled on cornhusks and shreds of soft inner bark, the birds crisscrossed over my head, screaming.

What a thrill, that first close encounter with hawks!

The red-tailed hawks I met that spring day represented one of some 205 species in the family Accipitridae. Twenty-five of those species inhabit North America and are classified as either kites, harriers, accipiters, buteos, or eagles.

Largest of North American Accipitridae, the four eagles include the gray sea eagle, which breeds in Greenland and sometimes on Baffin Island; Steller's sea eagle, a winter resident of the Pribilofs, Aleutians, and Kodiak Island; and the bald eagle and golden eagle, described in the next chapter.

Fiercest in the family, the three accipiters are bird eaters. Short-winged, they are adept at dodging through brush and branches. Walking quietly through dense cover, I have had a sharp-shinned hawk almost fly into me as it came twisting through the vegetation, intent on surprising some small bird. The Cooper's hawk, attracted by the covey call of quail, will hop about in tall grass to flush these birds. The goshawk, largest and fiercest of the group, will dash into a brier patch after a rabbit, hobbling along on foot, if necessary, to secure its prey.

The female accipiters are considerably larger than the males—in some species twice as heavy. Why is this? We are not sure, but it may be because the males of fiercely predatory species, if they were the more aggressive and stronger sex, might destroy the females and young. Among the accipiters the pendulum has swung so far the other way that it is difficult to keep pairs of them in captivity because the male, unable to flee, is killed and devoured by his mate.

Interestingly, mousers and insect eaters have a more placid disposition. Species such as the Mississippi kite, which is entirely insectivorous, or the Everglade kite, which feeds exclusively on freshwater snails, are almost gentle. And, unlike the solitary goshawk, the four North American species of kites are sociable. These birds have long wings and a swooping style of flight. The kites that children fly got their name from this group of birds because they dip and soar the same way.

North America's only harrier, the marsh hawk, resembles the kites with its slender body, long wings and tail, light, buoyant manner of flight, and sociable habits.

Largest of the four groups, the buteos number 13 species in North America. Members of this group have broad wings, wheel and soar high in the sky, and close in on their prey with less dash than the accipiters. My red-tailed hawks were buteos.

I revisited that first nest several times and learned more of hawk behavior. Eggs of medium-size hawks like the redtail take about a month to hatch. The female usually does most of the incubation, while her mate brings food. The hatchlings, wearing soft coats of down, are very feeble and their mother feeds them by holding out bits of flesh in the tip of her bill. But after a week or so they develop tremendous appetites and she is forced to leave the nest and help her mate search for food. The youngsters no longer require constant sheltering from cold, rain, or sun.

As soon as the young learn to tear prey and feed themselves, they begin to quarrel over food. When one seizes booty, he "mantles" over it, spreading wings and tail and turning his back on his nestmates. By now the little hawks frequently jump in the air, exercising their wings. They venture onto nearby limbs and after the fifth week may begin flying from tree to tree.

As a young naturalist I was puzzled by ringing cries, and finally learned they were the food cries of the young, newly on the wing. The parents continue to feed the fledglings several more weeks, for it takes time to gain the coordination needed to capture live prey. The young hawks make a game of plunging and veering, increasing their skills while playing, as kittens do when they pounce on a ball of yarn.

The second hawk's nest that I found required no climb at all. It lay on the ground, a shallow cup of grass stems in the weeds—the home of marsh hawks. Several times I watched the female fly up to take a mouse from her mate as he flew over, or to catch it as he dropped it. Marsh hawk pairs sometimes nest near one another. They also tend to congregate in winter. I recall one evening visiting a weedy, snow-

covered field near the Delaware River. Toward dark, marsh hawks began to come in singly from various directions with their low, irregular flight. I saw 25 or 30 settle to rest on the ground, sheltered from the chill wind by the dead vegetation. At the same time the "night shift," short-eared owls roosting in that very field, began flying out on their hunting patrols. The field mice had no respite, day or night.

The eyes of a hawk are justly famous and help explain the bird's success as a predator. Though a hawk is only a fraction the size of a man, it has eyeballs as large as a man's—sometimes larger! And the greatest density of nerve receptors known for any eye is recorded for a hawk.

These birds can spot even small prey at a fantastic distance. I have seen an Everglade kite flying 50 feet above a marsh suddenly veer down to seize a snail from its resting place in discolored water! The eyes are specially adapted for rapid change of focus and, unlike most birds, hawks have binocular vision. A Cooper's hawk could never pursue a bird at breakneck speed through dense brush if it had to peer now from one eye, now from the other, like a barnyard chicken.

Coupled with extraordinary sight, the hawk has sharp talons that operate with bone-cracking force. When it extends its legs fully in a dive, tendons spread the claws. When the bird strikes its prey, the legs double under the force of impact. This automatically clenches the toes and talons and they pierce the vitals of the victim, bringing almost instant death.

When I was a boy I captured an adult redtail whose wing was broken. I kept the bird in a shed and soon found myself hard put to find food for it. Occasionally I succeeded in shooting a woodchuck. An old chuck has a pretty tough hide, as I know, having skinned a few, but that bird had no trouble ripping into what must have been the biggest meals it ever ate. One day I was careless and the hawk drove a talon into one of my fingers. It swelled so I could not bend it at all. My father, already disenchanted with this hawk rescue operation, decreed an immediate release for the prisoner—fortunately by this time able to fly.

The legs of a hawk, the eyes, and the bill with its waxy growth at the base called the cere are often bright yellow. With maturity the eyes of a goshawk become deep red and fairly blaze as this fierce bird plunges after its prey. In hawk plumage, on the other hand, bright colors are entirely lacking. But so harmoniously are the grays, browns, and whites shaded and mottled that many hawks are extremely handsome.

The buteo hawks in particular often have a dark phase, common in one part of the range and perhaps virtually unknown in another. Some species even have a rufous phase, such as that displayed by the ferruginous hawk of the West. Add to

SWOOPING IN FOR THE KILL, *a female marsh hawk (opposite) swings her legs forward to deliver the stiff-legged smash that sinks talons deep. This time her prey is only a stuffed owl at Sapsucker Woods in New York. Elsewhere in Cornell's famed refuge an immature goshawk (below) pounces on a female mallard. This quarry proves too heavy for the young hunter; quacking and struggling, the duck gets away.*

Arthur A. Allen. Opposite: David G. Allen

these phases the immature and intermediate plumages, and small wonder that hawk identification presents a challenge. With practice, however, it is possible to recognize the birds by subtle differences in flight, profile, voice, and behavior.

Recently, driving near Tucson, Arizona, I saw a few turkey vultures quartering above the arid hillsides that flank the road. I stopped to look about and one of the birds happened to fly across the field of my binoculars. It had white bands across the tail—this could not be a vulture! Instead it was the relatively uncommon zone-tailed hawk, which tilts and veers with upswept wings in the manner of a turkey vulture. Small birds and mammals learn to ignore turkey vultures, which are scavengers, so the zonetail may have evolved into a mimic of this vulture. At least it is mistaken for one until it plunges upon the unsuspecting chipmunk or sparrow.

Most hawks are hardy, and those that migrate south apparently leave more because of food shortage than inability to withstand cold. When winter comes and

GLARING DEFIANCE, *young female goshawk feeds on a plump grouse. These big northern predators, ranging across Eurasia and North America, forget fear when attacking prey or defending young. Baby ferruginous hawks (opposite) in a Montana nest call for dinner—morsels of squirrel.*
Teuvo Suominen. Opposite: Frederick Kent Truslow

grasshoppers and small ground squirrels are no longer available in the western habitat of Swainson's hawk, the bird moves out completely. Most of these birds go all the way to Argentina, where they flock after the local migratory locusts. A few winter in southern Florida. There, instead of chasing locusts they follow farmers plowing fields and hunt mice as the rodents run for cover.

Although the Swainson's is the champion long-distance migrant among North American hawks, it travels up and down the vast interior of the continent often unseen. No one can predict exactly where the flocks will pass. In the East, however, hawk flights concentrate along such southward trending ridges as Hawk Mountain in eastern Pennsylvania, now a sanctuary. On a fine autumn day several hundred people may climb to this rocky prominence to watch the hawks glide and circle southward, almost without effort, on updrafts created as a brisk northwest wind strikes the steep slopes. Broad-winged hawks are commonest early in the season; then in late October and November redtails, sharp-shinned, and other species drift by. One day 11,392 hawks were counted!

Some hawks migrate along the shore. Southbound sharp-shinned hawks and songbirds sometimes fairly swarm around Point Pelee on the north shore of Lake Erie. Here they pause, confronted by the great lake. A melee results, with the little "sharpies" plunging through the brush after the warblers and sparrows, while bluejays, pinned down to the thickest brier patches, scream with alarm.

The rough-legged hawk, a northland species, never joins these early migrations. Later, in midwinter, you may see it—legs feathered right down to the toes—soaring gracefully above the snow-covered fields, or hovering to see whether a movement indicates the presence of a mouse.

Each in its own way, the hawks are admirably adapted for a predatory life. They are proud in carriage as they perch on crag or limb, spectacular in courtship flight where the male plunges earthward in a tremendous dive only to shoot skyward again. Keen, vigilant, and efficient, they demonstrate anew that even the harsher members of nature's community possess a certain charm and beauty.

Length 24"; Walter A. Weber, National Geographic staff artist (also opposite)

LIKE CAREFREE BACHELORS *in evening dress, swallow-tailed kites effortlessly trace patterns in the sky above the Florida Everglades. Fearless, they often zoom close to hunters.*

Swallow-tailed Kite
Elanoïdes forficatus

AS SUNSET COMES to the Everglades, three kites stage a ballet on air. Black-and-white plumage flashing, they arrow through shadowed groves, skim tranquil ponds and prairie, and dip and float and climb in the darkening sky.

Many observers consider the swallow-tailed kite the loveliest aerialist in North America. With a beat of slender wings or a flick of the deeply cleft tail, the kite swishes this way and that—or hangs suspended in the heavens for an eternal, breathtaking second.

At one time swallowtails nested throughout most of the eastern United States. Drainage, lumbering, and wanton shooting changed that. Today some of these migrants remain to breed in the South Atlantic and Gulf Coast states, but they nest in numbers only in southern Florida. They prefer swamp forests, river bottoms, lake shores, and freshwater marshes.

Large insects make up much of the swallow-tail's diet—grasshoppers, beetles, and dragon-flies. But it also dines on lizards, frogs, and small snakes—an item that has earned this bird the nickname "snake hawk."

Hunting in small groups, swallowtails fly low, back and forth, in a systematic search of the terrain. They usually seize prey with their feet, then, still airborne, tear and eat with their bills. They even drink and bathe on the wing, skittering gracefully across the water like swallows.

After an elegant aerial courtship a pair of swallowtails pick the crown of a tall tree for their home. They weave a flat, rather loose nest of twigs and moss collected on their flights. The mileage flown during nest-building can be enormous. One observer found more than 200 pieces in a nest located a mile from the source of the materials; to make that nest the birds had to fly at least 400 air miles!

Both parents incubate their two or three creamy, brown-marked eggs. They change the guard in spectacular fashion. The sitter rises straight up—as though on a spring. The incoming parent hovers a moment over the nest, then settles so slowly that it is hard to say just when the bird touches the eggs.

When several swallowtails fly together, they frequently twitter softly. But these birds utter loud and shrill squealing or whistling calls during the breeding season. If disturbed on the nest they will defend their young fiercely.

A few may winter in southern Florida but most migrate south of the United States.

Range: central Texas and Louisiana, also South Carolina, south to Argentina; migratory in the north. *Characteristics:* white head and underparts, black upperparts and deeply forked tail. Young have spotted black upperparts.

White-tailed Kite
Elanus leucurus

FROM THE MEADOW'S EDGE they look like gulls, these two pale birds breasting the high wind with ease. But their dark-shouldered, down-curved wings, long tails, and dangling yellow feet mark them as white-tailed kites.

Whitetails breed widely through South and Central America but now rarely as far north as the United States. Their whistles—sometimes ospreylike but ending in a guttural tone—sound only in California, Texas, and very rarely Florida.

These falcon-shaped predators inhabit open grassy country: prairies, marshes, savannas, alfalfa fields. Flying gracefully back and forth over their hunting ground, they look for mice and other small mammals.

Once the whitetail sights prey, it hovers a moment—kiting, or soaring, when the wind blows hard and beating slowly when it lulls. Then, holding up long pointed wings in a V, the kite slips down for the kill.

The nest, a loose mass of twigs, usually sits 12 to 60 feet up in a deciduous tree near a stream or marsh. Jays, magpies, and crows sometimes raid the finely lined cup and puncture the four or five whitish, brown-marked eggs.

Range: W. California, S. E. Texas, and peninsular Florida south to Chile. *Characteristics:* white head, tail, and underparts; pale gray upperparts; black patch on leading edge of wing.

White-tailed kites, length 15-17"; courtesy National Park Service

Everglade Kite
Rostrhamus sociabilis

FORTY YEARS AGO you could find an Everglade kite in almost any freshwater marsh on the Florida peninsula. You could hear its rasping chatter and watch it skim over the long grass, head tilted down and broad wings beating heavily.

In the cool early mornings and late afternoons the apple snails left the water and crawled on the grass. The kite, or snail hawk, seized them in its claws, flew to a perch, and drew the meat from the shell with its slender hooked beak.

Gunners took potshots at the bird and fishermen disturbed its nesting areas. Men drained the marshes, the snails died, and, too specialized to eat anything else, *sociabilis* faded. Surveys show fewer than 20 of these birds in the United States, most of them at the Loxahatchee National Wildlife Refuge in Florida. U. S. Fish and Wildlife Service men carefully guard them in breeding season and a successful nesting makes news.

Fortunately, the Everglade kite still ranges widely in Latin America. Conservationists hope to preserve the species in the United States by providing suitable freshwater marshes where kites can feed on apple snails and nest in peace. Their twiggy nests in willows or reeds hold three or four brown-spotted white eggs.

Range: S. Florida, and S. Mexico and Cuba to Argentina. *Characteristics:* slender hooked beak with red on base; white on base and tip of tail; orange legs. Male is dark gray. Female (page 202) has blackish head, white line over eye, brownish back, streaked buffy underparts.

Male Everglade kite, length 18"; Walter A. Weber courtesy National Park Service

Mississippi Kite
Ictinia misisippiensis

THIS MASTER of marathon flight spends most of its waking hours aloft. The falcon-shaped Mississippi kite soars and zigzags, tumbles over and over in breathtaking somersaults, and dives to within inches of the ground. Its black tail moves constantly during the stunting.

The sharp-eyed bird even eats most of its meals while soaring on rising air currents. It often swoops to snatch grasshoppers stirred up by grazing stock, or to pick cicadas from bushes.

In spring small flocks of these blue-gray birds, nicknamed "blue kites" or "mosquito hawks," return to their old treetop nests in dwarf elms, scrub oaks, or tall pines, usually near a lake or river. Paired birds line a twiggy platform with fresh leaves. Both sexes also incubate the one or two bluish-white eggs. Normally silent, a nesting Mississippi kite sounds a thin, ospreylike whistle when danger threatens.

Range: Iowa to Tennessee and South Carolina, south to Texas and N. Florida; winters to Paraguay. *Characteristics:* pearl-gray head, bluish-gray upperparts, paler gray underparts and wing patch, square or slightly forked black tail. Young have streaked buffy underparts, barred tail.

Mississippi kite, length 14"; Allan Brooks

Goshawk
Accipiter gentilis

ON STEADY STROKES of rounded wings a slate-gray bird cruises swiftly above an Alaskan meadow awakening to the touch of spring. Suddenly a male ptarmigan leaps up to rattle a breeding season challenge to all rivals.

The gray bird flips his long tail to change direction, then sails in low and fast. At the last moment he sets his wings and throws his sharp-taloned feet forward. He strikes the ptarmigan under one of its wings and drives his talons home with terrible force. Thus the goshawk kills.

This bird—largest of the Accipiter group of long-tailed, short-winged hawks—breeds over much of North America, from Alaska and Canada to central Mexico. But it is primarily a bird of the northern woodlands, living in and around heavy stands of timber.

The goshawk seems to migrate far only when its food supply runs short. In "flight years," when such staple prey as ptarmigan, lemmings, and hares are scarce, goshawks come south in large numbers. Then bird watchers in the United States can see one of the finest winged hunters, a hawk that is strong, fast, agile, fierce, and fearless. Medieval hawkers saw these traits and taught the bird to fly from the hand at flushed game.

Hunting, the goshawk dashes across clearings, around thickets, through tangled forest limbs, chasing small mammals and birds. Wide wings and a long tail provide perfect control. Tenacious to a foolhardy degree, this bird often hunts on foot when the quarry takes to cover. And it will seize poultry even after being stung by shot.

Ornithologist Edward Howe Forbush offered two examples of this bird's relentless hunting instinct. In one case a goshawk followed a hen into the kitchen of a Connecticut home and killed her in front of two people. In Maine a frantic hen ran under a woman's skirt; the pursuing hawk was trampled underfoot.

The goshawk's barnyard raids, though not so numerous as often portrayed, have earned it the usual family nicknames "chicken hawk" and "hen hawk."

Goshawks generally set their huge nest of sticks and twigs 20 to 60 feet up in a tree. The female, who averages two inches more in length and about a third more in weight than her mate, incubates the three or four bluish-white eggs. Intruders ignoring the harsh warning, *ca ca ca ca ca ca ca*, face a ferocious assault. Ornithologist George Miksch Sutton, studying a nest, was almost constantly attacked and screamed at by the female for eight hours!

Range: N. W. Alaska to Newfoundland, south to central California, S. E. Arizona, N. Minnesota, and W. Maryland; winters to Texas and Virginia. Also found in central Mexico, Europe, Asia, and N. Africa. *Characteristics:* slaty crown, white stripe above eye, blue-gray back, whitish underparts mottled with gray, rounded wings, long barred tail. Young have brownish upperparts, striped whitish underparts.

Goshawk, length 20-26"; G. Ronald Austing

Sharp-shinned hawk, length 10-14"; John Craighead   *Cooper's hawk, length 14-20"; Karl Maslowski*

Sharp-shinned Hawk
Accipiter striatus

A SUDDEN BREEZE, riffling the long grass of a sun-drenched field, betrays a feeding sparrow. For the sharp-shinned hawk perched in a nearby pine, an hour's vigil suddenly ends.

Down swoops the little hawk, beating his rounded wings, then gliding. He brakes by spreading his long, squarish tail, then sinks his sharp talons in the bird. The kill is quick.

The sharpshin, or "bullet hawk," hunts in remote woodlands through most of Canada and the United States. It eats rodents and insects but prefers small birds and may attack young poultry.

A mated pair usually place their nest of twigs lined with stems in the crotch of a conifer. The four or five whitish eggs, handsomely marked with brown, hatch in 35 days. Both adults, cackling shrilly, dive at any intruder.

Range: N. Alaska to Newfoundland, south to central Mexico, Louisiana, South Carolina, and the West Indies; winters to Panama. *Characteristics:* blue-gray upperparts, white underparts with reddish-brown crossbars; short rounded wings, long tail, square or slightly notched. Young have brownish upperparts, streaked underparts.

Cooper's Hawk
Accipiter cooperii

THE BAD NAME hawks have among poultry farmers stems largely from the deeds of this bird, named in 1828 for William Cooper, a New York naturalist. The swift, crafty predator not only raids chicken yards throughout its range but devours teal, grouse, quail, and small birds and mammals. Perhaps more than any of its kin it deserves the epithet "chicken hawk." Yet some Cooper's hawks become so selective in feeding habits that they nest near barnyards for years without molesting a single fowl.

Except for its tail, rounded instead of squarish, the Cooper's looks as well as acts like a larger version of the sharp-shinned hawk. Females of both species are larger than their mates, and the male Cooper's hawk is about the size of the female sharpshin.

Around the nest, usually built in a tree, *cooperii* makes a loud cackle. Both parents incubate the four or five whitish, sometimes spotted, eggs.

Range: S. British Columbia to New Brunswick, south to Baja California and central Florida; winters to Central America. *Characteristics:* like sharp-shinned hawk but has rounded tail.

Red-tailed hawks at two weeks ...   *... at three weeks ..*

♫♪ Red-tailed Hawk
Buteo jamaicensis

HIGH IN THE SKY a brownish hawk with a short reddish tail wheels on wide wings. Far below, a Cooper's hawk sails into a farmyard, seizes a chicken, and flies to the nearby woods.

The uproar in the hen yard brings the farmer with his gun. He looks up and sees, not the culprit but the red-tailed hawk. He fires, and the redtail falls. The farmer hangs up the body of the bird he calls "hen hawk." But strangely, he continues to lose chickens, and small rodents now despoil his garden.

The redtail is no hen hawk. It sails too slowly to catch any but sluggish or sick birds and eats mainly mammals, reptiles, frogs, and insects. It spots prey from a high perch or while soaring. Coursing over meadows, this hunter sometimes pounces on an animal before the victim can find refuge. Two redtails may team up to harry a squirrel dodging round a tree. If the prey is light, the hawk carries it to a feeding perch. Otherwise the bird shreds and gulps it on the spot.

Courting birds often mount high above the nesting area and wing buoyantly in great circles, crossing and recrossing each other's path. Legs dangling, the male sometimes zooms close to the larger female, seeming to graze her back.

The pair normally nest in a tall tree near the edge of a woodland. In prairies and deserts, however, they may dwell on a ledge or in a low tree or cactus. Redtails tend to occupy the same bulky twig nest year after year, lining it with bark and redecorating it with green sprigs.

For about a month both parents incubate the two or three whitish eggs, spotted or blotched with brown. The birds usually greet an intruder with prolonged squeals like the sound of escaping steam. They may attack—or abandon the nest, leaving their eggs to the mercy of jays.

After nesting, redtails wander widely. Most migrate from the colder regions in winter.

...at five weeks

Adult red-tailed hawk, light phase, length 19-25"; Walter A. Weber, National Geographic staff artist. Left: John H. Gerard

A related species, Harlan's hawk (*Buteo harlani*), nests in western Canada and winters in the lower Mississippi River basin and Texas. This blackish bird has a whitish tail mottled or streaked with black. The species has light and dark color phases, as does the redtail.

Range: central Alaska to Nova Scotia, south to Panama. *Characteristics:* broad wings, large size; brown upperparts, whitish breast, streaked belly, rounded tail red on top. Dark phase has dark underparts. Young have gray-brown tail.

Broad-winged Hawk
Buteo platypterus

SEVERAL FROGS in a woodland pool croak endlessly in the warm sun. A chunky crow-size bird in a nearby tree leans forward, twitching his black-and-white tail. Finally he leaps.

His quiet glide takes him 30 yards to a fat and careless croaker. Claws clutch, there's a splash, and before the ripples can spread to shore the broad-winged hawk flaps off with his victim.

Except for its specialties — frogs and toads plus an occasional snake or small bird — the broadwing kills no creature considered beneficial to man. In deep forests, wooded hills, and swamplands over most of eastern North America, it destroys many rodents and harmful insects.

The hawk gulps down insects and small animals whole and cleanly strips larger victims to the bone. With quick jerks of the bill the broadwing plucks a bird before devouring it.

In May the screams of the broadwing fill the woods. The clear notes, whiny yet musical, dispel the dank gloom of the forest and herald the nuptial season. A pair of the birds cavort in the sky, flapping, soaring, circling, skimming past one another.

Broadwings place their loose nest of sticks 15 to 50 feet up in a tree and line it with bark, lichens, and sometimes green leaves. Small and relatively tame, these hawks may utter a long whistle of warning at a human intruder but they usually will not attack. Brooding birds have even been lifted from the nest.

Both parents take turns incubating the two or three white eggs marked with brown and purple. The young hatch in about three weeks.

Downy hatchlings begin to peep and show signs of hunger soon after leaving their shells. Their mouths fly open at the least sound. Ornithologist Franklin Lorenzo Burns reported that one chick less than a day old turned its head and bit at his thumb.

The adult birds carve morsels of food for the chicks to take from their beaks. The solicitous parents carefully guard their young throughout the nesting period. With spread wings, they protect their brood from sun, rain, or cold winds.

In autumn the broadwings begin their flight to South America. Hundreds, even thousands of hawks swirl high to ride the winds and updrafts. Along Appalachian ridges they sometimes fly low and many have been gunned down.

Range: Alberta to Nova Scotia, south to Texas and the West Indies; winters to Brazil.
Characteristics: broad wings, dark brown upperparts, barred white underparts, black-and-white bands on short tail. Young are streaked buffy.

Juvenile broadwing
Allan Brooks

Red-shouldered hawk, length 17-24"; Frederick Kent Truslow

Red-shouldered Hawk
Buteo lineatus

KEE-YAR! KEE-YAR! While a blue jay mimics their piercing whistles, two red-shouldered hawks frolic in the New England sky.

Though paired for years, they resume their familiar courtship rituals each season with raucous zest. Flaring their broad wings and long tails, they gracefully soar and dive.

Red-shouldered hawks breed in wet woodlands over most of the United States east of the Rockies and west of the Sierra Nevada. And pairs show the same loyalty to nesting areas that they do to each other—frequently staying in their chosen territory in spite of lumbering.

Red-shouldered hawks occasionally take over the abandoned nest of a Cooper's hawk, a barred owl, or a squirrel, staking their claim with a sprig of greenery. But usually they build their own nursery of twigs, leaves, lichens, and shredded bark, setting it 20 to 60 feet up in a tree crotch.

Both parents incubate the three or four whitish eggs marked with brown.

Chicks hatch in about a month, and five or six weeks later they leave the nest. At first they merely climb about on the branches, returning to the nest at night. But soon they flutter to another tree and, under the watchful eyes of their parents, flap awkwardly through the woods.

Despite the nickname "hen hawk," this bird rarely takes poultry. It varies its diet of rodents with rabbits, frogs, snakes, turtles, screech owls, robins, crows, wasps, and grasshoppers.

In autumn one race of *lineatus*, the northern red-shouldered hawk, migrates south. The western subspecies is known as the red-bellied hawk.

Range: N. California to Baja California, and from E. Nebraska to S. Quebec, south to central Mexico and S. Florida. *Characteristics:* reddish shoulders, brownish upperparts, barred rusty underparts, white streaking on upper surface of wing, light patch near tip of underwing; white-banded tail. Young have streaked underparts.

oad-winged hawk, length 13½-19"
hn B. Holt, Jr., National Audubon Society

Swainson's Hawk
Buteo swainsoni

ONE BRIGHT SPRING DAY a Great Plains farmer spies a wave of brownish-and-white raptors soaring in from the south on broad, rounded wings.

Swainson's hawks! Some have come all the way from Argentina, spiraling high again and again on thermal currents to hitch rides on the southerly winds. The flock may number as many as 2,000 birds.

The birds bode good days for the farmer. They will help rid his lands of rodents, rabbits, and grasshoppers. They also eat frogs, lizards, and snakes but usually will leave his poultry alone.

This broad-winged species – which includes sooty brown birds of a darker color phase – favors the open country of western North America. When hunting, these birds may perch for hours on roadside posts or, with wings held in a slight V, glide low over the meadows.

Swainson's hawk – named for William Swainson, a 19th century English ornithologist – is a tame, unaggressive creature easily approached by man. Pairs frequently nest near the homes of orioles, bluebirds, or larks. These hawks have

Short-tailed hawk light phase, length 17"

even permitted doves and house sparrows to build in the bottom of their bulky dwellings.

The stick nest of *swainsoni*, set in a tree or on a cliff, usually holds two whitish, brown-spotted eggs. Hatched after a month's incubation, the young may undergo several changes of voice – at one time sounding like crying kittens, at another like screaming gulls – before they ultimately achieve the drawn-out squeal of adults.

Range: E. Alaska to W. Minnesota, south to Baja California and central Texas; winters to Argentina. *Characteristics:* light phase has dark grayish-brown upperparts, white forehead and underparts with dark band across breast, buffy linings on broad, rounded wings; dark flight feathers, barred gray tail. Dark phase is sooty brown throughout. Young have brownish upperparts, streaked head and underparts.

Short-tailed Hawk
Buteo brachyurus

THIS BIRD'S TOEHOLD in the United States looked tenuous indeed in 1937. That year ornithologist Arthur Cleveland Bent, noting the decline of the shorttail in Florida, said, "I believe it has almost, if not quite, disappeared from that State."

Bent's fears did not materialize. This tropical hawk still resides no farther north than Florida. But since the establishment of Everglades National Park in 1947, it has recovered there.

The short-tailed hawk keeps to mangrove swamps and cypress country. It often soars high on midday air currents, but few observers have seen the bird feeding. Records show that it will eat snakes, lizards, mice, and rats.

Nicknamed "little black hawk," this sluggish, tame, crow-size species may be either dark or light. Birds of different color phases – they occur with equal frequency and in both sexes – interbreed. The bulky nest of twigs and Spanish moss

Swainson's hawk, light phase, length 19-22"
Thase Daniel, National Audubon Society

White-tailed hawk
length 23-24"

Zone-tailed hawk
length 18½-21½"
John W. Taylor

cradles the two white, sometimes brown-marked, eggs on a lining of green leaves. The parents may squeal like ospreys when disturbed.

Range: E. Mexico and Florida to Argentina. *Characteristics:* small size, banded grayish tail. Dark phase has brownish-black plumage; light phase has dark upperparts, white underparts.

White-tailed Hawk
Buteo albicaudatus

THE FIRE BEGINS as a bright ribbon coiling across the Texas prairie; soon it becomes a raging torrent, blasting the land. Now, in the darkening sky, dozens of white-tailed hawks appear, sailing silently on long, broad wings.

Pillars of smoke have signaled these big gray birds, miles away, inviting them to a feast. The animals of this blazing region are hopping, running, crawling in heedless flight. The whitetails dive, picking off a rabbit here, a gopher there, a frog, a lizard, a mouse.

This predominantly Central and South American bird nests in the crown of a yucca or other shrub, or in a scrub oak. The whitetail lays two whitish, often brown-marked, eggs in a loose nest of sticks lined with grass. Disturbed, this hawk sounds high-pitched cries that resemble the laugh of a gull or the bleat of a goat.

Range: N. W. Mexico to S. Texas and the West Indies, south to Argentina. *Characteristics:* gray upperparts, whitish underparts and rump, chestnut leading edge on wings; short white tail with black band near end. Young are brownish.

Zone-tailed Hawk
Buteo albonotatus

ON MAY 3, 1872, at Rillito Creek, Arizona, Charles Emil Bendire, a soldier in the U. S. Army, climbed 40 feet up a cottonwood tree to investigate a nest. As he examined an egg, he suddenly noticed, only 80 yards away, a group of Apaches watching him.

"In those days," Bendire noted, "Apache Indians were not the most desirable neighbors." He popped the egg into his mouth, slid down the tree —leisurely to avoid suspicion—then jumped on his horse and galloped away!

"I found it no easy matter to remove the egg from my mouth without injury," Bendire reported, "but I finally succeeded, though my jaws ached for some time afterward."

Eleven years later Bendire became one of the founders of the American Ornithologists' Union. The egg today is preserved at the Smithsonian Institution in Washington, D. C.

The bird that laid the egg, a zone-tailed hawk, is a tropical American species that ranges as far north as the wooded canyons and river bottoms of the southwestern United States.

Aloft, the zonetail looks like a turkey vulture. It flies sluggishly, often soaring with long wings angled high, triple-banded tail partly shut, and body tilting from side to side. Sighting prey, the hawk dives swiftly to seize it. The menu includes fish, frogs, lizards, birds, and small mammals. The zonetail's loud whistles recall those of the red-tailed and broad-winged hawks.

Green-leaved twigs line the stick nest, which shelters two white eggs in a tall tree high above the old Apache country.

Range: N. Baja California to W. Texas, south to N. South America; winters mainly south of the U. S. *Characteristics:* white forehead, black body, long wings, three light bands across tail; yellow legs and feet. Young have spotted underparts, narrower tail bands.

Ferruginous hawk
light phase
length 22½-25"

Ferruginous Hawk
Buteo regalis

So LARGE that it is often mistaken for an eagle, this mild-mannered raptor looks like the king of the buteo hawks. The name *regalis* fits.

Awkward on takeoff, the ferruginous hawk soon mounts high in great circles, parading the rust-colored mantle that explains the bird's common name. From below, the feathered legs appear to emblazon a chestnut V on the white belly.

In its scarce brown-gray dark phase this bird resembles the smaller rough-legged hawk but lacks the dark tail tip. In a variant of the dark phase *regalis* is more reddish.

On the Great Plains and in the Great Basin where it breeds, the ferruginous devours crop-destroying rodents and insects as well as snakes and a few birds. A fondness for ground squirrels has earned it the nickname "squirrel hawk."

Two of these birds may team up to catch a prairie dog. One bird gets between the rodent and its hole while the other makes the kill.

On their breeding grounds ferruginous hawks scream like herring gulls. Their stick nests, placed 6 to 60 feet up in a cliffside or a tree, hold three or four brown-spotted white eggs.

Range: E. Washington to S. W. Manitoba, south to New Mexico and W. Oklahoma; winters to central Mexico. *Characteristics:* large size. Light phase has streaked pale head, reddish-brown upperparts and legs, whitish underparts and wing patch, white or rusty tail. Dark phase is brownish gray with whitish tail, white area on underwing.

Rough-legged Hawk
Buteo lagopus

As WINTER WITHDRAWS its snowy tentacles from Alaska and Canada, exposing the runways of the mice and lemmings, the rough-legged hawk soars again to the bleak northern forests and tundra.

The big bird with feathered legs—the name *lagopus* comes from the Greek for hare-footed—often hunts by twilight. Scouting prey, it flaps and glides silently above open fields, hovers like a kingfisher, or perches on a stub.

The roughleg helps control rodents and other small mammals harmful to man. In addition to mice and lemmings it relishes young ground squirrels. Its relatively small feet limit the size of the roughleg's prey.

In breeding season these hawks whistle and mew. They build stick nests with commanding views—in a tree, on a cliff ledge, or on the shelf of a stream bank. The usual clutch is three or four whitish, brown-marked eggs.

Range: N. W. Alaska and N. Canada south to the Aleutian Islands and Newfoundland; winters to California and Virginia. Also found in Europe and Asia. *Characteristics:* legs feathered to toes. Light phase has streaked pale head and neck, dark brownish upperparts; black on belly, wrist and tip of whitish underwing, and white tail. Dark phase is blackish brown with white area on underwing and on tail.

Gray Hawk
Buteo nitidus

"LIKE SILVERY SAILING SHIPS of the sky." Thus ornithologist Herbert Brandt described gray hawks in flight, circling and banking high above a forest of mesquite and hackberry "with a lazy sense of ease."

Spring brings these small tropical hawks—once called "Mexican goshawks" because of their resemblance to the goshawk—north of the border into the open country of the Southwest. Piping flutelike calls and spreading their black-and-white banded tails, they chase each other down wooded river valleys in courtship gambols.

Gray hawks usually nest in the slender top branches of a mesquite or cottonwood along a large stream in the dry country. The two or three whitish eggs rest on a small platform of green twigs and leaves. Parents gather food for their nestlings in dartlike dives, seizing in their strong talons a mouse or a rabbit, a quail or a dove, a lizard, a grasshopper, a beetle—the insects often serving as in-flight snacks.

Range: S. Arizona to S. Texas, south to N. Argentina; migratory in the north. *Characteristics:* ashy upperparts, barred gray-and-white underparts, broad black-and-white tail bands. Young have brownish upperparts and streaked buffy underparts, narrower tail bands.

Black Hawk
Buteogallus anthracinus

SQUEALING IN THE SPRING SKY, a dark hawk with a white-banded tail circles high above the Rio Grande Valley. Suddenly *anthracinus* tucks his broad wings tightly and lances down toward the trees. At the last second he opens his wings, spreads his tail, and, with yellow legs a-dangle, sails just above a tree crown. His talons clutch. A dry branchlet cracks, and the black hawk wings on home with construction material.

Like the zone-tailed hawk, which it resembles, this tropical bird barely ranges into the southwestern United States. Also known as the Mexican black hawk, it lives in river-bottom forests and arroyos fed by mountain streams.

Much of the time these hawks quietly perch low in the limbs of trees near watercourses, resting or waiting for prey. But during nesting season they become more active, hunting fish, small reptiles, crustaceans, insects, young birds, and small mammals for their hungry broods.

A pair often uses the same large, stick nest in a cottonwood, a willow, or a mesquite year after year. The one to three white eggs may have brown or lavender spots.

Range: central Arizona to S. Texas, south to N. South America and the West Indies. *Characteristics:* slaty black with white bands across middle and tip of tail; white spot near tip of underwing; long yellow legs. Young have buffy head and underparts, narrower tail bands.

John W. Taylor

*Gray hawk
length 16-18"
Right: juvenile*

*Black hawk
length 20-23"*

Harris' Hawk
Parabuteo unicinctus

PERCHED ATOP a telephone pole in the noonday sun, a soot-hued hawk eyes the cars that whiz along the road through his scrubby homeland. Sometimes he circles high above. More often he just sits, chestnut shoulders and white tail tip standing out against the dark body.

But don't let the sluggish appearance of Harris' hawk fool you. During feeding periods in the early morning and evening this powerful bird dashes through mesquite thickets and along watercourses hunting for wood rats and ground squirrels. It also catches rabbits, lizards, small snakes, and a variety of birds.

Harris' hawks build a nest of sticks and weeds 5 to 50 feet up in a yucca, Spanish bayonet, or giant cactus. Three or four whitish eggs, occasionally spotted with brown or lavender, rest on a lining of grass, rootlets, bark, and leaves. Intruders frequently meet harsh, prolonged screams from the circling parents. In the fall these hawks wander in flocks.

Audubon named this hawk for naturalist Edward Harris, a friend who accompanied him on a trek up the Missouri River in 1843.

Range: S. E. California to S. Texas, south to Argentina. *Characteristics:* blackish body, reddish shoulders, wing linings, and thighs; white on rump and tip of tail. Young have reddish shoulders and streaked pale underparts.

Harris' hawk, length 17½-29"
Russ Kinne, Photo Researchers

Marsh Hawk
Circus cyaneus

SIXTY FEET ABOVE the marsh grass a bluish-gray hawk suddenly halts in midair and plummets. The dive ends, not in the thrust of black talons into flesh but in a graceful pullout and a few easy wingbeats that loft the bird high again. A stall upends him, and down he swoops once more —then again, and again.

More than 70 of these spectacular dives have been counted in the springtime courtship dance of the male marsh hawk. Sometimes the streaked brown female joins in, but more often she watches from the ground or hunts in low gliding zigzags while her smaller suitor stunts above her.

When courting ends, nesting begins. The male shuttles in and out of the nesting site, bringing

Female marsh hawk, length 17½-24"; Frederick Kent Truslow. Inset: male, G. Ronald Austing

his share of stems and weeds which the female shapes into a crude platform. She always builds it on the ground, well hidden by shrubs or grass.

Here she lays four to six bluish-white eggs, some faintly blotched with brown. Both sexes incubate the eggs and the female protects the little white balls of down that peck through in about four weeks.

She stays close to home while the male soars low over marsh and meadow, his wings angling upward in a shallow V as he quarters the area hour after hour, skimming the weed tops, searching with sharp eye, listening with keen ear.

A mouse! Slamming his long tail downward, the marsh hawk jolts to a stop and plunges for the kill with long legs outstretched. Now his nasal whistling tells his mate that a meal is on the way. As he drops the mouse overhead, she rises

from the nest to make a deft midair catch. He makes similar supply drops of frogs, insects, fish, snakes, and small birds.

Other hawks show a white rump in flight but none more plainly than *cyaneus*, the "blue hawk." Shunning the woodlands, this harrier makes its home on tidal flat, meadow, or prairie, where it seldom perches on anything higher than a fence post. Only during migration does the marsh hawk rise to any great height.

Range: N. Alaska to Labrador, south to Baja California, Ohio, and Virginia; winters to Colombia and the West Indies. Also found in Eurasia and N. Africa. *Characteristics:* owl-like facial disks, barred tail, white rump. Male has blue-gray head and back, whitish underparts, black on tip and rear edge of wing. Female and young are brown, streaked on head and underparts.

PROUD AND POWERFUL
PREDATORS

The Eagles
Family Accipitridae, Part 2

By FREDERICK KENT TRUSLOW

BALD EAGLE *assails an osprey*
for the loot in his talons.
No match for his cousin,
the fish hawk will drop his prey,
which the hijacker will snatch
in midair. An able fisherman,
the eagle ordinarily
catches his own fare.

Walter A. Weber, National
Geographic staff artist

I T WAS ONE OF NATURE'S most fascinating dramas, and I would have a reserved seat! This thought gripped me as, jammed in a ranger patrol boat with tools, wire, and a sectional tower, National Park Service biologist Bill Robertson and I churned through the shallow waters of Florida Bay in Everglades National Park. Ahead, awaiting capture by my cameras was that splendid bird of prey, the bald eagle!

Civilization's relentless pressures have driven *Haliaeetus leucocephalus*, often called the American eagle, from many of its former haunts, and conservationists fear for the bird's future. It occurs throughout the United States and Canada but is abundant only in Alaska. One of the few places where the species nests in numbers is the Everglades. So to this biological showcase of temperate and subtropical wildlife I came to record the nest life of a bald eagle family.

Through aerial surveys Robertson and I had studied some 50 eyries in the park, each capping a tall tree near a body of water. We were after a very special nest. It had to offer good sunlight for color photography, yet nearby foliage for concealing the blind. It had to be a nest in current use and one in which young had been successfully raised before. It also had to be within daily commuting range, so I could obtain a complete sequence of pictures from hatching to flight.

One eyrie seemed to meet all these requirements. It stood on a mile-long key off Florida's tip, only a five-mile boat run from Flamingo, one of the park centers (map, page 202). The nest perched 20 feet up in a black mangrove stub—not nearly as elevated as the eyries built by northern bald eagles at heights of 80 feet or more in towering trees and on cliffs, but this was the loftiest perch the island offered. Moreover, in this nest lay two dull white eggs!

We kept check on the nest by air. Neither of us wished the parents to abandon the clutch—as eagles may do if disturbed during the 35 days of incubation. Once the eggs had hatched, we approached the eyrie on foot and saw a pair of babies covered with light gray natal down. At sight of us the parents flew off, crying out with weak, high-pitched notes that sounded more like a squeal than a scream. We stayed only long enough to plan the arrangement of the blind, because at this stage the eaglets might perish in the hot January sun if deprived too long of their parents' protecting shade. Now we were back again with the blind.

Tying our boat to a lacework of roots and branches, we shouldered the tower and waded ashore. We threaded the thicket, then carried the structure the length of the key through waist-high weeds to the nest site. There we set it up, guyed its legs with wire to nearby mangrove trunks, and made sure the peephole of the blind was level with the nest. As we retreated into the mangroves at the far end of the key, I saw the adults stop hovering and return to the nest. They were accepting the blind!

Two days later I began shooting. My workshop for the next three months would be this four-legged tower, nearly 20 feet tall, built of two-by-twos with a plywood platform topped by a tent three feet square and five feet high.

Scientists believe that a mated pair of bald eagles stays together until one dies. The nest, as I could easily see from my hiding place some ten yards away, is a monument to their union. Returning to the same site again and again, the birds build a remarkable home over the years. Each season they add new sticks, trample in new grass, and sometimes introduce odd bric-a-brac. Observers have found fishing plugs, light bulbs, on one occasion even a tablecloth. In time the nest may grow to tremendous size. One measured 10 feet across and 20 feet deep. Another weighed two tons! In such mammoth nurseries infant eagles look small indeed.

Through much of its range the bald eagle feeds largely on fish; in this nest the young ate nothing else. And at first the feeding proceeded with the formality of a

ritual. The male would arrive at the eyrie and drop a squirming catfish. The female hooked into the gills and with a single rip laid the fish open to its tail. She then bit off a half-inch snippet of flesh and, holding the morsel, extended her beak at right angles to the wide-open mouth of the waiting baby. The eaglet then covered its mother's beak and raked in the bite.

At first the little ones sat patiently, each awaiting its turn. But after a few weeks they became impatient, pushing, tumbling, clamoring for the tidbits. Usually one eaglet is more aggressive and dominates its nestmate. In this nest it was the larger and darker of the two youngsters. I called this one "Blackie." At mealtime the smaller, lighter "Brownie" invariably took second place. Their father took second place too, for a time. During the first three weeks his mate permitted him to hunt but not to feed the young. After that both parents hunted and served, though one always remained near the brood. I rarely saw either of them eat anything at the nest other than an occasional piece of meat too large or tough for their offspring.

SOMETIMES I WOULD STAY in my tiny cubicle for nine hours at a stretch. I worked my cameras on days when the sun made the inside of the blind a veritable oven. I worked on days when the wind blew so hard I had to time my shooting to the moments when the tower's swaying brought the lens on line with the nest. Moreover, bald eagles never let down their guard—so little a thing as a change in the lens size might alarm them. So I cut the ends from a big tomato-juice can, painted it black, and fastened it as a permanent dummy to the front of the blind. Then I could poke any of my lenses into it without being noticed. In addition, each day District Ranger Ernie Borgman or Ranger Jim Arnott would accompany me to the blind and then leave, thus fooling the birds into thinking no human remained nearby. Without the help of these and other Park Service men I could never have done the job.

The spacious eyrie made an ideal gymnasium for the growing young. At first they scrabbled around on their wings and shanks, like children on hands and knees. Later they exercised foot and leg muscles by prancing about. Sometimes they would broad-jump across the nest in mock pounces or toss a twig into the air and then leap upon it. After exercise the young birds often rested, nodding their heads, blinking, drowsing. And during these quiet moments I sometimes daydreamed myself.

Some say the bald eagle is a coward. Ben Franklin thought so. And, in truth, crows and kingbirds sometimes harry it. But let

Male bald eagle, length 30-36", and (right) female, 33-42"

WINGS STRETCHING *nearly seven feet, tail fanned, a male bald eagle (opposite) comes in to land on a tiny island off the tip of Florida.*

Fifty feet from this perch his mate (above) sits on a limb of the mangrove stub that holds their nest. Irritated, she lifts a talon to scratch in her head plumage for the insect that spoiled her siesta.

During the first weeks after the eggs hatch, the male does the fishing, bringing his catch home for his mate to offer to the young. But once he sought to feed the babies directly (left). Here the irate mother shields her brood. Snubbed, the dejected male eats the morsel himself (lower).

To take these striking photographs and the ones on the next four pages, the author endured oven heat and numbing cramps for 12 weeks in a canvas blind erected just 33 feet away from the nest.

one of them approach the eagle's favorite perch or its eyrie when there are young in it, and the big bird will brook no nonsense. I've seen one with a broken wing fight like a demon against the efforts of three men to subdue him. Master of the domain it surveys, the eagle is not easily provoked. Cornered, it becomes a fury who will not willingly wear any man's shackles.

The eagle, in fact, has symbolized strength and courage since earliest history. It went into battle with the Persian hosts. Its likeness rode on the standards of Roman legions. So, appropriately, in 1782 the Continental Congress chose the bald eagle for our national emblem—even though Franklin preferred the wild turkey.

As THE DAYS PASSED, Blackie and Brownie grew strong. Desultory wing flapping became rhythmic beating, then powerful sweeps that raised the fledglings above the nest. They made brief flights straight up to a height of three or four feet and finally minute-long hovering hops that took them as much as ten feet into the air.

They had to learn to fly by themselves. The parents didn't help. When the right day came, the old birds simply stopped bringing food to the

CARVING WITH SCIMITAR BILL, *mother eagle prepares a fish feast for her nestlings, "Brownie" (nearest camera) and "Blackie." The twins, nicknamed by the author for their colors, lean forward in anticipation. Later, when they learned that a strip of skin could snap and deliver a stinging blow, they stood back. But nothing dulled their appetites, so after one meal Brownie (opposite) opens its bill and calls for more. In three months the eaglets grew in length from three inches to three feet!*

Frederick Kent Truslow

Frederick Kent Truslow

READY . . . GET SET! *Month-old Blackie (above) tries wings and legs atop the nest. But no—flight must wait for feathers, just now starting to push through the wool on head and neck. Fourteen days later (left) strength is the problem; the wings are so heavily feathered Blackie can't lift them both!*

At nine weeks the twins (right) doze after exercising; flight is now less than a month away. But three or four years must pass before they will acquire the yellow beak and iris and the emblematic white head and tail. The head won't lack feathers—when the bird was named, "bald" meant whit

nest. Instead they offered it at a distance—starving out their youngsters. This was a hard school but an effective one. When Blackie and Brownie passed these first tests of flight, they still hung around the eyrie with their parents, using it as a family dining room. They'd stay in the neighborhood for weeks before setting out on their own.

Today the bald eagle appears on dollar bills, coins, uniform buttons, medals, flagstaffs, public documents, the President's own seal. And yet, though Federal law has given this bird strict protection since 1940, glimpses of eagles are all too rare. Clambering down from my cramped spyplace for the last time, standing quietly on that tiny island and watching one of this grand family wheel high in the sky, I thought what a tragedy if his kind should vanish from the earth!

THE GOLDEN EAGLE might have been our national symbol. Beautiful, savage, far fiercer than the bald eagle, this majestic bird served royalty in the olden days of falconry. But since it ranges the Old World as well as the New, it could well be claimed by nations throughout most of the northern hemisphere.

My best chance for photographing the nest life of the golden eagle would be in the Rocky Mountains. And that is how I came to spend more than a month observing *Aquila chrysaëtos* from a blind lashed to a cliff ledge near Livingston, Montana.

Inching down the face of that cliff in predawn darkness, I was glad to have at my side Bill Staniger, a fine climber and eagle student made available to me by Dr. John Craighead, leader of the Montana Cooperative Wildlife Research Unit. The bulky nest sat on the same ledge 85 feet from our blind. Three eaglets, hatched from whitish, brown-splotched eggs, occupied it. Watching this family day after day, I began to compare it with the bald eagle family I had studied in Florida.

Besides their physical differences, the adult golden eagles were far wilder than the bald eagles. The Montana birds were extremely wary and we had to enter the blind before daylight to avoid being spotted. Moreover, in contrast to the Florida

birds, which had an easy trip to fish-filled waters, these parents spent long hours

searching the surrounding foothills to stock the family larder. Ninety percent of their diet was rabbit, though they also captured a wide variety of other prey. I once saw the eyrie jammed with a weasel, a gopher, a jackrabbit, and a magpie!

The youngsters, however, seemed much the same as Blackie and Brownie. Like that engaging twosome, they were forever preening feathers, vigorously testing wings, and clamoring as their parents arrived with food.

When their time for flight did come, my time for observation was over. With some sadness I packed my gear and made a wish that I might see these free

Bold scientists wrest life secrets from the golden eagle

ATOP A 300-FOOT CLIFF *in Montana Bill Staniger heaves a scaling line past a ledge 30 feet below. There in an eyrie three young eagles stir uneasily.*

Bill and fellow researcher Jerry McGahan clamber down to the nest to mark the screaming birds with numbered bands. Bill holds one eaglet's feet while Jerry bands the leg of a second (opposite).

Moments later the third bird struck. Talons which someday might rip the life from a fox or a rattlesnake now fastened in Jerry's bare arm. It took pliers to get them out.

The banding is one phase of a comprehensive study guided by John Craighead, leader of the Mòntana Cooperative Wildlife Research Unit.

Gunned down, poisoned, trapped for years—though the bird normally preys on destructive small mammals— the golden eagle declined drastically. Dr. Craighead's team gathers data on nesting, mortality, and feeding to determine how this magnificent predator fits into nature's balance in the western mountains.

Frederick Kent Truslow

spirits again some day. Perhaps I shall, for with luck eagles may live 30 years or more.

Bald eagle – *Range:* Bering Island and N. Alaska to Labrador, south to Baja California and Florida. *Characteristics:* white head and tail, brownish-black body. Female is larger. Young are gray or brownish-black, mottled with white.

Golden eagle – *Range:* N. Alaska to N. Saskatchewan and Quebec, south in west to central Mexico, in east to New York, and probably in Appalachians to North Carolina. Also found in Europe, Asia, and N. Africa. *Characteristics:* "golden" crown and nape, dark brown body, white tail base. Female is larger. Young have white patch on both wing surfaces, white tail with dark terminal band.

Frederick Kent Truslow

ME IS THE HUNTER (above),
krabbit in tow. Three
den eaglets jockey for
sition. The adult rides to
ledge on thermals. Without
ch updrafts it cannot lift
wy loads. The young can now
d themselves, so the parent
ds the food, checks the brood,
d is off in five or six seconds.

Adult golden eagle, length 30-41″, and juveniles

BILL OPEN, *tongue out, the adult (above) poises
for takeoff, while the runt in this peck order
sneaks a bite from the just-delivered rabbit.
The parent departs, and number one eaglet (below)
leaps from its high perch onto the carcass.
Wings flapping, talons grasping, the youngster
makes several practice "kills" before eating.*

By ROGER TORY PETERSON

HIGH-DIVING FISH EATER The Osprey
Family Pandionidae

I
N A CROTCH of a dead elm on a small island near my home rests a huge platform of sticks. As I approach the tree a large bird—gleaming white below, dark brown above—hovers over it, showing a distinctive crook or kink in its wings. Its sharp cheeping whistles change from an annoyed *chewk! chewk! chewk!* to a frenzied *cheereek!* as it protests my audacity. Concern, however, impels my visit. For this is one of the few active osprey eyries remaining in Connecticut today.

I moved to the lovely town of Old Lyme in 1954, largely because of the colony of ospreys around the broad lower reaches of the Connecticut River. There were 150 active nests within a ten-mile radius, and we could see a dozen of the birds in the air at one time. We even had a nest on our property, in a great oak on the crest of a hill. One of our neighbors put up a pole topped by a wagon wheel in April and a pair of ospreys claimed it almost immediately. In our community, having an osprey's nest within a stone's throw of your house became a status symbol!

The core of our colony was Great Island—a sprawling marshy tract near the river mouth. Here every duck blind and stranded snag supported a flat platform of sticks gathered by the ospreys. I never tired of watching the birds as I canoed in those quiet waters. With luck I would see one cruising along the island shores. It would check, perhaps 50 feet above the water, hover on laboring wings to scan the riffles, then plunge, feet thrown forward. The big bird would vanish in spray but a moment later would reappear to flap away with a fish. An osprey's outer toes can move forward and back like those of an owl. And behind the needle-sharp claws spiny pads give a pincerlike grip. The bird almost invariably carries its prey nose forward like a shiny torpedo, using both feet, one before the other, if the catch is large.

High over Great Island one laden "fish hawk" after another would wing homeward. Sometimes a herring gull would give hopeful chase, but I never saw an osprey lose its catch to a mere gull. Eagles are another matter. Where they share the same water they sometimes hijack the fish hawks. Swooping from above, an eagle forces an osprey to drop its prey, then catches it neatly (page 236).

The osprey (*Pandion haliaetus*) has succeeded in extending its dominion round the world. I have seen the great nests of this one-species family in pine trees on

International Magazine Service-Pix

WEAKFISH IN HIS TALONS, *an osprey returns to his perch to carve his share. Two-thirds goes to his mate and young. Diving talons-first (opposite), he hits prey with a splash. If he locks into too big a fish and can't relax his grip in time, he may be pulled under and drowned.*

Length 21-24½", Frederick Kent Truslow

Japanese islets, on sea cliffs near Gibraltar, on spruce islands in the Baltic, on Mexican headlands, and on eroded pinnacles in Yellowstone National Park.

In Connecticut, nests on telephone poles were common. One enterprising bird in Old Lyme made off with the top of a trash can, a perfect bowl for its sticks when it was placed on the crossbars of a power pole. Nest material under the metal cover insulated it. But the next downpour filled the cover, tipped it, the water short-circuited the wires, and the neighborhood was blacked out for an hour!

Inevitably power companies take a dim view of ospreys. Some destroy the nests as stubbornly as the birds build them; but one enlightened company lured the birds away from transformer sites by erecting special nesting platforms.

No eggs are more handsomely marked than the osprey's. Usually three in number, they vary from white to cinnamon in ground color and are daubed with chocolate brown. The male brings food to the nest; the female determines the proper bite size for her brood. After five or six weeks the young may help themselves when food is delivered. Always mannerly, they take turns standing on the fish and tearing it. By then they have lost their buffy down and look quite like their parents. They spend much time jumping up and down and exercising their wings.

STICKS AND STALKS *of a sturdy osprey nest support naturalist (right), come to band juveniles in a declining colony on Gardiners Island, New York. Fledglings (opposite) try wings that in maturity may span six feet. Many nests perch atop trees and ledges; this rests on a mangrove in Florida Bay. Ospreys drive crows and hawks away from the nest but sometimes let house sparrows room in its base. Herons and egrets may even nest in the same tree.*

Byron Porterfield, New York Times. Opposite: Frederick Kent Truslow

In late July, when the river swarms with sailboats and outboards, the young start flying. Catching fish comes naturally—down they plunge into the water. True, they miss at first, but hunger is a good teacher.

Only after we had lived several years in Connecticut did we realize that something was wrong with our summer resident ospreys. Apathetic pairs laid eggs on marsh grass, even where the tide could reach them. When Great Island should have erupted with fledglings, I found only adults. Parent birds sat on unhatched eggs 60 or 70 days, though babies usually pip their shells in 28 to 32. The number of active nests dropped from 150 in 1954 to 17 ten years later. Other nesting areas showed a similar decline.

Laboratory tests revealed insecticide in the eggs and in fish samples taken from nests. How did it get there? Fingerlings consume poisoned insects and are eaten by larger fish. Catching these, the osprey ingests the accumulated poisons, which may inhibit fertility.

One year soon, I fear, I shall find no ospreys at Great Island—not one. Part of the lovely valley will have died.

Range: N.W. Alaska to Newfoundland, south to Baja California and Florida; winters to Peru and Brazil. Also found on every other continent except Antarctica. *Characteristics:* white head, black mask, blackish upperparts, white underparts; long angular wings.

251

The Falcons

Family Falconidae

By FRANK and
JOHN CRAIGHEAD

HIGH OVER THE YELLOWSTONE RIVER a duck hawk streaked earthward in that graceful, high-speed attack that falconers call a "stoop." We paused in our fly casting to watch as he picked a cliff swallow out of the air with deceptive ease and zoomed up close to his former altitude, or "pitch." As he set his wings to glide downriver, we heard him give a high wailing call that brought the female from the nesting cliff. In midair the male, or tiercel, transferred the swallow in his talons to his larger mate. And we thrilled at the sight as men have through the ages.

"Duck hawk" is another name for peregrine falcon, one of 58 members of the family Falconidae. Seven of these species inhabit North America—the vulturelike caracara and six true falcons of the genus *Falco*. These vary in size and specialization from the little sparrow hawk, or American kestrel, which pounces on grasshoppers, field mice, and sparrows, to the powerful gyrfalcon, which hunts ptarmigan over the tundra. The prairie falcon patrols arid land where vegetation is sparse and rodents numerous. The peregrine searches open waterways to strike ducks and other birds that venture from the wooded shores.

Generally smaller and more streamlined than hawks in the family Accipitridae, the falcons have small heads, hard compact plumage, and long pointed wings—adaptations that enable them to fly at great speed. Females are larger than males; both sexes have dark mustaches. Short, strong, conspicuously notched bills and big powerful feet mark the falcons as predators, yet they have gentle dispositions. A trained falcon often seems to show real affection for its master. Little wonder that falcons have endeared themselves to men since antiquity (page 35).

A *National Geographic* article on falconry by Louis Agassiz Fuertes inspired us to take up the sport when we were 14. Taming, training, and flying the most spirited and courageous of birds—this had seemed to us a challenge beyond compare. But we captured our young birds and eventually taught ourselves the "noblest of Arts." Training a bird for falconry simply means channeling its natural ability by controlling its food supply. A hungry falcon quickly learns to jump or fly to its master's fist when he rewards it with food. And if its master moves calmly and handles it gently, the falcon gradually accepts him as a friend as well as a provider. The taming process is called "manning."

After catching a bird a falconer puts leather straps, or "jesses," around its legs, using a jess knot that neither tightens nor loosens. The ends of the jesses come together at a swivel that prevents them from twisting. A leash, also threaded through the swivel, ties the bird to its perch, usually a padded block of wood. In flight the jesses trail free, separated so they won't snag. Sometimes a falconer attaches a bell to the leg to help find the bird in case it strays. A leather hood keeps the bird quiet.

The falcon, sheltered in a shed, or "mew," is fed raw lean beef once or twice a day and an occasional mouse, starling, or sparrow. The trainer regulates the amount so that the bird is neither too hungry nor too satisfied but is keen and ready to fly and hunt at the time he chooses to release it.

In progressive steps the falconer trains his bird to fly from and return to his gloved hand. He tethers it with a "creance," a long string attached to the swivel. He teaches the bird to recognize the lure—usually a leather packet garnished with meat and feathers—and to strike it when he swings and throws it. Soon he can remove the creance and let the falcon fly free to stoop at the lure. Hunger and habit will bring the bird back to his glove. Now he can "enter," or train, it on the particular game it will hunt. Finally, he flies his falcon at live quarry.

Like all falconers, we acquired vast respect for the peregrine. As boys we had one that we called Ulysses because he kept wandering off. One afternoon as he was circling high above us a crow flew past, about 300 feet up. We thought it would go unmolested, but just as it crossed the center of the field, farthest from any cover, Ulysses banked and started down in a marvelous stoop. As he picked up momentum he pumped his wings a few times and seemed to double his speed. He expanded suddenly from a distant speck to a hurtling wedge of streamlined feathers, feet lying back against the tail, wings half-closed, beak cutting the air.

MORSEL OF PHEASANT *rewards the hunter that killed it — a young gyrfalcon in South Dakota. Immature peregrine (opposite), jesses trailing, "binds on" to a pigeon. Trained falcons usually smash prey with a half-closed foot, let it fall, and land beside it. Wild birds kill small prey with the talons.*

G. Ronald Austing

The whining of air through the tiercel's wing feathers warned the crow and it started to turn. It never completed the maneuver. Ulysses struck, and crow feathers exploded in every direction. Upward streaked the tiercel, ready to stoop again, but there was no need. Before the last feather reached the ground, Ulysses was standing beside his fallen quarry.

The *National Geographic* article we wrote about our boyhood falconry brought an invitation from an Indian prince to visit him. In India we saw falconry practiced in the grand manner. We watched the white-bearded master falconer at work, his fingers unbelievably adept at hooding. We learned secrets passed on only from prince to prince and father to son as each generation is taught the art.

Now our own children learn the old art. When young Lance Craighead gets off his school bus in the afternoon the wings of Grizzly, his male sparrow hawk, are already quivering in anticipation of the daily flight. Lance frees the jesses and

the tiercel rises and races him toward the hawthorn trees in a distant meadow. There Lance flushes some sparrows, and from a commanding perch or hovering pitch Grizzly stoops. Most of the time the sparrows elude him. Lance and Grizzly continue their adventure until dusk forces them home, the bird circling over the boy.

When we were boys we found peregrine falcon nests on cliffs above the Potomac and along the Susquehanna, but our sons have never seen an active duck hawk eyrie beside an eastern river. Despite some legal protection, falcons are widely persecuted. To survive they must have man's tolerance and an uncontaminated habitat.

In medieval times only the nobility could keep hunting falcons, and the birds were strictly protected. In our modern democracy, anyone who wants to can practice this sport of kings. But indiscriminate shooting and indirect poisoning from pesticides may be tolling an end to the ancient art of falconry.

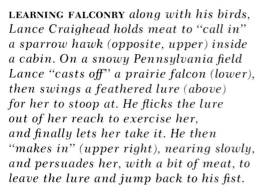

LEARNING FALCONRY *along with his birds, Lance Craighead holds meat to "call in" a sparrow hawk (opposite, upper) inside a cabin. On a snowy Pennsylvania field Lance "casts off" a prairie falcon (lower), then swings a feathered lure (above) for her to stoop at. He flicks the lure out of her reach to exercise her, and finally lets her take it. He then "makes in" (upper right), nearing slowly, and persuades her, with a bit of meat, to leave the lure and jump back to his fist.*

STOOPING TO CONQUER, *a prairie falcon strikes a ring-necked pheasant in South Dakota. "Stoop" mea*

Prairie Falcon
Falco mexicanus

OVER THE CLIFF you go, rappelling down to look at a windworn niche in the slickrock, a prairie falcon eyrie. As you slide and scuff toward it, the female bird vaults away. Screaming *kik-kik-kik-kik*, she mounts high into the Arizona sky with rapid strokes of her pointed, swept-back wings. At your feet lie four mottled brown eggs.

Abandon her clutch? Look up, quickly! Rocketing out of the sun, the falcon hurtles straight at you. Veering at the last instant, she whistles past your upthrown arm, then zooms back up to slash in again—and again. Wheeling above, her smaller mate chatters in excitement.

Only rarely does *mexicanus* strike a human intruder. But woe to the barn owl that flaps from its nest, disturbed by the commotion. Venting her wrath on this innocent neighbor, the falcon may dive savagely on it, breaking its wing, perhaps killing it with a single blow of her talons.

Though ravens are notorious nest robbers, prairie falcons often tolerate them on the same cliff with no apparent conflict. Each spring the falcons take first pick of nesting ledges, now and then annexing an abandoned raven eyrie. If the falcon pair finds no old nests to occupy, the female raises her fleecy young right on the bare floor of a rocky shelf or canyon crevice. Southern exposures are preferred, and usually the site affords a fine view of the surroundings.

From their box seat above the canyon the falcons dart out to hunt birds and rodents in morning and evening. Sometimes they fly low over arid plains or cruise above the timbered foothills. The brown thunderbolt that streaks out of the blue to strike a pheasant occasionally may shuffle along the ground after grasshoppers, or peer into tussocks for sparrows.

Length 17-20", Walter A. Weber
National Geographic staff artist

...live on prey.

Peregrine Falcon
Falco peregrinus

ON WINGS that span more than three feet, a peregrine falcon wheels half a mile above the mirror of a northern lake. Her dark eyes follow her mate, a tiny quiver in the green-and-silver tapestry below. He scouts while she "waits on."

Abundant waterfowl dot the lake, yet none flushes before the swooping male, or tiercel. The "duck hawk" rarely stoops on birds at rest, and the ducks seem to know this instinctively.

Suddenly an unwary mallard splashes up from a reedy cove and mounts into the morning air. The high-circling falcon half-rolls and shoots downward in a power dive, partly closed wings pointing straight back and whipping the air rapidly to build speed. Straight down she streaks, wind screaming past her sleek body at nearly three miles a minute.

The duck spots the hurtling speck and strains to sheer away, but in an instant lightning strikes. With a clawed fist the falcon knocks the mallard senseless. Pulling out of her dive, she turns and follows the shattered duck as it falls to a grassy bank in a shower of feathers. There she plucks and devours her kill.

Though swifts can outstrip her in level flight, the female peregrine in a stoop probably sets the speed record for all nature's creatures. On swept-back wings she arrows from the sky to bludgeon a sandpiper, split the skull of a marauding owl, or, in play, fetch a startled cormorant a puckish rap on the back.

Diving at 175 miles an hour, a falcon could not breathe without a system of baffles within its nostrils. Ancient falconers judged a bird's speed by the complexity of this structure. The peregrine was a favorite then, and modern falconers still prize the species and boast of its courage.

Southward goes *peregrinus*, "the wanderer," in autumn, not to escape winter's grasp but to follow the migratory birds that are its food supply. At his old ledge next spring the male courts his larger mate with awesome aerobatics and a

Slim and agile, this corsair of mountain range and prairie often hectors other birds. One target, the great blue heron, sometimes must drop to the ground, croaking in rage and ducking each pass, until the falcon finally flies away.

Range: British Columbia to North Dakota, south to Baja California and N. Texas; winters to central Mexico. *Characteristics:* dark brown eye stripe and mustache, pale gray-brown upperparts, white chin and throat, whitish underparts spotted with gray-brown; bare yellow feet. Young have darker upperparts, brownish streaks on face.

YOUNG PEREGRINE *trails falconer's bells and jesses, leg straps little changed for centuries. Adult perches on a crag (right).*

Length 15-21", G. Ronald Austing
Right: Allan Brooks

rusty-hinge *wichew* call. She broods four or five mottled mahogany eggs on a rock shelf. He feeds her with air-dropped kills, which she fields in midair with her talons. A few pairs nest on skyscrapers and prey on city pigeons.

Range: Alaska to Greenland, south to Baja California, S. W. Texas, Colorado, N. Louisiana, and N. Georgia; winters to Argentina. Also found nearly worldwide. *Characteristics:* blue-black cap and mustache, slaty back, white chin, buffy underparts barred with brown. Young have brownish upperparts, streaked underparts.

Aplomado Falcon
Falco femoralis

As BATS FLIT through the New Mexico twilight, two swift falcons dart among them and emerge with squeaking prey. Seldom seen singly, the graceful, slender aplomado falcons hunt in pairs, often over brush fires where they pounce on fleeing prey. While insects and rodents comprise their chief food, they occasionally ambush small birds, streaking from a secluded perch to make a midair kill.

Rare north of Mexico, this desert raptor makes little protest when you find its nest—a twiggy, grass-lined platform in a yucca crotch, cradling three brown-dotted whitish eggs.

Range: S. Arizona and S. Texas south to Argentina. *Characteristics:* dark gray cap, eye stripe, mustache, and upperparts; buffy "eyebrows," whitish throat and breast, dark wing linings, black belly, orange-brown thighs and undertail coverts, white bands on tail. Young have brownish upperparts, streaked breast.

Gyrfalcon
Falco rusticolus

GRAY WINGS BEATING with slow, shallow strokes, a large, heavily built falcon skims with surprising speed along the north face of an Arctic cliff. Ruddering with a long, squarish tail, the bird angles up to a shelf. Here it alights on a huge mound of sticks, bones, excrement, and the pellets of indigestible matter coughed up, or "cast," by generations of nesting gyrfalcons.

Though the icicles of May festoon its ramparts, the nest already cradles four creamy eggs blotched with rich reddish browns.

As the female settles to brood, the male sweeps over the tundra in ground-hugging flight. Far ahead of him a kittiwake beats up from the edge of an icy inlet, and the tiercel dashes in for the kill. But the quarry dodges and streaks seaward. The gyr swerves abruptly and the chase is on.

For long minutes the two split the air in headlong flight and wild gyrations. Then the kittiwake tires and the gyrfalcon bores in. Talons lash out and pluck the smaller bird from the air. On powerful wings the victor beats shoreward and drops his kill to his mate.

Off he goes again, this time in quest of a meal for himself. Soon he returns with a lemming dangling from his claws. Perching on a pinnacle, he snaps the rodent's neck with his notched beak and mantles his meal with outspread wings as he feeds. Then he spirals high, or "rings to his pitch," and "waits on" for his next victim.

What the peregrine catches by sheer speed the gyrfalcon often brings down by dogged endurance. Yet the kings of old preferred the gyr for its size and the crashing power of its stoop, and none but royalty could own one. A kingly gift indeed was the white gyrfalcon. Once classed as a distinct Greenland race, these striking gyrs are but one extreme of *rusticolus*, a species that includes white and nearly black phases and almost every shade in between. Sometimes variation occurs within a single brood.

While ptarmigan eggs are only beginning to hatch, the young gyrfalcons are already shuffling to the nest edge, flapping their wings, and launching into the air. Soon they try hunting, and the ptarmigan chicks scurrying through the

grass and blending with the lichen-covered rocks make good prey on which to sharpen their hunting skills. Later they attack hares and other small mammals and a variety of seabirds. When the ptarmigan wander, some of the gyrs tag along. In years when Arctic prey is scarce, bird watchers far to the south may get a glimpse of the lordly heavyweight of the hunting falcons.

Range: N. Alaska to Greenland; winters sporadically southward to Oregon, North Dakota, and Rhode Island. Also found in N. Europe and Asia. *Characteristics:* most commonly has white forehead, throat, and underparts; gray-brown mustache, upperparts, and spots on breast and belly; back feathers are white-edged. Phases vary from blackish to pure white.

light phase

dark phase

Gyrfalcons, length 20-25"
Right: dark phase
James Simon, Photo Researchers

259

Pigeon hawk landing
C. G. Hampson

Pigeon Hawk
Falco columbarius

CALLING TO HIS MATE in a rasping chatter, a male pigeon hawk streaks over a spruce-ringed clearing with a freshly killed bird in his claws. The female springs from her nest and flies out to meet him. His claws open; down plummets the prize toward the female 50 feet below. Darting under it, she rolls onto her back, reaches up, and deftly binds to her meal.

A moment later she settles back on her four or five brown-dotted buffy eggs as her smaller mate whirs away on fast, deep wingbeats. Heading for the base of a dead stub as if to ram it, he swoops up the trunk at the last instant and alights nimbly on his favorite hunting perch. Here he watches over lake or clearing. Smaller birds prove no match for the pigeon hawk, one of the speediest of the falcons. Small mammals and large insects also are on its menu.

At times this falcon resembles a pigeon in posture and flight style; hence the name. Its Old World cousins, the female "merlin" and the male "jack," rode the wrists of medieval ladies, who flew the pugnacious falcons at small birds. Mary Queen of Scots enlivened her days of captivity by lark hunting with a merlin.

Range: N. Alaska to Labrador, south to N. California, N. North Dakota, Iowa, and Nova Scotia; winters to Peru. Also found in Europe, Asia, and Africa. *Characteristics:* male has slaty upperparts streaked with black; white throat; tawny cheeks, collar, and underparts streaked with brown; black-banded tail with white tip. Female and young are more brownish.

Sparrow Hawk
Falco sparverius

WHIZZING PAST your head, a pair of sparrow hawks shrill their *killy-killy-killy* in your ear as you approach a dead tree at the edge of a meadow. Unlike most others in their family, these smallest and commonest of the New World falcons prefer to nest in cavities, often choosing abandoned holes of flickers and other woodpeckers.

The female "killy hawk," with some help from the male, incubates the four or five creamy-white eggs dotted and blotched with brown. Reach into the hollow after the young hatch and they will tip onto their backs, wings spread, to greet you with tiny, needlelike claws.

With young to feed, the parents expand their usual diet of mice and large insects. Now they stoop at sparrows and other small birds. Perching with flicking tail on treetops and power lines, these bold and aggressive falcons drop like a flash on small mammals and lizards. Like many

Pigeon hawks, female (left) and male length 10-13½", Allan Brooks

of their relatives, they often have favorite hunting perches which they use at regular intervals. Nicknamed "windhover," the sparrow hawk also hovers on shallow, rapid wingbeats, facing upwind as it scans a meadow or harvested field for prey. Slightly larger than a robin, *sparverius* occurs commonly in cities, where it preys on the abundant house sparrows.

Twentieth century falconers in the New World often start out with this nimble, vigorous little bird—the American kestrel—just as medieval falconers did with its near-twin, the Old World kestrel. Readily trained by the novice, this gentle and tractable falcon will fly to the hand or lure from a quarter mile away and strike down sparrows flushed by its trainer.

Range: N. Alaska to Nova Scotia, south to S. Chile. *Characteristics:* male (page 254) has black-and-white face, blue-gray crown and wings, rust-red back and tail, whitish underparts; black band on tail. Female is brownish and slightly larger.

Female sparrow hawk, length 9-12"; Eliot Porter

Caracara
Caracara cheriway

CIRCLING in the Texas sunrise, two black vultures settle awkwardly on a dead raccoon and begin to feed. Suddenly a red-faced, black-crested caracara streaks in low with deep, powerful wingbeats. Often this carrion eater will share a large animal with the vultures. But this time its long yellow legs lash out at the larger birds.

After a brief scuffle the vultures skulk on the sidelines while the victorious "Mexican eagle" calmly devours the prize.

Surely such a bird deserves respect. And this vulturelike member of the falcon family gets it—from the brown pelican that coughs up a gulletful of fish under fierce attack; from the vulture that surrenders its feast rather than tangle with the scrappy caracara; even from the lordly bald eagle, which the caracara may harry in hopes of stealing its prey.

Oddly, *cheriway* does not find the little scissor-tailed flycatcher so respectful. One observer in Texas watched the flycatcher drive the larger bird away by riding on its back for as much as a mile. Yet the caracara seldom preys on flycatchers or other birds, preferring carrion varied with small mammals, fish, frogs, snakes, turtles, insects, and even baby alligators. A swift runner, it does much of its hunting on foot.

Find a caracara and often you will see its mate nearby. These early nesters sometimes hide their deep, bulky bowl of sticks and broomweed so well in a treetop that you must climb the tree to find it. In arid country, however, they may build it atop a giant cactus where it can be seen from afar. Both sexes incubate the two or three brown-blotched whitish eggs. In about 28 days the hatchlings appear, decked out in jaunty brown caps and buffy down patched with brown on shoulders, thighs, and rump.

The adult bird is usually silent. But in early morning or late afternoon you may see one raise its crest, throw back its head, and squawk. To some listeners the call sounds like *caracara*.

Range: Arizona to Texas, south to Peru; also central Florida to Cuba. *Characteristics:* bluish bill, naked red face, black crest; whitish cheeks and neck speckling into blackish body; white tail with black tip; whitish patches near wing tips.

CACKLER OF THE TREETOPS The Chachalaca Family Cracidae 🎵

CHACHALAC! The rattling cry echoes through the chaparral along the lower Rio Grande at dawn and dusk, for spring has come to Texas and with it the noisy courtship of the chachalaca (*Ortalis vetula*). This chickenlike bird is the smallest member of the family Cracidae and the only one that breeds north of the Mexican border. The rest of the family—43 species including curassows and guans—dwell in the jungles and grasslands of Central and South America.

Like their relatives, chachalacas flock in treetops, where their drab plumage blends with the foliage. They feed on berries, buds, tender leaves, and insects and generally avoid long flights. Farming now threatens their brushy habitat.

In breeding season the female answers the male's strident call in her higher-pitched voice and climbs to a bough beneath his. He descends and struts along her branch, murmuring. An intruding rival may get his back pecked bald.

Home is a twig-laced, leaf-lined nest 5 to 15 feet up in a dwarf tree. The three white eggs have thick, rough shells. By the time the chicks are one week old they can elude pursuers by flitting through the underbrush.

Range: lower Rio Grande Valley in Texas to Nicaragua. *Characteristics:* gray brown with orange throat skin, long white-tipped tail. Young are barred with cinnamon buff.

Chachalaca, length 20-24"; David G. Allen

Caracaras, length 20-25"; Frederick Kent Truslow and (opposite) John H. Gerard

LIKE A VULTURE, *a caracara holds its raccoon dinner with one foot. In the United States the red-faced bird is called Audubon's caracara.*

263

PLUMP UPLAND GAME BIRDS

Grouse, Ptarmigan, and Prairie Chickens

Family Tetraonidae

By GEORGE MIKSCH SUTTON

I N MY EARLY CHILDHOOD my family spent the summers in the woods of northern Minnesota. I remember a ruffed grouse that came daily to our cabin. Why the bird liked this spot no one could say, but morning after morning he visited a wide windowsill where he marched back and forth, back and forth, with tail grandly spread and wings drooping.

Occasionally, tail down, he stood very straight, lifted his crest and fluffy neck plumage, and pounded the air with his powerful wings. *Thump, thump, thump,* each performance started, ending with a muffled roar that filled the cabin. While he was drumming I could move quite near the closed window. But if between performances I so much as batted an eye, off he went.

In time I learned that a male ruffed grouse may have more than one drumming spot, often fallen logs in deep woods; that in winter his toes have comblike fringes serving as snowshoes; that when the snow is fresh and deep he sometimes plunges into it to escape from a goshawk or to spend the night. If a crust forms while he is asleep in the drift he may have a hard time getting out.

At the height of the mating season

PTARMIGAN EXPLODE *from snowy camouflage under the feet of a hunter on Banks Island in the Canadian Arctic. Both willow (inset) and rock species fan their black tails in flight.*

ruffed grouse drum at any hour. One spring night at Cornell University in upstate New York I walked along a wooded road with some fellow graduate students. Suddenly drumming sounded ahead of us, close to the road. We approached cautiously and snapped on a flashlight. There stood the drummer as if transfixed by the glare. On all fours I crept closer, put my hand out slowly, and nearly touched the bird's toes before he blundered up through the shrubbery and rocketed off.

All 18 species of the grouse family inhabit the northern hemisphere. They are chickenlike ground dwellers characterized by feather-covered nostrils, feathered legs, and a well-developed crop. Of the ten New World species of Tetraonidae, only the willow ptarmigan and rock ptarmigan also occur in the Old World.

Prairie chickens, sharptails, and sage grouse are polygamous, and their famed courtship rites enliven the American prairies and brushlands. Cocks gather in spring to hoot, boom, coo, strut, and simulate fierce combat to attract hens. Prairie chickens lift feather tufts that resemble ears and inflate huge neck sacs. Sage grouse puff out wobbly foreparts and fan pointed tail feathers—and look like monsters from another world. Sharp-tailed grouse hold their wings out, stick their tails straight up, and patter around with mincing steps as if they were square dancing. They pause momentarily, then start again, all at the same time.

At sunrise one May morning in the rolling shinnery oak country of western Oklahoma I saw lesser prairie chickens perform. Some 20 cocks, scattered in twosomes on a bare circular area about 30 yards across, were dancing and booming. Nearby a burrowing owl displayed with fluttering flights, its wings luminous in the early sunlight that turned a jack rabbit's ears a delicate pink. Suddenly a pair of the chickens stopped their pantomime as a big skunk darted out after a grasshopper.

The cock grouse in a polygamous species takes no part in caring for the chicks. He probably does not even know where the nest is. The chicks hatch virtually simultaneously and well covered with down. Their first wing feathers develop so fast that the birds can fly while still quite small.

One summer I wanted to find the nest of a lesser prairie chicken, for the plumage of the hatchling had never been described. With a rancher friend I covered miles

PUFFING, BOOMING, AND STRUTTING, *cocks of the grouse family woo their mates with colorful rituals. Sage grouse (left) swells his neck sacs and splays spiked tail feathers. Sharp-tailed grouse (below) dances and postures with tail erect. Ruffed grouse (opposite) spreads tail and ruff and parades up and down a log, pausing to drum with his wings.*

Joe Van Wormer, Photo Researchers
Right: C. G. Hampson
Opposite: David G. Allen

on horseback with no luck. Then a mother chicken flounced out from under us, followed by several small chicks, all but one of which flew. The one that didn't, poor thing, was under my horse's hoof.

Those wonderful arctic grouse, the ptarmigan, whose plumage changes with the seasons (page 28), are monogamous. The cock may defend the nest and brood valiantly. And the hen is so devoted to her eggs that she waits almost until stepped on before she runs off, hissing and feigning injury. On the shore of Hudson Bay I found a willow ptarmigan hen that let me pet her, pick her up, and take the eggs from under her. If I placed an egg on the nest's rim, she pulled it back with her bill. If I put it just beyond her reach, she would ignore it and stay with her clutch.

Ptarmigan have no communal courting ground, but if several males display at once the whole tundra echoes. *Go back! Go back! Go back!* cackle the willow ptarmigan cocks as they whir upward 30 or 40 feet and sail back down. And the rock ptarmigan utters a hollow rattle well described by the Eskimos as belching.

Spruce grouse, male (left) and female, length 15-17"; Walter A. Weber, National Geographic staff artist

Spruce Grouse
Canachites canadensis

DEEP IN the north woods, lumberjacks call the spruce grouse "fool hen." The name is sadly apt; unlike the wily ruffed grouse, this bird does not flush straightaway. Instead it whirs up to the nearest limb to crane its neck naïvely at an intruder. Whole coveys have perched stolidly until all were clubbed or noosed.

In cool dark forests the spruce grouse seeks out boggy places overgrown with spruce, tamarack, or white cedar. For much of the year *canadensis* remains solitary or in small family groups, staying well up in thick evergreens and dining on needles, which give the flesh a strong, resinous flavor. Summer's bounty adds berries and tender herbaceous leaves to the menu.

In spring each male claims a mossy glade for a courting ground. Here he flutters on drumming wings to nearby branches and down again, and struts about with wings dragging and tail spread.

Beneath a concealing spruce the hen lines a mossy hollow with leaves and grass for her 10 to 12 brown-splotched buffy eggs. The chicks relish insects, and a large toadstool is a feast. With excited *oinks* the whole brood surrounds the delicacy as children do a birthday cake.

In one western race, called Franklin's grouse, the male has white spots on the base of his tail and lacks the brown band on the tip.

Range: W. Alaska to Labrador, south to N. E. Oregon, N. W. Wyoming, S. Manitoba, N. Wisconsin, and Nova Scotia. *Characteristics:* male has red "eyebrows," mottled grayish crown, nape, collar, and back; black chin outlined with white; black breast, mottled black-and-white belly, black tail with brown tip. Female is brown with whitish underparts, black streaks and bars, tawny tip on tail.

Blue grouse, male and (upper) female, length 15½-21"

 Blue Grouse
Dendragapus obscurus

DOWN FROM the high country they come, just as the first grass is sprouting in the valleys. The straggling companies sail across canyons but seldom fly over ridges. Tiring quickly, the birds drop to the ground and leave long trails in the snow as they walk to the next launching point.

Soon the blue grouse reach their breeding grounds on the more open slopes of the foothills. Inflating air sacs on the sides of their necks, the cocks pump out a resonant, low-pitched mating call. The nearby forests throb with the hoots, *humph-humph-humph-ma-humph-humph.*

Males of the Rocky Mountain races, also called dusky grouse, hoot from a log or rock, their normally concealed air sacs showing reddish purple within a frame of white feathers. Farther west, cocks perform while crouching on limbs high in

Douglas firs. The air sacs of these birds, often called sooty grouse, are bright yellow.

After a brief courtship with a single hen the male's family duties are over. His mate scrapes out a depression at the base of a tree or rock, or near a log. On a lining of pine needles she lays seven to ten buff eggs dotted with brown.

Some three weeks later they hatch. The hen leads her brood to verdant glades and streamside willows where they gorge on the insects of early summer. Ornithologist Aretas A. Saunders watched a hen and her young form a circle in a meadow, then close in, forcing grasshoppers into the center where they could be caught easily.

In the lowlands the adults add flowers and evergreen cones to their diet of leaves, buds, and fern fronds. By midsummer they have begun to follow the ripening berry patches back up the mountainsides. Males lead the way in small bachelor flocks, finally venturing into alpine meadows above treeline. Cold weather forces a retreat into the stands of fir on the slopes below. The big trees screen them from storms and provide a never-failing food supply of needles.

Range: S. E. Alaska and S. Yukon south to S. California and W. New Mexico. *Characteristics:* tail usually has light band on tip. Male has dark gray upperparts, bluish-gray underparts, yellow "eyebrows," whitish chin and flank spots, blackish tail. Female is mottled brown, black, and white, with dark gray tail.

Ruffed Grouse
Bonasa umbellus

DAWN OUTLINES the leafless tracery of the March woods. At his roost on a large mossy log a ruffed grouse stirs. The lengthening days have aroused an urge that demands expression. He stands athwart the log and leans on his tail. His cupped wings begin to beat the air, slowly at first, then faster and faster until they vanish in a blur. The strokes make a hollow thumping sound, filling the forest with a muffled drum roll: *bup . . . bup . . . bup . . . bup . . . bup-bup-bup-up-urrr.*

To ornithologist Arthur Cleveland Bent this was "the throbbing heart of awakening spring." But to the grouse this flourish is a warning to rivals that he has staked a territory and will defend it against all comers. A sound causes the bantam-size bird to freeze, crest bristling, tail raised in a fan marked by a broad black band near the tip. A circlet of dark neck feathers stands erect, framing his head in a ruff.

Hissing loudly, head swaying from side to side, the male struts to a nearby hemlock. There a hen crouches beneath the branches. Lured by his drumming, she is ready to be bred. But the master of the log regards her as a challenger and forces her into retreat. Days later the persistent hen finally catches her lord in a mating mood.

The hen selects a nest site at the base of a tree or stump among second-growth hardwoods, usually near a brushy pasture or other forest opening. She scratches a hollow in the duff and lines it with leaves. Blending quietly with the April woodland, the hen incubates 11 to 15 buffy eggs, some occasionally speckled with brown.

When the downy chicks hatch, she leads them to the edge of the woods where succulent insects swarm in the sunshine. The hen warns of danger with a sharp *pe-e-e-u-r-r*, and the youngsters stay under cover. She may drag a wing to feign injury, luring away a fox or other predator.

Yet her solicitude cannot prevent the loss of more than half the chicks by midsummer. Weaker ones fail to keep up with the family. Some fall into holes. Sharp-shinned and Cooper's hawks take a severe toll. But rain and cold are the worst killers. Young grouse chill easily, and whole broods sometimes die of exposure.

Surviving juveniles prosper on a summer diet of berries, becoming quarrelsome loners by early fall. They sometimes give in to "crazy flight," breaking their necks against village houses or smashing into picture windows.

Ruffed grouse, red phase, male (left) and female, length 16-19"; Walter A. Weber, National Geographic staff artist

In autumn, along woodland edges and on abandoned farms, ruffed grouse feast on wild grapes, apples, and the fruit of the flowering dogwood. When abundant, acorns furnish a staple.

At winter's approach the birds find shelter among conifers deep in the forest and feed on buds of birch and aspen. They grow "snowshoes," comblike projections on the toes, and dig into snowbanks to ride out storms. With spring they return to the forest edge. The cocks seek conspicuous drumming logs and a new cycle begins.

Known to New Englanders as "partridge" and to Southern mountaineers as "pheasant," the ruffed grouse shows geographic color variations. Reddish-brown birds prevail along the coasts and gray-brown ones inland. Within these regional differences there are also red and gray color

Ruffed grouse
gray phase

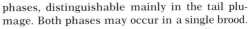

phases, distinguishable mainly in the tail plumage. Both phases may occur in a single brood.

Colonial settlers relished the absurdly tame "wood hen." As many as 40 grouse in a tree would sit quietly while men knocked them off limbs with sticks. Market hunting and farming pushed the species out of settled areas. Today it prospers under sound wildlife management and the reforesting of worn-out farmland.

For the sportsman few woodland thrills equal that of flushing grouse. Literally from your feet the bird rockets off with an explosive roar of wings and darts away under cover. The cocks rise steeply toward the treetops while the hens keep low. Pennsylvania has named *umbellus*, king of game birds, its state bird.

Though few dogs can find and hold a grouse, hunters manage to bag three or four million of the birds each year. This is only the surplus; by summer the breeding stock has replaced the losses. But about once a decade grouse numbers plummet, then gradually build again. Several cold, wet breeding seasons combined with hard winters may be the cause of a crash.

Range: central Alaska to S. Labrador, south to N. California, N. Arkansas, N. Georgia, and N. E. Virginia. *Characteristics:* chickenlike; dark ruff; mottled reddish-brown or gray upperparts, barred grayish or buff underparts; black band near tip of long tail. Female has shorter tail with broken band. Gray phase has gray tail; red phase has reddish-brown tail.

Willow ptarmigan, males (foreground) and females in summer plumage, length 15-17"
Allan Brooks. Above: Walter A. Weber, National Geographic staff artist

Rock ptarmigan
*male (left) and female
in fall plumage
length 13"*

White-tailed ptarmigan
*male and (left) female
in summer plumage
length 12-13"*

Juvenile whitetail
in fall plumage

Willow Ptarmigan
Lagopus lagopus

CIRCLING HUNGRILY, a trio of mew gulls scouts the tundra with its inlay of marshy ponds. One gull makes a sudden swoop, trying to startle a willow ptarmigan from her nest in a clump of grass. The other two gulls follow, looking for a chance to slip in and steal an exposed egg.

Sitting tight, the hen utters a distinctive cry. It brings an instant reaction from a pondside thicket of dwarf willows some 50 feet away. A cock ptarmigan hurtles forth like a rocket and smashes into a gull. Knocked head over heels in a cloud of feathers, the marauder drops. His confederates wing away. Having assured the safety of his family, the cock resumes his vigil.

Brave and vigilant though they are, cocks cannot always shield their families from the incessant attacks of jaegers, hawks, owls, and foxes. Many ptarmigan fall to the guns of Eskimos, who consider the birds an important source of food.

Cradled in a bowl of grass and leaves, a brood hatches from 8 to 13 buffy eggs boldly marked with brown. The parents lead their chicks to the shelter of river bottom willows. Risking attack by ravens, the youngsters leap to pluck insects from twigs. The family explores sunny hillsides to glean spiders, crowberries, and leaves.

State bird of Alaska, the willow ptarmigan ranges across the North American Arctic, summering on grassy tundra and marshy flats. Fall snowstorms cover food supplies, driving the bird back to the willows bordering rivers, where *lagopus* sometimes mingles with that hardy highlander, the rock ptarmigan.

Through the winter, willow ptarmigan dine on birds and twigs. They dig out snow chambers and passages in which to roost. The birds blend with the landscape by turning completely white except for black tails. These may serve as markers to keep the birds together in flight.

As spring days lengthen, the territorial challenge of the willow ptarmigan rings out across the blossoming tundra. The strutting cocks, red combs swollen and conspicuous, cackle and shout their varied calls. Now one bird leaps into the air, flapping upward, then spiraling down on set wings. Rivals follow suit. The hens, loitering under cover, gradually acknowledge the charms of the cocks. Spirited battles sometimes follow, with male adversaries bumping chests.

Range: N. Alaska to Greenland, south to S. E. Alaska and Newfoundland; also found in N. Eurasia. *Characteristics:* black bill and tail. Male has reddish-brown head, breast, and back; white wings. Female, nearly identical to the rock ptarmigan, is yellow-brown barred with black. Winter birds are white; black tail is mainly concealed except in flight (pages 264-5).

Rock Ptarmigan
Lagopus mutus

WHEN ARCTIC BLIZZARDS scour the tundra, the rock ptarmigan rides them out in fine style. Equipped with sharp claws and feathered to the toes, the bird burrows into the snow and sleeps in a cozy igloo, heated by its own warmth.

Hunger drives the bird into the open to forage for willow tips and dried berries. It also digs for moss and other plants under the white mantle. To descend a slope these plump "snow birds" often slide down with legs thrust forward and tail spread behind. While some "rockers" winter on exposed uplands, others move to sheltered valleys. From Arctic islands the birds wing south of the regions of continuous night. Gyrfalcons and snowy owls follow, picking off stragglers.

In summer, blending with her rocky habitat, the hen scratches a hollow on open ground for her 8 to 13 buffy eggs spotted with brown.

Range: N. Alaska to N. Greenland, south to S. W. British Columbia, Great Slave Lake, and Newfoundland; also found in Europe and Asia. *Characteristics:* buffy brown barred with black; white chin, wings, and belly; black bill and tail. Male is darker with red "eyebrows." Winter birds are white with black eye stripe and tail.

White-tailed Ptarmigan
Lagopus leucurus

HIKING TO TIMBERLINE, a Colorado naturalist once reached for a loose stone to mark a junco's nest. The "stone" turned out to be a nesting white-tailed ptarmigan, her mottled plumage blending with the ground. Noting that her grass-lined hollow lay three paces and one foot from a big rock, he went for his camera. Returning, he searched ten minutes. Finally a glint from her eye betrayed her, just inches from his foot!

With little help from her equally well-camouflaged mate, the hen incubates 7 to 12 pinkish-buff eggs dotted with brown. In late summer she leads her chicks to the high ridges, dining on insects, leaves, and berries as they climb.

In the southern Rockies this species does well at nearly 14,000 feet. Only severe snows force these truly alpine birds down to timberline to forage for fir needles. Now plumed in pure white, they are no easier to see than they were when brown against the summer barrens.

Range: central Alaska to Great Slave Lake region, south in coastal mountains to S. Washington and along the Rockies from British Columbia to N. New Mexico. *Characteristics:* coarsely mottled in white, brown, and black, with white wings, belly, and tail. Breeding males have red "eyebrows"; winter birds are pure white with black bill and eye.

Greater prairie chickens, length 16¾-18"
Walter A. Weber, National Geographic staff artist
(also opposite, upper)

♪♪ Greater Prairie Chicken
Tympanuchus cupido

BLOW ACROSS the top of an empty bottle and you mimic the nuptial booming of the male greater prairie chicken. Watch the crouching, foot-stamping dances of some of the Plains Indians and you see a direct imitation of the dance that goes with the booming in the courtship rites of *cupido*. Then, before daybreak on a March morning, slip into a canvas blind next to one of its booming grounds and you soon witness a spectacle that defies mimicry.

With the first glimmer of light the males begin to arrive at this open stretch of prairie perhaps as big as a city block. Each cock goes straight to his own territory, a few square yards won through several weeks of squabbling, bluffing, and beak-and-claw dueling.

One of them starts the dance with a dash forward, head low and tail high, wing tips dragging on the grass. Suddenly his feet blur as he stamps a tattoo, pivoting and at the same time raising a pair of plume tufts on his neck that look like satanic horns. Two vivid orange air sacs the size of big plums burgeon from the sides of his neck – the "drums" that explain his generic name.

Then comes a sound you will never forget, a sound unique to the prairies – a hollow, eerie *whoo-hoo-hoo* that booms from the bird's inflated throat sacs, sometimes rising like *do re mi* on a large ocarina.

But the dance isn't over. Deflating the sacs, the bird leaps a foot or so off the ground, cackles, and lands, usually facing in the opposite direction. Singling out a nearby cock, he charges in challenge. They exchange a few perfunctory pecks, but the time for territorial battling is over. On with the dance! Every cock takes it up, booming a chorus that can be heard a mile away.

Here come the hens! Instantly all the cocks desert their territories and rush to show off, scrambling for position, hooting, stamping, fighting, jumping up and down like popcorn on a griddle. Unimpressed, the hens straggle through the booming ground. Soon after sunrise the birds leave. The males may perform again at sunset, but again the hens appear indifferent.

Return to the blind in April and you will see a different show. Now the hens come to be mated, not mobbed. Each cock stays strictly within his claim and does his best to woo and win every hen that strolls past. Most of the females head for the center, where the strongest cocks have long since hammered out their claims. These few champions do most of the breeding.

In her own time each hen picks a mate, then waits while he struts a while longer and goes through a drawn-out ritual, bowing before her. Bred at last, she wanders into the dense grass to hollow out a well-hidden nest, lay a dozen brown-flecked olive eggs, and raise her brood on a diet of bugs, leaves, seeds, berries, and grains.

Prairie chickens in Boston? Indeed the colonists owed many a meal to the heath hen, a prairie chicken that once roamed the northeastern seaboard. Pressed by gun and plow, the heath hen had vanished by 1932; it may soon be joined in extinction by the Attwater's prairie chicken, a subspecies found along the Texas coast. But, helped by wise hunting laws and sound land use, the greater prairie chicken still holds its own as an unforgettable trademark of the prairie.

Range: central Alberta to S. Ontario, south to E. Colorado, N. E. Oklahoma, and S. Illinois; also coast of S. E. Texas. *Characteristics:* brown with strongly barred underparts; short round tail, black in male, barred in female. Male has yellow "eyebrows" and when breeding inflates orange air sacs on sides of neck.

Lesser Prairie Chicken
Tympanuchus pallidicinctus

ON AN OPEN KNOLL trampled to hard earth by generations of displaying, a dozen male lesser prairie chickens prance and hoot. Though the booming is not as loud or rolling as that of the greater prairie chicken, it brings the females out of the weeds to be courted and abandoned.

Suddenly an ominous silhouette appears—a hawk migrating northward. The bird of prey sees only a drab knoll covered with lumps or clods of earth. After it has passed, the "lumps" inflate their dull red neck sacs, erect their nape tufts, and take up the chorus anew.

Although smaller and paler, the well-camouflaged *pallidicinctus* is difficult to distinguish from the greater prairie chicken. One way to tell them apart is to know where each species dwells. The lesser prairie chicken ranges only through a narrow strip in the central Southwest. Here sagebrush and bunchgrass conceal the 11 to 13 faintly dotted buff eggs resting in a grass-lined hollow in the sand.

This once common grouse suffered as plowshares carved its habitat and birdshot tore into its flocks. Now it is barely holding its own. Efforts to widen its range often end in frustration when transplanted birds show up the following year,

Male lesser prairie chicken, length 16″

whooping and prancing, at the same old knoll.

Range: S. E. Colorado, W. Kansas, W. Oklahoma, E. New Mexico, and N. W. Texas; winters in central Texas. *Characteristics:* like greater prairie chicken but slightly smaller and paler with dull red neck sacs. Female has very small sacs, shorter nape tufts than male.

Male greater prairie chickens displaying; Walter A. Weber, courtesy National Park Service

Sharp-tailed Grouse
Pedioecetes phasianellus

IN THE MORNING SUN, powdery snow erupts from a drift as a sharp-tailed grouse blasts out of his night's lodgings. Nine more white puffs explode and soon the small flock whirs through the western hardwoods at better than 40 miles an hour. Settling in the branches, the birds breakfast on dried buds and berries. Later they may move to a nearby field or grain elevator to lunch on whatever grains they find.

When the snows melt, *phasianellus* – the "little pheasant" – returns to the brushland, where it feeds on seeds, tender leaves, and insects. Spring also draws the bird to its ancestral mating ground, an open knoll soon trodden bare.

Tooting hollowly from small, purplish neck sacs, the cocks stamp their feet, leap into the air, rustle their tails, and bluff each other with charges that end in beak-to-beak staring bouts. Drawn by the din, the hens stroll amid the competing males and finally squat before the chosen one. In a well-hidden hollow lined with grass and feathers the hen lays 10 to 15 olive-brown eggs. The chicks, raised by the hen alone, can fly a little in only ten days.

Range: N. Alaska to N. W. Quebec, south to N. Nevada, N. New Mexico, N. Minnesota, and N. Michigan. *Characteristics:* yellowish "eyebrows," brownish upperparts mottled with buff and black; whitish underparts with brownish V's; whitish belly and legs, short pointed tail.

Sage Grouse
Centrocercus urophasianus

AT THE EDGE of a dusty clearing on the sage-tufted Wyoming prairie, a female sage grouse stands in the April sunrise and watches several dozen cocks parading. For the past month the males from as far as a mile away have been blustering and scrapping here each morning and evening, trampling half an acre into an arena of bare earth, exchanging threatening clucks and cackles, pecking and bloodying each other. Now each male has his own strutting spot, and the battlefield has become a courting ground.

The hen walks toward the center of the arena. All around stand young cocks with pointed tail feathers rayed in courtship splendor, handsome heads crowned with "lyres" of black nape feathers, snowy chest puffed out, and inflated neck sacs hanging heavily (page 266).

While some strut others dance – three quick dashes forward, with drooping wings rasping against stiff neck feathers. Now the huge air sacs are bouncing. The birds contract their neck muscles and the sacs resound with a plopping noise that carries for a mile.

Some cocks, at the zenith of courting fervor, repeat their dance as often as 12 times a minute. Yet as the hen passes among them, not one approaches her. She enters a loose ring of half a dozen big males. They let her pass unmolested. But when a young cock tries to follow, one of the big males promptly beats him off.

Inside the circle she joins a group of other females, milling, preening, resting on the dusty earth. Two splendid males mingle with them. Most of the hens ignore one of the males, for he is only the "sub-cock."

There is no mistaking the flockmaster. Ringed by guard cocks, attended by his closest rival, this magnificent sage grouse struts around his hard-won harem. Through weeks of pecking and wing-flapping he has brawled his way to the top of the male hierarchy. Next year the throne will again be contested. But for the rest of this season the victor claims the spoils unchallenged. One by one the hens squat spread-winged before him. A few breed with his sub-cock or perhaps a guard, but only if the monarch is busy.

In flocks of three or four hundred birds several flockmasters may reign jointly. One flock of 800 had five, each with his harem and retinue, each breeding day after day on the same site.

As mated hens drift away to nest, the cocks strut and plop for a dwindling audience. Finally their hierarchy crumbles. Unopposed at last, the yearling males emerge from the bushes to practice for their next year's debut. Then folding their finery, the males all adjourn for a summer of good-fellowship and of feasting on fat insects, tasty weeds, and sagebrush leaves. Help raise the chicks? Why, that's hens' work!

Bred and abandoned, the hens seek nest sites. In a shallow, grass-lined dimple under a shrub, each female lays six to eight olive-buff eggs speckled with brown. They hatch in 22 days.

Through the warm months she rears her brood. As summer ends, the sexes flock together again. Rising heavily on short, blunt wings, the birds soon fly at 50 miles an hour or more on their "vertical migration" from the foothill prairie lands down to the warmer sagebrush deserts.

Eating mostly sage leaves, *urophasianus* has only a soft, membranous gizzard – in contrast to the hard, muscular organ other grouse use to grind grains. But the bird's dependence on sagebrush could endanger the species if brush removal continues to despoil its domain.

Range: locally, central Washington to S. Idaho and S. Saskatchewan, south to E. California, W. Colorado, and N. W. Nebraska. *Characteristics:* large size; mottled gray-brown and buff with blackish belly, whitish leg feathers; long spiked tail feathers. Adult male has yellow eye spot, black bib with white V, white breast; inflated neck sacs are yellowish.

Sage grouse: male (left), length 26-⟨⟩
and female, 22-23"; Allan Bro⟨⟩

Sharp-tailed grouse, length 15-20"; Walter A. Weber, National Geographic staff artist, courtesy Washington State University

GROUND-DWELLING GAME BIRDS

Quail, Partridges, and Pheasants
Family Phasianidae

By JOHN W. ALDRICH

EARLY ONE MORNING in late November I walked across frosted brown fields near Buffalo, New York. In all directions I could see hunters, their gun barrels glinting in the low sun's rays. This was one of only two days in the year when pheasants could be hunted in that region, and these pheasant days were virtually holidays there in the late 1920's.

As I contemplated the beauty of the quiet frosty morning I was startled by an explosive rush of wings and a rattling cackle. A cock pheasant shot into the air. Its

Tom McHugh, National Audubon Society
Left: Ozzie Sweet, Shostal

WINGS WHIR; *the startled hunter
swings toward a big brown shape,
suddenly gleaming like burnished
copper as it rockets from cover and
heads across a Vermont field.
Whether or not the shot rings out
and the bird drops, the sportsman
will long remember the glitter of the
autumn scene, the crispness of
the air, and the lustrous beauty
of a ring-necked pheasant cock (above).*

coppery body gleamed in the sun, contrasting with the flashing light gray wings. Its long streaming tail undulated with every wing stroke.

I started to raise my gun, but before I could take aim I heard a loud bang from the opposite side of a hedgerow and saw "my" pheasant topple into the weeds. Then as now, pheasant hunting was a highly competitive sport in western New York!

To sportsmen the ring-necked pheasant is one of the favorite and most familiar members of the Phasianidae. But the family is better known for another member—the domestic rooster with his clarion call, or as Shakespeare described him, "The cock, that is the trumpet to the morn." Since the dawn of history men have awakened to his crowing, and even before that to the voice of his remote ancestor, the wild jungle fowl of southern Asia. The Phasianidae number 165 species, and they appear in the utmost variety in almost every corner of the world.

Before Europeans settled in the New World, various species of upland game birds representing the order of gallinaceous, or chickenlike, birds were abundant. Grouse ranged through northern forests and uplands; turkeys flourished in southern forests as well; and quail inhabited a variety of brushy areas in temperate regions and in

MOTHER BOBWHITE *guards two sleepy-eyed hatchlings fresh from their shells. One by one the other ten eggs will hatch, boosting the upland game population of New York State.*

the tropics. North America had six species of quail: bobwhite, scaled, California, Gambel's, mountain, and harlequin. Unlike grouse, the Phasianidae lack feathering on nostrils and lower leg and have no inflatable air sacs on the neck. Unlike turkeys, they have rounded, not square-tipped, body feathers.

Settlers changed the natural habitats, planting large expanses of single crops. Game birds disappeared from many of those areas. But two Old World species – the ring-necked pheasant of Asia and the gray partridge of Europe – were introduced to fill the niches. They have thrived.

When I lived in the Chagrin Valley of northern Ohio I used to be attracted to the window overlooking the garden by the sound of a hoarse crowing note. Morning after morning as I watched, a cock pheasant would emerge stealthily from the hedgerow at the side of the garden and slowly walk out onto the dewy lawn. He would stand for a moment, his plumage gleaming, then disappear as quietly as he had come with only that short, rasping note to indicate his passage.

Although the gray, or Hungarian, partridge frequents alfalfa or clover fields, I always associate the bird with the open wheat country of the northern plains. Many times in the Dakotas I have watched partridges walking about in the vast stubble fields. Here, in a habitat that native members of the family find inhospitable, these imports reach their maximum abundance in North America. The "huns," as hunters call them, supply a much-needed game bird.

A third Old World member of the pheasant clan, the chukar or rock partridge, has filled another vacant habitat niche. This bird dwells in the most barren northern desert country of the Great Basin where no native game bird species has ever taken hold. Sportsmen constantly seek other prospects among the Old World pheasants, francolins, and partridges to provide additional game, particularly in the South. The Cooperative Federal-State Foreign Game Importation Program will almost certainly succeed in adding new species to North America, and most of them are likely to be from the diverse and prolific Phasianidae.

ONE OF MY EARLIEST RECOLLECTIONS is the sound of the crisply articulated whistle of the northern bobwhite. I still associate the call with the smell of new-mown hay and the sight of white daisies in the meadows of rural Rhode Island. Yet the bobwhite is the most generally distributed of the native New World quail, extending, in its great variety of racial forms, from the northern border of the United States south into tropical Mexico and Guatemala.

Most hunters know the bobwhite as a covey of plump-bodied birds bursting simultaneously, like fragments of an exploding bomb, from the dense covert ahead of a pointing bird dog. I knew this fine game bird in quite a different way in northern Ohio. Authorities there considered it a songbird and permitted no hunting season. A covey of bobwhites roamed our suburban neighborhood and came to our yard, where they joined the cardinals and juncos at the banquet of scattered bird feed.

In the land of cactus, chili peppers, and tortillas along the Mexican border I made the acquaintance of the scaled quail, whose appearance matches the drab aspect of the desert. Picking their way through thorny scrub, a group of them came in a long single file. One after another, white topknots erect, they emerged from a patch of brush. Alert to danger, they crossed a stony opening. Then they silently disappeared into a thicket beyond.

These trim creatures seemed perfectly adapted to their inhospitable environment. To me they emphasized that even the most unlikely habitat may prove a home to one of the representatives of this versatile family of ground dwellers.

Bobwhite

Colinus virginianus

NO BIRD PROCLAIMS its name more distinctly and persistently than the bobwhite. Its plumage may vary from the pinkish brown of the northeastern race to the red and black of Mexican races, but the whistling of its name remains the same.

Yet this familiar quail goes by other names as well. To Mark Catesby, the colonial naturalist, this was the "American partridge." He evidently associated the bobwhite with a relative, the partridge of the Old World. There "quail" referred to a group of smaller migratory birds.

The bobwhite is still "partridge" in the South, and to many hunters it's just "bird." New Englanders call it "quail."

The bobwhite thrives in small cultivated areas, weedy fence borders, and hedgerows such as were common on colonial farms. When settlers hacked out their clearings in the primeval forest,

quail populations mushroomed. But with the decline of small farms in the East and with the trend toward cleaning out brushy field borders on large midwestern farms, the quail decreased. In the southeastern states, however, the bobwhite remains the chief upland game bird.

With a setter or pointer the quail hunter scouts a wet creek bottom or woodland edge. Following the thunderclap of a flushing covey, his aim, if good, will contribute to an annual hunting toll of ten to fifteen million bobwhites.

The pursuit of *virginianus* dates from colonial days, when it became a staple food of the Atlantic coast settlements. Taken in large numbers by guns and later by nets, bobwhites sold for as little as a cent apiece. In recent years the birds have helped pay taxes, for southern farmers sell shooting rights to sportsmen.

In the restricted hunting season gunners may shoot as many as half a local population and discover a year later that the birds are back in

Bobwhites, males (white throats) and females, length 8½-10½"; Walter A. Weber, National Geographic staff artist

force. The guns clean out the surplus—many would not have survived the winter anyway. In mild climates this prolific species can absorb the loss along with that inflicted by hawks, foxes, skunks, and domestic cats.

In fall and winter bobwhites range in coveys. They travel on foot through fields and adjacent woods, walking quietly while in cover, running with necks erect and crests raised as they cross little openings. Flush them and they erupt into the air or scatter in the brush. When danger passes they sound a conversational call and slowly reassemble. If you imitate this call you may bring a nervous bird or two almost to your feet.

Toward evening the covey enters thick cover. There they roost in a compact circle, heads out, tails toward the center, resting against one another for warmth. Alarmed, all can fly straight off without colliding.

In the North drifting snow sometimes buries these coveys. If sleet doesn't form a crust and trap them, the birds sleep in warmth and safety.

As spring approaches, cocks which have been peaceable all winter become aggressive. They puff out their feathers and fight, sometimes so viciously that one of the antagonists dies from bites on the neck.

Finally the coveys break up and the birds sound the familiar bobwhite calls as they pair off. After being mated a few days the cocks lose their belligerence. When the paired birds begin to nest, two weeks to a month after mating, several families may live peacefully as close neighbors.

Bobwhites most commonly nest on the ground in grassy growth at the edge of an open area. The cock scratches out a hollow and lines it with grasses and weed stalks. Many nests have arched roofs of grass which help conceal the white eggs when the parent is not sitting on them.

The bobwhites usually approach their nest on foot. The cock waits a few yards off while the hen lays an egg. Then the two depart together.

This continues day after day until the set — usually 14 or 15 — is complete.

Several days or even a week may elapse before incubation begins. This lasts 22 or 23 days. Though the male normally sits on the eggs only about one quarter of the time, he will take over and hatch the brood alone if his mate is killed. The young leave the nest almost immediately and by the third week are able to fly. Parents and young stay together, joining other families in a small flock until spring. When courting begins, mated birds keep their partners.

Friends of the farmer, bobwhites eat weed seeds, weevils, locusts, and potato beetles.

Range: S. W. Wyoming and North Dakota to S. Maine, south to Guatemala and Florida; introduced in Pacific Northwest, West Indies, Hawaii, and New Zealand. *Characteristics:* small, chickenlike; short dark tail; mottled ruddy upperparts, barred grayish underparts, reddish-brown stripes on flanks. Eye stripe and throat are white in male, buffy in female.

284

California Quail
Lophortyx californicus

JAUNTY TOPKNOT BOBBING, a plump California quail scouts warily along a brushy slope. He flutters into a scrub oak, looks about for danger, and finally squawks a low, guttural call.

Out come 20 to 30 birds, following the sentry into the new feeding ground. They amble past his tree, gabbling softly, foraging for seeds and greens. But the silent lookout remains alert.

Then another male scouts ahead. Posting himself atop a shrub, he sounds the "all clear." The flock moves in, rejoined by the first sentry.

Suddenly the lookout spots a man with a gun. *Whit-whit-whit,* calls the sentry, and the others scamper into the brush. The sentinel whirs away a few yards, then glides to a landing, his black legs running as soon as they touch the ground.

Up runs the hunter. Refusing to flush, the birds scuttle away or hide in trees until he hikes home empty-handed. Then they sound the *step-right-*

up call and reassemble. For their elusiveness and flavor these quail are ranked by many hunters as the finest of western game birds.

Though *californicus* fell by the thousands to Gold Rush hunters and to vintners who resented its fondness for grapes, this quail is making a comeback. Now California's state bird, it flocks to "gallinaceous guzzlers," man-made water holes created to expand its habitat.

Flocks break up as the birds pair off in spring. The hen lays 10 to 17 brown-marked buff eggs in a concealed hollow, or sometimes in the nest of the blue grouse or white-crowned sparrow.

Range: S. Oregon and W. Nevada south to Baja California; introduced in S. British Columbia and south to Utah, also in Hawaii, New Zealand, Australia, and Chile. *Characteristics:* gray-brown upperparts; grayish nape, breast, and tail; dark scalelike lines on nape and belly; white flank stripes. Male has black plume and throat, reddish-brown crown, white "eyebrows" and bib line. Female has mottled brownish head.

Gambel's quail, male (right) and female length 10-11½", Allan Brooks

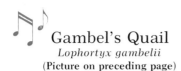 Gambel's Quail
Lophortyx gambelii
(Picture on preceding page)

LIKE A KNIGHT in armor with a black-plumed helmet, a male Gambel's quail perches atop a desert bush, its branches aflame with the blossoms of spring. The desert rings with his calls as he broadcasts a challenge to rivals and an invitation to females.

In answer, another male intrudes into his territory. The perching quail goes forth to drive out the interloper, then returns and sounds a call. Finally a hen approaches quietly. Hopping from his perch, he courts her by strutting around her with his head bobbing rhythmically. Soon the hen is mated and left to nest alone.

On rare occasions she annexes the old nest of a roadrunner or cactus wren. Usually she incubates her 10 to 12 brown-splotched buffy eggs in a scantily lined hollow that she scrapes out under a thorny bush. Once the downy youngsters hatch, the male helps in their upbringing.

Though more likely to flush than the scaled quail, *gambelii* prefers to escape on foot. Stalking about in the scant shade of prickly cactus and thorny shrubs, this desert denizen dines on weed seeds, berries, and succulent shoots. When the heat becomes intolerable, the bird resorts to the shade of streamside willows.

Dr. William Gambel, a pioneer ornithologist of the West, discovered the species in 1841.

Range: N. Nevada to S. Colorado, south to N. Mexico; introduced in Hawaii. *Characteristics:* similar to California quail but female also has plume. Male has buffy-white belly with black patch. Female lacks black throat, belly patch.

Scaled Quail
Callipepla squamata

THROWING BACK his white-crested head, a grayish bird barks a loud *kuk-yur* into the dry desert air. As the call resounds again and again, a hungry coyote pads through the thorny scrub, homing in on the sound of a possible meal.

Fifty yards from the bird the coyote's foot snaps a twig. Instantly alert, the quail dashes away in a blur of running feet, its drab plumage blending into the harsh southwestern landscape.

Even a well-trained hunting dog is no match for the swift and wily scaled quail, so named for its scalelike breast pattern. Instead of standing to a point, *squamata* sprints away, forcing the dog's master to give chase over the rough desert.

The "cotton top" or "blue quail" thrives farther from water than any of its American relatives. Its diet of insects, wild fruits, and juicy shoots gives it much of the moisture it needs.

But the chicks must have water, so nesting coincides with the rainy season. In the shelter of a low bush, or sometimes in the open among rocks, the hen lines a hollow with grass and incubates 9 to 16 brown-flecked buffy eggs. Those that are not devoured by roadrunners and skunks hatch in three weeks.

When nesting ends, these quail gather in coveys, calling a nasal *pay-cos, pay-cos* that oddly suggests the Pecos region where many dwell.

Range: central Arizona to S. W. Kansas, south to central Mexico; introduced in Washington. *Characteristics:* white-tipped crest, bluish-gray head and underparts, brownish upperparts with white stripes on sides; black scalelike markings on neck, back, and underparts.

Scaled quail, length 10-12"; Walter A. Weber, National Geographic staff artist

Mountain quail, males (long plume) and females, length 10½-11½″; courtesy Washington State University

Mountain Quail
Oreortyx pictus

HIGH IN THE SIERRA NEVADA a handsome mountain quail convoys a dozen chicks through the dense brush. His long black head plume flattens in the breeze as he dashes across clearings seeking seeds, bulbs, fruits, tender leaves, and insects for himself and his offspring.

A weasel bursts from cover and bounds toward the brood. The watchful cock cackles an alarm and the chicks squat quietly, their downy coats of chestnut, buff, and black blending with the forest floor. Then the cock flounders away, feigning a broken wing. But this weasel is not to be fooled; trailing the cock a short distance, the predator doubles back and seizes a chick.

As the chicks mature, they learn to run and hide in thick cover. Difficult to find and flush, the ground-nesting "plumed quail" or "mountain partridge" rises strongly when hard-pressed and flies swiftly, then alights and flees on foot. This bird mingles with its foothill and desert relatives when winter's approach nudges it off the mountain. In these vertical migrations *pictus* sometimes walks as much as 40 miles.

Range: S. W. Washington to S. W. Idaho, south to N. Baja California; introduced on Vancouver Island. *Characteristics:* blue-gray crown, neck, and breast; chestnut throat and white-barred flanks, brownish back. Male has long black head plume; female has short plume.

Harlequin Quail
Cyrtonyx montezumae

NOT UNTIL AUGUST, when rains pelt the dry, scrubby hills of its southwestern habitat, does this clown-faced bird nest. Both sexes incubate the 8 to 14 whitish eggs in a hollow hidden by overhanging grass or dead branches.

With its large, heavy-clawed feet the harlequin, or Mearns's, quail unearths plant bulbs. It also feeds on acorns, piñon nuts, seeds, berries, and insects. When danger nears, *montezumae* squats, relying on camouflage. Though a strong flyer, the "fool quail" flushes or runs only as a last resort. Like all quail, parent harlequins pretend injury when their broods are threatened.

Range: central Arizona to central Texas, south to S. Mexico. *Characteristics:* chunky; black-and-white striped face, pale brown bushy crest, streaky black-and-brownish upperparts. Male has chestnut breast, white spots on grayish sides; black lower belly. Female lacks strong face pattern, has brownish-pink underparts, belly spotted with black.

Harlequin quail
male (left) and female, length 8-9½″

RING-NECKED PHEASANTS, *sportsman's delight,
burst from a midwestern grainfield.
Introduced from Asia, this handsome, tasty
bird is one of North America's favorite game species.
The male's neck ring, iridescent head, and longer
tail distinguish him from the smaller female.*

Male, length 30-36"; female, 21-25"
Walter A. Weber, National Geographic staff artist

289

Ring-necked Pheasant

Phasianus colchicus

(Picture on preceding page)

To SOME PEOPLE the word pheasant means an epicurean delight. To others it brings memories of days afield with gun and dog. So well established is this popular and handsome game bird that Americans easily forget it's an import.

Phasianus colchicus, its scientific name, evokes the ancient land of Colchis, on the Black Sea at the foot of the Caucasus Mountains, where Jason and the Argonauts sought the Golden Fleece. A race of pheasants from here was reared for food by ancient Greeks. Romans brought the bird into western Europe.

This race, eventually known as the English black-necked pheasant, came to the New World as early as 1790 in attempts to stock the Atlantic coast states. It didn't do well in this forested region. Yet to this day our eastern pheasants tend to be darker than those in the West, perhaps because of the dark plumage characteristic of those European immigrants.

In the early 1880's Judge Owen N. Denny, U. S. Consul General at Shanghai, shipped several dozen Chinese pheasants to Oregon, where they were liberated in the Willamette Valley. Later introductions came from other stocks, but today's typical American ringneck with its light, burnished plumage most closely resembles the ring-necked pheasant native to northern China.

In 1892, only a decade after Judge Denny's birds were introduced, the species was so abundant in Oregon that a 75-day hunting season was declared. On opening day hunters killed 50,000 birds!

Gunners in the United States now bag between sixteen and eighteen million ringnecks in a good year. South Dakota, which honors the pheasant as its state bird, tops the list with a million to a million and a half cock pheasants taken annually; in 1946 the state's total soared to seven and a half million!

It's a wonder any pheasants survive. Yet here in the grain belt of the northern plains the ringneck thrives, fattening on grains, seeds, berries, grasshoppers, and snails. In other areas the local pheasant population requires a periodic boost from restocking and a shortened hunting season. In the southern states, an unfavorable habitat for the Chinese birds, game managers are introducing other strains, including an Iranian subspecies, adapted to warm climates.

The ring-necked pheasant, adept at skulking through low cover, presents a challenge to the sportsman. Hunters quip that a cock pheasant can hide on a golf green! Generally it takes a well-trained dog to find the birds and make them flush. Cackling noisily, they rise on whirring wings, fly fast and low, and soon glide to a landing in cover where they can scuttle off on foot.

During fall and winter pheasants flock in separate groups. The hens and cocks tend to keep apart unless forced to share the same cover for roosting or lured together by a patch of standing corn or by some other good food supply.

At the first suggestion of spring the cocks begin to crow and fight among themselves when near the females. On warmer days their activity increases. The cocks establish crowing areas and defend them against each other.

In courtship the cock pheasant is a grand sight! Feather tufts rise over his ears; the bare skin of his face turns bright red. He struts before the hens, turning this way and that to display his brilliant plumage to best advantage, walking with an exaggerated bobbing motion. Sometimes he runs in a circle around a hen, leaning in her direction with the tip of one outstretched wing dragging on the ground.

By such displays the cocks lure the hens to their crowing areas. A cock's harem may vary from two to five hens or more.

The female pheasant usually selects a grassy area in which to scratch out her nest hollow. Hayfields are a favorite choice, but this leads to heavy losses from early mowing. To avoid killing the sitting hens, some farmers install a "flushing bar" on their mowers. This scares the birds off their nests ahead of the cutting blades.

A hen lays 10 to 12 brownish-olive eggs over a two-week period and normally incubates them alone, though one cock was observed not only to build the nest but to incubate the eggs. In 23 to 25 days the chicks begin to hatch. Fully clothed with down, they can run about after their mother and pick up food. She helps her brood find small seeds and insects, much as a domestic hen does. She protects them from the cold by nestling them under her wings and breast feathers. If a skunk or fox approaches, she tries to lure it away with the broken-wing act.

The young pheasants stay with their mother until fully grown. Their father, meanwhile, has long since gone off to undergo the annual molt of his feathers and mingle with the masculine fraternity until the next mating season.

Range: established from British Columbia south to N. Baja California and S. E. Arizona, also from S. Alberta to S. Manitoba, central Michigan and Nova Scotia, south to New Mexico, N. W. Missouri, S. Illinois, and New Jersey. Also introduced in Hawaii and New Zealand. Native in Europe and Asia. *Characteristics:* large, chicken-like, with long pointed tail. Male has glossy green head, red face patch, white ring around neck; mottled reddish-brown upperparts, golden flanks, grayish wings and rump. Female is mottled buffy brown, lacks neck ring.

Gray Partridge
Perdix perdix

ANOTHER NATURALIZED CITIZEN, the gray or Hungarian partridge of Europe is now widely established in North America. Sportsmen give the wary "hun" high honors as a game bird.

Since the late 18th century men have tried in vain to transplant this bird to the Atlantic coastal region. Yet, introduced into Alberta in 1908-9, *perdix* quickly spread on the open grainfields and grasslands of the northern plains.

The gregarious gray partridge eats shoots and leaves as well as seeds and waste grain, and thrives in an intensively cultivated habitat unfavorable to native species. In spring and summer insects supplement the fare.

Courting begins in early March. Feathers and wattles bristling, cocks face off and leap at each other with buffeting wings, while the hen feeds unconcernedly. The duel may continue on and off for a week before one cock retires.

The hen alone incubates the 8 to 20 olive eggs in a grass- or leaf-lined scrape concealed among bushes or tall grass. When the downy chicks hatch in about two weeks, both parents tend them. The high reproductive rate offsets losses from plowing, mowing, and predators.

By hunting season the brood has joined with one or more groups. The coveys flush explosively, speeding off on thundering wings.

Range: established from British Columbia to Nova Scotia, south to N. E. California and N. New York. Native in Europe and Asia. *Characteristics:* chunky; gray with mottled brownish upperparts, tawny face, chestnut breast patch, tail, and bars on flanks; white belly.

Chukar, length 13"; Karl Maslowski, Photo Researchers

Chukar
Alectoris graeca

KA-KA-KA-KA-KA-KA, a chukar cackles. Other cocks take up the call until the canyon walls ring. The males gather at a water hole in the heat of summer while their mates are incubating.

An immigrant from the foothills of the Himalayas, the chukar failed to take hold in the eastern United States. But the handsome gray-brown bird found rugged country to its liking in the Great Basin, where the thin, arid soil of canyons and mesas supports only a meager cover of bunchgrass and sagebrush. Within a few years "rock partridges" became numerous enough here to allow a hunting season.

What sport the birds bring! They are hard to flush, preferring to run. They dash away, always uphill and screened by boulders. And when they do take off it's with an explosion of drumming wings as the covey disperses. The birds fly fast, then glide downhill, veer, and land.

Winter snows send the birds to low country to find their grass and weed seeds. Spring lures them back to higher altitudes, where the flocks break up. Crowing *cha-cha-cha-ker, cha-ker*, the cocks chase and fight each other for territories. In nests well hidden under scrawny sage bushes, the 15 or more spotted buffy eggs hatch.

Range: established from N. Washington to N. W. Wyoming, south to S. California and S. W. Colorado; further introductions in the Southwest. Native in Europe and Asia. *Characteristics:* red beak, eye rings, and legs; brownish-gray upperparts, gray chest, buffy throat and underparts with black "necklace" and flank stripes.

Gray partridge, length 12-14"; C. G. Hampson

BIGGEST OF UPLAND GAME BIRDS The Turkey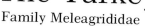

Family Meleagrididae

BEFORE THE COMING of the white man, a great bird with bronzed feathers and a gobbling call strutted widely through the New World wilderness. From Mexico, where Aztecs domesticated it, to the northern forests, where other Indians hunted it with bow and arrow, the haughty turkey flourished.

Europe first learned of it early in the 16th century, when conquistadores brought some back to Spain. By the 1540's the "turkie-fowle" graced many English tables, including the royal board of Henry VIII. Apparently this New World bird was confused with the African guinea fowl, which had come to Europe via the Turkish Empire. Both imports were called "turkey." Thus a bird so American that Benjamin Franklin wanted it proclaimed our national symbol took the name of a distant land!

When the Pilgrims celebrated the first Thanksgiving, in 1621, they drew on a "great store of wild Turkies." The great store was not destined to continue. The last wild turkey in Connecticut was recorded in 1813; in Massachusetts in 1851.

Overshooting, clearing of open woodlands, and the loss of a staple food by chestnut blight drove *Meleagris gallopavo* from much of its original northeastern range. But this largest of North American game birds is staging a comeback there, aided by stocking, managed hunting, and habitat improvement. In the West it has become established beyond its former range. Upwards of 75,000 are killed annually in 23 states with open seasons. Hunters lure the now-shy birds by sounding *keow, keow, keow,* a flock's assembly summons. Sometimes they imitate the female's mating cry on a call made from the wingbone of a hen turkey—and a cock may step out from the forest gloom, his iridescent plumage glistening in the sun.

Strong flyers, turkeys can clear treetops swiftly and sail a mile or more with only occasional wingbeats. More often they run, sometimes at 15 miles an hour. Audu-

Opposite: male turkey, length 48". Above: female, length 36", and displaying male.
Walter A. Weber, National Geographic staff artist (opposite, courtesy Claude D. Kelley)

"Turkey Shoot" by John W. Ehninger, 1879. M. & M. Karolik Collection, Museum of Fine Arts, Boston

bon, on a good horse, trailed several turkeys for hours. He couldn't overtake them.

Some wild turkeys dwell on mountain slopes, others around swamps. All roost in the upper branches of trees, usually changing perches nightly except in severe weather. They do not migrate, but a foraging flock may wander widely. From early morning, while one or more turkeys keep watch, the flock combs half an acre at a time, scratching for tubers, picking up grasshoppers and beetles, eating berries, grapes, grass, and seeds. Then all move on. In midday they seek an open area where they can roll in dry earth or ashes, apparently to get rid of vermin. Toward evening they feed again on the way to roosting sites. They compete with deer for the mast of oak and beech, and will scratch through a foot of snow to steal a rodent's cache of nuts. Acorns are a major food. In a single feeding one bird ate 221!

After wintering in flocks separate from those of the females and young, the old toms open courtship—a ritual always flamboyant and occasionally violent. A big male, chest padded with fat to sustain him through the weeks of display, stands in a forest opening and gobbles. Other toms come running, wattles gorged with blood, heads turned bright blue, white, and red with excitement. All gobble, competing furiously for the attention of the hens. The tom that started the uproar may try to drive off the other males, pecking their heads bloody.

Morning after morning, as spring spreads green fingers over the land, the prideful promenade continues. Tails fanned, wings dragging the ground, the males strut, flaming cravats quivering. Finally captivated by the big male's performance, a hen throws herself at his feet. Hens invariably take the initiative, as if they sensed that

"The Pioneer's Home," lithograph by Currier & Ives, 1867
Harry T. Peters Collection, Museum of the City of New York

TURKEY SHOOTING *spelled survival to pioneers, sport to settlers. At 100 yards competing marksmen with muzzle-loading rifles tried to clip off the heads of staked-out gobblers. Today's shoots still boast turkeys, but usually as prizes, not targets.*

otherwise the vain males would go on strutting forever. In his excitement the cock may trample his harem of three to five hens before mating with them.

Bred at last, the hen slips away to nest, ignoring the male's frantic gobbling to lure her back. She scoops out a hollow in a dense thicket for her 8 to 15 cream-colored eggs spotted with reddish brown and lilac. When she goes off to feed she carefully covers them with leaves and grass. Sometimes two or three hens share a single nest and take turns tending it during the 28 days of incubation. They guard against foxes, raccoons, skunks, bobcats, crows, and owls. One observer saw a turkey mother rise to meet a hawk, knock it to the ground, and pursue it until the raptor withdrew, leaving plucked feathers behind. Female turkeys also must shield eggs and young from the toms, who might destroy them.

The poults, as young turkeys are called, roost beneath their mother's wings for several weeks. Cold rains endanger them most; if chilled, they quickly die. Within a month the young birds begin to roost in trees. Those that escape the banquet board and predators may live 12 years and weigh as much as 35 pounds.

The only other species of Meleagrididae is the ocellated turkey of the Yucatán Peninsula, with eyespots on its tail. It is smaller than the common turkey.

Range: locally from central California and N. Arizona to S. E. Montana, W. North Dakota, S. Wisconsin, S. Michigan, and S. New York, south to S. Mexico and Florida.
Characteristics: slender version of barnyard turkey; iridescent brownish body, black wings barred with white, red wattles. Male has bare bluish head, black "beard" or tuft on breast, and spurs. Female is smaller, with light tips on dark body plumage.

By ROBERT PORTER ALLEN

TALL LORDS OF THE MARSHES **The Cranes**

Family Gruidae

ACROSS DUN-COLORED MARSHES, half a mile away, we saw two white forms, seemingly too big to be real. "There they are!" I whispered to Fred Truslow. "There's your first pair of whooping cranes!" We moved cautiously toward them. Whooping cranes stand about five feet tall, and in the flat country of coastal Texas they can spot anything out of the ordinary as much as a mile away. With our telescope we could see the carmine patch of bare skin on the crown, the broad mustache of stiff black feathers across the face and cheek, and the plumelike feathers of the lower back and tail. We could sense the gloriously wild, fierce nature of the big birds.

"Do you think we could get closer?" Fred whispered.

"Not a chance. Just stand up and see what happens."

Fred stepped a few paces clear of the oak brush. Immediately the male whooper lifted his head and glared at us. The female followed suit, and both took a few steps in the opposite direction. Suddenly the male whooped—a buglelike alarm note that sent a tingle along our spines—*kerloo! ker-lee-oo!* The female's voice echoed his. The birds spread their great satin-white, black-tipped wings, ran several steps, and took off. I knew that they would put at least a mile and perhaps a stretch of deep water between them and us. Then they would land with slow, graceful flaps of their wings, running a few strides with unruffled poise.

"What a bird!" said Fred, staring in awe. "What a bird!"

He might well have said it about any of the world's 14 species of cranes —the Gruidae. All are spectacular birds, strutting on long legs, trumpeting far-reaching calls, frequently cavorting and leaping in wild dances. Civilization has almost wiped out several of them, including the whooper.

The other North American crane, the sandhill (*Grus canadensis*), breeds on wild prairies, muskeg, and tundra. A rare subspecies dwells in Florida. Another race, the greater sandhill crane of the northern United States and southern Canada, is more common. The most numerous subspecies, the lesser sandhill, nests farther north and winters chiefly in the Southwest, where limited hunting of the bird is permitted. Unfortunately the sandhills relish grain and have been shot by farmers in areas where whooping cranes migrate. The gunners have brought down whoopers as well.

Few birds can match the nobility of the whooping crane (*Grus americana*). Pairs mate for life and live in privacy with a decorum almost unique among birds. The male is undisputed head of the family, always ready to challenge an enemy with loud bugle calls and a head-on charge. The female is free to devote herself to the ungainly but rapidly developing youngster. When there are twin youngsters the male helps care for one.

Like the sandhill, the whooper once nested in the prairie country. Then settlers drained the sloughs and the birds moved off. After 1922 no more nests were found on the prairies. Yet the species hung on, wintering at the Aransas National Wildlife Refuge in Texas, where Fred Truslow and I had

YOUNG WHOOPING CRANE, *welcome addition to a rare species, gives a piping cry. When adult, this tallest of North American*
296 *birds bugles a mile or more with its coiled, five-foot windpipe.*

Length 49-56", Frederick Kent Truslow

come to photograph them for *National Geographic*. Until our visit no outsider had been permitted to take photographs in the closed portion of the refuge for ten years.

From my work with the Cooperative Whooping Crane Project set up by the U. S. Fish and Wildlife Service and the National Audubon Society, I knew that each pair would occupy a territory of about 400 acres providing the essentials for winter life —food, water, preening ground, bathing place, and a safe roosting pond. Just before sunup the birds leave the sleeping area, walking slowly and probing for blue crabs and other marine fare, and a few vegetable items. After feeding, the cranes stand on a slight elevation and preen. At day's end they return to the roost.

Each morning that fall we haunted the vicinity of Mustang Lake, climbing the observation tower with hopeful steps. Each day we searched along shoreline and salt flats for arriving whoopers. After spotting our first pair, on October 19th, we saw a few more arrive from the north, and one fledgling. But when a whole week passed, overcast and rainy, without new arrivals, we began to worry.

October 31 dawned still cold and wet. Then about midmorning the sun broke through. In late afternoon we sighted a family with two young, then another pair with a single youngster. Just for luck we made a last run along East Shore Road. The sun was riding close to the rim of the coastal prairie, and flocks of sandhill cranes were piling into their roosts at shallow ponds, their guttural notes rising on the warm air. From heavy oak clumps horned owls called in the semidarkness. Sweeping with the telescope from atop our truck, I saw a pair of whooping cranes with

two rusty-plumaged young. I moved the scope and spotted another pair with twins. Farther to the left I saw another adult and, a moment later, two more youngsters!

"Fred! You'll never believe this unless you look!" Six young whoopers before our eyes. Three others within the last hour. Nine young. This was a record!

To photograph them we had to wait a couple of months until they had settled down for the winter. We found a family of three feeding daily at a spot where we could set up Fred's blind. We scattered corn in front of it. Would the birds come to the bait? They did. All we needed now was sunshine. Instead we had rain, fog, temperatures down to 40°—and endless days to recall the whooping crane's long struggle for survival and the dramatic discovery of its secret nesting grounds in Canada.

IN 1954 A FOREST FIRE broke out in Wood Buffalo National Park, 17,300 square miles of wilderness sprawling across northern Alberta and into the Northwest Territories. Returning from the blaze in a helicopter, a forester radioed Fort Smith with an urgent message for a Canadian Wildlife Service biologist there—he had seen two adult whooping cranes and one fledgling. The next spring aerial observers saw a pair of whoopers and a rough circle of weeds and rushes with a hollow in the center. Here would soon lie two brownish eggs, darker than those of the sandhill crane. This was the first whooping crane nest seen by anyone since 1922!

I was named leader of a ground expedition. We tried to reach the site by canoe and were turned back by log jams in the river. We tried again by helicopter and were

SOARING *stiff-legged before his entranced mate at left, a male whooper displays his seven-foot wingspan in the prenuptial ballet. Both carmine-crowned adults will bow, pirouette, and leap. Their youngster, no longer a gawky chick like the one below, prepares to mimic the dance.*

U. S. Fish and Wildlife Service
Left: Frederick Kent Truslow

landed at the wrong site. After 16 days in the wilderness we struggled back to Fort Smith. It was getting to be a habit! We made one more try. This time a helicopter landed us within half a mile of a nest. Three other pairs nested nearby. For ten wonderful days we explored the breeding ground of the whooping cranes—bulrush bogs, muskegs, and tangles of birch, tamarack, and spruce. We crossed the tracks of whoopers many times, but the birds usually slipped away unseen in the thickets.

THE CRANES are wary at Aransas too. Waiting our chance to photograph them, Fred and I would reach our hideout by 6:30 every morning, put out our corn, then retreat—Fred to his blind, I behind a screen of oak brush. On February 4, I awoke at 5:10 a.m. and saw stars shining outside. I shook Fred awake; this was our day. By 6:40 Fred was installed in his blind. It was now up to the whoopers—and Fred.

By 7:15 the sun broke through with a blinding glare. Behind my screen I paced back and forth like a football coach. Through his peepholes Fred could see whoopers only when they were on the bait. At 8:20 the crane family walked majestically past the blind. Had Fred seen them? The male bird resolved that by bugling! When at day's end the birds finally left I joined Fred. His grin spoke volumes!

We were especially lucky, for at one point the male whooper made a few brief leaps, the beginning of the courtship dance. Later in the winter mated pairs renew their bond. One bird approaches the other with a series of grave nods while skipping and flapping in a half circle and back again. Both leap with legs stiff, bills pointed skyward, and necks arched over the back. They gyrate, jump higher and higher, nod and circle frantically. And then it is over as suddenly as it began.

If the whoopers have a youngster, one parent may drive it away. But when the adults are ready to migrate, they relent and readmit junior to the fold. Before they reach the nest site the young one is driven off again—this time for good.

Whooping crane—*Range:* Wood Buffalo National Park, Canada; winters on the Gulf Coast of Texas. *Characteristics:* tall, white with red crown, black wing tips. Young have rusty head and neck.

Sandhill crane—*Range:* N. E. Siberia, N. Alaska, and N. Canada, south to N. E. California, Wyoming, Minnesota, and Michigan; also S. Mississippi to S. Georgia, south to Cuba; winters to central Mexico. *Characteristics:* tall, gray, often stained rusty; adults have red crown. Young are brownish.

♪♪ **SANDHILL CRANE,** *smaller cousin of the whooper, also has retreated before encroaching civilization but remains much more abundant. Thousand migrate together, trumpeting on high, then swarm onto fields to feed*

Length 34-48", Luther Goldman (also upper

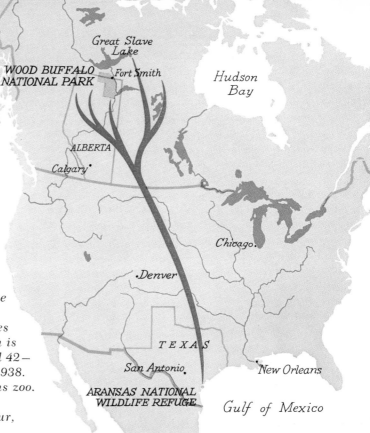

"HOW MANY WHOOPERS THIS YEAR?" *the world asks as adults and young fly 2,500 miles from Canadian nest sites to winter home in Texas. Protection is paying off. In 1964 Aransas counted 42— highest since the census began in 1938. Seven others live in the New Orleans zoo.*

On wings beating twice a second, the cranes cruise at 45 miles an hour, averaging 200 miles a day.

National Geographic map by John D. Garst

BROWN WADER IN SOUTHERN SWAMPS

The Limpkin ♫♪
Family Aramidae

MARCH MOON glints on the black water of a Florida swamp. Life rustles in the predawn twilight as you stand quietly on a wharf. Suddenly a dark shape leaps straight up from a nearby weed patch. Long legs dangling, a cranelike bird flaps to the far shore and drops among some cypress knees. Then comes a loud, almost incredible cry, a wail of unutterable sadness.

"That's a limpkin," says your guide, untying a rowboat. "Folks used to think they was little boys a-cryin', little boys lost in the swamps forever."

You climb aboard and he poles the boat to a weedy inlet. Ahead another limpkin vaults into the sunrise and alights in a moss-draped tree, flapping and floundering along a limb to feign injury. Soon you find her nest, a shallow basket of stems and leaves resting above the water on grass stalks and vine tangles.

The brown-splashed buffy eggs, usually numbering four to eight, hatch in March. The downy blackish youngsters leave the nest in a matter of hours. Though they look like young rails and grow up to fly like cranes, science classes the limpkin (*Aramus guarauna*) as the sole member of the Aramidae family, found only in the New World. No longer hunted, the once common limpkins still dwindle as swamp-drainage projects and dry spells diminish their habitat.

Your boat moves on. As you pass a mudbank you spot a heap of shells of the apple snail, favorite food of the "crying bird." You beach the boat nearby, determined to see how *guarauna* removes the meat without breaking the shell, despite the snail's tough operculum, or trapdoor. You crouch in the boat, waiting.

Two hours later you hear something land on the shore to your left. Slowly you turn your head. It's a limpkin! He stands on one leg looking at you, resting the other leg slackly then tucking it up under him as other wading birds do. After long minutes the bird relaxes and scratches his head with a long middle toe. He walks to the water, favoring his slack leg — this is the famous limp for which the limpkin is named. He wades in up to his belly, probing the bottom with feet and bill.

Down goes his head and up it comes grasping a snail by the lip of the shell. The limpkin wades ashore and lodges the snail in the mud, its opening upward. One leg limp, the bird waits until the snail begins to emerge. Then his beak stabs behind the trapdoor and tears it off. He seizes the exposed tidbit, gives a little sideways jerk of his head — and the meat pops right out of the shell.

Instead of bolting the morsel, he stands slack-legged for a few minutes like a gourmet pausing with a delicacy on his fork. Then the bird gulps his prize. Soon other limpkins come to feed, twitching tails punctuating their jerky movements. You watch in fascination until a late-morning shower finally calls a halt.

That night, as you watch ragged clouds scud across the moon, a shrill cry drifts from the depths of the swamp. Is it the drab, gangling bird you watched that day? Or a little boy calling plaintively, a little boy lost in the swamp forever?

Range: S. E. Georgia to the West Indies, and S. Mexico to Uruguay. *Characteristics:* brown with white streaks on head, back, and breast; long bill, neck, and legs.

A TIMID GOURMET *of the Florida swamps wades ashore with an apple snail. Shells litter the bank. Gulping an occasional frog or lizard, the limpkin hunts the snails by day and rends the night with bansheelike wails.*

Length 28"; Frederick Kent Truslow

MYSTERIOUS VOICES OF THE SWAMP

Rails, Gallinules, and Coots
Family Rallidae

"BE HEARD AND NOT SEEN" may be poor counsel for children. For rails it is a guide to survival. Hearing these chickenlike birds is no problem. Wander through a marsh at dawn or dusk and they will serenade you with a cacophony that comes close to drowning out every other voice in the swamp chorus. Seeing them, however, is something else again.

Rails spend their lives scuttling through the cattails and rank weeds that beard the face of the marsh. They tramp out thousands of hidden, crisscross paths that they can scamper down in time of danger rather than taking to their short, rounded wings. If there is no path, they can squeeze their remarkably compressed bodies through seemingly impenetrable sedge tangles without quivering a single telltale blade. The expression "thin as a rail" originally referred not to a fence but a bird.

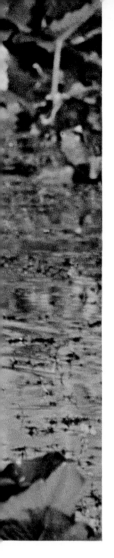

JUST ONE MORE? *A purple gallinule edges closer, begging another tidbit. Naturalist-photographer Fred Truslow, who took many of the pictures in this volume, held peanuts in his mouth to win the bird's confidence. Usually the telescopic lens is needed to photograph this family's retiring members — like the American coots (left) swimming nearby in Everglades National Park.*

In North America we know only nine of the Rallidae, a worldwide family comprising 132 species of rails, gallinules, and coots. Gallinules are less wary than rails; their extra long toes (page 20) enable them to skip across the broad pads of water lilies, where fewer predators can reach them. Most rails wear drab, gray-brown monk's robes. The purple gallinule, in colorful contrast, sports fop's garb. The American coot dresses in sooty hues. Like ducks, coots flock on open lakes and bays. To take off they run into the wind, splashing through the water and rising higher and higher until they are actually running along the surface.

Only the coot has lobed toes, but rails and gallinules also swim and dive with ease. All normally nest on or near the water, building basins of reeds and grasses that cradle their large clutches of eggs and their broods of downy chicks. They forage successfully on land and water, thriving on a variety of plants, insects, worms, and mollusks. And though awkward and slow on short, leg-dangling flights, many of these birds migrate long distances.

Highly adaptable, the Rallidae have established colonies in tropical jungles, mountain forests, and on most oceanic islands. The flightless weka of New Zealand runs down rats and has acquired the habit of slipping into homes and making off with trinkets. Bonaparte's horned coot lives on frigid lakes more than 13,000 feet high in the Andes. Vegetation is sparse there, so this bird builds its nest of stones!

King rail, length 15-19"; Frederick Kent Truslow

 ## King Rail
Rallus elegans

SHY AND FURTIVE, these cinnamon-breasted birds skulk in freshwater marshes in the eastern United States. They announce their presence with *hip-hip* or *chuck-chuck* calls. The latter sounds like a teamster clucking to his horses, so Illinois farmers named the bird "stage driver."

Among rank grasses and sluggish shallows king rails hunt crayfish, aquatic insects, and seeds. Winter may drive them to raid wheat and oat crops, and in the South cars have hit many of the big birds crossing roads to rice fields.

When flushed, *elegans* usually runs off at a surprising clip or swims away. If it must fly, it leaps up, legs dangling, and heads for the nearest cover with choppy strokes of its short wings.

On a hummock or in a clump of cattails the king rail fashions a well-made cup of leaves and stalks, sometimes weaving a canopy of vegetation over it. Both sexes incubate the 6 to 15 buff eggs spotted with brown.

Range: E. Nebraska and central Minnesota to Massachusetts, south to S. Texas, Florida, and Cuba; winters to S. Mexico. *Characteristics:* chicken-size; long beak; rusty brown with streaked upperparts, white chin, barred gray flanks, white patch under short tail.

Clapper Rail
Rallus longirostris

MANY ENEMIES plague the clapper rail. Mink and raccoon stalk the bird by night. Hawks hunt it by day. Turtles, snakes, and big fish prey on the young. But the worst enemy is man.

Tidal marshes from New England to Texas once teemed with these timid grayish birds. Their very numbers and the easy targets they offered in their slow, lumbering flight invited slaughter. Audubon reported hundreds being shot by a few hunters in a matter of hours. He also boasted of collecting 72 *dozen* clapper rail eggs in one day in the salt marshes of New Jersey and pointed out that 100 dozen a day was not uncommon for local eggers. Still another enemy, the tempestuous sea, occasionally devastates clapper rail populations. These birds build their grass and reed nests

Clapper rail, length 14-16½"
Allan Brooks

amid clumps of marsh growth where the highest point is often only inches above normal high tide. When storms goad the tides to exceptional heights, the water sweeps away nests and eggs. With stubborn instinct the rails build and lay again. If the sea should strike once more, these tenacious birds will sometimes build and stock their nests a third time.

Despite the depredations of man and nature salt marshes in nesting season still echo with the long rolling cry of clappers. The *cac cac cac cac ca caha caha* calls still draw gunners, but not to unlimited slaughter as in former days. In recent years man has added new menaces – drainage of marshes and pesticide spraying.

The clapper rail lays 6 to 14 buff eggs, usually darker and more heavily blotched with brown than those of the king rail. Both sexes incubate the clutch, which hatches in 14 days. The downy black young leave the nest almost immediately. They quickly learn to swim, dive, and find small crabs, snails, insects, fish fry, and tasty plants. And when danger threatens, they learn to lower their heads, stretch out their necks, and scurry along runways through the rank herbage.

Ten clapper subspecies breed in North America. Those birds in the northern regions migrate. *Range:* coastal areas from N. California to Peru and Connecticut to Brazil; also in lower Colorado River region. *Characteristics:* large size, long bill; grayish-brown upperparts, white chin, brownish or tawny breast, barred grayish flanks, white patch under short tail.

Virginia Rail
Rallus limicola

IF THIS "LITTLE RED RAIL" shows itself at all in its marshy domain, it looks like a pocket edition of the king rail. The Virginia rail is better known for its voice and a vocabulary that includes squeaks, chatters, moans, and piglike grunts.

During courtship the male sounds a metallic note like the pounding of iron on an anvil, repeating it day and night. The female replies with a lisping *kee-a*. Still singing, the couple weaves a grassy nest a few inches above water. Supporting sedges shield the 7 to 12 eggs, pale buff with a few brown freckles.

The downy black chicks hatch ready to run, swim, and dive. Down the hidden aisles of the marsh they run after their mother, plaintively crying while searching for snails, slugs, earthworms, and insects. Their big feet and the tiny claws that tip the outer digits of their wings help them clamber over tangled vegetation.

A feeble short-distance flyer, the Virginia rail stirs little interest in sportsmen. On migration, however, the birds fly with speed and assurance, usually traveling at night. Some fly so low that they run afoul of utility lines and wire fences.

Range: British Columbia to Nova Scotia, south to N. Baja California, Illinois, N. Alabama, and North Carolina, and in central Mexico; winters to Guatemala. Also found in South America. *Characteristics:* similar to king rail but about half the size; gray cheeks.

Virginia rail, length 9-10½"; John H. Gerard

Yellow Rail
Coturnicops noveboracensis

MYSTERY SHROUDS this little bird, for it rarely shows itself. Yet it lives in many parts of North America, feeding on snails in freshwater marshes and wet meadows.

Approach a yellow rail and it will generally run or hide. Even if a dog comes near the bird it may refuse to fly. Instead it freezes — so stubbornly that a man can actually pick it up!

People may dismiss this rail's clicking note as a tree toad's. Yet the grass nest with its eight to ten buff, brown-specked eggs could lie close by.

Range: Great Slave Lake to New Brunswick, south to S. Alberta, Ohio, and Connecticut; locally in E. California. Winters in Oregon, California, and S. Louisiana to S. Florida. *Characteristics:* yellowish with dark stripes on back, buffy underparts; white wing patch shows in flight.

Black Rail
Laterallus jamaicensis

TINIEST in this group, *jamaicensis* remained unknown in the United States until Audubon identified the bird in 1836. Rarely seen, it darts through the sedges in marshes, preferably brackish, where it eats small crustaceans.

Normally silent as a mouse, the male in breeding season utters a series of *kiks* or *kuks* and the female answers *croo-croo-croo-o*. The roofed nest they weave into the marsh grasses hides six to ten brown-spotted, pink-white eggs.

Range: coastal California and locally from Kansas to Massachusetts, south through the Atlantic states to central Florida; winters to S. Louisiana and S. Florida. Also found in the West Indies, Peru, and Chile. *Characteristics:* black bill, red eyes, slaty head and underparts, sepia nape, dark brownish back with white specks.

Sora
Porzana carolina

AS LATE AS 1908 sora rails nested within sight of New York City's 207th Street subway station. Time has erased these marshes and their soras from Manhattan, but across North America the black-faced birds remain the most abundant and best known of all rails.

On fall evenings fresh marshes and reedy riversides, even those near large cities, ring with sora *keeks*. Spring brings an ascending, plaintive *ker-wee*. The most characteristic call, however, is a series of descending, "whinnying" whistles.

Soras conceal their nest of cattail leaves in a hummock or anchor it to marsh plants a few inches above water. The parents take turns incubating the giant clutch — as many as 18 buffy, brown-spotted eggs arranged in layers.

The hatchlings can swim immediately. Ornithologist William Leon Dawson came upon a hatching sora egg and watched as the chick "rolled out, shook itself, grasped the situation, promptly tumbled over the side of the nest, and started to swim across a 6-foot pool to safety."

In late fall soras forsake mollusks and insects to gorge on wild rice. Fattened, they become targets for sportsmen. But this seasonal obesity serves nature's needs. On the night of the first frost these birds, flying without their usual awkwardness, set out on long migrations. En route to South America and Bermuda they cross large stretches of ocean without food.

Range: British Columbia and Great Slave Lake region to Prince Edward Island, south to Baja California, Oklahoma, Ohio, West Virginia, and Pennsylvania; winters to Peru and British Guiana. *Characteristics:* yellow bill, black face, gray cheeks and breast, brownish upperparts, barred flanks, white spots on back and breast. Young have buffy face and breast.

Yellow rail, length 6-7½"   *Black rail, length 5-6"*   *Sora, length 8-9¾"; Allan Brooks*

Purple Gallinule
Porphyrula martinica

THE EXOTIC COLORS of this marshland gem reveal its tropical origins. Tennessee marks the northern limits of its breeding range, though the purple gallinule may wander as far north as Canada. Strays have been recorded even on Tristan da Cunha in the middle of the South Atlantic, proof of this bird's capacity for long flights.

In favorite haunts—deep swamps abounding in pickerelweed, whose blue flowers provide camouflage—the purple gallinule treads lightly over lily pads, weight distributed by its long toes. As the bird walks it nods and bows with the grace of a dove, all the while twitching the white "flag" in its tail. To cross open water the bird usually swims, but it may fly in the labored, legs-down fashion of its relatives.

Like most of the family, this gallinule is a noisy bird. Aloft it sounds a barnyard cackle. Perhaps the commonest call is a rapid, laughing *hiddy-hiddy-hiddy, hit-up, hit-up, hit-up*. Near its nest the bird becomes unusually raucous, calling loudly as it attacks intruders.

Purple gallinules usually nest in patches of high, thick marsh growth. They weave a platform of decaying leaves and stalks into a clump of living reeds. Some ornithologists believe heat from the decomposing matter helps incubate the

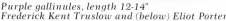

Purple gallinules, length 12-14"
Frederick Kent Truslow and (below) Eliot Porter

Common gallinules, length 12-14½"; Frederick Kent Truslow

five to ten eggs – pink or buff, spotted with brown.

Frogs, small snails, aquatic insects, and seeds from spatterdock and water lettuce form this bird's regular diet. Rice is another favorite, and purple gallinules sometimes make a nuisance of themselves by bending and breaking stalks to get at the seeds. In Louisiana these birds have been found to prey on the eggs and young of other small marsh birds.

Range: Louisiana to Tennessee and South Carolina, south through the West Indies; also W. Mexico to S. Texas, south to E. Argentina. *Characteristics:* yellow-tipped red bill, pale blue frontal shield, purplish head and underparts, olive upperparts, yellow legs, white under tail.

Common Gallinule
Gallinula chloropus

SWITCHING a comically short tail, curling long toes before every stride, the common gallinule wades gracefully into a pool. It stops to nip grass and seeds from the bank, then bends to snatch a mollusk from the muddy bottom. Reaching a carpet of lily pads, it runs lightly over the broad leaves, fluttering its wings to keep balance. Now in deep water it bobs its head in rhythm to the paddling, swimming almost as easily as a duck, though its feet are not webbed.

In breeding season the male turns his bit of water into a stage and performs in swanlike splendor for an audience of one, who may be hiding coyly in nearby reeds. Uttering harsh *tick-et-ticket* wooing notes and raising his head to show off the brilliant red of his bill and forehead shield, he sails serenely toward his mate. A foot or two from her he reverses course, drops his head, partly opens his wings, and erects his stub tail to flash the white feathers beneath.

Common gallinules wedge their nest, a shallow basin of dry cattail leaves and rushes, into marsh vegetation, usually several inches above the water. Sometimes they simply tramp down grasses to make a platform, then place a cradle of dead rushes on it. Often a "gangplank" of stalks and reeds leads from nest to water.

The female lays 10 to 12 eggs, colored various shades of buff and dotted with brown. Incubation lasts about three weeks.

The hatchlings leave the nest almost immediately and take to the water as if they were born to it. For about a month the mother gallinule cares for them tenderly, frequently calling them ashore to be dried and warmed under her body and wings. Then she abandons them and breeds again, leaving the youngsters to fend for themselves. A sharp spur at the bend of the wing helps the chicks get about among reeds and lily pads in their search for grasses, seeds, water insects, and worms. Those youngsters that escape snakes and crows grow surprisingly fast.

The common gallinule – also called the Florida

310

gallinule in the United States—ranges farthest of the family. It lives throughout the world, except for Australia and Antarctica. In England the "moorhen" ornaments ponds in city parks.

Range: California and Arizona, and from Texas to Nebraska, Minnesota, and S. Quebec, south to Argentina. Also found in most other parts of the world. *Characteristics:* yellow-tipped red bill, red forehead, slaty head and underparts, brown back; white band on flanks and under tail.

American Coot
Fulica americana

Coots belong to the rail family, but they might just as well be ducks. Scorning the weedy cover preferred by their more retiring brethren, they congregate on open water. Long, lobed toes help coots swim as well as most ducks. They dive even more abruptly, sometimes going down 25 feet.

The American coot dwells on marsh-fringed lakes and rivers over most of North America. Capable of taking food on or below the water's surface as well as on land, the omnivorous birds eat seeds, leaves, roots, insects, snails, worms, and small fishes. They sometimes steal wild celery and waterweed from canvasbacks.

At times coots anger hunters by taking over feeding areas that would otherwise draw ducks. Some duck clubs have even inaugurated coot-killing days. But the despised "mud hen" or "blue peter" swimming or pattering across the water presents too easy a target for most sportsmen, and its numbers wax rather than wane.

In breeding season these normally gregarious birds tolerate no intruders in their reedy domains. Backing water, flapping wings, they sit on their tails, slash at one another with heavy, taloned feet, and thrust with their bills. They further vent their feelings in explosive cacks, clucks, coos, and wails. A courting male swims back and forth in front of the female, fanning his white-patched tail with every pass.

The coot usually moors its nest of reeds and grass to bulrush or cattail clumps to prevent it from drifting in the shallow water. Both sexes warm the 8 to 12 buffy eggs specked with brown or black. Because incubation begins before the entire clutch is laid, some chicks emerge before others. The male takes the firstcomers into the marsh to feed while the female continues sitting.

To take off, the coot gallops over the water with thrashing wings and feet. In flight, the outstretched feet serve as a rudder in place of the useless little tail.

The bald eagle preys on this species, diving on a group of coots as they swim in a lake. One threatened flock drew together and flailed furiously, kicking up a blanket of spray. This hid individual birds and foiled the eagle. Despite its stupid facial expression and clownish behavior, *americana* is not really "silly as a coot."

Range: British Columbia and Great Slave Lake region to New Brunswick, south locally to Nicaragua and West Indies; winters to Panama. *Characteristics:* slaty with darker head and neck, brown-black back; red frontal shield, white bill, white under tail and on trailing edge of wings.

American coot, length 13-16"; Eliot Porter

SOUTHERN LILY-TROTTER

The Jaçana

Family Jacanidae

SHARING *a Mexican marsh with a swimming grebe, jaçanas stroll across the lily pads, weight distributed on extra-long toes. Pausing to raise wings, they reveal bright flight feathers.*

RAFTS OF WATER PLANTS half choke the shallow marshy pond. Walking atop the buoyant mass, seeming almost to tread across the dark surface of the water, come several chestnut-caped birds with yellow forehead shields, probing and pecking for aquatic insects and seeds.

Nature has endowed these exotic little bogtrotters—as it has the gallinules—with toes and claws that extend an extraordinary length. Just as a man on skis can cross thin ice because his weight is spread over a broad area, so the jaçana can stride over mats of floating vegetation.

Seven slender, long-necked members of the Jacanidae frequent freshwater marshes in tropical or semitropical regions of the world. Only occasionally does one species, *Jacana spinosa*, come as far north as the Rio Grande delta in Texas; the name jaçana stems from the language of the Tupi Indians of the Amazon region.

This marvelously adapted bird has little reason to be shy. When endangered it freezes, blending with its setting, or skips away over water hyacinths and lilies like a lumberjack on a log raft. If forced to fly, it flaps off on fluttering wings, trailing its huge feet and cackling noisily, but soon flops awkwardly back to its marsh. If harried to the edge of the pads, it takes to the water like a grebe, swimming submerged and even clinging to vegetation on the bottom to hold itself down out of sight.

In courtship the female, larger and more aggressive, takes the lead. The birds raise their wings and feint at one another as if to strike with the long, sharp spurs that jut from the bend in the wing. This action recalls a common gesture as the birds feed. They lift their wings until the tips all but touch above their backs, thus displaying the greenish-yellow patch on the trailing edge of the wing. Pierre Louis Jouy, a 19th century ornithologist, suggested that this might be a signal, for the coloration is visible at a great distance.

The jaçana builds a small cuplike nest of leaves out amid the floating vegetation, and the four glossy, brownish eggs scrawled with black are often wet. The henpecked male does much of the incubating. Soon after hatching, the downy young can follow their father nimbly across the lily pads or dive into the water and swim.

Range: W. central Mexico to N. E. Mexico and the West Indies, south to W. Panama; casual in S. Texas. *Characteristics:* chestnut with blackish head and neck, yellow bill, frontal shield, and wing spur; greenish-yellow wing patch, greenish legs with very long toes and nails. Young have gray-brown upperparts, white underparts.

Length 8-9", Allan Brooks
Opposite: Arthur A. Allen

313

Black oystercatcher, length 17-17½"; Karl W. Kenyon

SHOREBIRDS WITH CHISEL BILLS

The Oystercatchers

Family Haematopodidae

EVERY CREATURE with a taste for shellfish faces the same problem: how to breach the shell. Gulls break it by dropping it on rocks. Starfish pull it open with suction-cupped arms. Some snails bore a hole. But the oystercatcher uses nature's oyster knife, a long hard bill, flattened vertically and colored bright red.

The ebbing tide signals banquet time for the oystercatchers. Out from the rocks and dunes they fly, dropping in twos and threes on the emerging sandbars. Along the Atlantic and Gulf coasts bird watchers glimpse the showy but shy American oystercatcher (*Haematopus palliatus*), unmistakable as it wings swiftly to the feast on long, white-patched wings. Observers along our Pacific coast watch the slower, tamer black oystercatcher (*Haematopus bachmani*), somber in plumage but with the same three-toed foot and red bill and eye ring as its cousin. Several other species of Haematopodidae range widely along seashores of the world.

At the feet of the assembling birds lies a smorgasbord of oysters and other mollusks, the oysters' valves still parted as they sift the receding water for plankton. Into an open shell goes the red knife, and with a deft snip the bird cuts the adductor muscle before it can slam the door. Then, with vigorous sidewise twists of its head, the "oyster plover" works the half shells apart and gulps the meat inside. Sometimes the bivalve clamps shut on the bird's bill. The oystercatcher then finds a rock, swings its burdened bill like a baseball bat, and shatters its quarry's armor.

The versatile bill also comes in handy for digging fiddler crabs out of their burrows, probing deep into wet sand for worms, sand fleas, and shrimp, and for chipping limpets off rocks. The black oystercatcher feeds more on limpets than the American, as it frequents surf-hammered rocks and reefs along a coast where clinging shellfish are plentiful and sandbars few. Sluggish in flight, grave and stilted in gait, *bachmani* greets intruders with piercing whistles but is slow to flee.

Wild and wary, the American oystercatcher can still be fooled. One photographer, unable to approach without flushing the nesters, set up his camera near a nest and camouflaged it with seaweed. While the parent birds flew in wide circles and piped their *wheep-wheep-wheep* distress call, he tied a string to the camera's shutter, backed off a few paces, and had friends bury him in the sand. With his head and one arm protruding, he waited while his companions left.

Soon the birds returned to the nest, a shallow shell-girt depression in the sand atop a low rise, where they could keep a lookout over the area. Walking with dignity past the disembodied head, the female, similar in plumage but larger than her mate, settled on her two buffy eggs, camouflaged among the pebbles with scrawls and blotches of brownish black. The disconnected arm gave a yank, and a happy photographer sprouted from the sand!

Young oystercatchers leave the nest shortly after they hatch. Like the adult black oystercatchers, the downy young of both species react to danger by squatting in a depression, relying on protective coloration for their defense. Young black oystercatchers sometimes hide only their heads among the rocks.

American oystercatcher—*Range:* coastal areas from N. Baja California to Chile, and New Jersey to Argentina. *Characteristics:* large size; long red bill, black head and neck, brownish back, white wing patches, underparts, and rump.

Black oystercatcher—*Range:* coastal areas from W. Aleutians to Baja California. *Characteristics:* long red bill, black head and underparts, dark brown back.

RED OYSTER KNIVES AGAPE, *American oystercatchers (below) rove rocky shores on three-toed feet. Beaks often show signs of wear from shucking shellfish, cracking crabs, and chiseling limpets from reefs. Black oystercatcher (opposite) has a solemn manner to match his somber hue. He and a few companions are sometimes seen on an Aleutian ledge gravely nodding at their bleak world.*

American oystercatchers, length 17-21"; Robert I. Bowman

WADERS IN THE SURF

Plovers, Turnstones, and Surfbirds

Family Charadriidae

"A MOST PLAGUEY SORT of public-spirited individual that follows you everywhere, flying overhead, and is most persevering in his attempts to give fair warning to all animals within hearing to flee from the approach of danger." Thus Dr. David Livingstone, writing about an African kinsman of the North American plovers, expressed in gentler tongue the bitter complaint of generations of hunters. But these alert, noisy birds can claim good reason to be suspicious; before game laws, gunners in the United States overshot several species nearly to extinction.

Stocky, boldly patterned birds with long wings and short, pigeonlike bills, Chara-

driidae range throughout the world except Antarctica. Fourteen of the 61 species breed in North America. The Eurasian golden plover visits Greenland during migration; the lapwing, also from the Old World, appears only irregularly. Large flocks of lapwings crossed the Atlantic into Canada in 1927, but all apparently perished. Since ancient times a belief has persisted that an African relative, the spur-winged plover, or crocodile bird, searches for leeches in the open jaws of crocodiles. Some scientific observations support the story, but the issue is still in dispute.

Being shorebirds, most plovers keep close to the sea or lakes. But some, like the mountain plover, scorn the waterside. Others, like the killdeer, make themselves at home in almost any habitat. Plovers nest in scantily lined depressions in the ground. Both sexes incubate the brown- or black-blotched eggs. Both care for the chicks, which run about and find their own food immediately.

Animal behaviorists have long considered the plover's "crippled-bird act" a ruse to decoy a threatening enemy away from the nest. But some of these experts now maintain that the bird is showing distress at being torn between two drives—to defend the nest and to flee in fear. Trick or trauma, the act often works.

The long-legged plovers trot along the glistening sand in the seething wake of a wave, bobbing now and then to snatch up some minute crustacean. These birds tend to pick food from the surface rather than probe. But the turnstone, besides moving pebbles and debris with its bill, sends sand showering as it roots piglike for worms —sometimes digging so deep that its neck disappears into the hole. A New Zealand relative, the crook-billed or wry-billed plover, has a beak that bends to the right— perhaps an adaption to help the bird catch insects that scurry under stones on beaches.

IN "BROKEN-WING" DISPLAY, *a female killdeer flutters away from her nest. Grayer upperparts mark the young killdeer (top), who wears two breast bands like those of adults. Ruddy turnstones (left), unlike shorebirds generally, often perch above the ground or water.*

Frederick Kent Truslow. Opposite and top: Arthur A. Allen

Killdeer
Charadrius vociferus

LET MAN OR DOG approach a killdeer's nest, and this ever-alert shorebird takes off, flying frantically in circles, warning *killdee-eee, killdee* to all the creatures of the meadow.

Its common name derives from that call. And the killdeer has such a noisy repertoire of other notes that its scientific title is *vociferus*. Sometimes on the breeding ground and often hundreds of yards in the air, while hovering on almost motionless wings, it trills a long *t-r-r-rrrr*.

At the first cry of alarm from its mate, an incubating parent scurries away and either pretends to brood elsewhere or flies up to circle with its partner. If danger to the nest is imminent, the brooding bird returns, flops on the ground, and fakes injury, holding one wing up and beating the dust with the other. If this lures the intruder, the bird gets up and runs, sometimes dragging a wing—always away from the nest.

When surprised by a grazing animal, the killdeer straddles its nest with outspread wings and scolds vigorously. The bird may even run or fly into the face of a cow or horse to startle and chase the beast away.

Perhaps the most widely distributed of the family, killdeers are as well known to the California schoolboy as to the vacationer on Cape Cod. The double-collared birds are less associated with beaches than most plovers. Although they join other shorebirds on the mud flats in migration, they pick nest sites in uplands, sometimes far from water. They favor open locations with an extended view—pastures, cultivated fields, moist grassy flats, gravelly ground. They even use gravel roads, driveways, and roofs, and cinder beds between railroad ties.

The nest, a shallow hollow with a few stones, wood chips, or weed stalks scattered in and about it, holds four buff eggs blotched or scrawled with black. Both parents share the incubation, which takes about 25 days. They sometimes rear two broods in a season.

Around the turn of the century sportsmen almost wiped out this species in some areas. Nowadays farmers and conservationists hail the game laws that protect it, for *vociferus* dines heartily on beetles, grasshoppers, and weevils. It also helps domestic animals by eating ticks, flies, and mosquitoes.

In winter killdeers retreat south to escape the snows, moving in loose flocks.

Range: N. British Columbia to New Brunswick, south to central Mexico and central Florida; winters to Ecuador. Also found in Peru and N. Chile. *Characteristics:* olive-brown upperparts, white underparts and wing stripes, two black breast bands, orange-brownish rump.

Killdeers, length 9-11"; Frederick Kent Truslow

Piping plover, length 6-7½"; Olin Sewall Pettingill, Jr. National Audubon Society

Piping Plover
Charadrius melodus

Now you see them, now you don't, as these pale little birds run nimbly along the shore. Sometimes they leap lightly into the air to skim the crest of a breaker.

As you approach, piping plovers often flee on foot rather than fly. Or, relying on their coloration, they crouch, blending with the sandy lakeshore or ocean beach where they breed.

Because of its ventriloquial quality, this plover's whistle rarely helps locate the bird in hiding. The sweet, bell-like *peep-lo* earned *melodus* both a common and a scientific name.

The male starts a number of shallow nest holes, usually well above the high-water mark on an open beach away from busy resort areas. The female chooses one and completes the digging while her mate, like a machine that won't stop, sometimes keeps on scraping new holes. The four buffy, speckled eggs are almost invisible against the bits of shell and driftwood and the pebbles that line the sandy nest.

Extremely wary, incubating birds steal off the nest and distract an intruder. Within 24 hours after hatching, the chicks run, swim, and forage. Sometimes several adults herd a single brood up the beach to a hiding place in time of danger.

The piping plover eats marine worms, crustaceans, and insects.

Range: central Alberta and N. Michigan to S. W. Newfoundland, south to central Nebraska and Virginia; winters along coast from Texas to South Carolina. *Characteristics:* small size; black-and-yellow bill, black forehead and neck ring, pale ashy upperparts, white underparts, orange-yellow legs. Winter birds have less distinct black markings.

Semipalmated Plover
Charadrius semipalmatus

Partly webbed toes inspired the name of the semipalmated plover, a small shorebird with a back the color of mud.

Like a miniature sandpiper, which it resembles, *semipalmatus* hunts along beaches and tidal flats for mollusks, crustaceans, and marine worms. Inland it dines on aquatic insects.

Searching behind receding waves, dashing back a step ahead of the returning froth, these plovers rely on their fleet legs rather than their long, pointed wings to escape a drenching. They sleep in groups well above high water, and when alarmed they whistle a clear, plaintive *chee-wee* as they fly off in tight formation.

Over their Far North breeding grounds the males swoop, uttering harsh, whinnylike songs. Often, to win a mate or a nest site, they puff out their feathers and fight each other like gamecocks. The nest, a depression in the sand, may be located near a piece of driftwood or other landmark. It cradles four buffy, spotted eggs.

The ringed plover (*Charadrius hiaticula*) of the Old World breeds also on Ellesmere and Baffin Islands and Greenland. Except for less prominent foot webs, it resembles the semipalmated.

Range: Alaska to N. Labrador, south to N. W. British Columbia, Nova Scotia, and Newfoundland; winters from central California and South Carolina to S. South America. *Characteristics:* small size; black-and-orange bill, black crown bar and breast band, gray-brown upperparts, white underparts, orange-yellow legs. Winter birds have black bill, brownish chest band.

Semipalmated plover, length 6½-8"; Alfred M. Bailey

Snowy plover, length 6-7"; Alexander Sprunt IV, National Audubon Society

Snowy Plover
Charadrius alexandrinus

"WE WERE DRIVING one June day to the Bear River Marshes north of Great Salt Lake in Utah," wrote Dr. Arthur A. Allen in *National Geographic.* "Suddenly, a few feet in front of the car, a queer-looking pebble rolled off to the side of the road.

"I stopped the car as quickly as I could and watched my rolling stone turn into a pale, graceful little snowy plover – now much perturbed. It was not until after a half hour of diligent search that we found the protectively colored eggs... halfway between our front wheels."

As often occurs with the three buffy, black-marked eggs of *alexandrinus*, these were nearly invisible among the pebbles lining the gravelly nest. Both the western subspecies and the "Cuban Snowy" of the Gulf Coast frequently make their nest hollows on stretches of upper beach and on salt flats. They may also utilize dikes between the ponds of commercial saltworks.

The voice of this cosmopolitan bird is less melodious than that of its very similar cousin, the piping plover: a rapid trill in flight and a low, three-note whistle for its common call.

Small and pale, snowy plovers can stand as inconspicuously as driftwood on a beach. They forage in tight bunches, sometimes running after the waves, sometimes hopping on one leg as they feed on marine worms and small crustaceans. Inland their diet consists of insects.

Range: S. W. Washington and W. Nevada to S. W. Kansas, south to S. Baja California; along the Gulf Coast and in the West Indies. Winters to Venezuela. Also found in Peru and Chile, Europe, Africa, Asia, and Australia. *Characteristics:* small size; like piping plover but has whiter plumage, broken breast band, black bill, and dusky legs. Winter birds lack black band.

Wilson's Plover
Charadrius wilsonia

A LONELY SOUTHERN COAST, the sound of surf, a soft sea breeze – these characterize the world of the Wilson's plover. If you stroll here in spring, you will see this little ashy bird running up the beach, pale legs twinkling so fast you can hardly see them. Once or twice it stops and turns to watch you. Then it flies away, fast and low, calling a clear, ternlike *quip.*

Named for ornithologist Alexander Wilson, *wilsonia* has an outsize bill. This feature distinguishes the bird within the family and prompted a frequently used name, "thick-billed plover."

Though they usually live singly or in pairs, Wilson's plovers sometimes gather in loose groups on inlets with storm-washed sandbars and mud flats. Here they feed on small crabs, shrimp, crayfish, mollusks, spiders, insects, and worms.

The three pale buff eggs marked with black rest in a depression on the open beach. Returning from feeding, a parent sometimes finds them drifted over with windblown sand and must excavate them. Incubation lasts about 24 days. In fall many Wilson's plovers remain on the Gulf Coast, but some head for more southerly climes.

Range: along coast from Texas to Virginia; winters to Brazil. *Characteristics:* small size, thick black bill; sandy upperparts, white underparts, pinkish legs. Male has black patch on crown and eyes, and black collar. Female, young, and winter male lack black markings.

Male Wilson's plover, length 7-8"; David G. Allen

Mountain Plover
Eupoda montana

Don't look for the mountain plover in the mountains, nor for this tawny shorebird along the shore. It breeds in dry prairie and sagebrush country, often far from water. And those that migrate to the Pacific coast region stay inland instead of joining other plovers on the beach.

This species was first described from a bird collected in the tablelands of the Rockies.

Long-legged and fleet, *montana* prefers to run from an intruder rather than fly. When the plover does take off, the undersides of its wings flash silvery white—brightening its otherwise drab dress. The bird flies low, alternately flapping and sailing for short distances; it lands with a few mincing steps and squats in an attempt to hide. Such habits made this plover easy game until laws stopped its slaughter.

Mountain plovers place their three spotted, olive-buff eggs on bare ground, then build a nest of dirt, grass, and weeds around them. Sometimes rain turns the soil into mud. When the mud dries it may grip the eggs so firmly that the sitting bird cannot move them.

These plovers often feed in freshly sown grainfields, uttering lisping whistles while they search for grasshoppers, crickets, and flies. In late summer they gather in flocks at water holes and flooded fields before migrating.

Range: N. Montana to W. Kansas, south to S. E. Mexico and W. Texas; winters from central California and Texas to S. Baja California and E. Mexico. *Characteristics:* black crown patch and eye stripe, grayish brown upperparts, white underparts with buff-gray wash on breast. Winter birds lack black marks.

Mountain plover, length 8-9½"; Patricia Bailey Witherspoon

Female Wilson's, Allan D. Cruickshank
National Audubon Society

American Golden Plover
Pluvialis dominica

GOLDEN LEAVES and American golden plovers may appear simultaneously in New England, especially if September gales blow the birds inshore. Leaving their arctic nest sites in late summer, the adults, still clad in gold-spangled breeding coats, make phenomenal overwater flights from Nova Scotia to South America.

The young move south later and on a broader front, some taking a more westerly route. On deep-stroking wings they fly over sea and land to rejoin their elders, wintering on the pampas.

A smaller, western subspecies of this plover breeds in Siberia and Alaska and migrates over Asia as well as directly down the central Pacific to Hawaii and New Zealand.

Golden plovers leaving gaucho country in South America for their breeding grounds in spring take an entirely inland route. On this northward journey, still mostly in dull winter plumage, they frequent prairies, pasturelands, and newly plowed fields chiefly west of the Mississippi. Scattering to feed, they run gracefully and rapidly, stop suddenly to look around with head held high, then strike at an insect. They help farmers by devouring grasshoppers, grubs, cutworms, and wireworms. In the Far North they also feast on the abundant crowberries.

Besides their migration flight call, a harsh, quavering *que-e-e-a*, golden plovers utter a loud but melodious cry of *tud'ling* during the mating season. For a nest they usually select a ridgetop in open tundra, scratching a hollow in the gray reindeer moss and lining it with other lichens. These birds make no attempt at concealment, but their four buffy eggs marked with brownish black are difficult to see.

At the turn of the century hunters nearly wiped out the golden species, once one of the most abundant plovers. Boys in the Midwest killed the confiding birds with whips and sold them in Chicago streets for 50 cents a hundred. One commercial shipment of game birds to Boston comprised 40 barrels, each containing 300 Eskimo curlews and 720 golden plovers. But with protection *dominica* is now recovering.

An Old World relative, the Eurasian golden plover (*Pluvialis apricaria*) breeds from Iceland to Siberia. In migration it reaches Greenland, where *dominica* appears infrequently.

Range: Arctic coasts of Siberia, Alaska, and Canada south to central Siberia, S. Alaska, N. Manitoba, and S. Baffin Island; winters in S. Asia, Australasia, central Pacific islands, and S. South America. *Characteristics:* dusky upperparts speckled with yellow, white stripe on face and side of neck, black underparts. Winter birds have brownish upperparts, lighter underparts.

Black-bellied Plover
Squatarola squatarola

A PLAINTIVE WHISTLE, *pee-u-wee*, interrupts the metronomic lapping of the waves, and the naturalist tenses in his blind. Overhead sweeps a crescent-shaped formation of plump plovers, the adults still wearing their black-breasted breeding dress. The flock dips momentarily, and a few pale young peel off and head for the decoys.

The naturalist clicks his camera again and again—good shots of the juveniles on the beach. But the old black-bellied plovers speed on. Even before protective laws, these largest and wariest of North American plovers managed to keep their ranks filled. Fleet wings helped.

Along with two cinnamon-vested Old World relatives that reach Alaska—the dotterel (*Eudromias morinellus*) and the Mongolian plover (*Charadrius mongolus*)—*squatarola* breeds on the tundra. This nearly worldwide migrant usually arrives in flocks of 20 to 50. After an aerial

Golden plovers in winter plumage, Thase Daniel

courtship blackbellies hollow out a nest on the ground or in the tundra moss, often on a ridge or a bluff. The four black-spotted eggs, varying from buff or gray to pinkish or greenish, rest on a lining of lichens or grass.

On tidal flats, sandbars, and salt-marsh meadows this plover feeds on worms, crustaceans, and small mollusks. Inland it thrives on insects.

While wintering on more southerly coasts, the blackbelly wears a grayish coat. This gave rise to the nickname "gray plover."

Range: Alaska and N. Canada; winters along coasts from S. W. British Columbia, Louisiana, and New Jersey to Chile and S. Brazil. Also found in Europe, Africa, Asia, and Australasia. *Characteristics:* large size; whitish upperparts mottled with black; black bill, face, and underparts; white rump and tail. Winter birds and young are grayish with black underwing patch.

olden plover in breeding plumage, length 9½-11"; Russ Kinne, Photo Researchers. Inset: juvenile, Allan Brooks

elow: black-bellied plover, length 10½-13½"; Arthur A. Allen. Inset: juvenile, Allan Brooks

Surfbird, length 10"; Adolph Murie

Surfbird
Aphriza virgata

FOR 46 WEEKS A YEAR surfbirds frequent the wave-washed rocks and reefs of the Pacific coast from Alaska to the Strait of Magellan. Then for six weeks in summer they disappear.

The stocky, grayish species was first described in 1789, but its breeding grounds remained a mystery till 1921. Then biologist Olaus J. Murie stumbled upon two adults and a downy hatchling in Mount McKinley National Park, Alaska. Five years later ornithologists Joseph Dixon and George M. Wright, searching the same area, found the first surfbird nest. They could barely see the four buffy, chestnut-marked eggs, so well did these blend with the moss of the tundra.

Sharing its lofty Shangri-la with mountain sheep, the shy surfbird circles the crags in swift, ploverlike flight, calling *tee-tee-teet*. Here *virgata* dines on insects. In its coastal haunts, it eats mollusks and crustaceans. Some surfbirds log as much as 24,000 miles a year on migration.

Range: mountains of central Alaska; winters along coast from S. E. Alaska to S. Chile. *Characteristics:* ashy-brown upperparts speckled with black, white underparts heavily spotted with black; white wing stripe, black-tipped white tail, yellowish legs. Winter birds have uniformly dusky upperparts and breast.

Ruddy turnstone, length 8-10"; Arthur A. Allen

324

Black turnstone, length 9"; Arthur A. Allen

Ruddy Turnstone
Arenaria interpres

IN ITS LOVELY HARLEQUIN spring coat, the ruddy turnstone runs little risk of being misidentified. Especially striking when the stocky arctic breeder wings swiftly along the shore chattering metallic *kek* notes, this sporty garb has prompted such picturesque nicknames as "calico back" and "checkered snipe."

True to its name, the turnstone uses its bill to flip over stones, shells, mud clods, and seaweed, snapping up any worms or insects that hide beneath. It pushes heavier stones out of the way with its breast, and climbs bushes to gobble berries. In Massachusetts *interpres* digs the eggs of horseshoe crabs out of the sand. And on Laysan Island in the Pacific two ruddies were seen to push aside the feathers of an incubating tern, drag the egg from beneath her, and eat it.

The pugnacious turnstones defend their own nests fiercely, attacking skuas, Arctic foxes, even men. The four olive-buff eggs, boldly marked with brown, rest in a well-lined depression in open tundra, along a river, or in a coastal dune. In fall the ruddy migrates south in large flocks, often with black-bellied plovers.

Range: Alaska to Greenland; winters from central California, the Gulf Coast, and South Carolina to central Chile and S. Brazil. Also found in Europe, Africa, Asia, Australia, and Oceania. *Characteristics:* upperparts patterned with black, white, brown, and chestnut; black breast, white belly, orange legs. Winter birds are duller and lack chestnut.

Black Turnstone
Arenaria melanocephala

STANDING MOTIONLESS on a barnacle-covered reef along the Pacific coast, the black turnstone looks like a rock or a clump of seaweed. But when it leaps into flight, its black-and-white pattern flashes as brightly as that of its cosmopolitan relative, the ruddy turnstone.

And like the ruddy, *melanocephala* leaves no stone unturned to find a meal. But it limits its breeding grounds to the coasts of Alaska. Here in courtship flights the female zigzags through the sky with the male in hot pursuit. Often he climbs alone into the heavens till he's out of sight. Then he dives, making a peculiar winnowing sound— *zum, zum, zum*—as the air rushes by his feathers.

An unlined depression near the edge of a tundra pond holds the four olive eggs that often look as if the turnstone rolled them in the mud. Alert and noisy, the parents allow no interloper near the nest without protest. As soon as the eggs hatch, adults and young move to the seashore to feed along the tide line on small aquatic animals.

During southward migration this species may travel part of the way with the ruddy. But when the ruddy veers westward for the Pacific islands, the black turnstone ends its journey in northern Mexico. In winter it shares the rocky coast with the surfbird and the rock sandpiper.

Range: coasts of western and southern Alaska; winters to Baja California. *Characteristics:* blackish upperparts and breast with white spot before eye and white speckling; white belly. Winter birds lack speckling.

SLENDER-BILLED SHOREBIRDS

Woodcock, Curlews, and Sandpipers

Family Scolopacidae

By OLIN SEWALL PETTINGILL, JR.

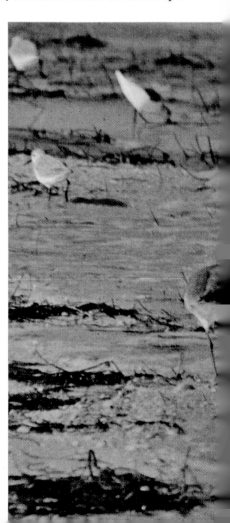

W HEN I FISHED as a youngster at my favorite lake in Maine, a spotted sandpiper
was always along the shore. I took for
granted its pleasant, inquiring *peet-tweet, peet-
tweet*. One day I found its nest, a leaf- and
grass-lined depression with four eggs so well camouflaged that I didn't see them at
first. The bird returned as soon as I withdrew, and this gave me an idea. I set up my
Kodak, tied a long string to the shutter, and released it the next time the bird came
back. Thus I took my first bird portrait, such as it was. A few days later I found four
chicks, lively and utterly appealing. They could already run like streaks.

Of all the members of the huge sandpiper family—the Scolopacidae—only the
spotted sandpiper, the little "teetertail," is generally familiar. Yet 33 of the 82 spe-

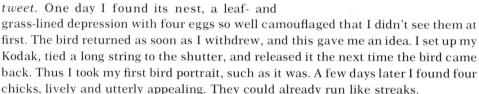

COMMON SNIPE *alighting in an Ohio field
and willets combing a Florida beach blend
with their surroundings just as the long-billed
curlew does, nesting amid Colorado cactus.*

G. Ronald Austing. Right: Russ Kinne, Photo Researchers
Upper: Patricia Bailey Witherspoon

326

cies breed in North America, ranging in size from the least sandpiper, barely six inches long, to the long-billed curlew, about two feet long. Many are so similar that they challenge the bird watcher's skill. One of the most remarkable members of the family, the ruff, carries on a ritualistic courtship, the males wearing huge erectile plumes around their heads and shoulders. But the species is European, a mere casual visitor along our East Coast, usually in its drab winter plumage.

Most North American shorebirds nest inland, many on the tundra of the Far North. The American woodcock has left the shore entirely and frequents woodland edges and thickets. I chose this bird as the subject for my doctoral thesis, and there were times when I wished I hadn't. Most active at twilight, the woodcock walks quietly, crouches motionless, and blends perfectly with the forest floor. Finding it is hard enough; finding its nest is even harder. Studying the chicks was another problem, for the female leads them away soon after they hatch. Luckily, a friend found a nest on a small island, where the brood had no place to go. Each day I weighed and measured the chicks. To my astonishment they grew so fast that they were able to fly away from the island when they were but 14 days old.

One spring I joined Dr. George Miksch Sutton on an expedition to the Churchill area on Hudson Bay. Here we met many sandpipers and other Scolopacidae as they arrived from the south to nest. I saw one ecstatic performer after another take wing, climb, circle or hover, and pour forth a trilling song. This time I had no trouble finding nests to photograph. I recall setting up a blind and very quietly taking pictures of a least sandpiper, careful not to frighten it. Finally I stepped out to make a close-up of the eggs. The bird had no intention of budging. I had to shoo it away!

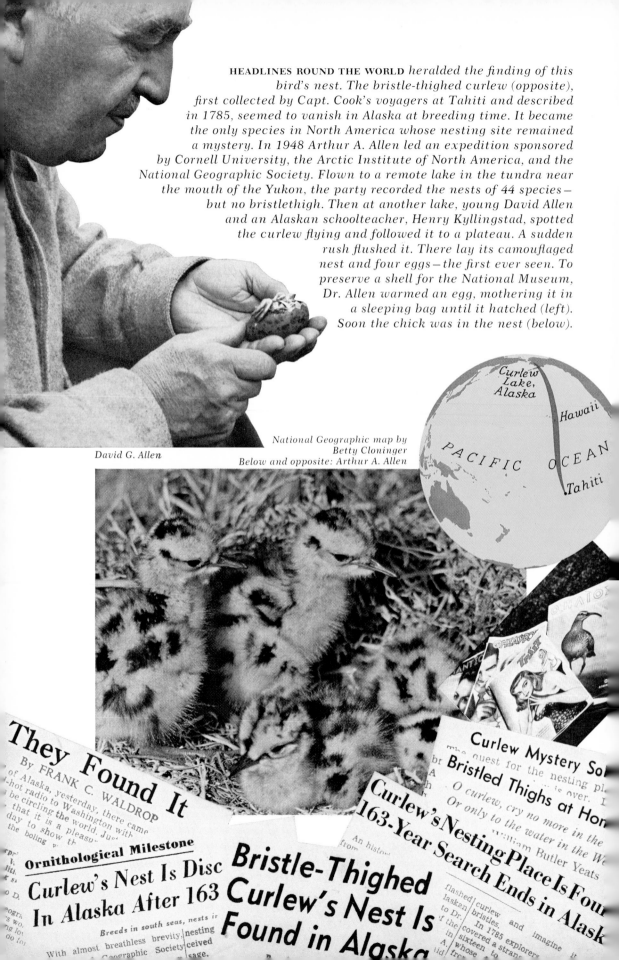

HEADLINES ROUND THE WORLD *heralded the finding of this bird's nest. The bristle-thighed curlew (opposite), first collected by Capt. Cook's voyagers at Tahiti and described in 1785, seemed to vanish in Alaska at breeding time. It became the only species in North America whose nesting site remained a mystery. In 1948 Arthur A. Allen led an expedition sponsored by Cornell University, the Arctic Institute of North America, and the National Geographic Society. Flown to a remote lake in the tundra near the mouth of the Yukon, the party recorded the nests of 44 species — but no bristlethigh. Then at another lake, young David Allen and an Alaskan schoolteacher, Henry Kyllingstad, spotted the curlew flying and followed it to a plateau. A sudden rush flushed it. There lay its camouflaged nest and four eggs — the first ever seen. To preserve a shell for the National Museum, Dr. Allen warmed an egg, mothering it in a sleeping bag until it hatched (left). Soon the chick was in the nest (below).*

David G. Allen

National Geographic map by Betty Cloninger
Below and opposite: Arthur A. Allen

Curlew Lake, Alaska

Hawaii

PACIFIC OCEAN

Tahiti

They Found It

By FRANK C. WALDROP

Ornithological Milestone

Curlew's Nest Is Disc In Alaska After 163

Bristle-Thighed Curlew's Nest Is Found in Alaska

Curlew's Nesting Place Is Four 163-Year Search Ends in Alask

Curlew Mystery So Bristled Thighs at Hon

O curlew, cry no more in the Or only to the water in the W
— William Butler Yeats

A shorebird's eggs are large in proportion to its body and lie with the pointed ends meeting in the center of the scrape. Thus they fit a space small enough for the parent to cover —two eggs under each side of the breast. The eggs hatch more slowly than jay or crow eggs of the same size, for the embryos develop further. Instead of being blind and helpless at birth, the chicks can pick up their own food. Their wings grow fully before they lose all their down, and in 10 to 12 days they can fly short distances. They can swim even sooner. I have seen a week-old spotted sandpiper dive underwater to escape a gull.

The parent birds cover their brood at night and in chilly weather; they also warn of danger. At the alarm note the chicks freeze. This worries me when I search for them, for so strong is their response to the signal that they would let me step on them without moving. At Churchill I wanted desperately to find chicks of the lesser yellowlegs, but do you think

I could? If I got near the breeding area the adults yammered wildly from the treetops, following me as I moved about. I couldn't even tell by the noise whether I was "getting hot."

Once in North Dakota a pair of marbled godwits circled over me with piercing alarm calls. This time I found the chicks and expected the parents to die of despair. But they had apparently exhausted all their protestations!

Young shorebirds are on their own within a month. In the Far North they migrate without leadership, having inherited the trait. In winter and when migrating they grow comparatively silent and once solitary pairs flock together. In May or September, during migration, no North American beach or tidal flat is without them.

The sanderlings follow the edge of a receding wave picking up crustaceans, then scurry away from the next breaker, their legs a blur. Knots and pectoral sandpipers doze at low tide, balancing on one foot, bills tucked under shoulders. Throngs of "peeps"— the little look-alike sandpipers, the white-rumped, Baird's, least, semipalmated, and western— mill over a mud flat, picking and dabbling. And as they wing off in a tight, wheeling flock, I see all their white bellies, then all their backs, then all their bellies again.

American Woodcock
Philohela minor

As DUSK SETTLES on a woodland opening, the *peent, peent* of the male woodcock seems just another song at twilight. Suddenly the singer takes off from his courting territory and spirals up on whistling wings, then hovers about 200 feet above the ground as the trilling note floats down: *chickaree, chickaree, chickaree!*

At the peak of this ecstatic performance the woodcock zigzags rapidly down to earth with chirping notes. He struts across a patch of open ground, sounds his *peent* notes again, then soars to repeat the aerial act. Under a bright moon he may perform all night.

Often a female joins him on the field and watches the show. Finally he mates with her and perhaps with others. The females then nest and rear the broods with no help from the male. They may choose a site far from the singing field. One observer painstakingly scoured the vicinity of a courting ground; when he finally found a nest, the performing male was out of earshot.

The three or four eggs, buffy with brownish spots, lie on the ground among leaves and twigs. The hatchlings need brooding for a day or two while gaining strength. They grow fast and soon are as fluffy and perky as barnyard chicks. In two weeks they can fly.

The woodcock's favorite food—earthworms—explains its nocturnal habits and its early nesting and breeding. The birds follow the thaws of late winter northward, searching for worms in the softening ground. Late snow may almost cover the mother birds on their nests.

A woodcock may consume half its weight in worms in a single day. Earthworms are most active at night, so the birds hunt them then, probing in the soil with their long, sensitive bills. The end of their upper mandible is flexible; they can open it under the mud, grip their prey, and draw it forth. Even with the bill submerged they can keep a good watch on their surroundings. A woodcock's eyes are set so far back on its head that the bird can scan a full circle.

By morning only a series of holes in the ground tells of the presence of woodcock. In a boggy thicket the birds doze through the day, so marvelously camouflaged that they simply vanish unless you know exactly where to look for them.

When drought drives earthworms far below the surface, woodcock shift to insect larvae and beetles. They also eat seeds and berries.

Fall sends the more northern of these birds southward. Night migrants and low flyers, they sometimes hit wires. Hunters also take a toll. With its explosive way of taking off and streaking through the woods, the woodcock makes an exciting and challenging target.

Before Federal regulations set bag limits, hunters bragged of shooting more than a hundred woodcock a day. Dogs come in handy to flush the game and locate it if it falls among leaves.

Range: S. E. Manitoba to Newfoundland, south to Louisiana and Florida; migratory in the north. *Characteristics:* cinnamon brown with black bars on back of head and black-and-gray variegated pattern on back and wings; long bill, short neck and tail, chunky body.

Common Snipe
Capella gallinago

FOR AS FAR as the eye can see the sky is clear. Yet from somewhere above comes a distant eerie sound like the sigh of a lost soul.

You crane upward and search the blue. And at last you make out a high circling speck, dipping and rising erratically. As it comes closer you see a brown, long-billed bird with a light belly. It resembles a woodcock but is trimmer. When it dives, the rush of air through the outer feathers of its spread tail produces strange, pulsating notes, the mating "song" of the common snipe.

The North American race of this circumpolar species is often called Wilson's snipe. It usually frequents low wet places such as swampy meadows. During migration it will find a marshy patch even amid rocky, arid hills.

In the United States the common snipe and the American woodcock are the only members of their family that may be hunted legally. Unlike the woodcock, the "jacksnipe" prefers open country. Twisting and skidding as it rockets into the air, this bird makes a sporty target.

Like the woodcock, the snipe probes for worms with its slender bill. A common daylight feeder, it also consumes snails, small crustaceans, and aquatic insect larvae. The snipe usually enters

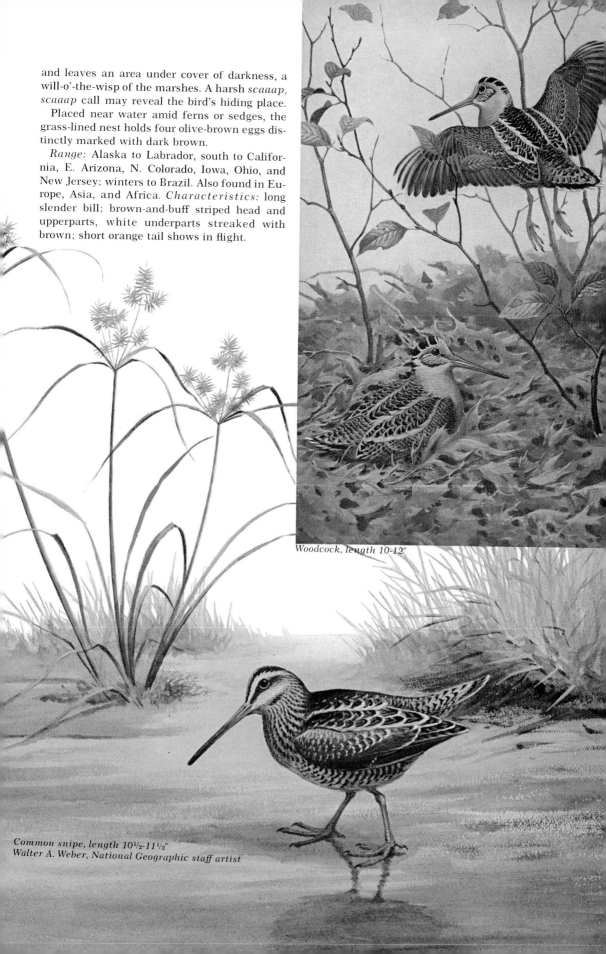

and leaves an area under cover of darkness, a will-o'-the-wisp of the marshes. A harsh *scaaap, scaaap* call may reveal the bird's hiding place.

Placed near water amid ferns or sedges, the grass-lined nest holds four olive-brown eggs distinctly marked with dark brown.

Range: Alaska to Labrador, south to California, E. Arizona, N. Colorado, Iowa, Ohio, and New Jersey; winters to Brazil. Also found in Europe, Asia, and Africa. *Characteristics:* long slender bill; brown-and-buff striped head and upperparts, white underparts streaked with brown; short orange tail shows in flight.

Woodcock, length 10-12"

Common snipe, length 10½-11½"
Walter A. Weber, National Geographic staff artist

Long-billed Curlew
Numenius americanus

LARGEST in its family and pre-eminently a bird of the grasslands, the magnificent "sicklebill" was once abundant on the prairies and migrated through the eastern states. The V-shaped flights were a common sight along the Massachusetts coast and stirred gunners to set out decoys. When the curlews swept in, the guns would roar. A handful of birds would drop, and others would wheel over them, keening. Again the guns would speak. Eventually these flocks disappeared.

As farmers turned the prairie sod, *americanus* retreated to the plains west of the Missouri River. There, under protection, it ranges in vastly reduced numbers.

The curlew's curved bill may measure eight inches. Using it as a forceps, the longbill extracts shellfish from tidal flats and beaches it frequents while migrating. On the plains it eats insects.

Longbills incubate their four spotted olive-buff eggs in a grassy hollow. When an intruder approaches, birds from the scattered colony rally overhead, crying their haunting *curleeuu!*

Range: S. British Columbia to S. Manitoba, south to N. E. California and S. Texas; winters to Guatemala. *Characteristics:* very long sickle-shaped bill, mottled buffy upperparts, streaked underparts, cinnamon underwings.

Bristle-thighed Curlew
Numenius tahitiensis

FEW PEOPLE have seen this curlew, but millions heard of it when newspapers trumpeted the discovery of its nesting grounds in Alaska (page 328). The bristle-thighed curlew comes into contact with man only on Pacific islands from Hawaii to Tahiti, where it spends most of the year.

Named for a few stiff feathers on its flanks and thighs, this big, long-billed bird plays the part of a South Sea pirate. Watch one slip up behind a nesting frigatebird. As the sitter raises momentarily the curlew sneaks an egg out from under her so slickly she may not even miss it. Again, finding a red-footed booby's nest untended, the bandit impales an egg with a quick stab of that rapier bill and carries it off.

In late May the bristlethighs begin arriving at their Alaskan nesting grounds. Dr. Arthur A. Allen, leader of the expedition that found the first nests, wrote in *National Geographic:* "Why these curlews should want to leave the warm, luxurious shores of Tahiti and the other South Sea islands, fly 5,500 miles over the open sea, and arrive at one of the most forlorn stretches of tundra in North America, deserted by all other birds and still largely covered by snow, just to lay four eggs, is hard to understand."

The eggs are brownish-green with dark brown

Long-billed curlew, length 20-26"; Bill Reasons, National Audubon Society

Eskimo curlew
length 12-14"
Allan Brooks

Karl W. Kenyon

Bristle-thighed curlew, length 17"; Arthur A. Allen

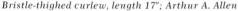

Whimbrels in winter plumage, length 15-18¾"

spots. Many fall prey to marauding jaegers. Sometimes the parents drive away a jaeger by flying at it with piercing whistles.

In early August, when the young birds are well grown, the bristlethighs gather along Alaska's western coast. They fill up on berries in preparation for flying once more to their Pacific paradise.

Range: W. Alaska; winters from Marshall Islands and Hawaii south to Santa Cruz and Tonga Islands, and the Tuamotu Archipelago. *Characteristics:* long curved bill, brown-and-buffy striped crown, brown mottled upperparts, buff underparts, tawny rump and tail.

Whimbrel
Numenius phaeopus

ONE LOOK at that long, curved bill and you know this is a curlew. Formerly named the Hudsonian curlew, the bird is now classified as an American subspecies of the Old World's whimbrel.

While other North American curlews have diminished in number, *phaeopus* has increased. Bird refuges and laws against market gunning helped turn the tide for this migrant. Relatively unmolested, it often travels in enormous flocks. Over land whimbrels fly high in V's; over water they sometimes skim the surface in long lines.

Venturing into shallows for insects, they may stand storklike on one leg. On tidal flats their bills thrust deep into the mud for shellfish.

Whimbrels nest in the open, choosing a depression in the tundra to hold the four olive-buff eggs marked with brown. While incubating and while brooding their young, the parents will fly screaming in the face of any intruder.

Range: N. W. Alaska to N. W. Canada, south to central Alaska and S. W. Yukon; also along the S. W. shore of Hudson Bay; winters along coasts from central California to S. Chile and from Colombia to E. Brazil. Also found in Eurasia, Africa, and Australia. *Characteristics:* long curved bill, striped crown; mottled grayish-brown upperparts, brown-streaked whitish underparts.

Eskimo Curlew
Numenius borealis

NEARLY EXTINCT NOW, the "prairie pigeon" or "dough bird" was the most numerous of the curlews in the 1880's. In migration they swarmed southward off the East Coast to winter in Argentina, where they were shot for game. Spring sent them north up the Mississippi Valley.

Traveling by the millions in dense flocks, they faced slaughter. A single blast from a muzzle-loading shotgun once brought down 23 curlews. Hunters on the prairies loaded wagons with the plump birds and trundled them to market, piling the overflow on the grass like mounds of coal.

Still occasionally sighted, *borealis* is easily confused with a young whimbrel, but has a unique, squeaking flight call. Its nest on the tundra holds four brown-marked olive-buff eggs.

Range: formerly N. W. Canada; wintered in S. South America. *Characteristics:* slightly curved bill; buffy-brown with darker upperparts, cinnamon-buff wing linings.

Upland Plover
Bartramia longicauda

PERCHED ON A POLE, a big brownish
sandpiper surveys the hayfield
and utters a mellow courtship song,
whoooleeeee, wheeeeloooooooooo.
This upland plover, once known
as the Bartramian sandpiper, runs over
pasturelands and prairies where it hunts
insects and breeds. When flushed from the
grassy hollow containing its four spotted
buffy eggs, the bird flies off, fluttering
the tips of its long, pointed wings.
Range: S. Alaska to central Maine,
south to Texas and Maryland; winters
on the pampas of S. South America.
Characteristics: streaked buffy-
brown with dark rump; short bill,
small head, thin neck, long tail.

Spotted Sandpiper
Actitis macularia

TAILS WAGGING, spotted sandpipers teeter
as they walk on logs and rocks or perch
on wires and branches near ponds, lakes,
and streams over most of North America.
Wearing distinctive spots on its breast in
summer, the "teetertail" uses a grass-lined
depression or a deep cup of moss and
seaweed, normally in a field near water, to
hold its four spotted buffy eggs. Downy
young can swim and adults occasionally flee
by swimming underwater or walking on the

bottom. Spotted sandpipers even dive straight
into the water. If flushed they fly up with short,
quick wing strokes and utter *peet-weet* calls.
They dine on crustaceans, fish, and insects.
Range: N.W. Alaska to Labrador, south to S.
California and Virginia; winters to central South
America. *Characteristics:* olive-brown upperparts, black-spotted white underparts, white "eyebrows" and wing stripe. Winter birds lack spots.

Wandering Tattler
Heteroscelus incanum
(Picture on page 337)

LEAVING CORAL-FRINGED winter havens on South
Sea islands in March, wandering tattlers live up
to their name by winging thousands of miles to
mountain streams in Alaska and Canada.

Wearing nuptial stripes of black across their
pale breasts and bellies, these grayish birds nest
in a depression on a gravel bar. The four greenish, brown-spotted eggs rest on a lining of twigs.
When flushed, *incanum* flies a short distance on
downcurved wings. Its loud whistles tattle a
warning to other animals nearby.

With its head often underwater, the wandering
tattler searches for insects among the pebbles in
stream shallows. Along rocky shores it teeters on
yellow legs and, drenched in spray, probes amid
kelp for crustaceans.
Range: E. Alaska to N.W. Canada; winters
along coast from California to Ecuador and on
South Pacific islands. *Characteristics:* grayish
upperparts, pale barred underparts, white line
over eye, yellow legs. Winter birds lack barring.

Above: upland plover, length 11-12½"; Karl Maslowski   *Below: spotted sandpiper, length 7-8"; Eliot Porter*

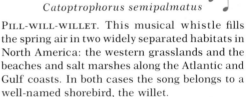

Inset: Russ Kinne, Photo Researchers.

Willets, length 14-17"; Karl W. Kenyon

Willet
Catoptrophorus semipalmatus

PILL-WILL-WILLET. This musical whistle fills the spring air in two widely separated habitats in North America: the western grasslands and the beaches and salt marshes along the Atlantic and Gulf coasts. In both cases the song belongs to a well-named shorebird, the willet.

On their breeding grounds the two races of this clamorous gray bird also utter a series of *whee-wee-wee-wee* notes. Less frequently they make a call that sounds like *beat it, beat it*. In courtship the male stands behind his mate, waving his flashy parti-colored wings, and both birds cry *kuk-kuk-kuk-kuk-kuk.*

The coastal bird picks nest sites atop dunes and along marsh embankments. The inland subspecies prefers sloughs and alkaline flats, usually near shallow lakes. Nests for the four spotted olive-buff eggs vary from sparsely lined depressions to bulky cups of grass and weeds.

Perching on boulders, trees, fences, and telephone poles, willets often scold the human intruder. Man, in fact, has been this bird's greatest enemy. During the early years of this century hunters nearly extirpated it along the East Coast. Nova Scotians and Virginians ate its eggs in large numbers. But in recent years, under protection, it has made a comeback.

The willet feeds on mollusks, fiddler crabs, crayfish, small fish, insects, grass roots and seeds, and cultivated rice. Its partially webbed feet give it the name *semipalmatus*.

Range: E. Oregon and central Alberta to S. Manitoba, south to N. E. California and E. South Dakota; also along coast from Nova Scotia to Texas. Winters to central South America. *Characteristics:* gray with black-and-white wing patches, white tail, bluish legs.

Solitary sandpiper, length 7½-9"; David G. Allen

Solitary Sandpiper
Tringa solitaria

WADING IN THE SHALLOWS of a secluded woodland pool, a solitary sandpiper gently stirs the mud with one dark foot, agitating water insects and pecking them when they try to dart away.

If disturbed, the dainty bird takes off, piping *weep* notes. It crosses the pool with deep strokes of its dark, pointed wings, which it extends above its back momentarily after landing.

This bird of the northern wilderness breeds mainly near ponds and bogs. Unlike other shorebirds, *solitaria* nests in trees, placing its four brown-spotted green or buffy eggs in the deserted dwellings of robins and blackbirds.

Range: central Alaska to central Labrador, south to central British Columbia and central Quebec; winters from Gulf Coast and S. Georgia to Argentina. *Characteristics:* small size; blackish upperparts with light speckles, whitish breast with dark speckles; white belly and eye ring, barred white tail, dark legs. Young are paler.

Greater yellowlegs, length 12½-15"; Hamilton Rice

 ## Greater Yellowlegs
Totanus melanoleucus

A SKILLFUL WHISTLER can mimic the plaintive *whew-whew-whew* of the greater yellowlegs and cause it to circle close overhead, crying and peering down curiously. This early spring migrant frequents marshes and tidal creeks on its way to remote northern nesting grounds.

High-flying flocks spiral down to feed, wings set and long yellow legs trailing. Landing beside a marshy pool, the hungry travelers team up to catch minnows and other small fish. Perhaps a dozen will form in line abreast and wade or swim through the pool. Driving their prey before them, they maneuver the fish into a cul-de-sac where they can dine at leisure. They also eat tadpoles, crustaceans, and aquatic insects.

These birds feed with noisy gabbles, but they are wary, quick to flush if an intruder appears. Because their raucous calls spread the alarm to other birds, hunters dub the yellowlegs "tattler" and "telltale." Now protected, this big sandpiper once was considered game and shot down as it planed in to decoys.

Greater yellowlegs breed across Canada in regions of marshes and pools surrounded by forests. They scratch out nest hollows on hummocks near water or on gravelly ridges among scattered trees and fallen logs. The four orange-brown eggs are marked with reddish brown.

Range: S. Alaska and central British Columbia to N. Quebec and Newfoundland; winters from Oregon, S. W. Arizona, and South Carolina to S. South America. *Characteristics:* dark grayish upperparts, light underparts speckled on neck and chest, whitish rump, barred whitish tail, bright yellow legs.

Lesser Yellowlegs
Totanus flavipes

THIS BIRD shares many habits with the greater yellowlegs and covers much the same territory. But it's about one-quarter smaller. And instead of the greater's three-syllable whistle, the lesser sounds a harsher cry, *cu* or *cu-cu*. You may compare these calls on the records—or at shallow marshy pools where both species often pluck small fish and tadpoles from the surface.

The lesser yellowlegs heads south earlier than the greater, and returns north later. North American gunners used to call it the "summer yellowlegs," since *flavipes* begins its southward flight in summer. The larger species, which may linger almost into winter, is known as the "winter yellowlegs." In spring the lesser usually follows a Mississippi Valley route; in fall it frequently migrates along the Atlantic coast.

The lesser occurs singly or in flocks of up to 100. Small groups are usually the rule. In their northern breeding range the birds keep south of the tundra but avoid densely timbered regions. They nest in meadows and bogs, also in open aspen and poplar stands that sprout in the ashy devastation of a burned forest. The nest hollow holds four buffy eggs blotched with brown.

Range: N. Alaska to N. W. Quebec, south to E. British Columbia and central Quebec; winters from the Gulf Coast and South Carolina to central South America. *Characteristics:* like the greater yellowlegs but smaller.

Lesser yellowlegs, length 9½-11"; Thase Daniel

unison, showing alternately the gray backs and brick-red bellies of the breeding season which explain the nickname "robin snipe." The name "knot" imitates the bird's croaking call. The lichen-lined nest holds four spotted olive-buff eggs.

Range: N. Alaska, Arctic Canada, and Greenland; winters from S. California and Massachusetts to S. South America. Also found in northern Europe and Asia, wintering to Africa, southern Asia, and Australasia. *Characteristics:* stocky, short-billed with mottled gray upperparts; breast red in spring, whitish in fall.

Knot
Calidris canutus

ROBERT E. PEARY, returning from his discovery of the North Pole in 1909, found the first authentic knot's nest, with eggs, on northern Ellesmere Island. This was in June, about a month before the knots begin a migration that takes some of them on a 19,000-mile round trip to Tierra del Fuego in southernmost South America.

They travel in dense flocks, moving gradually along the coast, feeding on mollusks. In spring the flocks return, wheeling and dipping in

Purple Sandpiper
Erolia maritima

THE WAVE-LASHED New England coast hardly ranks as a southern resort, but it's balmy enough for purple sandpipers arriving in December from Baffin Island and Greenland.

The slaty birds blend with the offshore rocks where they feed, and you may not see them until they wheel away, flashing their white bellies. The four green or buff eggs are spotted with brown.

Range: Arctic Canada and Greenland; winters along Atlantic coast to Maryland. Also found in northern Europe and Asia. *Characteristics:* slaty upperparts, white belly, yellow legs.

Rock Sandpiper
Erolia ptilocnemis

ALSO CALLED Aleutian sandpiper, this rock-feeding bird has been considered by some as a race of *maritima*, which it resembles in winter.

The courting male rises 30 to 40 feet in the air, then flutters down with a twittering song. The tundra nest holds four spotted buffy eggs.

Range: N. E. Siberia and Bering Sea islands to W. Alaska; winters to the Kuril Islands and Oregon. *Characteristics:* mottled brown upperparts, whitish underparts with dark breast splotch; in winter similar to purple sandpiper.

*Wandering tattler
in breeding plumage
length 10½-11¼"
Allan Brooks*

*Rock sandpipers
in winter (above left)
and breeding plumages
length 8-9"*

*Knots
adult in breeding plumage (left)
and juvenile, length 10-11"*

*Purple sandpiper, length 8-9½"
Helen Cruickshank
National Audubon Society*

Pectoral Sandpiper
Erolia melanotos

STRUTTING about his breeding ground on the tundra, the male pectoral sandpiper brings to mind a bagpiper. With throat and breast ballooned to twice their normal size, he pours forth deep, hollow notes like the hooting of air across the top of a bottle: *too-u, too-u, too-u.*

He may fly 40 feet high, then sail to the ground on set wings, jerking his head as he gives the call. Tootling, prancing, and ardently bowing, the gallant windbag courts the female. She lays four buff eggs blotched with brown in a leaf- or grass-lined depression in a tussock.

On migration the "grass snipe" is most often seen in the Mississippi Valley, hunting insects and crustaceans in wet fields and rainpools. It flushes in zigzag snipelike fashion with a harsh call that explains another nickname—"krieker."

Range: Arctic coasts from N. E. Siberia to Hudson Bay, south to S. W. Alaska and N. Ontario; winters in South America. *Characteristics:* mottled brown upperparts, dark breast streaks, white belly. Young are tawnier.

cle overhead in twisting, erratic flight, protesting with a soft *pleep, pleep.* They often return to the same spot once the observer has passed.

Range: N. Siberia; winters in Australasia. Seen in coastal Alaska and British Columbia. *Characteristics:* like the pectoral but ruddier and lacks sharp contrast between breast and belly.

Baird's Sandpiper
Erolia bairdii

SEARCHING the shores of an inland pond, Baird's sandpiper weaves through the other "peeps"—small, very similar sandpipers which often flock together—as it energetically picks up crustaceans and insects. Its nest on dry tundra holds four buffy, brown-spotted eggs. If disturbed, the bird flies off with a trilling *kreep!* On its long migrations it traverses the Mississippi Valley; in fall it is also seen along both coasts.

Range: N. E. Siberia to N. W. Greenland, south to S. W. Alaska and S. W. Baffin Island; winters in South America. *Characteristics:* short bill, buffy head and breast, brownish scale-patterned back, gray belly, dark legs.

*Pectoral sandpipers
adult (left) and juvenile
length 8-9½"*

*Sharp-tailed sandpipers
adult in breeding plumage (right)
and juvenile, length 8½"*

Sharp-tailed Sandpiper
Erolia acuminata

OLD WORLD COUNTERPART of the pectoral sandpiper, this bird breeds in Siberia and winters in the South Pacific. In migration a few sharptails fly down the American coast for varying distances before heading out over the ocean.

In early September sharptails appear along the coasts of Alaska and British Columbia, generally in flocks of 10 to 50. Some straggle south to Washington and California. They hunt for insects and mollusks along the borders of salt marshes and on moist meadows. Only when an intruder comes close do these birds rise and cir-

Least Sandpiper
Erolia minutilla

A FLOCK of least sandpipers, smallest of North American shorebirds, pecks at bits of life stranded on a mud flat. The mud-colored peeps are hard to see until in flight their silvery breasts wink, all at once, as they swerve in unison.

Least sandpipers migrate along both coasts and in the interior. A grassy hollow near water holds the four buffy, brown-blotched eggs.

Range: N. W. Canada to N. Labrador, south to S. Alaska, also to N. E. Manitoba, N. Ontario, and Nova Scotia; winters from Oregon and California to Louisiana and North Carolina, south to Brazil. *Characteristics:* small size, short thin bill; streaked brown upperparts, white breast streaked with brown, yellowish or greenish legs.

Dunlins
winter-clad (left and on wing)
and in breeding plumage
length 8-9"

Baird's sandpipers
adult in breeding plumage
and (above) juvenile
length 7-7½"

Least sandpipers
adult in breeding plumage (left)
and juvenile, length 5-6½"

White-rumped sandpipers
adult in breeding plumage (upper)
and juvenile, length 7-8"

Allan Brooks

 Dunlin
Erolia alpina

TWISTING AND TURNING as though drilled to act as one bird, dunlin flocks sweep south in late autumn, usually after other sandpipers have departed for winter quarters.

Alighting on beaches, the dunlins search for crustaceans and insects, moving deliberately and showing little fear of humans. Inland, they probe the muddy banks of pools and rivers.

The dunlin is the most abundant sandpiper in Europe and one of the commonest in western North America. In spring it wears a distinctive black belly patch and the reddish plumage that gives it the name red-backed sandpiper.

Courting dunlins chase each other in the air, singing a tinkling song. In a tussock near a tundra pool the female lays the usual four eggs, greenish-buff with brown spots.

Range: N. W. Alaska to Somerset Island, south to S. W. Alaska and the W. shore of Hudson Bay; winters along coasts from British Columbia to Baja California and from Massachusetts to Texas. Also found in N. Eurasia. *Characteristics:* long bill curved at tip, reddish upperparts, light underparts with black patch. Winter birds have brown-gray upperparts, gray chest, white belly.

White-rumped Sandpiper
Erolia fuscicollis

IT'S JUST ANOTHER PEEP until it flies away. Then the white patch on the little bird's posterior distinguishes the species.

The white-rumped sandpiper breeds along the bleak shores of the Arctic Ocean and migrates as far south as the equally bleak terrain of Tierra del Fuego. It is rare in much of the United States. Only in fall along the Mississippi Valley and the New England coast is this migrant frequently seen. In meadows, rainpools, and mud flats, the whiterump plunges its beak deep as it feeds on crustaceans and insects.

Mingling with other peeps, this sandpiper reveals its presence with a thin sharp call, like the click of two marbles hitting each other. If approached, it may fly only a few feet off, then return to its feeding.

The whiterump nests in a hollow on a dry slope or beside an Arctic pond. Its four eggs are olive green with brown splotches.

Range: Melville Island to N. Baffin Island, south to N. Alaska and S. W. Baffin Island; winters in S. South America. *Characteristics:* streaked rusty upperparts, grayish underparts, white rump. Winter birds are grayer.

339

Curlew Sandpiper
Erolia ferruginea

Curlew sandpiper in breeding plumage length 7-9"

FOR YEARS the curlew sandpiper, a Siberian breeder, rarely even visited Alaska. Then in 1962 Richard T. Holmes and Frank A. Pitelka discovered two nests and a small population of the little reddish sandpipers on the coastal tundra near Point Barrow.

The American ornithologists seized the chance to study the little-known courtship antics of the male: his trilling as he rockets off the ground; his plaintive *whaay, whaay* as he descends; his head-up, swaying walk on long legs around the female, displaying his white rump. The four eggs are yellowish with blackish spots.

Range: N. Siberia and N. Alaska; winters in Europe, Africa, Asia, and Australasia. *Characteristics:* small size, long curved bill; chestnut with black-mottled crown and back, white rump. Winter birds are grayish.

Short-billed Dowitcher
Limnodromus griseus

A FAMILIAR SIGHT along many a coastal bay or inland lake, marsh, creek, or rainpool in spring, a cluster of short-billed dowitchers wade belly-high in the shallows, pecking the bottom with sewing-machine speed. Probing the mud with a snipelike bill and often dunking its head, *griseus* feeds on insect larvae, tiny snails, and seeds. Along coasts it eats crustaceans and clam worms, and so absorbed is the bird in its feeding that it seldom panics when people approach.

On its northern breeding grounds the male often hovers 50 feet in the air, gurgling musically. The female incubates the four greenish, brown-spotted eggs in a mossy depression and tends the handsome downy hatchlings. In early summer the birds begin to migrate south, uttering *dowitch* notes in flight.

Range: S. Alaska to N. Quebec; winters from central California, the Gulf Coast, and South Carolina to N. South America. *Characteristics:* long bill; speckled reddish-brown neck, breast, and sides; dark mottled back, white rump and belly. Winter birds have gray back and breast.

Long-billed Dowitcher
Limnodromus scolopaceus

FROM THE MIDDLE OF MAY till early June the Alaskan tundra resounds with the mating cries of the long-billed dowitcher. Two or three males often fly after a female, twisting and turning as they speed over marsh and stream. Sometimes a male pauses, calls *peet-u-weet, wee-too, wee-too,* then resumes the chase.

This "red-breasted snipe" closely resembles *griseus* in looks and habits. But its plumage is darker and its bill – measuring about three inches – is a shade longer.

Range: N. E. Siberia to N. W. Alaska; winters from central California and the Gulf Coast to Guatemala. *Characteristics:* like short-billed dowitcher but slightly larger with longer bill, darker back and underparts, and barred sides.

Stilt Sandpiper
Micropalama himantopus

As SOON AS THE SNOW disappears, stilt sandpipers arrive at Churchill on Hudson Bay, winging in small fast flocks, rocking as they alight on the tundra. Here, and westerly along the arctic reaches of the continent, this salt-and-pepper wader with stilty legs nests in a mossy depression near lakes, ponds, and marshes. Its four olive eggs are boldly marked with black.

If you approach the handsome chicks, the parent will drop before you, rump feathers lifted and tail spread, and attempt to lure you away by crawling on its belly, flopping and dragging both wings, and squealing as if in agony.

Generally sedate, the stilt sandpiper walks up to its breast in shallow pools, probing the mud in dowitcher fashion or sweeping its bill from side to side like a roseate spoonbill. It also may kick the water to stir up insect larvae and small mollusks. Seeds round out its fare. This sandpiper sounds hoarse call notes on shore and takes wing with a soft *purwee* call. On migration *himantopus* usually flies over the Great Plains.

Range: N. E. Alaska to W. shore of Hudson Bay; winters in South America. *Characteristics:*

Long-billed dowitcher, length 11-12½"; Walter A. Weber National Geographic staff artist (also top)

long bill; rusty facial stripes, mottled grayish upperparts, barred white underparts, long greenish-yellow legs. Winter birds have gray upperparts, white eye stripe, underparts, and rump.

Semipalmated Sandpiper
Ereunetes pusillus

SPRINGING 30 FEET into the air on quivering wings, this little sandpiper utters a high-pitched trill that ends in sweet-flowing notes. It is mating season along the Arctic coast, and soon the four pale, brown-blotched eggs will rest in a tundra hollow or on a grassy dune.

At other times *pusillus* takes off with a *chip*. In fast, erratic flight it may give a sharp *churk*. In spring and late summer these abundant peeps flock along the East Coast. Scurrying before the waves on toes that are semipalmated, or partially webbed, they probe for insects and crustaceans.

A relative, the rufous-necked sandpiper (*Erolia ruficollis*) breeds in Siberia and western Alaska. In winter it resembles the semipalmated.

Range: N. W. Alaska to Baffin Island and N. Labrador, south to Hudson Bay; winters from the Gulf Coast and South Carolina to S. Brazil. *Characteristics:* very small size, short bill; blackish-and-buffy upperparts, speckled chest, white belly, black legs. Winter birds lack speckling.

Western Sandpiper
Ereunetes mauri

APPROPRIATELY NAMED, the western sandpiper breeds abundantly in northwestern Alaska and migrates up and down the Pacific coast.

This little rusty-and-gray peep begins nesting as soon as the tundra emerges from snow. Giving preliminary *tee* notes, *mauri* mounts to perhaps 20 feet, hovers and trills, and then—still trilling —glides down with wings held in a shallow V. Neighboring birds join in, rising and singing together as skylarks do on Scottish moors.

Flight songs end as pairs settle down to tend the four creamy, brown-blotched eggs and the chicks that arrive before mid-June. By the end of July all have abandoned their grass-lined depressions and are winging south—some by way of East and Gulf Coast beaches, where the migrants feed on tiny crustaceans and insects at low tide. Their flight call, *creep,* is more plaintive than the semipalmated sandpiper's, and shorter than the least's.

Range: coast of N. W. Alaska; winters from California, the Gulf Coast, and North Carolina to Peru and Venezuela. *Characteristics:* similar to the semipalmated sandpiper but slightly larger and rustier with coarser markings and longer bill. Winter birds are rusty only on shoulders.

Juvenile stilt

Stilt sandpiper
breeding plumage
length 7½-9"

Short-billed dowitchers
adults (in fall plumage, left;
breeding plumage, center) and
juvenile, length 10½-12"

Western sandpipers
adult in breeding plumage
and (left) juvenile, length 6-7"

Semipalmated
sandpipers
adult in breeding
plumage (right)
and juvenile, length 5½-6¾"

Allan Brooks

Buff-breasted sandpiper, length 7½-8¾"
G. Ronald Austing, Photo Researchers

Buff-breasted Sandpiper
Tryngites subruficollis

UNLIKE MOST shorebirds, this sandpiper tends to feed in dry fields. But it likes company and if its only companions flock to the usual wet meadow or marsh, the buffbreast will join the crowd. Migrating northward over the plains, these sociable sandpipers begin courtship. One will interrupt his search for insects to stretch to full height, cock his wings, often raising them until the tips almost touch, and utter a rapid ticking.

Market gunners nearly wiped out the species during its migrations, for the dense flocks would return again and again to their wounded members. These sandpipers were so fat they would ooze grease when shot. In the distant Arctic the buffbreasts line a depression in the tundra for their four pale buff eggs blotched with brown.

Range: N. Alaska to Melville, Bathurst, and King William Islands in Arctic Canada; winters in central Argentina. *Characteristics:* brown-and-buff upperparts, buff underparts, white wing linings, yellow legs.

Bar-tailed Godwit
Limosa lapponica

ABUNDANT in the Old World, this large shorebird also nests in northwestern Alaska. But it migrates along the Asian coast, so few Americans see the bar-tailed godwit. On downcurved wings *lapponica* speeds through the air, then glides to a landing on a mud flat or sandbar. Energetically it probes for insects, worms, or crustaceans, pausing to

Bar-tailed godwit
length 15-18"
Allan Brooks

raise its wings, then slowly fold them again.

Bartails lay four greenish or brownish eggs in a moss-lined cavity in a dry tundra ridge. Let an intruder approach and they rise and circle, shrilling *krick* and *ku-wew, ku-wew.*

Range: northwestern coast of Alaska; winters to S. E. Asia and Australasia. Also found in Europe and Africa. *Characteristics:* long, slightly upturned bill; brownish upperparts, reddish underparts and head, gray wing linings, whitish rump and barred tail; female is duller. Winter birds have grayish upperparts, white underparts.

Marbled Godwit
Limosa fedoa

LISTEN! This bird tells you who he is. *God-wit! god-wit!* he calls, accenting the last syllable.

He also makes himself known by the marbled pattern of black that weaves through his brownish plumage. And except for the long-billed curlew, he is the largest of our shorebirds.

Like the big curlew, the marbled godwit was hunted almost to extinction and has vanished from most of the Atlantic coast. You may see the godwit, however, on migration along California beaches and tidal flats, and around ponds and sloughs in the Mississippi Valley. Stalking about on long legs, it hunts insects, worms, mollusks, and crustaceans. If you try to get near, *fedoa* leaps into the air with shrill alarm notes.

In a grassy hollow on the northern plains the female lays four olive-buff, brown-blotched eggs.

Godwits are similar in habits to the curlews, whose bills inexplicably curve downward while the godwits' bills turn up.

Range: central Alberta to S. Saskatchewan and S. Manitoba, south to central Montana and W. Minnesota; winters from central California and South Carolina along the coasts to Guatemala. *Characteristics:* long, slightly upturned bill; mottled buff-brown upperparts, buff underparts, cinnamon wing linings.

Marbled godwit, length 16-20"; Karl W. Kenyon

Hudsonian godwit, length 14-16¾"; Walter A. Weber, courtesy National Park Service

Hudsonian Godwit
Limosa haemastica

RARELY SEEN, the handsome Hudsonian was long considered a rare bird. A generation ago men forecast its demise. But in its remote breeding haunts on the tundra, the species thrives.

Placed in a hollow, the four spotted, olive-buff eggs hatch in July. Southbound flocks migrate off the Atlantic coast. In spring they return over the Great Plains. Occasionally the Hudsonians utter a low *qua qua* or chatter *ta-it* in flight. They probe shorelines for small shellfish and explore grasslands for insects.

Range: N. W. Canada locally to W. shore of Hudson Bay; winters in S. South America. *Characteristics:* long, slightly upturned bill; dark brown upperparts, chestnut underparts, blackish wing linings, white rump, black tail. Winter birds have gray upperparts, whitish underparts.

Sanderling
Crocethia alba

FOR A STROLL along the beach, what a delightful companion the sanderling makes! It darts after the receding waves, snatching tiny mollusks and shrimps from the wet sand, and trots back as the next wave crashes ashore.

Sanderlings nest on arctic islands, migrate far into the southern hemisphere, and visit just about every beach in the world. They also frequent North America's inland waters. Their pale winter plumage, blending with the sand, ex-

plains the nickname "whitey." In their darker spring garb they court with curious snarling calls. The nest, set in a clump of vegetation on dry tundra, holds four brown-spotted olive eggs.

Range: N. W. Canada to N. Greenland, south to Southampton Island; winters along coasts from British Columbia and Massachusetts to S. South America. Found worldwide except Antarctica. *Characteristics:* mottled rusty upperparts, white underparts, black wings with white stripe; black legs. Winter birds are pale gray and white.

Sanderling, length 7-8¾"; William J. Bolte

By FREDERICK KENT TRUSLOW

SLEEK, SLIM WADERS # Stilts and Avocets
Family Recurvirostridae

T HIS IS THE STORY OF A BATTLE between a pair of small birds and an implacable enemy. It happened at the Bear River Migratory Bird Refuge – 100 square miles stretching over the marshy delta where the Bear River empties into Utah's Great Salt Lake. Glassy waters reflect the Promontory Mountains to the west and the abrupt crest of the Wasatch Range to the east (page 196). Here at this cross-roads of the flyways birds by the hundreds of thousands breed or rest, filling the air with a babel of sounds day and night.

For weeks I had been photographing wildlife in the marshes. I had watched squads of handsome avocets (*Recurvirostra americana*) pacing side by side through the deeper pools, cinnamon heads wagging sideways as they snatched small aquatic animals and insects from the ooze with their long, upturned bills. Startled by my movements, they would sometimes bark harsh alarm notes, flap into the air on strong, pointed wings, and swirl overhead in a gracefully maneuvering flock. These long-stemmed waders and the somewhat smaller stilts (*Himantopus mexicanus*) are the only North American members of the Recurvirostridae, a family that spreads its seven species throughout most of the temperate regions of the world.

One hot cloudless morning my stilt adventure began. A refuge biologist rolled up in a pickup truck, trailing a long streamer of dust. "Fred," he called, "I think I've found that black-necked stilt's nest you've been hoping to photograph."

Excited, I helped load a skiff into the truck and we took off down a gravel road that topped a six-foot dike along the water's edge. Half a mile later we pulled up. "Over there," he pointed, "in those bunches of grass beside that pool."

Two stilts were fidgeting about, their slender bodies held high on pink pipestem legs. Their bills jutted from their round heads like toothpicks from cherries. With my binoculars I finally spotted a nest partly hidden in a clump of grass nearby.

We launched the skiff and my companion drove off. Thirty yards of poling brought me to the expanse of muddy tussocks and inches-deep pools that surrounded the nest. The birds were feeding on aquatic insects and larvae a few yards away, seemingly unconcerned with my approach. I knew then that they had not yet hatched their four buffy eggs speckled with dark brown. Otherwise they would have tried to draw my attention away from the nest by stalking into the open, bending and straightening their long legs suddenly so that their bodies bobbed up and down, breasts slapping the water. Or they would have staged a broken-wing act.

I pitched my canvas blind 18 feet from the nest and ate my lunch. The flats stretched out before me as smooth as a billiard table, while along the dikes new hatches of insects rose and fell like billowing curtains. As I watched the stilts through a slit I noticed that the sky was clouding over. A strong west wind built up, blowing from the direction of the water-filled marshes.

Suddenly one of the stilts ran and looked into the grass where the nest lay. Its *pep-pep* calls rose in tone and volume to a startled *yip-yip-yip*. Only then did I realize that my feet were wet. I could well understand the bird's alarm.

Blown from the marshes, the water had been driven across the flats and now stood an inch and a half deep in my blind. What had been a nearly dry mud flat when I arrived was now a broad lake. Worse, wind and water were still rising.

BLACK-NECKED STILT *frantically builds up her nest with muddy leaves as rising waters threaten her speckled treasures. After the chicks hatch the parents often fly out to distract intruders a quarter mile or more away.*   345

Length 13½-15½", Frederick Kent Truslow

The two stilts studied their nest for a moment, then burst into frantic action. They rushed about within a circle ten feet around the nest, yanking up small sticks and leaves and strewing them about. After 15 minutes of this frenzied dashing they seemed satisfied with the amount of debris dislodged. The female ran to the nest and rolled the eggs to one side. Then, as her mate hustled the material to her, she began to build up the level of the nest's other half.

Fine grass and small stems had made up the original nest. Now big muddy leaves were crammed in, with just enough twigs to bind the wet mass. When the cleared side had been raised about an inch, the mother stilt hopped across and deftly rolled each egg up beside her with her bill. Then she started building up the lower half.

The male, running with unbelievably long strides, brought in the debris from the perimeter first. Gradually his circle shrank. When he had worked to within two feet

Length 16-20", Frederick Kent Truslow. Opposite: Thase Daniel

AMERICAN AVOCET *(opposite) often feeds in groups, marching shoulder to shoulder through the shallows, swinging upturned bills sideways like farmers scything hay. Bulleting into the sky (above), they wheel with drill-team precision. Like stilts, they build up their nests to keep the four spotted buffy eggs above water.*

of the nest, he changed his method. Planting his feet well apart, he reached away from the nest as far as his neck would stretch, picked up a leaf, and tossed it over his shoulder to his mate. Running time was thus cut. The frenzied building continued for 90 minutes, the birds just managing to keep the eggs above the rising water. I marveled at the efficiency and stamina of these frail-looking creatures.

Altogether four and a half inches were added to the height of the nest before the water stopped rising. When at last I came out of the blind, the nest top was still perilously close to the flood level. With good intentions I put three more inches into the pile. As I left, I was happy to see the female back on the nest.

Two days later, however, I saw that some predator had destroyed the eggs. Possibly the extra height I had added had made the nest too conspicuous—the birds had known when to stop building. Yet within a week my stilts, recognizable by a dark stain on the breast of one, had built again. This time the nest was on a little embankment, safe from the water. When I finally packed my cameras, the four youngsters were running about on long stilt legs, just like their parents.

Black-necked stilt—*Range:* S. Oregon and S. Idaho to S. Saskatchewan and the Gulf Coast of Texas and Louisiana, south to Peru; and from South Carolina south to N. Brazil. *Characteristics:* long bill, long pink legs; black upperparts, red eye, white face, eye spot, and underparts.

American avocet—*Range:* central Washington to S. Idaho, central Alberta, and S. Manitoba, south to S. California, N. Utah, and S. Texas; winters to Guatemala. *Characteristics:* long upturned bill, long gray legs; cinnamon-buff head, neck, and breast; white back and belly, black outer wing and diagonal stripe on inner wing; cinnamon fades to gray in winter.

HANDSOME FEMALES
AND HENPECKED MALES

The Phalaropes
Family Phalaropodidae

Suddenly the Arctic awakens. Rivers cast off their shrouds of ice. The tundra stirs with life. And answering the summons of the short northern spring, the dainty phalaropes return to their birthplace.

In their reddish nuptial plumage all three species of Phalaropodidae breed in the northern hemisphere. Some of the red and the northern phalaropes head for polar lands, others for islands and shores south of the Arctic Circle. The Wilson's phalarope nests mainly on the North American plains.

In a droll domestic comedy the domineering, brilliantly colored female chases the smaller, comparatively drab male—a reversal of the normal sexual roles. Though he flees her attentions, she usually captures him and he submits to his fate.

Nest building, incubating, and rearing the young the female leaves to her mate, one of the most henpecked birds in the avian

Allan D. Cruickshank, National Audubon Society

LEFT AT HOME *with the eggs, a male Wilson's phalarope in Utah takes up the yoke of incubation. Unmotherly types, female phalaropes normally abandon all domestic chores after laying their eggs and retire to little hen parties on the water. The migrating northern phalaropes (above), resting and feeding at the foot of Montana's Mission Range, float buoyantly and swim erratically, like all members of the family.*

world. Two lady bird watchers saw a pair of phalaropes (pronounced *fal*-uh-ropes) walking through a marsh in the Hebrides. They reported that the male was "apparently tired out, and whenever the hen stopped, as she frequently did, to preen herself or feed, he sat down where he was, and tucking his bill under his feathers, went to sleep. Before he had dozed for more than a minute, however, the female would peck him awake, and, calling querulously, force him to follow her."

In August, their plumage fading to wintry gray, the two polar-breeding phalaropes head back to sea. Migrating southward in the Atlantic and Pacific, the great swirling flocks wheel, twist, and turn like a drill team. En route, as many as 250,000 gather in the Bay of Fundy. The northern phalarope, wrote Roger Tory Peterson, flies to a "winter *Shangri-la* in the South Atlantic." So does the red phalarope. And in the Pacific both species find similarly mystifying winter sanctums.

Red Phalarope
Phalaropus fulicarius

FISHERMEN CALL red phalaropes "whale birds." As soon as these stocky little rovers see a whale blowing, they fly quickly to it and join it in feeding on crustaceans. They may even land on Leviathan's back to hunt parasites.

Red phalaropes also feast on tiny marine animals that live on floating masses of seaweed. On shore they devour gnats and kelp flies. The birds stab rapidly at the water with spikelike bills, gobbling victims one at a time. In shallows they may tip up to feed on the bottom.

Circumpolar breeders, red phalaropes migrate mainly to tundra near the coast. The resplendent female courts the smaller, paler male with aquatic and aerial ballets. She first tries swimming in tight circles near him. If that doesn't work she flies toward him, whipping the air with her wings and crying *clink, clink.* Bullying and cajoling, she pushes and pecks him until he joins her in a whirling dance on the water. Then she takes to the air and flies off to the mating place she has chosen, the captivated male at her side.

The male conceals the nest in marshy ground, scratching out a shallow hole, shaping it with his body, and lining it with grass. He usually does the incubating as well, although the female sometimes will spell him on the three or four olive-buff eggs spotted with brown.

As though reluctant to venture from the land of their birth, the young remain behind when the adults begin their early migration south. Last of the waders to leave the Arctic in the fall, these loitering juveniles rise from already ice-locked lakes and harbors.

For many months the red phalaropes will rarely touch land again. Like the northern phalaropes, they pass the winter months on the open sea in the southern hemisphere. Their dense breast feathers and undercoating of down are fully as waterproof as those of ducks.

During the long migration most remain far at sea. But some stray over land, often driven shoreward by storms. Audubon reported seeing *fulicarius* for the first time on the Ohio River near Louisville, Kentucky; he said he killed 17 of the birds with a single shot!

In fall both sexes lose their bright colors. Most people see the bird in its pale plumage, which gave it the nickname "gray phalarope."

Range: Arctic coasts from Alaska to Greenland; winters to S. Atlantic and S. Pacific. Also found in Europe and Asia. *Characteristics:* blackish head, white cheeks and wing stripe, striped brown back, reddish underparts, yellow legs. Male is duller than female and has brown streaks on head. Winter adults and young have blue-gray upperparts, white underparts.

Wilson's Phalarope
Steganopus tricolor

"DURING MY VARIOUS SEASONS spent on the western plains," reminisced ornithologist Arthur Cleveland Bent, "I have frequently seen these phalaropes flying about in trios, consisting of one male and two females, the male always in the lead, as if pursued."

The beautiful tricolored rivals, wings trembling and feet dangling, swell their necks during the chase and fill the air with nasal grunts. Finally the harried male accepts one as a mate, and the pair join other Wilson's phalaropes in a scattered breeding colony.

In a meadow near water or in tall grasses on the edge of a fresh-mown field, the male hides the nest so well that ornithologists usually find it only by stumbling upon it. The grass-lined depression, three or four inches in diameter, holds four dark-spotted buffy eggs. After the chicks hatch, the father continues to watch over them. Yet the female often stays nearby and, despite her unmaternal reputation, tries to protect the nest if danger threatens.

Unlike the other phalaropes, *tricolor* wades or walks far more than it swims. With feet less broadly lobed and longer neck, bill, and legs, the bird is better adapted for feeding in marshes, mud flats, and shallows than on the open ocean.

Wilson's phalarope follows the family trait of whirling on water—one was observed to spin 247 times in succession. This stirs up the bottom of shallow pools, bringing mosquito and midge larvae to the surface in the vortex so that the graceful little birds can pick them up without having to submerge their dainty heads.

But *tricolor* also dips its head like a spoonbill, swings its long thin bill from side to side, and pokes vehemently in the mud. And it feeds on insects around rain pools in pastures.

As soon as the young can fend for themselves the adult males join the flocks of females. In August all wing southward, mainly along both coasts of Mexico, to their winter quarters in southern South America. The Wilson's, named in honor of pioneer ornithologist Alexander Wilson, is the only one of the three phalaropes restricted to the New World. It lacks the white wing stripe of its relatives.

Range: British Columbia to N. E. Manitoba, S. Wisconsin, and S. Ontario, south to central California and central Kansas; winters in Chile and Argentina. *Characteristics:* long needlelike bill, pale crown, cinnamon neck stripe shading to black eye stripe; gray back, dark wings, white rump and underparts, black legs. Male is duller than female. Winter adults and young have gray upperparts paler than red phalarope's, white underparts, yellowish or greenish legs.

Red phalaropes
female (below) in breeding
plumage, length 7½-9"
juvenile (above) in winter plumage

Wilson's phalaropes
male (left) and female in
breeding plumage, length 8½-10";
juvenile (upper) in winter plumage

Northern phalaropes
male (above left) and
female in breeding plumage
length 6½-8"; juvenile at left

Allan Brooks

Northern Phalarope
Lobipes lobatus

FEEDING ON BRIT near the surface in the Bay of Fundy, a school of mackerel suddenly vanishes. Northern phalaropes, competing for the crustaceans, have scared the fish away.

Thus fishermen consider these thin-billed birds a mixed blessing. They help locate mackerel, but they also drive the fish below.

Smallest and most abundant in its lobe-toed family, *lobatus* flocks in large numbers off North America's Atlantic and Pacific coasts in spring. Ten thousand of the birds have been seen off Swampscott, Massachusetts.

Though its migratory pattern resembles the red phalarope's, this species appears more often on inland waters and frequently passes over the Great Plains. Despite its name, the northern nests somewhat farther south than the red.

In May the northern begins to arrive on the breeding grounds, winging in close formations just above the marshes and lakes. The female, in phalarope tradition, takes the initiative in courtship. Bowing her head, she glides to the side of a male on the water. If he turns away to peck at a mosquito larva or water bug, she follows him. If he flies to another pool, she tags along. Eventually he accepts her.

The male builds a grass-lined nest—a hollow in a marshy mound or tussock—for the four olive-buff, brown-spotted eggs. He also performs most if not all the incubation. The female, however, does remain close to the nest and warns him of danger by taking wing and uttering a low cry, *plip, plip*. And she helps rear the young.

Gentle and fearless, the northern phalarope sometimes allows itself to be picked out of the water. The birds have frequented a lake in the middle of Reykjavik, Iceland's capital.

Rufous neck patches give this bird the nickname "red-necked phalarope." But after the breeding season the colors fade and the northern could pass for the red phalarope in winter attire.

Range: N. Alaska to Greenland, south to S. Alaska and Labrador; winters at sea off Atlantic and Pacific coasts of South America. Also breeds in Eurasia, wintering in E. Atlantic, Indian, and W. Pacific Oceans. *Characteristics:* gray head, buff-striped gray back, reddish neck patches, white throat, wing stripe, and belly. Male is browner than female, has less red on neck.

ACROSS TRACKLESS SKIES
ON BEATING WINGS

The Mysteries of Migration

By GEORGE H. LOWERY, JR., and ROBERT J. NEWMAN

MYRIAD WINGS SPARKLE as snow geese,
viewed from a plane, rise in a
great white arrow from Malheur
refuge in Oregon, way station
on their spring migration
to arctic shores.

David B. Marshall
U. S. Fish and Wildlife Service

OUT OF NOWHERE! That's where the birds seemed to come from back in the days when we first began to study the small spring migrants that now and again deluge the Gulf Coast of the United States with startling suddenness. We would stroll a mile among the live oak and hackberry trees on a ridge and see scarcely a migrant. Then we would turn toward the beach to look for shorebirds. All at once storm clouds dulled the bright day. Thunder rumbled and rain pattered on the sand. The wind shifted, now rustling through the trees from the north.

We would hurry back to the woods. Migrants were everywhere! Whenever we raised binoculars to look twice at the same limb, we saw different birds – thrushes, warblers, orioles. Birds of a dozen species might perch on a fence as close together as swallows on a wire. Branches might flame with the red of tanagers, or tree after tree explode into bomb bursts of beating wings as yellow-billed and black-billed cuckoos flew out by the dozen. From roadsides blue with birds, buntings and grosbeaks sometimes swarmed into the air. And the glowing yellow of prothonotary warblers once ornamented bushes so richly that we seemed to be in a forest of Christmas trees decked with burning candles.

We knew that most of these birds wintered deep in the tropics and many nested to the north. The storm had interrupted their journey and forced them to seek shelter. A long-held belief was that such birds flew directly across the Gulf of Mexico. But at that time – the 1940's – some ornithologists strongly challenged the idea. They felt that migrants from South and Central America moved north exclusively overland through Mexico and Texas or island-hopped up the West Indies through Florida. According to one version of this theory, coastal pileups occurred when a cold front caught the birds inland and forced them southward to the coast.

How to settle the matter? We thought and thought. Once we even released eight male purple martins from an airliner over the middle of the Gulf to find out how long they would take to return to their nests in Baton Rouge. The answer might give us an idea of a timetable for trans-Gulf migrants. But a cold front moved in and when none of the birds showed up after a few days, one newspaper headlined the story: "WIVES OF MARTINS MOURN FOR HUBBIES LOST AT SEA." Three finally returned and all probably made it safely to land, but the experiment added little to our knowledge and we still wince at the thought of that headline.

Then one of us, Lowery, recalled reading as a boy an article by Frank M. Chapman that described how he had pointed a telescope at the moon and watched night migrants on the wing cross this illuminated disk. So one April night in 1948 Lowery positioned himself with a 20-power telescope at the end of a pier jutting out from the northern coast of the Yucatán peninsula. As the full moon rose, he kept his eye pressed to the ocular. Now and again silhouettes of birds flashed across the moon's face. Then around midnight scores of birds passed before his eyes.

Using a mathematical formula developed by a colleague at Louisiana State University, he determined that birds were departing at a rate of thousands per mile of shore, headed out across 500 miles of open water for the United States.

But a mystery remained. Assuming an average speed of 30 miles per hour, and considering that most could not rest on the water, these birds should reach Louisiana the next afternoon. Yet, except for the coastal pileups, we had seldom seen migrants arriving there. Chance provided an answer. Newman flew to an oil drilling rig 34 miles off the Louisiana coast to watch the moon. A cloudy sky gave him an unexpected rest. The next day he idly aimed his telescope at the sky. He tensed. For four and a half hours he scarcely took his eye from the ocular. Almost 1,000 birds flashed northward through the sliver of sky framed in his scope. Now we

Farrell Grehan, courtesy Massachusetts Audubon Society

EPTEMBER MORN *brings birds*
nd bird watchers to the
ational wildlife refuge on
Monomoy Island, a lonely spit
f sand jutting southward
ff the Massachusetts coast
rom the elbow of Cape Cod.
Here at summer's end birds
y the thousand pause to feed
nd rest during fall migration.
Here too come members of the
Massachusetts Audubon Society,
rmed with cameras, binoculars,
potting scopes, and checklists,
or a strenuous two-day outing.
They splash happily across
he tidal flats, observing
eabirds, ducks, geese, herons,
parrows—even golden plovers,
esting before their nonstop
cean flight all the way
o South America.

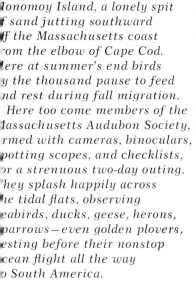

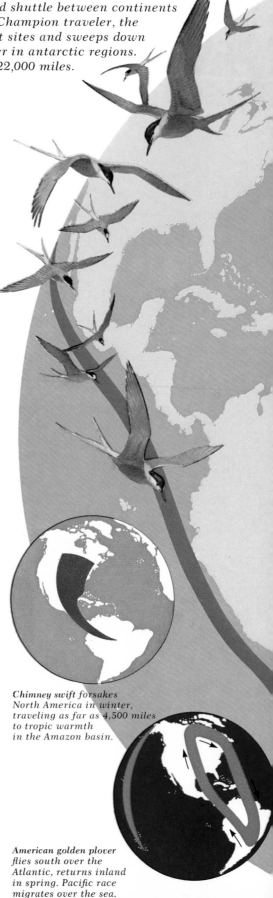

knew why the incoming migrants eluded us. They flew too high to be seen with the naked eye or ordinary binoculars. And they proceeded well inland before alighting, unless they met adverse weather. Then they frequently dived almost vertically to the ground. These discoveries heartened us. But we had thrown light on only a tiny part of the total mystery of migration.

Eᴀᴄʜ ʏᴇᴀʀ billions of birds make flights of hundreds or thousands of miles as they alternate between winter and breeding territories. Some species cover staggering distances. Arctic terns nest partly within the Arctic Circle and winter partly within the Antarctic Circle; some bobolinks wing from the prairies of Canada to the pampas of Argentina, more than 6,000 miles; millions of greater shearwaters roam most of the Atlantic before returning to tiny nesting islands in the remote Tristan da Cunha group.

Hundreds of experiments have demonstrated the amazing ability of birds to find their way back to the same breeding or winter territories year after year. One winter Dr. L. Richard Mewaldt of San Jose, California, captured and banded 400 white-crowned and golden-crowned sparrows in his backyard, daubed them red and blue, and air-expressed them 1,800 miles to us at Baton Rouge. There, far from their normal territories or migration paths, we set them free. Next winter 26 of the birds turned up again in Dr. Mewaldt's backyard—presumably after spending the summer in their usual breeding territories between Alaska and the State of Washington. A year later some of these same sparrows outdid themselves by finding their way back from Maryland.

Seabirds have set even more dramatic records. A Manx shearwater was taken from its nest on an island off the coast of Wales, flown to Boston, and released. In 12½ days the bird was back across the Atlantic in its burrow. A Laysan albatross, released 3,200

Chimney swift forsakes North America in winter, traveling as far as 4,500 miles to tropic warmth in the Amazon basin.

American golden plover flies south over the Atlantic, returns inland in spring. Pacific race migrates over the sea.

Arctic tern, nesting on Cape Cod, gets a leg band
*be*fore flying south. Recovery of banded birds
helps scientists map
migration "highways."

Greater shearwater circles
Atlantic, returning to breed
on Tristan da Cunha islets.

Slender-billed shearwater of the Australian
region rides winds clockwise round
the Pacific on its migration flights.

Pectoral sandpiper nests along
*Arct*ic shores, migrates in fall
as far south as Patagonia.

*National Geographic map
by Isaac Ortiz
Research by John D. Garst*

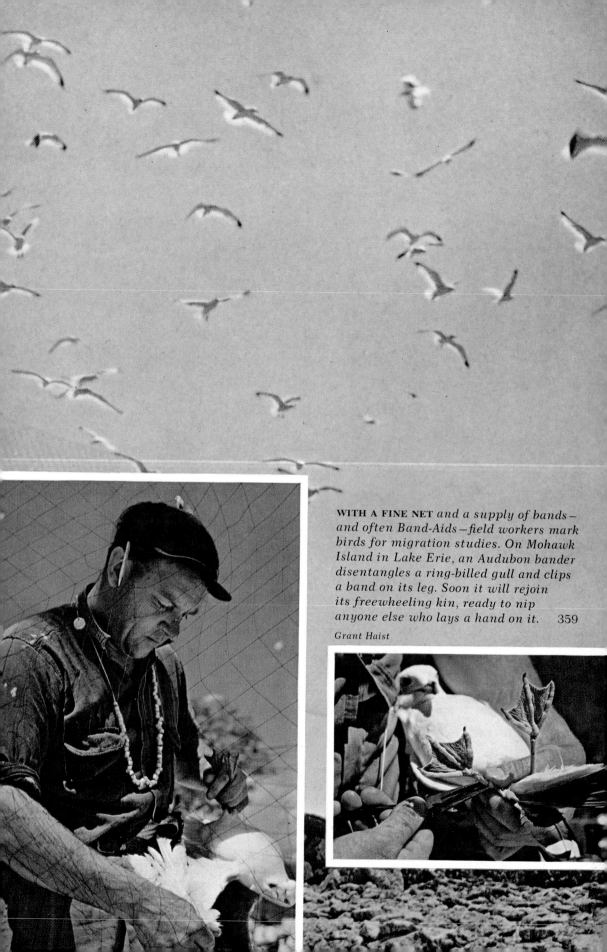

WITH A FINE NET *and a supply of bands — and often Band-Aids — field workers mark birds for migration studies. On Mohawk Island in Lake Erie, an Audubon bander disentangles a ring-billed gull and clips a band on its leg. Soon it will rejoin its freewheeling kin, ready to nip anyone else who lays a hand on it.* 359

Grant Haist

John Craighead (also opposite). Below: Robert F. Sisson and (left) George F. Mobley, National Geographic photographers

miles from its nest in the Midway Islands in the Pacific, returned home in 10 days!

Why do birds migrate? In spring and summer the temperate latitudes of North America offer a rich banquet of plant and insect food, longer days in which to gather it, and broad living space for migrants and their offspring. But many birds would starve or freeze in a northern winter; they must fly south.

We saw another reason for migration while making a bird survey in the Mexican state of San Luis Potosí. When we visited a nest the second time in the state's tropical areas, more often than not we found the eggs or young gone. The tropics swarm with predators. In temperate areas the drastic reduction of their food supply in winter holds their numbers in check. Clearly, some birds gain a greater measure of safety for their young by nesting in the north.

Some authorities say bird migration is as old as bird flight, others that it evolved independently many times. One theory is that the great glaciers which once covered much of North America forced resident birds south, and now each spring they return to their ancestral homes.

A SHOT *of red dye in Canada goose eggs marks goslings for a study of preflight journeys. To chart migrations scientists spray bright colors on grown birds or record numbers on leg bands, sized to fit all from tiny hummingbird to majestic eagle (bottom left).*

Each fall small land birds of more than 200 species pour southward from the United States and Canada. Half the species go no farther than Mexico and the West Indies, some 60 reach Central America, and at least 50 travel as far as South America. The resulting compression of populations in the tropics produces an ornithological time bomb whose fuse is set for the coming of spring.

How does the fuse work? Laboratory experiments have suggested that the lengthening days of late winter and spring stimulate endocrine glands in the brain of the bird. These glands feed hormones into the blood stream. Soon the body begins to store fat for use as fuel during migration, sex organs grow larger, and the bird seems to acquire a psychological readiness to move on. Caged birds at migration time show a great restlessness—*Zugunruhe*, German ornithologists call it.

The trouble with the day-length theory is that birds wintering in the southern hemisphere are experiencing decreasing day lengths in the period before migrating. One suggestion is that birds may respond to the *total* amount of daylight between phases of their annual cycle. But the sooty terns that migrate to Ascension Island in the South Atlantic to breed operate on an "annual" cycle of nine months. They can hardly be responding to regulation by light. Since birds possess their own internal "clocks," perhaps they need no external regulator like the sun. Most birds also sense favorable meteorological conditions: in spring the surge of tropical air northward, in fall polar air rolling southward.

Not all birds migrate north and south. One year as we worked on the lower slopes of a great massif in central Mexico, we were pleasantly surprised by the appearance

of birds that nest on the heights – black robins, spotted woodhewers, and shrike-vireos. When winter struck the summit, they simply moved down the mountainside. The rosy finches of our West are among other altitudinal migrants.

Many birds, such as most house sparrows, do not migrate. In northern regions of the United States where ruffed grouse reside, temperatures plunge from a summer high of more than 90° to 40° below zero in winter. On midwinter nights the grouse burrow into snowbanks to sleep; in daytime they emerge to feed. Song sparrows are partially migratory. Some remain in their breeding territory to face winter's blasts; others fly south to join resident song sparrows in warmer climates.

Unusually severe weather or periodic food shortages may alter normal migration habits, or cause some birds to migrate which might not have done so. One memorable day when snow powdered the Spanish moss around Baton Rouge, one of our colleagues collected a Lapland longspur. He rushed back excitedly with his prize,

but when he opened the refrigerator where we keep specimens, his face fell. There lay a whole row of Lapland longspurs. Everybody had collected one. These birds seldom visit us, but when they do they come by the thousands.

BANDING HAS revealed a great deal about migration routes. In past autumns we used to band chimney swifts — the last North American species whose wintering range remained unknown. We would trap them in the chimneys of large buildings in Baton Rouge where they thronged to roost, capturing as many as 7,000 in a night. We hoped that one would be recovered somewhere in winter, and we were thrilled when in 1944 Peruvian Indians turned in 13 chimney swift bands apparently acquired the previous year. The six points of origin represented virtually all major banders of swifts in the United States — except ourselves! Just how the Indians got hold of those 13 bands in the wilderness of the upper Amazon Basin we don't know, but they had solved a long-standing ornithological mystery.

Some 13 million birds have been banded in North America. For songbirds the rate of recovery is only a fraction of one percent. Hunting boosts the rate for game birds — mallards yield a 16.3 percent return. Some years ago analysis of banding data for ducks and geese led to the idea that North American migration follows four mighty flyways — the Atlantic, Mississippi, Central, and Pacific. Each covers a vast geo-

"BIRD!" *cries the student observer at the telescope as a tiny silhouette flashes across the face of the moon (opposite). An assistant records her estimates of the migrating heron's size, speed, and direction. The authors developed moonwatching techniques to measure migration at night, when most birds travel. Some, like the swallows above at right, migrate by day, feeding on the wing. Others, like the green heron at left and the geese at top, travel by day or night.*

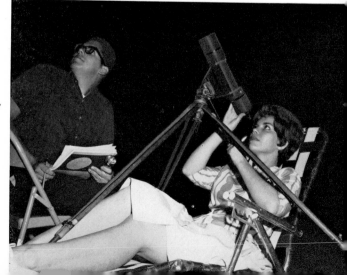

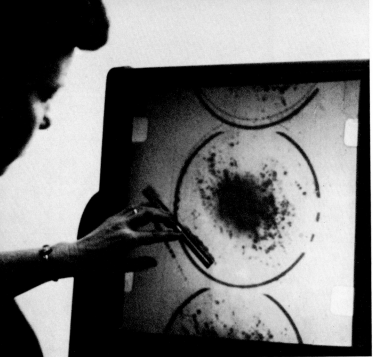

RADAR REVEALS *many secrets of night migration. With each sweep of the antenna the scope shows a fresh dot reflected by a flock. Measuring a two-minute "track" recorded on film, the technician at left learns the migrants' course and speed. Dark area in center represents the ground near the station. Altitude-measuring radar indicates that most migrants fly between 2,000 and 6,000 feet high, some shorebirds at 20,000 feet!*

Frank Belrose, Jr.

TINY TRANSMITTER *attached to a Canada goose by an antenna loop around its body (right) enables researchers to follow its travels over Illinois wintering grounds. A cartop receiver can pick up the signals five to ten miles away. Plastic nasal disks and green dye on neck and underparts permit quick visual identification.*

Parabolic reflector (below), so sensitive it can pick up normal conversation two miles away, reaches into the night sky to detect the flight calls of unseen migrants. Bales of straw shield it from ground noises. Tape recorder registers nightlong results. Analysis shows that flight calls can be heard throughout the night but often reach a peak in predawn hours. Birds may use the calls to keep in contact during darkness.

Illinois Natural History Survey

Wendell Crews, Southern Illinois University

graphic region with breeding and wintering areas connected by a complex route system. The Mississippi flyway as depicted on maps looks like a tree, the lower valley forming the trunk, the tributaries making up the branches.

Separate maps have been prepared to show specific routes of many individual species. Such route and flyway maps can be misleading. Migrating ducks and geese do congregate along waterways to rest. Soaring birds like hawks travel year after year along mountain ridges, where they take advantage of thermal updrafts; seabirds often follow coastlines. But continued study enlarges our knowledge of the myriad pathways of migrants. One year more than 1,000 moonwatchers joined us in a nationwide study of nocturnal migration. Analyzing the data, we discovered that birds were moving south in great numbers, not only along the traditional flyways but on broad fronts stretching from the Great Plains to the Atlantic seaboard.

The case of the Kirtland's warbler demonstrates the difficulties in mapping the routes of some migrants. This little bird has a tiny breeding range; no nest has ever been found more than 60 miles from the spot in central Michigan where the first was discovered in July, 1903. Each autumn the entire population of some 1,000 birds moves to the Bahamas for the winter. But despite an army of enthusiasts that scours the countryside, these warblers have completed their journey every fall for the past 50 years with few positively identified along the way. Apparently 1,000 birds form such a tiny fraction of the whole migration that most go unnoticed.

The bobolink within historic times has established nesting colonies as far west as Oregon. A lack of observations in the southwestern states has led to the belief that in fall these birds backtrack eastward before turning south along traditional migration routes. The elusiveness of the Kirtland's warbler suggests, however, that the western bobolinks may fly directly to South America without being seen.

B IRDS DO NOT ALWAYS FLY straight as an arrow from winter to summer territories. Some detour to avoid mountains, deserts, and bodies of water. Europe's white storks provide a classic example of route preference. Instead of flying directly across the Mediterranean to winter in Africa, they tend to skirt it. Some swing to the west to cross the Strait of Gibraltar; others veer east to come down through Turkey.

Like a swimmer in a strong current, a bird may be pushed off course by crosswinds. Such drift helps account for many puzzling features of migration: the straying of migrants from the Far West to the eastern United States and vice versa; the fall concentrations of migratory land birds along the Atlantic coast of North America during northwest winds; the appearance in the British Isles of migrants bound for the Continent.

Our studies indicate that birds adjust their flight plans to weather conditions. After a night when fall migration was heavy across the entire eastern half of the United States, winds in the Mississippi Valley swung round from north to south. Migration lessened in this area, while large concentrations were reported along the East Coast. Apparently the migrants in the valley simply sat out the night awaiting more favorable winds.

Radar today helps chart migrations. But years went by before anyone realized its possibilities. World War II radarmen saw mysterious spots on their scopes, knew they couldn't be aircraft, storms, or clouds, and simply dubbed them "ghosts" or "angels." Finally European investigators matched visual sightings against radar returns and confirmed that the mystery objects were indeed winged creatures, though not angels. Often a flock appeared on radar as a "doughnut," a bright ring dark in the middle. These proved to be starlings, swirling up from their roosts.

Radar records are still difficult to decode without visual correlation. Yet investigators in some areas have identified large, intense spots as goose flights; compact, fast-moving returns as plovers, sandpipers, and other shorebirds; and a scattering of tiny, weak specks as songbirds.

The Illinois Natural History Survey has provided much useful information by recording and analyzing calls from birds passing overhead in the night. The Survey gathers its data with a huge ear, a parabolic reflector that can record thrush calls from as high as 10,000 feet! At times we find an uncanny contrast between birds seen against the moon and birds heard—lunar silhouettes decrease during the very hours when the volume of flight calls is on the rise.

Diurnal, or daytime, migrants are mostly the larger birds or those that can feed on the wing. We see them often. Widely separated V's of geese go honking by. Blackbirds pass in dense recurrent clouds, now on one side of us, now on the other. Herons, in companies of five to fifty, beat their way slowly along a line of surf. Swallows in an unending stream course low along the levees.

B UT HOW DO BIRDS NAVIGATE? This is the question our beginning students most frequently ask us. It has mystified man for centuries. Many day migrants seem to follow landmarks; we see kingbirds flying high along the Mississippi, apparently following its course. But birds crossing the sea have no landmarks, and night migrants would be hard put to discern guideposts in the inky darkness below.

The German ornithologist Gustav Kramer demonstrated that birds can orient themselves by the sun. He built a cage with six windows, each revealing a patch of sky. In it he placed a starling during its period of migratory restlessness. The bird aligned itself in its normal migration direction. Kramer attached mirrors to the windows and reflected the sunlight into the cage from an angle of 90 degrees from its true direction. The starling shifted its direction approximately 90 degrees.

Kramer devised another test to demonstrate that birds can compensate for the daily movement of the sun. He trained a starling to select food from one of six feeders, the correct one placed so that the feeding bird would be almost facing the morning sun. For the critical test the cage and bird were moved several miles, the cage was rotated, and the experiment was run in the afternoon with the sun at the opposite end of the sky. The bird went to the correct feeder, although to do so it had to face *away* from the sun.

Another German experimenter, E. G. Franz Sauer, undertook to discover if birds could guide by the stars. Placing warblers in a cage exposed only to the night sky, he noted that many aligned themselves in their normal migratory direction. He took the birds to a planetarium and shifted the normal pattern of constellations. One bird was presented with an artificial sky that indicated it was in Siberia. The bird appeared disturbed, then headed westward, a course that would have taken it back toward cen-

E. G. Franz Sauer, University of Florida

Tricked by science, golden plovers reveal migration secrets

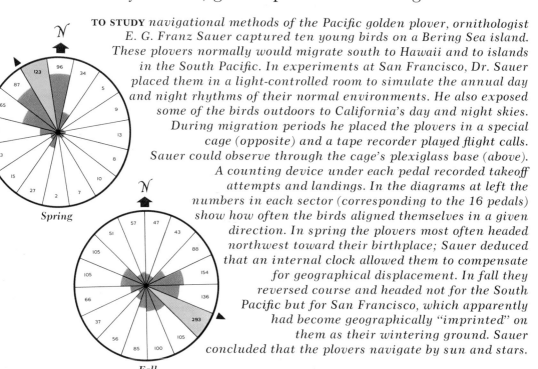

Spring

Fall

TO STUDY *navigational methods of the Pacific golden plover, ornithologist E. G. Franz Sauer captured ten young birds on a Bering Sea island. These plovers normally would migrate south to Hawaii and to islands in the South Pacific. In experiments at San Francisco, Dr. Sauer placed them in a light-controlled room to simulate the annual day and night rhythms of their normal environments. He also exposed some of the birds outdoors to California's day and night skies. During migration periods he placed the plovers in a special cage (opposite) and a tape recorder played flight calls. Sauer could observe through the cage's plexiglass base (above). A counting device under each pedal recorded takeoff attempts and landings. In the diagrams at left the numbers in each sector (corresponding to the 16 pedals) show how often the birds aligned themselves in a given direction. In spring the plovers most often headed northwest toward their birthplace; Sauer deduced that an internal clock allowed them to compensate for geographical displacement. In fall they reversed course and headed not for the South Pacific but for San Francisco, which apparently had become geographically "imprinted" on them as their wintering ground. Sauer concluded that the plovers navigate by sun and stars.*

In war and sport pigeons yearn for home

SINCE THE DAYS OF SOLOMON, men have domesticated pigeons, bred and trained them, and utilized their homing ability. Winged couriers sped news of Olympic victories to Greeks waiting anxiously at home. Pigeons helped Caesar conquer Gaul, and served Saracen against Crusader. The Sultan of Baghdad set up a pigeon post in 1150 to link his empire.

Parisians, besieged by the Prussian army in 1870-71, sent out crated pigeons by balloon. The birds flew back with more than a million messages. A single bird could carry 40,000 dispatches, reduced by microphotography.

In World War I thousands of combat pigeons darted above the trenches (below) with messages that sometimes turned defeat into victory. One, Cher Ami, won the Croix de Guerre for carrying the message that saved the American "Lost Battalion." Though badly wounded, the bird flew 25 miles in 25 minutes. Another war hero, The Mocker, earned a Distinguished Service Cross for delivering information that enabled American artillery to pinpoint and si-

lence enemy guns that had halted an advance.

In World War II an American pigeon, G.I. Joe, brought word in the nick of time to call off an Allied air strike on an Italian town that British infantry had just captured. The British, crediting him with saving 1,000 lives, awarded Joe the Dickin Medal, the pigeon's equivalent of a Victoria Cross, in a Tower of London ceremony (below). In 1957 the last U.S. Army pigeons were distributed to zoos and pigeon fanciers—ending a service that started in the Indian Wars of the 1870's.

In civilian life specially bred racing birds bring delight to sportsmen. Owners rendezvous with crated birds 100 or more miles from home. Doors swing open; a cloud of beating wings catches the sunrise (upper right). Hours later the birds begin to come in. Each pigeon wheels over a certain house and flutters down. A sealed timer box records its arrival in the loft. Officials tabulate time, airline distance, and speed in yards per minute and proclaim the winner at the clubhouse (right). As many as 5,000 birds compete, clocking from 30 to 70 miles an hour, depending on the wind.

What brings a homer back? Hunger, desire to return to its mate, an inherited gift of nature, centuries of breeding, and expert schooling. Daily the trainer takes a young bird to progressively more distant points and releases it, rewarding it with grain on its return. Second-year training becomes more strenuous until the bird can fly 1,000 miles. Top-notch homers, air-expressed 1,500 miles, can return to their lofts in just three days!

National Archives. Top: Bettmann Archive
Right: United Press International

Arthur E. Block

tral Europe. Sauer concluded that the warblers are born with a remarkable mechanism for orienting themselves: "a detailed image of the starry configuration of the sky coupled with a precise time sense which relates the heavenly canopy to the geography of the earth at every time and season." The skilled mariner would gladly swap his sextant, chronometer, astronomical tables, and chart for such an ability!

But often when overcast blots out sun and stars, birds are observed migrating along their normal routes. How do they navigate then? Some investigators have suggested that birds find their way by sensing the varying forces of gravity and magnetic attraction around the earth, or by reacting to the Coriolis force arising from the earth's rotation. But these theories remain uncertain.

Navigation and "homing," once considered separate functions, now generally are thought to be applications of the same faculty. How does a bird know its "home," or breeding territory, after an absence? There is growing evidence that after a bird learns to fly it spends late summer and early autumn wandering aimlessly. At a certain time in its life there comes a day or span of days when the bird is "imprinted" with its locality. To this locality the bird will return the following spring.

In some species parents may guide the young on their first fall migration. At Baton Rouge we see migrant geese fly over in family groups. Sometimes they get separated. One fall day a lone blue goose youngster dropped exhausted on our campus and stalled traffic along Dalrymple Drive. The young bird could not have had more than 15 hours of flying experience before departing Hudson Bay with its family on a nonstop flight to its Louisiana winter home. Yet it had almost made it.

Adult American golden plovers desert their young at migration time. Somehow the youngsters of the eastern population find their way 8,000 miles from above Hudson Bay deep into South America, where they join the adults. Experiments indicate that on their first flight to winter quarters some birds rely on an inherited tendency to fly an appropriate distance in an appropriate standard direction.

If a young migrant errs in its first fall jour-

369

ney, chances are it will repeat the error the following year. We see evidence of this in Louisiana, which of all states along the Mississippi most often receives strays from the Far West. Spotted towhees had never been reported here before 1950. Then in the autumn of 1952 some unusual occurrence, probably a quirk in the weather, shunted many of these westerners into this state. They wintered here for several years, apparently until the last of this "misguided generation" died.

Migrants face natural and man-made perils night and day. Night flyers sometimes collide with lighted structures—television towers, lighthouses, the Empire State Building, the Washington Monument. Casualties for one night at television towers have been estimated as high as 20,000 birds. Attraction toward light seems to be a common reaction. Caged migrants turn to face a falling star, the moon, city lights. One night in Baton Rouge flaming gas shot 150 feet into the air from an oil refinery stack. Soon the stack began to belch blazing chunks. These were small birds—a migratory wave was passing over. Hour after hour more and more birds circled the flame like moths drawn to a candle.

Ceilometers, powerful mercury-vapor lamps used by airports and weather stations to measure the height of clouds, are a serious hazard. Sometimes birds fly round and round in the beams as though trapped in a cage of light. Occasionally they seem to become confused or blinded; then they power-dive into the ground. One night some 50,000 birds were killed at a ceilometer in Georgia.

Though seldom observed, natural disasters take the greatest tolls. Birds migrating over water may tire or be driven off course by winds and fall into the sea. A fisheries biologist told us of slitting open sharks and finding songbirds inside. Birds often take refuge aboard ships. One night hailstones as large as hen's

NOVEMBER SUNSET *silhouettes Canada geese above their winter quarters at Blackwater refuge in Maryland. Heeding the urge of spring, the honkers will depart northward, re-enacting the age-old drama of migration.*

370

Albert Moldvay, National Geographic photographer

eggs bombarded migrants passing over Baton Rouge, leaving our campus littered with dead and dying birds. During spring migration in 1904 a blinding, wet snowstorm caught Lapland longspurs over Minnesota and Iowa; more than a million died. Some springs a late cold snap destroys food supplies and new arrivals starve. We estimate that only half the birds that migrate one season return the next. Yet the benefits of migration more than compensate for the loss.

If migration ceased, we humans would be losers too. No longer could we look forward to the bright harbingers of spring. No longer could we welcome in fall the arrival of ducks and geese, the array of sandpipers, plovers, swallows, warblers. Gone would be the anticipation of something new: a transient off its normal route, a straggler from the distant north. Bird migration lends flavor and color to all our lives, and its mysteries provide a continuing challenge to men of science.

Jaegers and Skuas

Family Stercorariidae

CROUCHED IN THE MIST, a weasel hungrily eyes two large olive-gray eggs in a hollow atop a cliff in the Shetland Islands. Suddenly a whirring shriek cuts the air, and down through the mist a brown bird plummets like a feathered bomb. There is a thud, wild screeching, a frantic flurry of feathers and fur – and in a moment the battle ends. Its back broken, the weasel feebly struggles to get away. The mighty skua stands over its victim, impassive as a bronze statue.

In defense of their nests skuas may be the most courageous of all birds. Even man, treading too close, is not safe from their hooked beaks, slashing claws, and knife-edged wings. One collector, attempting to gather eggs from a skua nest in the Kerguelen Islands in the Indian Ocean, had to take cover and fight back with pistol and stones, so fiercely did the parents attack.

In search of a meal these bold fighters and their kin the jaegers, which together comprise the family Stercorariidae, rank among the most rapacious of birds. Over the ocean they play the role of the hawk, falcon, and vulture. When skuas and jaegers fly near, no other bird can be sure of its dinner – whether in its beak or in its stomach. Let a tern seize a fish from the sea, let a gull gulp down a chunk of carrion, and immediately one of these freebooters wheels to the attack. Few birds can match such speed or agility on the wing. Under relentless harassment the tern eventually drops the fish, the gull finally regurgitates the morsel. And the pirate usually catches the booty before it hits the water.

These winged raiders will eat almost anything – garbage, carrion, the eggs and young of other birds, weak birds of any species, berries, insects, and small mammals. Skuas will crowd around a fisherman and boldly snatch bait from his hand. They are so voracious that they will even eat their own young. Should a hatchling wander too far from the nest to be recognized, it is quickly gobbled by the parent. Yet the same adult will defend to the death its chick in the nest.

Jaegers and skuas range all the world's coasts, particularly within the Arctic and Antarctic, where they breed. Skuas have been observed flying within 160 miles of the South Pole, closer than any other bird, and they show a remarkable homing instinct. One banded bird, carried by plane 850 miles from its nest on Ross Island, was released at the Pole, and though there were no landmarks within hundreds of miles and every direction was north, it found its way back to the nest!

Science knows little of the movements of jaegers and skuas in winter, when they roam the oceans. These birds spend more time at sea than their close relatives the gulls. In North America a few jaegers visit the Great Lakes.

Long, pointed, falconlike wings mark the three species of jaegers; wider wings with rounded tips distinguish the skua. All members of the family boast a flash of white in the wings. But only the jaegers have elongated central tail feathers and distinct color phases – a light one generally with black cap, grayish back, and whitish underparts, and a dark one uniformly sooty. Seen streaking through the distant sky like feathered lightning, these birds are difficult to tell apart. Even the expert often can make only a one-word notation in his record book: "jaegers."

SCOURGE *of the polar regions, skuas attack birds on the wing and plunder their nests. Here, in Antarctica, one swoops down on a penguin chick.*

Richard C. Penney

Pomarine jaeger, dark phase, length 20-23"
Helen Cruickshank, National Audubon Society

Pomarine Jaeger
Stercorarius pomarinus

IN AUGUST, when bluefish and mackerel run off the New England coast and frighten smaller fish to the surface, gulls and terns flock to feed. The pomarine, largest of jaegers, joins the feast, stealing the food from the other birds' mouths or forcing them to disgorge in flight.

The ocean-roving pomarine executes backflips and half-rolls, while vertically planed central tail feathers enable it to make quick turns. Rare is the tern that eludes its relentless pursuit.

On their Arctic breeding grounds pomarines feed on lemmings, eggs, small birds, and carrion. They nest in solitary pairs on cliffs or tundra, incubating two brown-spotted olive eggs on a ledge or in a ground hollow for three or four weeks.

Range: Arctic coasts of North America and Eurasia; winters to tropical seas. *Characteristics:* projecting central tail feathers are stubby and turned vertically. Dark phase is sooty throughout. Light phase has sooty cap and back, yellow sides of neck, white underparts. Young are barred dusky and buff, lack long tail.

Parasitic Jaeger
Stercorarius parasiticus

TERRORS OF THE TUNDRA, these sharp-tailed freebooters work in pairs or small groups, quartering their arctic breeding grounds in search of plunder. Parasitic jaegers eat the eggs and young of ducks and geese, prey on mice and lemmings, and bully seabirds into surrendering their food. They even join flocks of migrating Arctic terns to continue their piracy on long ocean journeys. Gluttons, they often swallow their meal whole and sometimes eat so much that they must disgorge to take to the air.

Wailing cries and shrieks erupt at dusk from their nesting colonies near the coast or inland around a lake. A depression on a hummock cradles the two olive eggs scrawled with brown.

Most common of the family, the parasitic jaeger is the one usually seen in fall migration along American coasts.

Range: Arctic coasts of North America south to S. Alaska and Labrador; also N. Eurasia. Winters offshore in Pacific from S. California to S. Chile and E. Australia, in Atlantic from Maine to Argentina and S. Africa. *Characteristics:* projecting central tail feathers are short and pointed. Light phase has black cap, yellow sides of neck, white nape and underparts, grayish upperparts. Dark phase is sooty throughout. Young are barred brown and buffy, lack long tail.

Long-tailed Jaeger
Stercorarius longicaudus

AS GRACEFUL AND BUOYANT in flight as a swallow-tailed kite, this small-bodied jaeger darts through the air with the speed of an arrow. Pointed wings and central tail feathers thrash as it flies, giving the bird an undulating motion. The tail feathers, three to ten inches long, also serve as a rudder as *longicaudus* chases wildly across the sky, sometimes in pursuit of another bird's dinner, sometimes simply in play.

In May longtails reach the northern breeding grounds, where males noisily vie for mates. A depression on a mossy knoll holds the two brown-splotched olive eggs, incubated by both parents. To draw off intruders the adult longtail, like other jaegers, feigns injury, thrashing on the ground and staggering away from the nest. Summering

Parasitic jaeger, light phase, length 16-21"; Arthur A. Allen

Long-tailed jaeger, length 20-23"; Adolph Murie

longtails devote little time to robbing seabirds. Instead they hunt insects and rodents and fatten on crowberries for the long fall migration.

Range: Arctic coasts of North America south to central British Columbia and N. Quebec; also N. Eurasia. Winters in Atlantic from latitude 40° N. to 50° S., in Pacific from 10° to 50° S. *Characteristics:* long, pointed central tail feathers. Light phase has black cap, yellow neck, grayish back and belly. Dark phase is extremely rare. Young have brownish upperparts, lack long tail.

Skua

Catharacta skua

A CHUNKY, clumsy-looking body belies the strength and aerial skill of this master pirate. With its short tail it looks like a gull, in contrast to the falconlike jaegers. But the skua flies with surprising speed and, armed with sharp talons and a stout hooked beak, fears no other seabird.

In its quest for food it will attack the great black-backed gull. And in defense of its young it knows no equal for ferocity. One nesting skua even tackled a golden eagle that ventured near.

On forays the skua, voicing a cry that sounds like its common name, sometimes seizes other birds by the wing, wrestles them down to the water, and pins them there until they give up their catch of fish. It also feeds on carrion, birds' eggs, and small seabirds.

Skuas breed as far south as Antarctica, as far north as Iceland. They incubate their two brownish-splotched olive-gray eggs in a scrape lined with grass or moss, often on a cliff near the sea. After nesting some birds migrate to the coasts of New England and the Pacific Northwest.

In southern seas the skua has earned the title "eagle of the Antarctic" for its boldness, but it has a bad reputation as a raider of penguin colo-nies. The British, who term all jaegers skuas, call this bird the "great skua."

Range: Iceland to islands off Scotland; and from S. Chile and islands in the southern oceans to Antarctica. Northern birds wander to Baffin Island, Massachusetts, the Sargasso Sea, and the Canaries; southern birds wander to British Columbia, Brazil, S. Africa, the S. Indian Ocean, and Japan. *Characteristics:* hooked bill, brownish body lightly streaked with cinnamon or buff; white wing patch, short blunt tail.

Skua, length 20-22"; Russ Kinne, Photo Researchers

By AUSTIN L. RAND

RAUCOUS COAST WATCHERS # Gulls and Terns
Family Laridae

I STILL THINK OF GULLS as "sea gulls," for I grew up in Nova Scotia on the edge of the sea where herring gulls followed the tide, patrolled the beaches, escorted ships in and out of port, and swarmed about homeward-bound fishing boats. The squealing, yelping, laughing medley of calls from a feeding flock of these long-winged gray-and-white birds recalls this coast to me as much as the sound of the lapping waves and the odors of mud flat, seaweed, and fish.

From a rocky point I often watched the gulls feed on mussels. The strong, tightly closed shells of these bivalves protect them against the gulls' bills but not against their ingenuity. A gull flies up with a mussel, drops it onto the rocks or hard sand, then swoops down to peck and pull the flesh from the cracked shell.

Though popularly known as "sea gulls," herring gulls do not venture far out to sea. When I first sailed for Europe I watched the escorting gulls drop away and turn back as the coast began to sink below the horizon. The days in mid-Atlantic were

enlivened only by the sight of an occasional kittiwake, which is a pelagic bird—a true sea gull. Not until we approached the English Channel did the coastal gulls, the herring and the black-backed, come out to join the ship.

Though few gulls visit the empty stretches of the ocean, many live far inland. One May when motoring to Yukon Territory, I stopped at Edmonton, in central Alberta. Overhead a dozen Bonaparte's gulls darted and swooped, veered and fluttered, catching insects as swallows do. These birds had the black heads of their breeding plumage and were on their way north. Two months later I overtook them in the little valleys of the Mackenzie Mountains. Here the gulls nested in the spruces. Their young, nearly able to fly, remained in the trees while the parents fed them, gathering insects on the wing and from the surface of willow-fringed lakes nearby.

The next summer I visited gull colonies on the prairies, where I was counting antelope for the Canadian Government. I found the prairie itself almost empty of birds, but each slough in a fold of the land held a veritable bird metropolis. Here ducks, grebes, and blackbirds swarmed. As I walked along the water's edge, marbled godwits, avocets, willets, killdeers, and black terns, anxious about their young, circled and scolded. Franklin's gulls nested in colonies of thousands in the reedy

FEEDING GULLS, *a childhood joy, brings seaside visitor and wild birds together in mutual trust amid the wash of sun-warmed wind and wave.*

Ringbills and a laughing gull (dark wing tips, flying at left) on Anna Maria Key at the mouth of Tampa Bay, Florida
Frank A. Muth, Photo Researchers

shallows, while ring-billed gulls occupied dry, bare islets. The ringbills were exploiting a new source of food: ground squirrels killed by traffic on nearby roads.

Though I have seen terns over many of the waters that gulls patrol, I remember most vividly those I have watched over tropical seas that gulls rarely frequent: around Australia's Great Barrier Reef, where dark-colored noddy terns fish; on Wake Island, where the noddies come in to their stick nests in the low trees; and along the Madagascar coast, where terns whiten the sandbars with their numbers.

Once, crossing a wide bay by dugout in northwest Madagascar, I watched the behavior of crested terns and frigatebirds. One tern found a school of fish and plunged into the water, rising quickly with its prey. From near and far others gathered to share the abundance. Frigatebirds, soaring high above, watching, now zoomed down—but not to catch fish themselves. A frigatebird would chase and harry a tern until it dropped its catch, then snap up the fish before it hit the water.

Gulls and terns form the family Laridae, which numbers about 80 to 85 species in the world. Some, like the herring and California gulls, are so similar that ornithologists still puzzle over where one species ends and the next begins. Sixteen of the gulls and 13 terns breed in North America north of Mexico. All these long-winged, web-footed species can fly great distances. Typically, adults wear white with a gray mantle, a plumage which may take the brownish young of the larger gulls several years to acquire. Only on their bills, eyelids, and feet do the Laridae flash bright colors—yellows and reds, sometimes tints of green.

The smallest tern is barely as large as a thrush; the largest gull is larger than any hawk. Their lengths range from 8½ to 32 inches. Generally the gulls are coarser and sturdier than the terns, with heavier bills, hooked at the tip, and square or rounded tails. They often alight to feed, and walk and swim freely. Terns, in contrast, are lighter and more delicate in build, with slender, pointed bills. With their pointed wings and forked tails they fly more gracefully than gulls. Terns ordinarily do not light on the water. They sit on shore or on floating objects, walk little, and feed either on the wing or by plunging into the water.

Though the Laridae occur from the Arctic to the Antarctic, gulls make their headquarters in the North Temperate and Arctic Zones, while most species of terns live in tropical waters. Gulls and terns nesting in the colder regions usually migrate in winter. The ivory gull, however, winters along cracks in the Arctic ice fields and

Herring gull, Grant Haist

WITH RAUCOUS CRIES *gulls patrol seacoast, lakeshore, and hinterland — perching on pilings in Lake Erie, riding salty air currents behind boats to steal bait from Maine lobstermen, swooping behind harrows in Maryland cornfields to snap up earthworms.*

scavenges behind the polar bear. Champion migrant is the Arctic tern, which nests as far north as Greenland and winters as far south as Antarctica, thus spending more of its life in daylight than any other bird.

At nesting time both sexes of the Laridae, alike in plumage, share domestic duties, tending the one to four eggs and feeding the downy young. Typically, the birds gather in colonies of scores, hundreds, even thousands. On islets off the coast from Virginia to Texas, royal terns scrape out close-spaced hollows in the sand that serve as nests. Walk among them and the screaming birds rise like a dense cloud. You must tread carefully to avoid stepping on the eggs.   379

Bates Littlehales, National Geographic photographer. Above left: Kosti Ruohomaa, Black Star

Herring Gull
Larus argentatus

RIDING AN UPDRAFT, a male herring gull glides away from the island gullery where his mate guards their nest. A small fish ripples the water below. The gull darts down, but the fish dodges his shallow dive. Airborne again, he sees another gull drop a mussel on a rock. He races in, but the other bird reaches the shattered morsel first.

With leisurely wingbeats the gull heads for a colony of cormorants. Though the big black birds sometimes suffer from nest-robbing "sea gulls," they often nest nearby in peace.

Alighting, the gull preens, locking together with his beak the tiny hooks on the filaments of his feathers. This helps to keep water out so the bird can float. Flocks often sleep on quiet water, floating high with wing tips cocked up.

As some of the cormorants brood, others flap in from their feeding grounds to take over the nesting chores. Alert now, the gull watches for a momentarily unguarded nest.

There's one! Darting in, he pecks open an egg and gulps the embryo. Seizing a hatchling, he gobbles it whole and beats away on long, slender wings, squawking a harsh *kakakaka* as its parents rush too late to its defense.

Moments later the plunderer drops to his own nest, a low heap of seaweed and trash surrounded by thousands like it. Weaker males, unable to win sites near the colony's hub, have to nest near the edges, where predators threaten and storms blow eggs and chicks into the sea. Even at the center this dominant male must defend his territory against other males and even against juveniles who gang up to cannibalize eggs and chicks. Not until their fourth year do these dusky young acquire adult plumage. Some live to 28 years.

While the female swells her neck menacingly and squawks at a claim-jumping neighbor, her mate walks to their fuzzy brown chick, first to hatch from a clutch of three brown-blotched olive eggs. The nestling pecks at a red spot on the parent's lower mandible. The adult responds by feeding the chick a bit of regurgitated food.

The intruding male steps into the pair's territory. Half opening his wings, the defending male

Herring gull, length 22½-26"; Allan D. Cruickshank, National Audubon Society

confronts him. The bluff fails, so he advances slowly, tearing up grass with his beak. His foe starts tearing grass too.

Most arguments over territory end here. But when the trespasser keeps inching forward, the defender seizes his bill and wrestles him to the ground. The loser flails free and flies off to scavenge along the beach or tread the mud in the tidal flats to force worms to the surface.

If a nestling weakens or strays, one of its own parents may eat it. For every five eggs, usually only one chick finally flies. When it does, at six weeks, the adults abandon it forever and go their separate ways, often roaming many miles from their summer haunts.

Returning next spring, the gulls parade about and chase each other through the air. The female walks around her mate, stretching her neck and cooing until he feeds her a regurgitated morsel. They all wing to the gullery in a great flock, where the males battle each other for territory.

Seldom venturing seaward beyond landfall, *argentatus* often shows up hundreds of miles inland to scavenge at garbage dumps, hunt worms behind plows, even nest in trees.

Range: Alaska to W. Greenland, south to S. British Columbia, N. Ohio, N. New York, and E. Virginia; winters to El Salvador. Also found in Europe, Asia, and Africa. *Characteristics:* white with red spot on beak, gray back, white-spotted black wing tips, pinkish legs and feet; head streaked with brown in winter. Immature birds are dusky grayish, becoming whiter with age.

Juvenile herring gull, William J. Bolte

Glaucous gull
length 26-32"
Allan Brooks

Glaucous Gull
Larus hyperboreus

THE STARTLED DOVEKIE speeds toward a rocky Greenland cliff, but the huge glaucous gull flies faster. The dovekie shrills but once as the gull seizes it in midair, carries it to a ledge, and swallows it whole. On the predator's breast is a blue stain from tundra berries feasted on earlier, between meals of lemmings.

Deferring only to the powerful skua and sometimes to the great black-backed gull, the "burgomaster" lords it over the other sea and shore birds, stealing fish and mollusks, preying on eggs and young, sometimes devouring the adults. One, shot by Arctic explorers, was carrying an auklet in its crop and another in its stomach.

In April *hyperboreus* returns to its arctic breeding grounds ahead of most other migrants. The vanguard subsists on dead fish and anything else it can scavenge along the shore until the sun unlocks the sea's icebound larder and brings the other coastal birds to nest. By then the glaucous gulls have claimed the highest nest sites on crags and cliffs, where they build basins of grass, seaweed, and moss. Guarded by her mate, the female incubates two or three grayish-brown eggs blotched with dark brown.

The ravenous chicks soon grow fat. Then, in some areas, the robber may become the robbed as Eskimos climb up the rocks or trek to nests on the tundra and help themselves to the tender squabs, while the parents dive and scream in protest.

Range: N. Alaska to N. Greenland, south to Hudson Bay and Labrador; winters to S. California, Great Lakes region, and New York. Also found in Europe and Asia. *Characteristics:* large size; white with red beak spot, pale gray back, and white-tipped wings. Immature birds are mottled buff-and-brown, lack beak spot.

Iceland gulls, length 23-26"; Arthur A. Allen

Glaucous-winged Gull
Larus glaucescens

ALARMED by an intruder, three downy young glaucous-winged gulls plunge off a rock, splash into the sea, and swim to safety. Behind, in a seaweed nest, lie fragments of their brown-spotted buffy eggshells. Ahead stretches a life of scavenging cannery refuse, fishing, robbing birds of catches, and shattering shellfish on rocks.

Soaring buoyantly on pale-tipped wings that span 4½ feet, *glaucescens* follows outbound ships but seldom ventures far inland. It is the common gull of the Pacific Northwest coast.

Range: Bering Sea islands and W. Alaska to N.W. Washington; winters to Japan and N.W. Mexico. *Characteristics:* white with pale gray mantle; whitish spots at wing tips, red spot on yellow beak. Young are mottled grayish brown.

Iceland Gull
Larus glaucoides

FROM EGG TO ADULT, the ghostly Iceland gull resembles a scaled-down version of the glaucous gull, whose boreal domain it shares. But it is less inclined to prey on other birds, feeding mainly on fish, carrion, and tundra berries.

Often the two species nest in the same mixed colony on the ledges of a cliff. Here the gentler Iceland gull yields the upper stories in the bird apartment to its predatory relative. The grass-and-seaweed nest sometimes rests on a ledge so narrow that *glaucoides* has to stand sideways, its small head, slender beak, and long wings giving the gull a curiously dovelike profile.

A subspecies, the Kumlien's gull of Canadian arctic islands, differs in its grayish wing tips.

Range: W. Greenland south to N. Quebec; winters to Great Lakes, Virginia, Iceland, and N. Europe. *Characteristics:* like glaucous gull but smaller and proportionately longer winged.

Glaucous-winged gull, length 24-27"; Karl W. Kenyon

Western Gull
Larus occidentalis

THE ONLY GULL to nest on the coasts of Oregon and California, *occidentalis* lays its two or three brown-spotted olive eggs in a seaweed nest near a colony of murres or cormorants. If these neighbors leave a nest unguarded, the dark-mantled gull devours eggs and chicks.

In winter this marine bird is joined on its fishing grounds by the glaucous-winged gull from the north and the California gull from inland. When fresh water is handy, the western drinks and bathes in it; when not, seawater will do.

Range: N. Washington to N.W. Mexico. *Characteristics:* white with red beak spot, slaty mantle, mostly blackish wing tips. Young are brownish.

Western gull, length 24-27"
L. R. Owen, National Audubon Society

Great black-backed gull, length 28-31"; Helen Cruickshank, National Audubon Society

Great Black-backed Gull
Larus marinus

ON DARK WINGS that span 5½ feet, this majestic gull rides the air currents with a grace and mastery that recall the bald eagle. But when the updrafts and buoying breezes die down, *marinus* must pump along with laborious strokes as it roams Atlantic coasts in search of food.

One of the larger North American gulls, the great blackback is both scavenger and predator. Along the beaches it pulls the meat from crab shells, drags dead fish into the shallows to wash or soften the dried flesh, picks at whale carcasses, and sometimes flaps offshore to catch fish near the surface. In summer it preys on the eggs and young of terns, eiders, and other birds, few of whom can do more than wheel and cry in protest. Often it hunts down crippled adults of these species. It also eats small mammals and even kills sickly ewes and lambs.

Benefiting from laws that protect gulls from gunners and eggers, the great black-backed gull is slowly extending its range northward and southward. The increase of refuse from coastal cities and the gradual warming of the North Atlantic climate probably help. But the bird's predations make it a problem.

On rocky islands offshore or in a lake, noisy "saddlebacks" build bulky basins of grass and seaweed for their three brown-spotted, buffy-olive eggs. Hatching in four weeks, the young fly when about eight weeks old. They acquire adult plumage in about four years.

Range: E. Labrador and W. Greenland south to New York; winters to Great Lakes and North Carolina. Also found in Europe. *Characteristics:* large size; white with blackish mantle. Young are dark brown with paler underparts.

Mew Gull
Larus canus

WHEELING IN FLOCKS, these small gulls repeat their name in shrill *meew* calls. The "shortbills" dive for fish more than do most gulls but are first to quit the sea when storms approach. They often range inland to feed behind plows or hunt insects near ponds. Nests for their three spotted buff eggs may be on islets in lakes or on cliffs.

Range: N. Alaska south to S. British Columbia and N. Saskatchewan; winters to S. California. Also found in Europe and Asia. *Characteristics:* like ringbill but smaller with unmarked bill.

Mew gull, length 16-18"; Charles J. Ott, Photo Researchers

ancestral Quebec nursery. The rest had vanished.

Had predators, a lack of small fish, or other natural threat forced the gulls into exile? Or had the birds finally caught on to the human nest robbing? No one knew for sure, but human encroachments had caused ringbills elsewhere to desert rocky islands and lonely beaches along the northeastern seaboard where they had nested since time unrecorded.

Audubon found the species so abundant that he called it "The Common American Gull." But early in this century ornithologist Arthur Cleveland Bent found not a single colony in the northeastern areas mentioned by Audubon. Inland, however, ringbill colonies are still common around lakes and sloughs.

In a nest of weeds and debris built on the ground or occasionally in a low tree, a pair incubates three eggs, which hatch in three weeks. Chicks in two color phases, grayish or buffy, may occur in the same nest. They venture from the nest a few days after hatching.

Swooping and wheeling, uttering their squeaky cries, the agile ringbills often seize insects on the wing. Singly or in flocks, they scavenge at garbage dumps, follow plow and trawler, pluck the fruits of cabbage palms, and sometimes dive on coots and mergansers to steal their catches of fish. They also catch their own, splashing in from a low hover but never immersing fully.

Along the beach they snatch small marine animals and bits of refuse from the breakers, sometimes plunging through waves like bathers.

On the East Coast in winter, ringbills often mingle with their look-alikes, the herring gulls. Bird watchers distinguish *delawarensis* by its smaller size, black-ringed beak, and yellow feet. West Coast gull spotters sort ringbills from their near-twins, the California gulls, by the same field marks.

Away from the breeding grounds, ringbills often seem bolder than herring gulls as they gobble handouts from human admirers. Yet the herring gulls stood their ground against eggers and gunners while the ringbills forsook many of their coastal gulleries.

Today, thanks to protective laws, the ringbills are increasing and a few breed once again on the seaboard. Among North American gulls, only the herring gull outnumbers them.

Range: central Washington to N. Saskatchewan, S. Ontario, and Newfoundland, south locally to N. E. California, S. Idaho, S. Colorado, N. E. South Dakota, N. Michigan, and N. New York; winters to S. Mexico. *Characteristics:* white with gray mantle, black-ringed yellow bill, yellowish feet, small white spots in black wing tips. Immature birds have brownish upperparts, whitish underparts, black band on tail.

Ring-billed gulls
Adult and (upper) immatures,
length 18-21"

Ring-billed Gull
Larus delawarensis

HERE, THEY SAID, was the "right way" to rob a colony of nesting birds. Each spring a flock of ring-billed gulls would nest on a small island in the Gulf of St. Lawrence. Egg hunters from the mainland would comb the colony and load their boats with buffy, brown-blotched delicacies. But they took only the first sets of eggs, allowing the gulls to lay again and raise their young in peace.

For many years ringbills by the hundreds seemed to thrive under this system of planned pilferage. Then in 1921 the eggers were surprised to find fewer than a dozen pairs nesting on this

California Gull
Larus californicus

IT IS 1848, year of the great "cricket" invasion, and day by day under the blazing Utah sun weary Mormon pioneers have been fighting the host of big black insects devouring their precious crops. A thousand miles from supplies, their struggling settlement near Great Salt Lake seems doomed.

Then, in the depths of gloom, recalled a pioneer, "I heard the voice of fowels flying overhead . . . and saw a flock of seven gulls. . . . They came faster and more of them until the heavens were darkened with them and they would eat crickets . . . . In the morning they came back again and continued that course until they had devoured the crickets."

Today two gilded California gulls surmount a monument to their kind in Salt Lake City, and *californicus* reigns as Utah's state bird.

More hungry than heroic, the providential gulls came from islands and marshes about Great Salt Lake where, now as then, the birds nest by the tens of thousands. With pelicans, herons, and cormorants as neighbors, these large gulls set up dense colonies and build basinlike nests of weeds and rubbish, often only two feet apart. The two or three eggs are pale olive spotted with dark brown. When an intruder approaches, the gulls swirl up in clouds and fill the air with a deafening clamor.

Like most gulls, the California eats almost anything. Grasshoppers, including the long-horned "Mormon crickets," bulk large in its summer diet. Farmers find this gull following the plow for grubs and worms, plucking cherries in the treetops, and seizing mice drowned out of their burrows in irrigated alfalfa fields. The birds flock to country schools for scraps from the children's lunches, and visit city garbage dumps.

As winter nears, *californicus* wings westward and joins other gulls along the Pacific coast, scavenging in the shallows and fishing in coastal waters until spring. Some winter instead on the larger lakes of the Southwest.

Range: N. W. Canada south to N. E. California, N. Utah, and central North Dakota; winters to Guatemala. *Characteristics:* like ring-billed gull but larger, with black-and-red spot on yellow bill, darker mantle, greenish legs. Young birds are mottled brown with black bill tip.

California gulls, length 20-23"; Bill Ratcliffe. Opposite: John Craighead

Black-headed Gull
Larus ridibundus

NINETY-NINE YEARS after California gulls saved the Mormon pioneers from a grasshopper invasion, this common Eurasian relative paralleled the feat. When caterpillars infested Perthshire's oak forests in 1947, black-headed gulls by the hundreds foraged deep into the Scottish woods, feasting on the pests and halting the plague.

Since its first sighting in North America—in the harbor at Newburyport, Massachusetts, in 1930—*ridibundus* has been reported as a rare but regular winter visitor in the Northeast. Its larger size, red bill, and whiter wings separate it from Bonaparte's gull, with which it often mingles. Also called brown-headed gulls, blackheads incubate two to four brown-marked olive-buff eggs in a grass-lined hollow.

Range: Europe and Asia; winters to Africa and along the North American coast from Labrador to New Jersey. *Characteristics:* red bill and feet, dark brown head, whitish neck and underparts, gray mantle, white wedge near black wing tips. Winter birds have duller bill and feet and a white head with dark patches.

Laughing Gull
Larus atricilla

HA-HA-HA-HAAH-HAAH-HAAH, cry the fluttering gulls. Or are they calling "half, half, half," as if demanding tribute from the pelicans diving below? Up comes one of the pelicans with a pouchful of fish. Instantly a laughing gull alights on the diver's head, thrusts its red beak down, and snaps up fish wriggling from the sides of the great scoop. Other gulls vie for scraps. To some observers the excited cries of the thieves sound like demoniac laughter trailing off in three drawn-out syllables.

With no pelicans to rob, the gulls wheel above the water and dip to catch small fry. Rarely do the birds immerse in their fishing.

Heavy rains draw these dark-hooded gulls inland in straggling squadrons to feed on worms brought to the surface of lawns and fields. Outbreaks of insect pests also bring the flocks to dine or gather cropfuls for their chicks, though the infested area may be miles from the nests.

Less of a scavenger than most gulls, *atricilla* picks at beached fish or forages in garbage dumps when other fare runs short. Terns often nest near its colonies, but the laughing gull usually lacks the aggressiveness to steal eggs from its smaller neighbors.

For breeding sites the gregarious laughing gulls choose sandy islands or weedy marshes. On warm days the nesters sometimes leave their two to four brown-spotted olive-buff eggs untended for long intervals. But chilly or rainy weather keeps them firmly aboard the nest or close by its edge, awaiting a turn at incubating. Chicks in southern regions usually hatch in a mere hollow in the sand. In northern areas hatchlings often emerge in a carefully woven cradle of beach grass and sticks built up several inches

Laughing gulls, length 15½-17"

Black-headed gull, length 14-15"; Arthur A. Allen

above the sand and roofed by a bush or the meshed blades of surrounding grass. Two tunnels lead through the grass in opposite directions, an arrangement that allows the parents to enter by one and leave by the other without having to ruffle their feathers in turning around.

Fledglings hide in the tall, thick grass when threatened, squatting quietly until touched. Then they scamper away, often nimbly enough to escape a human intruder. Some youngsters exercise on the beaches, running about or trying their wings in short flights from little rises.

As summer ends, laughing gulls quit their northern haunts and retire southward. Only a vague mottling and a dark spot behind the eye remain of the hood worn by adults in spring.

Before protective laws men shot laughing gulls for their feathers, depleting the vast colonies in the Northeast. In the southern part of its breeding range, *atricilla* is the only nesting gull.

Range: Atlantic and Gulf coastal areas from Nova Scotia to Venezuela and in the West Indies; in the west from S. California to N. W. Mexico. Winters to Peru and Brazil. *Characteristics:* dusky red bill and feet, black head and wing tips, white eye ring and rear wing edge, dark gray mantle, whitish neck and underparts. Winter birds have slaty bill and feet, white head with grayish markings. Young are mottled brownish with buffy chin, white rump, and blackish tail band.

Allan D. Cruickshank, National Audubon Society

Franklin's Gull
Larus pipixcan

A FEW HOURS out of its brown-scrawled buffy egg, a mottled brownish chick clambers to the edge of its reed-moored nest and tumbles into the Minnesota lake, home for hundreds of other Franklin's gulls. Its pink feet paddle to no avail as the breeze puffs it away from the nest. Bobbing through the shallows, it drifts into a strange nest, where a female broods her own three hatchlings. Instead of killing the chick as other gulls would do, she feeds it a disgorged dragonfly nymph and tucks it under her breast. A Franklin's gull may end the nesting season with as many as a dozen youngsters.

To retrieve a vagrant chick in open water, adults may even converge on it and in relays clutch the chick by the neck in their beaks and fling it toward the colony.

When winds and rising waters tear the floating cradles loose and jam them together, parents confuse both nests and chicks and squabbles break out. Normally Franklin's gulls, named for the 19th century English explorer Sir John Franklin, nest in harmony among themselves and with grebes, ducks, and other birds.

When autumn winds sweep the plains, the gulls flock south. With the spring thaw they return, seeking out the early plowman for the grubs and worms he unearths. In late summer the graceful flocks wheel in great eddying knots.

Range: S. Alberta to S. Manitoba, south to E. Oregon, N. W. Utah, S. Montana, and N. W. Iowa; winters along Texas and Louisiana coast and along Pacific coast from Guatemala to Chile. *Characteristics:* like laughing gull but has white spots in black tips of gray wings.

Franklin's gull, length 13½-15"; Frederick Kent Truslow

387

Bonaparte's gulls, length 12-14"; Hamilton Rice

Heermann's Gull
Larus heermanni

NAMED FOR THE 19TH CENTURY SURGEON and naturalist Adolphus Heermann, these striking gray-bellied gulls roam the Pacific coast when not breeding. They scavenge along the shore, fish, rob pelicans, and loaf.

In spring white-headed adults migrate north and south to nesting islands off western Mexico, leaving behind dark-headed offspring which have not yet reached breeding age.

As a colony forms, birds literally cover the ground, and whining calls fill the air day and night. Courting gulls dance about and tug each other's beaks. In closely spaced hollows pairs warm two or three brown-spotted grayish eggs.

Range: coast and islands of N.W. Mexico; winters along coast from Oregon to Guatemala. *Characteristics:* red bill, white head blending into dark gray mantle and ashy underparts; black band on tail. Immature birds have dark heads.

Bonaparte's Gull
Larus philadelphia

NEARLY ALL OF NORTH AMERICA sees Bonaparte's gulls at one season or another. From their northern nurseries these small native gulls drift southward in loose flocks in autumn, coursing down rivers and coasts and pausing to fish and scavenge. April's warmth draws them back before all the snow has gone. Handsome black-hooded adults arrive first, followed by hoodless juveniles led by one or two grown-ups.

A visit to their breeding grounds in a Canadian spruce forest brings screaming adults diving at your head, while others swirl and chatter protests as they defend the nesting colony.

You climb a spruce. Near the trunk 20 feet up you find a twig platform lined with weeds and moss. There, next to two brown-spotted buffy eggs, sits a downy yellowish chick. Clambering down, you retire to watch from a blind. Soon the parents settle to brood or wing away on ternlike strokes to nearby marshes and lakes. There they snatch flying insects or pick up larvae on the surface. Crying incessantly, they pluck insects from drifts of dead weeds on the shore.

This plump gull was named for Charles Lucien Bonaparte, eminent 19th century naturalist and nephew of Napoleon I.

Range: W. Alaska to N.W. Canada, south to central British Columbia and W. Ontario; winters to N.W. Mexico, the Gulf Coast, central Florida, and the West Indies. *Characteristics:* similar to Franklin's gull but smaller with black bill; white patch on upper surface covers most of area near black-edged wing tip. Immature birds have white head, black cheek spot, and narrow black band at tip of tail.

Heermann's gulls, length 18-21"
Roger Tory Peterson, Photo Researchers

Little gull
length 10½-11½"

Little Gull
Larus minutus

SMALLEST of its tribe, this Old World gull was known in North America only as a winter visitor until 1962. Then three nests, each holding three brownish eggs, were found in a Lake Ontario marsh. The bird feeds on fish and insects.

Range: S. Ontario; also Europe and Asia. Winters to S. Greenland and New Jersey. *Characteristics:* similar to Bonaparte's but with blackish wing linings, no black on wing tips. Immature birds have dark V on each wing.

Ivory Gull
Pagophila eburnea

SEEMING TO SUPPORT no body at all, two short black legs twinkle across the Arctic ice. But the body is there, pigeonlike and dainty, its pure white plumage blending with the snow.

The ivory gull lives farther north than most birds and has been seen near latitude 85°, only 350 miles from the Pole. It feeds on small marine animals, carrion,

Ivory gulls, adult (lower) juvenile length 15-17"
Allan Brooks

and offal, and follows Eskimo hunters for scraps of seal or bear. Nesting on mossy cliffs and rocks, the "ice partridge" tends two brown-marked olive eggs. In winter a few ivory gulls wander as far south as New Jersey.

Range: Arctic Canada and Eurasia. *Characteristics:* white with black feet. Immature birds have olive-gray spots, blackish bill.

Black-legged Kittiwake
Rissa tridactyla

SOME NEW ENGLANDERS say winter begins when the black-legged kittiwake arrives in mid-October, announcing itself with a shrill *kit-ti-wake*.

Most common far offshore, the "frost gull" swarms around fishing boats and follows ships out to sea for refuse. The swift, long-winged kittiwake seems to enjoy the howling autumn gales, dipping low into wave troughs and soaring high over the crests. Alone among the gulls it surface dives and swims underwater after fish. And when it tires, it settles on the waves, tucks its head under a wing, and sleeps.

Kittiwakes breed in vast colonies on northern sea cliffs. Each nest of seaweed and moss holds two spotted buffy or whitish eggs. The red-legged kittiwake (*Rissa brevirostris*) may share a cliff with the blackleg on Bering Sea islands.

Range: Alaska to Greenland, south in the east to Newfoundland; winters along coasts to Baja California, New Jersey, and Bermuda. Also found in Eurasia and Africa. *Characteristics:* similar to herring gull but much smaller with black feet, no white in wing tips. Immature birds have grayish nape and wing bands, black tail band.

Black-legged kittiwakes, length 16-18"; Frederick Kent Truslow. Top: Walter A. Weber, National Geographic staff artist

Ross' Gull

Rhodostethia rosea

VISIT Barrow in October when frigid gales rake this northernmost Alaskan village and look out beyond the ice forming along the shore. Against the leaden sky you may suddenly see thousands of Ross' gulls—pink-hued adults and white youngsters flying from boggy Siberian breeding grounds to winter on the polar seas. There, as wind and current shift the ice floes, these small, wedge-tailed gulls—named for James Clark Ross, the British Arctic explorer who discovered the species in 1823—pluck fry and plankton from patches of open water.

Winter over, they wing back to Siberia to hunt insects and build grassy nests. Each pair tends three brown-blotched olive eggs.

"Rosy gulls" move out over the Arctic Ocean in flocks as soon as the young can fly. En route a few may wander south of the Arctic Circle.

Range: N. Siberia; winter range uncertain, probably on open waters of the Arctic Ocean. *Characteristics:* pinkish with gray mantle, narrow black collar, wedge-shaped tail, red feet. Winter adults lack collar; young lack pink color.

Sabine's gull, length 13-14"; Arthur A. Allen

Sabine's Gull

Xema sabini

IN A THINLY LINED hollow on an Arctic island three sepia-spotted olive-buff eggs lie exposed while a pair of Sabine's gulls change the watch. A hungry glaucous gull soars in. From all over their loose colony Sabine's gulls rise to meet it with grating cries while their brownish chicks "freeze" or hide in the grass. The outnumbered pirate turns tail and flaps away. Ploverlike, the Sabine's gulls soon are running along tidal flats after sea animals and insects, or hovering over the water to snap up fish and plankton. Though they never dive, they look like terns as they flap without soaring, and their slightly forked tails add to the illusion. But their spread wings dispel it, boldly triangled with gray, white, and black.

In autumn Sabine's gulls—named for British Arctic explorer Edward Sabine—head down the coasts. Most "forktails" winter over cold currents off Peru, others in the Atlantic.

Range: locally in Arctic regions around the world; winters off Peru and in the Atlantic. *Characteristics:* dark gray head, paler mantle; gray, white, and black triangular wing patches; white underparts. Winter adults have whitish head. Young have grayish-brown upperparts.

390

Gull-billed tern, length 13-14½"

Gull-billed Tern
Gelochelidon nilotica

ITS HEAVY BLACK BEAK pointing straight down, a gull-billed tern hovers for a moment, sighting its prey. Suddenly it plunges, not into white-flecked waves in pursuit of a fish, but into waves of windblown grass after a spider or grasshopper. Rising heavily, it hawks over meadows and salt marshes to pick off flying insects. When winged prey is scarce, the gullbill scours the marsh edge for a frog, a lizard, even a mouse.

Sated, the tern skims away on steady wingbeats that carry it toward the sea. On a stretch of beach it drops down, rasping an insectlike *kay-ti-did* as it relieves its mate on the nest. Their stout bills and shallowly forked tails set them apart from other terns nesting nearby. A grass-lined scrape in the sand cradles the gullbills' three brown-spotted buffy eggs.

At times these terns hunt crabs along the beach and they may occasionally dive for fish, but in nesting season they prefer to forage inland around marshes. On the Middle Atlantic coast this cosmopolitan species once nested on the marshes in considerable numbers. Then in the 19th century men invaded the colonies, some to steal the eggs, others to gun down the nesters for milady's milliners. In many areas the "marsh terns" were nearly wiped out. With protection they have become more common.

Range: S. E. California to N. W. Mexico, and E. Texas to Florida and S. Maryland, south to Argentina; migratory in the north. Also found in Europe, Asia, Africa, and Australia. *Characteristics:* black gull-like bill, black cap and nape, pale gray mantle darker at wing tips; white underparts, slightly forked tail. Winter adults and young have whitish heads. Young have mottled buffy upperparts, brownish tail band.

Forster's Tern
Sterna forsteri

AT THE MARSH EDGE a medium-size black-capped tern stands preening in the spring sunshine. As the black-tipped orange bill passes over feather after feather, two nearby observers nod in agreement, "Common tern."

Common mistake. So alike are Forster's and common terns that not until the mid-19th century did ornithologists recognize *forsteri* as a distinct species. It was named for the 18th century naturalist Johann Reinhold Forster, who sailed round the world with Captain Cook.

Skilled tern watchers in summer note the outer edge of the forked tail, white in the Forster's, dark in the common. Forster's tern also has a harsher call. In winter *forsteri* sports black ear patches, the common a black half-collar.

A marsh nester, the Forster's tern hatches three brown-scrawled buffy eggs on a raft of floating plant debris. Sometimes as many as five pairs nest atop the same deserted muskrat house.

Range: S. Alberta to S. Manitoba, south to central California and S. Wisconsin; also S. Maryland and E. Virginia, and from N. E. Mexico to S. Louisiana; winters to Guatemala. *Characteristics:* black-tipped orange bill, black cap and nape, pale gray mantle with silvery wing tips, white underparts; forked tail. Young and winter adults have black ear patch on white head.

Forster's tern, length 14-16¼"
Allan D. Cruickshank, National Audubon Society

Common Tern
Sterna hirundo

ROUND AND ROUND the island ternery they go, a pair of common terns performing the "fish flight" that heralds their breeding season in May. One flies in silence, beak straight ahead; the other wings close behind, calling a slow *tee-arr* with a fish clamped in its down-pointing beak. In midair they pass the fish and exchange roles.

In graceful spirals the "sea swallows" land. Soon one darts off for another fish flight with a new partner. Now and then a third tern joins in.

Later, on the beach, the male parades for his chosen mate, tail cocked high, beak stretched skyward. He flies off, returns with a small fish, and struts while she begs with half-opened wings. They may pass the morsel back and forth before she finally gulps it. If she accepts offerings from two males, the suitors battle it out.

In a few weeks the islet is peppered with terns incubating their three brown-spotted olive-buff eggs in weed-lined hollows. Soon the young roam the colony, and parents make a chick-by-chick search to find and feed their own. Storm-driven tides may destroy thousands of eggs and young.

When fry roil the sea, *hirundo* flocks to dive for its staple fare. Fishermen know that a noisy mob of "mackerel gulls" means big fish below driving the small ones to the surface.

Range: N. W. Canada to Newfoundland, south to Montana, N. Ohio, central New York, and E. North Carolina; also on Texas coast and Dry Tortugas. Winters from Baja California and South Carolina to S. Chile. Also found in Europe, Asia, and Africa. *Characteristics:* like Forster's tern but has dark outer edge on outer tail feather. Winter birds have black on back of head.

Roseate Tern
Sterna dougallii

"THE GREYHOUND of its tribe," wrote ornithologist Arthur Cleveland Bent of this slender, buoyant tern. It whirls through aerial chases with effortless grace and dives swiftly for small fish.

You'll rarely notice the faint rosy tinge of breeding season that explains its name. But the roseate's calls—a ploverlike *chu-ick* and an alarmed *kraaak* that sounds like ripping cloth—easily distinguish it.

Both sexes incubate the two or three brown-dotted buffy eggs in a hollow either in the open or roofed by the weeds of a sandy islet.

Range: Nova Scotia locally to Virginia, also in the Dry Tortugas and the West Indies; winters to Brazil. Also found in Europe, Asia, and Africa. *Characteristics:* like common tern but with bill usually black, sometimes partly red, and longer tail with outer feathers entirely white.

Roseate tern, length 14-17"; Helen Cruickshank

Common tern, length 13-16"; Frederick Kent Truslow

Aleutian tern, length 15"; R. T. Wallen

Aleutian Tern
Sterna aleutica

DISCOVERED IN 1868 on Kodiak Island, this rare tern was not reported from its namesake islands until 1925. When a naturalist investigated the report, the breeding colony had disappeared. Finally in 1962 scientists came upon a small colony of Aleutian terns on Umnak Island. A member of that colony appears above.

In a tangle of grass and moss Aleutian terns lay two buffy eggs richly blotched with brown. These terns, whose *twee-e-e-e* call sounds like a shorebird note, winter in the western Pacific.

Range: scattered islands off W. and S. Alaska and E. Siberia; winters to Japan. *Characteristics:* like Arctic tern but darker gray with white forehead and black bill.

Arctic Tern
Sterna paradisaea

WORLD'S CHAMPION COMMUTER, the Arctic tern in the extremes of its range migrates from one polar region to the other. From Arctic nest sites where they spend the northern summer these terns stream south for a second summer near the Antarctic Circle. Some wing down the eastern Pacific past the Americas, some fly down the Atlantic past Europe and Africa (page 356). For a few the round trip may exceed 22,000 miles!

Alone or in colonies, pairs of Arctic terns nest in a scrape in sand or moss. The two or three eggs resemble those of common terns. Fearless around the nursery, Arctic terns scream and swoop at intruders. One pair struck naturalist Ira N. Gabrielson more than 20 times while he photographed their nest in Alaska.

Parents feed small fish and crustaceans to their chicks, who learn to swim and later become expert aeronauts. Soon the young feed themselves, diving after fish in typical tern fashion, shaking off the water with a shudder as they flap away. But, like many other seabirds, they often have to give up the catch to piratical jaegers.

Range: N. Alaska to N. Greenland, south to the Aleutians, Hudson Bay, and along the Atlantic coast to Massachusetts; also N. Eurasia. Winters in southern hemisphere to Antarctica. *Characteristics:* like common tern but has blood-red bill, grayer underparts, shorter legs.

Arctic tern, length 14-17"; Roger Tory Peterson, National Audubon Society

Sooty terns, length 15-17"; Frederick Kent Truslow

Sooty Tern
Sterna fuscata

WINGING THROUGH CLOUDS of birds, a sooty tern hovers over a tropic isle jam-packed with nests and drops toward its own two-foot-wide domain. But a gust spoils its aim and it plops a foot into a neighbor's claim. The neighbor leaps with a squawk from its lone brown-spotted creamy egg. The squabble spreads. Soon a dozen sooties peck, flap, and scream in an earsplitting rumpus.

An acre of nests—mere scrapes in the sand—may spawn hundreds of battles at a time. Multiply this by thousands of nests and you have the day-and-night bedlam of a colony of "wide-

awakes." Lacking waterproof plumage, these birds catch small fish and squid at the water's surface without submerging.

After nesting, sooties vanish abruptly. They have no known winter quarters on land and apparently remain at sea. It seems unlikely that they sleep on the ocean since their feathers would get waterlogged. Some scientists suggest that these birds may sleep on the wing.

A relative, the bridled tern (*Sterna anaethetus*), also breeds on warm islands and visits the Southeast coast. Its grayer back and light collar set it apart from the sooty.

Range: Dry Tortugas and tropic isles round the world; wanders at sea. *Characteristics:* white brow and underparts, black upperparts. Young are sooty brown with white-flecked back.

Least Tern
Sterna albifrons

THE LITTLE SEABIRDS swarm around and scold with a high-pitched *kreet* as you stroll a Cape Cod beach. Their size and their yellow beaks and legs mark them as least terns. Their anxiety tells you that nests are near.

Knowing that their clutches of two brown-sprinkled buffy eggs blend well with the sand, you tread carefully. Here and there an unlined hollow cradles two mottled buffy chicks. They lie so flat that they barely cast a shadow. Touch one and it scurries off with surprising speed. As you depart, the chick's mother marshals her

Royal terns, length 18-21"; Helen Cruickshank, National Audubon Society, and (lower) John H. Gerard

Least tern, length 8½-9½"; David G. Allen

Royal Tern
Thalasseus maximus

LIKE A SILVERY BLANKET, nesting royal terns cover the hot sand. The bustling ternery may hold as many as six incubating birds per square yard, each sitting on a pair of whitish eggs spotted with dark brown.

The colony seems charged with nervous excitement as birds come and go, often touching neighbors on landing and setting off squabbles. Sometimes, as if on signal, whole sections suddenly sweep into the sky at once with a great roar of wings. They fly around for a minute or two, excitedly screaming their harsh *kaak* calls, then settle on their nests. Like other terns they face the wind to take off, land, or rest.

On the Baja California coast and nearby islands royal terns nest in harmony among the smaller elegant terns (*Thalasseus elegans*). Both were known only as winter visitors along the California coast until 1959. In the spring of that year a small colony including both species was discovered at San Diego Bay.

Royal terns frequently fish in company with brown pelicans and now and then steal a morsel from the big-beaked birds. At times the thieving tern must surrender its booty to an attacking frigatebird. Usually *maximus* does its own fishing, diving straight down into the sea.

The second largest of our terns, the "big striker" escaped neither plume hunters nor eggers in their heyday. Law now restrains both, but tern colonies still suffer from thoughtless visitors who keep the birds in the air so long the sun addles their eggs. And storm-swept waves may wipe out a whole ternery. In 1947 high water inundated most of the 11,000 nests in one South Carolina colony.

Range: coastal areas from S. California to Baja California, E. Mexico to Louisiana, and Maryland to Georgia and the West Indies; winters to Argentina. Also found in Africa. *Characteristics:* large size; orange bill, black forehead (turns white early in breeding season), black crest and feet, pale gray mantle. Winter adults and young have white forehead.

brood and shades them with her wings. Offshore, her mate fishes with a squealing flock; from a hover the "little strikers" plunge to the water. Soon the male returns with food for the chicks.

Least terns often gather round a fallen member of a flock as if urging it to rise. Aware of this, gunners for the millinery trade bagged almost entire flocks by tossing up a white rag tied to a stick to simulate a fallen tern. The hunters and eggers nearly wiped out the species on the East Coast. Today, shielded by law, the least tern thrives on many Atlantic seaboard strands, outnumbering all other terns. Along inland rivers some wait until midsummer to nest on sandbars exposed after the floods of spring.

Range: along coasts from central California to Peru, and from Massachusetts to Brazil; inland along the Colorado, Red, Missouri, and Mississippi river systems. Migratory in north. Also found in Eurasia and Africa. *Characteristics:* small size; yellow bill and feet, white forehead and underparts, black cap and eye line, gray mantle. Winter birds have dark bill, whitish crown.

Sandwich terns, length 14-16"; Allan D. Cruickshank, National Audubon Society

Sandwich Tern
Thalasseus sandvicensis

SWIFT AND SKILLFUL, these noisy terns plummet into the sea for fry and shrimps. First described from a bird taken near Sandwich, England, the species is also known as Cabot's tern.

Sandwich terns lay two eggs – white, pink, or buff blotched with dark brown – on the bare sand of sea beaches. By the time the chicks hatch, some black-capped adults already have the white brow they wear all winter. Then they resemble the larger royal terns that often nest nearby.

Range: coasts of Texas, Louisiana, and the Carolinas; also in the Bahamas and islands off Yucatán; winters to Argentina. Also found in Europe, Africa, and Asia. *Characteristics:* yellow-tipped black bill, black forehead (turns white early in breeding season), black crest, pale gray mantle, white neck and underparts.

Caspian Tern
Hydroprogne caspia

LEAST SOCIABLE and largest of its clan in North America, the Caspian tern may breed alone or in colonies apart from other Laridae. On sandy or rocky islands pairs tend two or three spotted pinkish eggs in a weed-lined hollow. Some nest inland on floating weed beds, winging coastward in fall. Caspians dive for fish like other terns or ride the waves and feed like gulls.

Range: Great Slave Lake to central Manitoba, the Great Lakes, and Newfoundland, south in the west to central Baja California and Wyoming; also coasts of Virginia, South Carolina, Louisiana, and Texas; winters to S. Baja California and West Indies. Also found in Europe, Asia, Africa, and Australia. *Characteristics:* similar to royal tern but larger and has red bill. Winter birds have white-streaked cap.

Caspian tern, length 19-23"; Robert C. Hermes

Noddy terns, length 15"; Frederick Kent Truslow

Black tern, length 9-10"; David G. Allen

Black Tern
Chlidonias niger

WITH SHALLOW, irregular strokes of its gray wings, a black tern flies over a marshy pond. Hovering suddenly, it drops to the water and stabs in after a minnow, tadpole, or crayfish. But the prey darts away, so the bird wings to a nearby meadow. There it seizes a flitting dragonfly.

Morsel in bill, the small tern flies back to the reedy shallows where it is joined by another bird. The food carrier flies behind its partner in a pre-courtship rite like the "fish flight" performed by several other tern species. In courtship flight black terns fly high and fast, then sweep down to the marsh on set wings, the trailing bird hold-ing a constant distance as if on a towrope. In a shallow cup of reeds atop a muskrat house or low tussock, the female lays three olive-buff eggs blotched with dark browns.

When humans near the small, loose colony, the black terns flock out and shrill their metallic *keek* notes as they boldly dive and peck.

Range: E. British Columbia to New Brunswick, south to central California, Nebraska, and W. Kentucky; winters from Panama to Dutch Guiana and Chile. Also found in Europe, Asia, and Africa. *Characteristics:* small size; black with gray mantle, white under the short notched tail. Winter birds have white head and underparts; blackish on nape and side of breast.

Noddy Tern
Anoüs stolidus

WITH COURTLY POMP the noddy terns bow and scrape to one another throughout the breeding season. In the Dry Tortugas these fish eaters breed in spring and summer. On some equatorial islands they may nest at any time of year.

The only North American terns that nest above ground level, noddies often place their single speckled buffy egg on a bed of sticks and seaweed in a bush or low tree. Some pairs, however, build on the ground or on a beach rock. If you approach a nest, *stolidus* – the "stupid" tern – may stay put until you lift it. Like the sooty tern, which often shares its sandy islets, the noddy vanishes at sea after nesting.

Range: Dry Tortugas and warm islands over most of the world; wanders at sea. *Characteristics:* brown with white cap; rounded tail.

PLOWMAN
OF THE WATERS

♫ The Black Skimmer

Family Rynchopidae

EBBING FROM the salt marshes, the outgoing tide leaves sloping mud flats exposed to the early morning sun. Shrimp and small fish now must leave the shelter of flooded grass roots and venture into open water. Anticipating a feast, groups of black skimmers start tacking close above the shallows, their long, knife-edged lower bills cutting the water.

When one of these black-and-white fishermen touches prey, the shorter upper mandible clamps down to trap it and the bird's head jerks down under its breast. Then, dragging its bill from the water, the skimmer straightens out and swallows the morsel with an easy gulp in full flight.

Skimmers frequently feed in waters less than three inches deep. Occasionally the lower mandible strikes an obstacle, chipping the tip. The bird often furrows the sand near its nest, as well as the water, a trait that in Latin America earns it the name *rayador* – "one who draws lines."

During warm winter days large flocks of black skimmers rest quietly on sandbars, packed as tightly as sheep in a paddock. At dusk, when their quarry rises close to the surface, they scatter over coves and estuaries, sometimes to fish all night.

Three species of Rynchopidae, the only birds in the world with the lower mandible markedly longer than the upper, range the coastlines and rivers of Africa, Asia, and the New World. The American representative, and the largest, is the black skimmer (*Rynchops nigra*), which inhabits marsh channels, inlets, and river mouths as far north as New England. In eastern South America it also is found inland on the larger rivers. Caribbean hurricanes sometimes blow the birds north to Nova Scotia and Quebec.

Black skimmers nest in colonies, often choosing an expanse of shell-littered beach just above high-water mark on a sandy barrier island. An extra high tide can wash out an entire colony. Twisting and turning their plump breasts in the sand, the females fashion nest hollows in the open sun. The four or five eggs, white, buff, or pale blue and heavily spotted, blend with their surroundings. Male skimmers often stand dutifully beside their mates but take no part in incubation. After the eggs hatch, the parents carry fish to the brownish young, who soon roam the area in bands. When disturbed the nesters rise in a swirling, coordinated mass, their yelping cries recalling a pack of hounds hot on a scent.

Range: along coasts from Massachusetts to central Argentina, and from N. W. Mexico to S. Chile; winters from Gulf states and W. Mexico southward. *Characteristics:* red, scissorlike bill with lower mandible longer than upper; black upperparts, white underparts.

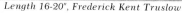
Length 16-20", Frederick Kent Truslow

ON SCIMITAR WINGS, *a black skimmer creases a canal in Florida's Everglades (left). This fishing bird repeatedly returned to furrow its own wake.*

A mother skimmer (above) broods two-hour-old chicks at Great Egg Harbor, New Jersey. When her web-footed young waddled away from the nest, the father, identical in plumage to his mate, kept an eye on them while she continued

to incubate the eggs that remained.

Showing paternal inexperience at first, this skimmer (upper right) persistently tried to feed his offspring a fish nearly the size of the chick. Finally the adult ate it himself, then went fishing for fry small enough to fit infant gullets.

In a blizzard of wings, skimmers cross a Florida inlet (below). Buoyant and graceful, the massed birds rise and wheel in unison.

UNDERWATER "FLYERS"

Auks, Murres, and Puffins

Family Alcidae

By PHILIP S. HUMPHREY

IT WAS A CHILLY GRAY DAWN in August when I slipped my canoe into the bay near Machias on the Maine coast and paddled out to look for birds. The wooded, rocky shoreline soon vanished in the swirling mist. As my canoe gently slap-slapped on the glass-calm water, I made my first acquaintance with the auk tribe—and with the game one can play with a guillemot.

I noticed my unwitting opponent—a compact black bird with pointed bill, short neck, and two large white patches on the back—resting on the water about 30 feet away. I no sooner got a close view in my binoculars than the guillemot splashed underwater with a flash of narrow wing tips and startlingly orange-red feet. As the circle of ripples widened I wondered where the bird would surface again. I waited endlessly, looking everywhere, half expecting it to appear directly behind me. Then I saw the prankster again, obscured by the mist, about 40 feet ahead of my canoe. At that moment the game began.

Cautiously Indian-paddling, I guided the canoe toward the guillemot. Twenty-five feet away the bird disappeared underwater again, apparently going off to my right if the little trail of bubbles meant anything. Hard paddling for 20 seconds sped me toward the spot where the guillemot was sure to emerge. I stopped. The bird popped to the surface barely ten feet from me and, with a harried look, was gone again. The first round was mine.

For the next half hour we maneuvered back and forth, I in the mist and the guillemot underwater. I got lots of exercise that morning, to say nothing of losing all sense of direction. I never again got as close as ten feet and finally lost touch with the bird altogether. Which way back to shore? I had no idea. So I tied up to a lobster buoy to wait for the morning sun to burn off the mist.

I had another memorable experience with alcids several years later at Monterey Bay, California. It was the end of December and huge flocks of Cassin's auklets were wintering a mile or so off-shore with marbled murrelets. As I approached in my skiff to observe them, the little gray auklets started up before me, sometimes by the scores. Some skittered and splashed along the wave tops as if uncertain whether it would be safer to escape in the air or underwater. Others submerged and I watched the in-

LOOKING LIKE DIPLOMATS *in formal attire, murres crowd atop a rock off the British coast. Incubating murres usually turn black backs to the sea. If disturbed, they face about as one, flashing myriad white shirtfronts. Bird protocol gives lower ledges to gray-and-white kittiwake gulls.* 401

credibly swift silvery forms plummet into the clear green depths.

Alcids actually do not swim underwater the way loons and grebes do; the feet are not used for propulsion. Instead their wings propel them in a kind of agile underwater flight.

I saw this remarkable method of locomotion demonstrated while Dr. Peter Stettenheim took slow-motion pictures of a pet murre in the aquarium at Tacoma, Washington. As we stood there in the cool dark interior of the room, looking into the brightly lighted, glass-fronted tank, we could see the white underside of the murre.

The bird floated on the surface, paddling its webbed feet. Then suddenly it sped underwater, weaving back and forth before our eyes — a gracefully undulating creature, trailing a stream of bubbles.

Several days later Peter projected his films. We could see clearly the murre's wing and foot movements as it dived. The bird plunged its head and breast in and with half-spread wings propelled itself downward, assisted by a backward flip of its feet. Below the surface the wings pumped

up and down and the murre "flew" through the water. The feet helped in steering.

All 22 species of the family Alcidae range in the northern hemisphere, 20 of them in North America. Three nest as far south as Baja California; one of these, Craveri's murrelet, only on islands in the Gulf of California. On the Atlantic coast only the common puffin, the black guillemot, and the razorbill breed as far south as Maine and no other alcid any farther. The truly great concentrations of this family occur in the Far North, especially in the Pacific Ocean and the Bering Sea area.

The auks, puffins, murres, and their allies are northern hemisphere counterparts of the penguins of the southern hemisphere. Penguins, like alcids, "fly" underwater. Both groups have dense, waterproof plumage and dive to considerable depths in search of food. Both stand nearly erect in crowded colonies. Differences? Certainly. Alcids can take to the air while penguins are flightless. Ancestry also distinguishes them. Alcids are related to gulls, terns, and shorebirds; penguins, to the great order of tube-nosed swimmers, including albatrosses, shearwaters, and petrels. In a fascinating case of evolutionary convergence, alcids and penguins have ended up with the same aquatic behavior from entirely different beginnings.

True mariners, alcids reach inland infrequently — usually only in the wake of an exceptionally violent winter storm. Only the marbled murrelet and Kittlitz's murrelet — until recently the mystery members of the family and still little known — nest away from the edge of the sea. As far as we know, both breed on rocky mountain

Robert C. Hermes. Opposite and below: Karl W. Kenyon

BIZARRE BILLS *and tufts mark the breeding season. The clownlike common puffin (above) rubs noses with his mate, wields his sturdy bill as a pickaxe to dig a burrow, snaps up fish, and sharply bites the hand that doesn't heed him. As summer wanes, the bright bill covering is shed; white cheeks turn gray; the eye loses its red rim.*

The horned puffin (left) can raise the fleshy papilla over its eye at will. The rhinoceros auklet (opposite, lower) sprouts a bill plate, while the tufted puffin (upper) sports nuptial plumes.

slopes, sometimes 2,000 feet or more above sea level. They appear to be solitary nesters, in contrast to most of their relatives, who pack together in hundreds of thousands on forbidding sea cliffs.

The murres and guillemots nest on open ledges. Others, such as the puffins and auklets, dig burrows. Some make do with crevices and sheltered spots under boulders. Though the guillemots lay two or even three pale eggs, most members of the auk tribe lay only one. Both sexes, identical in plumage, share the incubation, which takes up to five weeks. Hatchlings are charming little balls of down. The young of some species, such as the thick-billed murre and ancient murrelet, leave the nest a few days after hatching and swim out to sea with their parents. Others, like the Cassin's auklet, wait until almost fully grown before they leave the nest site.

403

Common Murre
Uria aalge

ALONG NORTHERN SEACOASTS common murres nest in dense throngs on cliffside ledges. Their summer chorus of hoarse moans and low murmuring calls, which perhaps inspired their name, can be heard for a mile or more.

Ornithologist Robert W. Storer suggests that crowding on the nest ledge may have forced the murre to develop its upright, penguinlike stance. And the sheer weight of numbers may have kept predatory birds in check, allowing the species to thrive with but one egg per season from each pair. Eggs range in color from white to buff, blue, and green, and are either plain or scrawled and blotched with gray, brown, and black.

When the murre takes off, head extended, feet trailing, and small wings flapping steadily and rapidly, the pear-shaped egg usually rolls in a tight circle instead of falling off the crag. But when a sudden disturbance flushes a nesting colony, a shower of eggs often results.

Nineteenth century eggers decimated the rookeries of this large, tame bird on both coasts of North America. In a six-year period more than three million murre eggs reportedly were sold in San Francisco for up to 20 cents a dozen.

Propelled underwater by its wings, the common murre hunts fish, crustaceans, and marine worms. In its rather long pointed bill *aalge* carries one fish at a time to the young. Unlike the razorbill, which holds several fish crosswise in its beak, the murre clamps its prey lengthwise, with only the tail hanging out.

Range: coastal areas from N. Japan to Bering Strait and central California, and from Nova Scotia to W. Greenland and N. Europe; winters offshore, in N. Atlantic to New Jersey. *Characteristics:* large size, long slim bill; blackish-brown upperparts, white underparts. Winter birds have white face and throat.

Common murre, length 16-17"; Robert I. Bowman

Thick-billed murres, length 17-19"; Karl W. Kenyon

Thick-billed Murre
Uria lomvia

AS SPRING BREAKS up the ice fields along the Arctic coasts, the thick-billed murre arrives in small flocks. Wings back-stroking rapidly and feet extended, it alights on sea cliffs. It may share a headland with the common murre, which it resembles, but usually breeds farther north. Eggs of the two species are indistinguishable.

The bleats and murmurs of the adults and the chirping of young thickbills fill the air as quarrels break out in the vast colonies. Youngsters flutter down to sea before they can fly, often with some nudging by their parents.

Thickbills dine mainly on fish and crustaceans and in turn are eaten by falcons nesting nearby.

Razorbills, length 16-18"; William J. Bolte

Also called Brünnich's murre, *lomvia* winters farther offshore than the common murre.

Range: N. Alaska to the Aleutian Islands, and from Ellesmere Island and N. Greenland to S. E. Quebec; winters offshore to British Columbia and South Carolina. Also found in N. Europe and Asia. *Characteristics:* like common murre but has a stouter bill with a pale line along the gape.

Razorbill
Alca torda

IN AND OUT of fog patches on the Gulf of St. Lawrence a razorbill swims, head retracted, tail cocked. Suddenly the blackish bird dives – for a fish, a shrimp, or a squid.

The razorbill can carry six or more fish crosswise in its bill. Even naturalists wonder how it keeps adding fish without losing those already caught. A cliff crevice holds the single bluish or greenish egg with dark scrawls and blotches.

Except for its swift flight, the penguinlike razorbill resembles in miniature the extinct great auk (page 194). That flightless seabird swam from northern nesting islands to winter havens off Florida and in the Mediterranean. Hunters slaughtered the helpless birds en masse for food, feathers, and fish bait. The last known pair was killed in 1844. Similarly persecuted, the razorbill survives in reduced numbers.

Range: along coasts from W. Greenland and E. Newfoundland to Maine; winters offshore to New York. Also found in Europe. *Characteristics:* large size, thick neck, deep, compressed bill with white vertical stripe; black upperparts, white underparts. Young have unmarked bill and more white about head and neck.

Dovekie
Plautus alle

WHEN WATERFALLS and gushing rivulets bring spring music to the Arctic, there comes a sudden chorus of chirrups, a roar of fluttering wings, and a swarm of chunky, quail-size birds beclouds the bright sky. The dovekies, smallest alcids on the Atlantic coast, have arrived to breed.

By the tens of thousands these black-and-white birds flock to cliffs and steep, rocky slopes. They build no nest; instead the single bluish-white egg of each pair lies in a crevice or tunnel among the boulders. The immense colonies hold their own despite the inroads of falcons and foxes, and of Eskimos who catch the dovekies with bird nets to lay in winter food supplies.

These hardy seafowl winter in rafts on the open ocean, feeding on minute marine life. Sometimes violent storms drive them far inland.

Range: along coasts from Ellesmere Island and Greenland to N. Russia; winters to waters off Southampton Island, New Jersey, the Canary Islands, and in the Baltic Sea. *Characteristics:* small size, stubby bill; black upperparts with white lines on wings, white underparts. Winter birds have white throat and sides of nape.

Black Guillemot
Cepphus grylle

AMONG THE VAST COLONIES of alcids that blanket the forbidding heights and shelves of sea crags you won't find many black guillemots. Less gregarious than its relatives, *grylle* prefers to breed in tunneled, rock-strewn cliff bases.

This dark "sea pigeon" places its pair of dull white, brown-blotched eggs under boulders or in talus on northeastern headlands and islands. Occasionally guillemots pick a wooded site. They leave the nest cavity bare or line it with bits of rock, shell, and grass. In some

areas the male incubates at night and the female during the day. When the downy black chicks appear, a parent delivers a beakful of squirming rock eels to them every hour from dawn to dusk.

Toward summer's end the guillemots move offshore, where they frolic and dive and twitter.

Range: along coasts from Melville Island to Greenland, south to James Bay and Maine; winters offshore to N. Alaska and Rhode Island. Also found in Eurasia. *Characteristics:* black with white shoulder patches, red feet. Winter adults have dark upperparts, white underparts. Young have white underparts with dusky markings.

Pigeon Guillemot
Cepphus columba

WINGING low and fast over water or standing in small groups on offshore rocks, this westerner hardly can be told apart from its Atlantic cousin, the black guillemot. Only the black wedges on the pigeon guillemot's white shoulder patch distinguish the two species. At a distance you'll probably miss these markings.

From rocky islands in the Bering Sea to the Farallons and the scenic Painted Cave on Santa

*Pigeon guillemots
in winter (adult, right
and juvenile) and breeding
plumages (lower), length 12-14"
Allan Brooks*

*Black guillemots
adult in breeding plumage
and (below) juvenile
length 12-14"*

*Dovekies
in breeding (left)
and winter plumages
length 7½-9"*

Cruz Island off California, *columba* uses a wide variety of nest sites: open ledges, grotto crannies, grassy ground. The female sometimes places her two eggs, colored like those of a black guillemot, in the abandoned burrow of a puffin or a rabbit, even beneath a railroad tie.

Unlike most alcids, pigeon guillemots feed mainly on bottom-dwelling marine life.

Range: coasts and islands from N. Japan and Siberia to S. Alaska and S. California; winters offshore south of the Aleutians. *Characteristics:* like black guillemot but has black markings on white shoulder patch.

Marbled Murrelet
Brachyramphus marmoratum

ALONG THE INSIDE PASSAGE off Canada's west coast chubby marbled murrelets skim swiftly over placid bays and channels, shrilling *meer, meer, meer.* Wings rowing rapidly, they hunt underwater for fish, crustaceans, and mollusks.

Where this shy bird lays its single egg—white marked with black and brown—is largely a mystery. Only three nests have been found, two in southeastern Alaska, one in Siberia. Unfledged young have been seen as far south as Oregon.

Range: S. Alaska perhaps to California. Also found in E. Asia. *Characteristics:* sooty-brown upperparts with rusty bars on back; white-and-sooty underparts. Winter birds have dusky upperparts, white neck band and underparts.

Kittlitz's murrelet in winter plumage length 9"

Marbled murrelets in winter (left) and breeding plumages length 9½-10"

Kittlitz's Murrelet
Brachyramphus brevirostre

THIS LITTLE-KNOWN NORTHERNER has a more restricted range than its relative, the marbled murrelet, perhaps because it prefers glacier-fed waters. Flocks of up to 500 Kittlitz's murrelets have been seen in Glacier Bay, Alaska.

Grayer than the marbled murrelet, *brevirostre* also has a shorter beak. It dives as quickly for crustaceans and other small marine animals. But when approached it flushes more wildly,

rocketing up from the water. Rarely has its nest been seen. Apparently it lays a single spotted buffy or olive egg on bare rock high in the mountains. Eskimos of St. Lawrence Island say the "fog bird" nests on misty slopes and cliffs.

In winter this species visits the waters of eastern Asia. Its name honors the 19th century German explorer, Baron Friedrich von Kittlitz.

Range: Alaskan coast south of Cape Prince of Wales. *Characteristics:* gray upperparts spotted and streaked with tan; white underparts spotted and streaked with black. Winter birds have white face and underparts and dark broken breastband.

Xántus' Murrelet
Endomychura hypoleuca

WHILE COLLECTING SPECIMENS for the Smithsonian Institution in 1859, Hungarian naturalist John Xántus de Vesey discovered this bird at the southern tip of Baja California.

Xántus' murrelet—and its close relative, Craveri's murrelet (*Endomychura craveri*)—dwell farther south than other members of the auk tribe. The Craveri's has a slightly longer bill and grayish rather than white wing linings. Both nest on islands, *craveri* in the Gulf of California and *hypoleuca* in the Pacific.

The two spotted bluish eggs of Xántus' murrelets lie in a shallow depression in a cave or pothole, or on the ground under thick vegetation. When changing shifts, after sunset and before dawn, incubating adults often chatter.

They feed at sea. Returning, these poor walkers crash clumsily to earth and scramble awkwardly to the nest.

Range: islands of S. California and N. W. Mexico; winters offshore.

Characteristics: small size; slim black bill, slaty upperparts, white underparts.

Xántus' murrelet, length 9½-10½", and downy chick

Cassin's auklet, length 8-9", and chick
Allan Brooks (also right)

Cassin's Auklet
Ptychoramphus aleutica

PROBABLY THE MOST ABUNDANT small alcid along the Pacific coast of North America, Cassin's auklet, named for 19th century ornithologist John Cassin, keeps out of sight around its breeding islands by day. Small wonder that scientists knew little of its nesting habits until recently.

In 1959 ornithologist Asa Thoresen was able to study these "night birds" without disturbing them in a lighted area around Coast Guard buildings on California's Farallon Islands.

Soon after the first December rains the nesters arrived and began refurbishing old burrows or digging new ones in the softened soil. Dirt flew in all directions as male and female took turns scratching at the earth with needle-sharp claws. Often they paused to bow to one another, exchange *kreek* notes, or fight with neighbors. The combatants stood face-to-face, then leaped to battle like fighting cocks.

Each pair dug night after night for two months or more until they completed a burrow up to four feet long. The single white egg hatched after five weeks. Then the parents began stuffing the dusky chick with small fish and shrimp. The arriving parent clicked its bill as a dinner signal. The chick's answering *chir* located it in the Stygian tunnel.

The fledgling's first flights often ended in a crash landing. Eventually it learned the swift, steady strokes of its parents, clocked by Thoresen at about 45 miles an hour.

Range: coastal islands from S. Alaska to Baja California; winters offshore mainly south of Puget Sound. *Characteristics:* small size; pointed black bill with light spot, dark gray upperparts and throat, white belly.

Ancient murrelet
length 9½-10½"

Ancient Murrelet
Synthliboramphus antiquum

DUSK BRINGS a startling change to tranquil islands off British Columbia. The air fills with murrelets whirring home after a day of foraging at sea. Thud follows thud as the dapper birds land, their white head streaks making them look "ancient."

Each scampers to a crevice or burrow to take a turn on the two eggs spotted with brown and gray and varying in ground color from white to cinnamon. A few days after hatching, the young leave home. Resting offshore, the parents chirp to trigger the midnight exodus. The chicks swarm down the hillsides and plunge into the surf. Then young and old swim out to sea.

Range: the Aleutians and Kodiak Island to N. W. Washington; winters to N. Baja California. Also found in E. Asia. *Characteristics:* pale bill, black head with white streaks at side, gray back, black throat, white underparts. Winter birds lack head streaks, black throat.

Parakeet auklet, length 10"; Karl W. Kenyon

Parakeet Auklet
Cyclorrhynchus psittacula

To LONELY, FOG-CLOAKED ISLANDS in the Bering Sea parakeet auklets return each spring, rolling from side to side as they fly. Often, like murres, they dangle their webbed feet to brake and steer.

These plumed birds don't travel far out to sea to feed. Naturalists once thought their peculiar upturned bill served to pry open shellfish or pick small animals out of rock crevices. But *psittacula*—little parrot—feeds in the manner of other auklets, diving for small crustaceans. The shape of its bill remains unexplained.

Perhaps the least gregarious member of its clan, this quail-size auklet strolls skillfully about rocky ledges alone or with a few companions. It may breed in a small colony but more often in solitary pairs scattered over long stretches of shoreline. On some islands parakeet auklets nest on sparsely vegetated slopes or, in company with horned puffins, near the tops of cliffs.

Nowhere do they provide much of a home. The single whitish egg is laid on bare rock in a cavity or crevice. Parents transport seafood for the young in a pouch under the tongue.

Though usually silent, these birds sometimes trill in a rising pitch: *chu-u-u-ee, chu-u-u-ee-ee*. They are the most migratory of the small auklets, most of which usually spend the winter in the southern part of their breeding range. Parakeet auklets begin leaving their nesting islands in August. By September they have disappeared. They ride out the cold months on the open ocean.

Range: capes and islands from N. E. Siberia to S. E. Alaska; winters offshore to Japan and central California. *Characteristics:* stubby upturned red bill, long white plumes behind white eye; black upperparts and throat, white belly. Winter birds have white throat, lack plumes.

Crested Auklet
Aethia cristatella

SHORTLY AFTER MID-MAY, hordes of dark birds wearing curly crests on their crowns swarm to breeding islands across the North Pacific. With loud honks or grunts, the crested auklets join tens of thousands of guillemots, puffins, and other auklets seeking nest sites.

Here *cristatella* finds sheltered crevices in the middle and lower levels of cliffs or among boulders along the beaches. The female places her single white egg on debris or naked rock. In the evening, when parents change places on the nest, vast numbers flock through the sky.

Normally, crested auklets fly close to the water, but on some days they rise high in swarms that blacken the sky. Parents off nest duty forage at sea, often many miles from the colony. They carry crustaceans to the nestling in a throat pouch like that of the parakeet auklet. Apparently crested auklets dive deep—their remains have been found in the stomachs of bottom-feeding codfish caught at a depth of 200 feet.

In a family notable for weird beaks, the crested auklet boasts a unique feature. Its orange bill gives off a pungent, citruslike odor. A large flock of these "sea quail" resting on the water exudes a scent so strong that you can smell it half a mile downwind. A soft semicircular growth at the corner of the mouth is shed in fall.

In September, when the young are on the wing, these auklets leave the nesting grounds. They winter well out at sea.

Range: coasts and islands from E. Siberia to S. Alaska; winters offshore to Japan. *Characteristics:* forward-curling blackish crest, orange bill, thin white plume behind eye; blackish upperparts, brownish-gray underparts. Winter birds have brown bill, shortened crest.

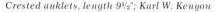

Crested auklets, length 9½"; Karl W. Kenyon

Least auklet, length 6"; Karl W. Kenyon

Least Auklet
Aethia pusilla

BERING SEA islands in June teem with millions of these starling-size birds, smallest of the alcids. On rapidly vibrating wings least auklets buzz through the air, their twitters and squeals sounding above the roar of pounding waves. To ornithologist Edward William Nelson in the 1880's the craggy skyline of Big Diomede Island resembled "a vast beehive, with the swarm of bees hovering about it."

Least auklets nest in bare, rocky crevices. While one bird incubates the single white egg the other feeds all day at sea, taking little leaps from the surface before diving after crustaceans. At dusk the feeder returns to relieve its mate. Soon the sky fills with off-duty auklets exercising their wings after a quiet day of incubation.

Range: coasts and islands from N. E. Siberia and N. W. Alaska south to the Aleutians; winters offshore to Japan. *Characteristics:* small size; black upperparts with white plumes on forehead and behind eye, and white shoulders; heavily mottled white-and-sooty underparts. Winter birds lack mottling and have shorter plumes.

Rhinoceros auklet length 14-15½" Allan Brooks

Whiskered auklet length 7"

Whiskered Auklet
Aethia pygmaea

DESPITE ITS SOMBER COAT the whiskered auklet in nuptial array ranks as one of the most attractive members of the family. Slender, dusky plumes curl rakishly over the bright red bill. And wispy white feathers sweep back from around the eye, giving the effect of grand, trailing eyebrows and mustachio.

Too bad *pygmaea* lives all its days on or near remote islands rimming the northwestern Pacific Ocean. Few ornithologists have seen it.

In a rocky crevice on a cliff or boulder-strewn shore whiskered auklets incubate a single white egg. They dine offshore on amphipods, snails, and crabs. They winter at sea but sometimes come to land, seeking shelter among the rocks. Young birds look much like young crested auklets.

Range: Kuril, Commander, and Aleutian Islands; winters offshore. *Characteristics:* curled dusky crest plumes, white plumes around eye; white-tipped red bill, blackish upperparts, grayish breast and belly. Winter birds have shorter plumes, brown bill. Young lack plumes.

Rhinoceros Auklet
Cerorhinca monocerata

FLYING fast and straight, the big, chunky birds flock in from the sea in early March and immediately begin staking claims to nest sites. Some rhinoceros auklets refurbish old burrows, others dig new ones. They work only at night and by the end of April their North Pacific breeding islands are riddled with tunnels.

Growls, barks, and shrieks fill the air as the energetic auklets scratch into steep slopes or among stands of spruce. They dig with beak and feet, throwing out loose dirt with backward kicks.

The odd little horn at the base of the beak which gives "rhino" auklets their name apparently neither helps nor hinders their labors. It seems to serve only for adornment during breeding.

Burrows may run 20 feet before widening into a nest chamber. There *monocerata* incubates its single lusterless white egg for three and a half weeks on a pad of grass, moss, spruce twigs, or fern. Bringing food to the nestling, a parent often carries a dozen or more smelt or sand launce in one trip. But the downy chick may have to wait through 18 hours of midsummer daylight between nightly feedings.

Range: islands from S. E. Alaska to N. Washington; winters offshore to Baja California. Also found in E. Asia. *Characteristics:* orange-brown bill with horn, white plumes behind eye and bill; blackish upperparts, gray throat and chest, white breast. Winter birds have brownish bill, lack horn. Young have dark bill, lack plumes.

Tufted Puffin
Lunda cirrhata

MEET THE MOST BIZARRE member of the Alcidae. With a bright red bill that seems too large for his white face, long yellow plumes that droop behind the head, and with red feet and dark body, the tufted puffin looks like a Halloween reveler who forgot to change his business suit.

If you meet this "sea parrot" around its nest you may get a far different impression. For Alexander Wetmore, searching the burrows on the grassy slopes of the Alaska Peninsula, it was a painful encounter. "Exploring these one by one with a long arm," Dr. Wetmore wrote, "I was finally rewarded by a savage bite that gashed my fingers, and with some difficulty I seized and dragged out a struggling tufted puffin."

Alaskan fishermen rage at the "old man of the sea" when it filches the bait off their hooks.

Normally silent, tufted puffins growl when captured. They burrow into turf to nest; when the turf is crowded some birds in the colony use rock crevices. Both adults incubate the single egg, plain white or lightly spotted. Later they feed the chick fish, mussels, and sea urchins.

Range: coasts and islands from N. Japan to N. W. Alaska and S. California; winters offshore. *Characteristics:* blackish with white face, large bill red at tip, yellowish at base, yellow plumes behind eye, red legs. Winter birds have dark face. lack plumes; young have dark bill.

Tufted puffin, length 14½-15½". Above: horned puffins, length 14½". Karl W. Kenyon, National Audubon Society

411

Horned Puffin
Fratercula corniculata
(Picture on preceding page)

FROM NUPTIAL CHAMBERS deep in the cliffs of the Pribilof Islands comes an endless chorus of harsh, querulous sounds. The horned puffins forever seem to be bickering.

But when they leave the burrows they show no sign of quarreling. You note an air of calm dignity as they stroll about their ledges on stiff toes. And you can't help but smile at those clownish faces with their brilliant beaks and the fleshy, movable "horn" above the eye.

Often one will plummet off the crag, then loop back up over the nest site, repeating the maneuver again and again.

Many of these puffins dig burrows with two entrances, one in the side of the cliff, the other at the top. Some nest in natural crevices among rocks at lower levels. The single whitish egg lies on bare ground or on a cushion of moss and feathers. When the chick emerges, the parents gather small fish in rapid underwater "flight" and return to the nest with the catch arrayed crosswise in the bill.

In many areas *corniculata* shares its breeding grounds with the tufted puffin, though it does not nest as far south. Horned puffins winter at sea in the vicinity of their nest sites, except in the northernmost areas where the waters freeze.

Range: coasts and islands from the Kurils to N. W. and S. E. Alaska; winters offshore to Oregon. *Characteristics:* large parrotlike bill, yellow at base, red at tip; fleshy papilla over eye; black upperparts and collar, white cheeks and belly, orange feet. Winter birds have gray cheeks and black bill base. Young lack red bill tip.

Common Puffin
Fratercula arctica

GENTLE SPRING BREEZES waft in from the ocean and a great raft of gay-beaked birds undulates in the bay. After eight months at sea a thousand common puffins have returned to their ancestral breeding island in the North Atlantic.

All pairing takes place in this offshore congregation. Rarely diving—they seem uninterested in food—the puffins paddle about like ducks. Several jerk back their heads, grotesque beaks pointing toward the sky. Couples bill each other, moving their heads and necks like doves. When a lone male tries to lure a mated female, her mate rushes up with flapping wings that churn the water into foam, and drives the tempter off.

Without a stiff wind these chunky birds must splash along for some distance to get airborne. Aloft they wheel on short, whirring wings with the precision of shorebirds; now you see the black

backs, now the white bellies. Moving ashore, they reconnoiter with droll gravity. In an upright stance they walk nimbly about on their toes. At times they settle on a rocky outcrop and stare for hours on end. Soon they begin to repair old burrows or dig new ones, sending up a shower of debris as they whack away with their strong beaks and scratch and kick with sharp claws. Often the entrance is concealed under a rock, and the tunnel follows a serpentine course.

On some islands foxes and other animals raid the burrows, and great black-backed gulls constantly harass the puffinries. Strangely, the puffins show more interest than alarm when the huge gull with its deadly bill walks among them. Such boldness often costs a puffin its life.

On Iceland and in the Faeroes man joins in the slaughter of the Atlantic puffin. Half a million birds are netted each year for food and feathers.

Though they incubate only one white egg, male and female each have two small brood spots on the sides of the lower breast. To incubate, the puffin must tuck the large egg partly under one wing and lean, rather than sit, upon it.

Reporting in *National Geographic* on his observations of a colony off Wales, ornithologist R. M. Lockley noted that the puffins hold to a definite daily schedule. Incubation, which lasts about a month, goes on from dawn to early afternoon. Then the sitters let the eggs cool for a few hours while they go outdoors to socialize.

Some perform mass "joy flights" about the island. Others bathe and preen. Frequently pairs nuzzle each other. But this draws a crowd and may provoke a fight. The male warns an intruder with a "threat" yawn. Then he lowers his head, bristles his neck feathers, and cocks his tail. Finally he opens his sharp beak and growls. Curious bystanders, however, crowd in and squelch the squabble.

Feeding themselves, the puffins swallow their seafood while cruising underwater. The first sign of hatching time comes with the appearance of fish in the adults' beaks. Lockley estimated that one chick ate nearly its own weight every 24 hours and consumed some 2,000 small fish during its sojourn in the burrow.

On a July night, deserted by its parents, the chick walks without hesitation over the side of the cliff. Gradually it works its way out to the open sea where, far from the sight of land, it learns for itself the art of fishing and flying.

Range: coasts and islands from N. W. Greenland to Maine; winters offshore from ice line south to Massachusetts. Also found in Europe. *Characteristics:* large bill with slaty base, red tip, and yellow trimming; black upperparts and collar, grayish face, white underparts, orange feet. Winter birds have darker face, smaller beak with brownish base. Young birds have dark beak.

LIKE DROOPING WHISKERS, *Atlantic needlefish hang from the gaudy beak of a common puffin. This expert angler caught them off the Maine coast and lined them up neatly for delivery to a hungry chick.*
Length 11½-13". Frederick Kent Truslow

Pigeons and Doves

Family Columbidae

A LOW, DOLEFUL CALL throbs across the ripening fields: *coo-coo, coo, coo*. It sounds far off, faint yet clear, evoking a mood of loneliness and reverie in the summer dawn. You cross the field, heading for the sound. Suddenly the mournful cooing gives way to low whistling sounds – the rush of air through beating wings as pairs of plump, gray-brown birds flash up from the ground.

No need to look twice. These are mourning doves, widespread, friendly, the most familiar of the native North American pigeons and doves. Their better known city cousin, the domestic or street pigeon (*Columba livia*), is one of three immigrants from the Old World. All subsist mainly on seed and grain, as do most others in the Columbidae, a family of nearly 300 species spread through the earth's temperate and tropical regions. Diverse in size and color, the family includes the fruit pigeons, radiant arboreal birds concentrated in the Indo-Malayan region, and the spectacular crowned pigeons of New Guinea, which grow up to 33 inches long and sport showy, filmy crests. The names "pigeon" and "dove" are used interchangeably without clear distinction throughout the family.

Pigeons and their relatives in the Old World sandgrouse family share the unique ability to drink water like a horse, with head down and bill immersed. Other birds must raise their heads to swallow. When walking, pigeons seem to nod their heads in time with their mincing gait. Actually the head moves out before each step, then remains fixed while the body catches up. This allows the pigeon a moment of steady vision, clearer than when the head is moving.

After a courtship marked by much billing and cooing, both adults, wearing almost identical markings on their firm, dense plumage, join in building a simple stick nest. As they incubate the white or buff eggs – usually two – their crop lining thickens. By the time the young hatch, the lining casts off a curdy secretion. This "pigeon's milk" provides nourishment for the hatchlings.

STREAKING SKYWARD *like a flight of arrows shot at random, mourning doves flush in all directions. Unlike most birds, which lift the head to swallow, a thirsty dove (opposite) drinks bill down.*

Walter A. Weber, National Geographic staff artist

Through the ages pigeons have served man in a variety of ways. With their phenomenal homing ability these winged couriers sped vital dispatches for armies ancient and modern (page 368). Men have hunted and raised them for food, and have fancied them as pets and for racing.

Descended from the rock dove of Europe and Asia and domesticated at least 5,000 years ago, the street pigeon dwells in cities the world over. To many people this gamin is a delightful companion of parks and sidewalks. Others condemn it as a pesky litterbug. Harried city officials have tried trapping, poisons, even birth control drugs to check its numbers.

Millions of passenger pigeons once ranged the United States. Men slaughtered them and cleared the forests where they bred, and so wiped them from the earth (page 192). But the smaller, similar mourning dove lives on, favored as a game bird in the South, protected as a songbird in the North, welcomed by birders everywhere.

Arthur A. Allen

White-winged Dove
Zenaida asiatica

BEFORE THE AX and the plow turned large stretches of the Rio Grande Valley into farmland, south Texas supported millions of white-winged doves. With the clearing of vast mesquite thickets which provided nest sites, these gregarious birds decreased in the entire Southwest.

Despite this decline, white-winged doves still gather in great flocks to clean stubble fields of weed seeds and waste grain. They also dine on nuts and wild fruits. They usually eat on the ground, then fly up into nearby trees and perch among the leaves. When feeding on the nectar of saguaro blooms, whitewings help cross-pollinate the towering cactus plants. On the wing these doves move swiftly and follow regular flight paths. Hunters consider them fine sport.

For nesting, whitewings prefer mesquite, mangrove, or other low trees, usually near water. Their colonies may cover many acres. Using sticks and weed stems, the doves build loose nests, bulkier than those of most of their relatives. They place these nests in forking branches some 6 to 15 feet above the ground. Some trees contain only one nest. Even in large colonies the doves seldom crowd together.

A big rookery, however, is a noisy place. Displaying males flap upward with a whistling sound and a great clapping of wings, then sail silently down to their favorite branches. Birds arrive or depart constantly on food-gathering missions. The musical cooing from hundreds of throats sounds like the gurgling of a large, swift-moving stream. Though never strident, the sound may carry as far as a mile.

The males often fight. But their battles usually amount only to a few guttural notes and a bit of wing flapping. Displaying before a female, the male spreads his tail to show its prominent black-and-white markings. Whitewings lay two eggs, varying in color from buff to white. They often raise two broods a season. After breeding, some whitewings in the United States head south. Others may wander as far north as Colorado and east to Florida. *Range:* S. E. California and S. Nevada to S. Texas, south to Panama; also in West Indies and from Ecuador to Chile. *Characteristics:* purplish-brown head and neck, brown back and breast, gray rump, tail sides, and belly; large white wing patch; rounded tail with white corners and broken black band.

White-winged doves, length 11-12½″
Walter A. Weber
National Geographic staff artist

Mourning doves, length 11-13"
Walter A. Weber, National Geographic staff artist

Mourning Dove
Zenaidura macroura

WITH VIGOROUS, whistling wingbeats flocks of ashy, slender-necked doves fly north across the land in spring. These trusting migrants seem to put down anywhere – by a water hole in the desert, by a dirt road in the corn belt, in an eastern barnyard to feed with the poultry or drink with the cattle, at a feeder on a suburban lawn.

Settled on their breeding grounds, these mourning doves begin their colorful courtship ritual. The male flies upward 100 feet or more, then glides back in sweeping circles on stiffly spread wings. He flutters once just before landing. On the ground he struts with nodding head and lures the female by bowing low, calling, and cocking his pointed tail.

At the first low *coo* of his nesting call he spreads his tail wide enough to display its black-and-white fringes. He then closes it for the last two notes, a high-pitched *coo* followed by a low one. He repeats this rhythm as he calls. The plaintive cooing gave the species its name.

Nesting doves usually place their flat and fragile platform of twigs in a shrub or tree. In treeless country the female deposits her two white eggs in a ground nest. Since the breeding season may start as early as February, a pair may rear three or even four broods in a spring and summer. As in nest building – where the male brings the materials and the female fashions them into a home – usually both partners share the chore of incubation. The male warms the eggs during the

day and his mate incubates by night. About two weeks after hatching, the young leave the nest.

The mourning dove dines on waste grains and other seeds. One stomach yielded 7,500 seeds of yellow wood sorrel. Although mainly a ground feeder, the bird sometimes flies to the upper branches of a pine tree to remove seeds from the cones. As grit to help grind its food the dove may take in snail shell and hard bits of beetles as well as the usual sand and gravel.

Like the rest of the Columbidae, the mourning dove needs plenty of water to help soften its dry, hard food. Travelers on the western plains used to welcome the sight of this bird as a sign of water nearby.

More widely distributed in the United States than any other native dove, *macroura* does not fear man's presence and has prospered from settlement of the land. Farms growing cereal crops provide a bountiful food source, and hedgerows, woodlots, and shade trees offer shelter and nest sites. Ponds maintained for livestock make ideal watering holes for the doves. Even overgrazing and soil erosion, which result in the growth of weeds, benefit these birds.

A few mourning doves winter in northern states but most retreat to warmer climes. They gather in large numbers wherever food is ample, especially near harvested fields. Protected in the northern states, the mourning dove is prized as a game bird in the South and West.

Range: S. E. Alaska to New Brunswick, south to Panama and the West Indies; migratory in the north. *Characteristics:* small head, slim neck; slaty-brownish upperparts with blackish spots on neck and wings, golden and reddish-brown sheen on neck; pale underparts, grayish wing linings, black-and-white edge on long pointed tail. Young lack black neck spots.

417

Band-tailed Pigeon
Columba fasciata

THE GREAT BULK of Pikes Peak loomed to the west beyond the red sandstone cliffs. At last Maj. Stephen Harriman Long neared his goal in 1820: the southern Rockies, whose snowy caps had appeared weeks before like cumulus clouds low on the horizon.

To the expedition's weary naturalists the rugged land was a treasure house of scientific discovery. Here Dr. Thomas Say recorded the rock wren, the lazuli bunting, the house finch, the dusky grouse. One day a hunter brought in still another bird new to science—a pigeon with a purplish head and a broad gray band on its tail.

The band-tailed pigeon, largest of its clan in North America, became an important game bird in the wooded, mountainous areas of the West. Great flocks wintered in the valleys of California, and hunters slew them by the thousands. Often a single load of shot knocked off an entire row of pigeons perched along the branch of a tree.

In later years naturalists feared that the band-tail would share the fate of the extinct passenger pigeon, which had filled a similar niche in the forests of the East. But protective laws intervened in time to check overshooting and permit the western species to recover.

Feeding in forests of oaks and conifers, the bandtail swallows acorns and other nuts whole, relying mainly on strong stomach muscles to grind them. While gathering food, *fasciata* flutters its wings to keep balance on the slender branches. If disturbed, it leaps into the air with a great clatter of wings. Swift, direct flight—like that of a hawk—carries the pigeon to a safe perch in the top of a lofty tree. In summer the bandtail feeds on wild peas, berries, and the buds of balsam poplar. When supplies peter out, bandtail flocks move to new feeding areas. At times farmers have complained of damage these pigeons have done to crops of fruit and grain.

Normally the bandtail's breeding season runs from April to June, but in the State of Washington young have been found in the nest in mid-October. Though colonies occasionally occur, flocks usually split up into pairs at nesting time.

A courting male sounds an owl-like *whoo-oo-whoo* from high in the trees, then launches out in a circular display flight. The loose twig nest, about 20 feet up in a tree, contains a single white egg. Bandtails may raise two broods in a season.

Range: S. British Columbia to central Colorado, south to W. Panama; migratory in the north. *Characteristics:* large size; purplish head and breast, white nape bar and lower belly, dark gray back, squarish tail with narrow blackish band above broad pale band at tip; dark-tipped yellow bill, yellow feet. Young are brownish gray.

*Red-billed pigeon
length 13-14"
Allan Brooks*

Red-billed Pigeon
Columba flavirostris

NATIVE to the tropical forests of Mexico and Central America, red-billed pigeons barely range across the border into southern Texas. To find these heavy-bodied birds, you must strike deep into the densely wooded bottomlands of the lower Rio Grande Valley.

Here the redbills frequent thickets of ebony, huisache, mesquite, and hackberry. Rising on clattering wings, flocks of 20 to 50 birds course the countryside in search of berries and other fruits. In Texas they resort to stubble fields to glean waste grain. In Central America their loud cooing often sounds in town gardens.

Fond of water, redbills can be spotted best during their daily visits to water holes and sandbars in streams. At a distance the "blue pigeon" looks uniformly dark.

Pairing may begin as early as February. George Miksch Sutton watched a male redbill deliver his courtship serenade, his chest so puffed up that his head could barely be seen. After a long windy *cooooooo*, the bird repeated *up, cup-a-coo* three times. He sang it several times facing north, and again to the northeast. "Then," wrote Dr. Sutton, "he about-faced in the manner of a baritone remembering the audience ... and sang it straight to the south."

Solitary nesters, redbills construct a frail stick cradle and sometimes line it with fibers. Placed in a snarl of vines or on a tree limb, this simple nest holds one or, rarely, two white eggs. Both parents share incubation duties. Redbills usually raise several broods in a season.

In Mexico this pigeon is hunted for sport and occasionally for meat. Observers have noted that hunters seeking food usually will not shoot at redbills unless they can bring down several with a single shot. The meat of one pigeon would not repay the cost of the ammunition.

Range: N. Mexico and S. Texas south to Costa Rica. *Characteristics:* large size; small red bill, purplish-red head, neck, and breast; blue-gray rump, sides, belly, and tail; brownish on back and adjacent wing areas. Young are duller.

*and-tailed pigeons (adults with white crescent on nape, and juvenile)
ngth 14-15½"; Walter A. Weber, courtesy Washington State University*

419

White-crowned pigeon, length 13½"; Robert C. Hermes

White-crowned Pigeon
Columba leucocephala

THESE ISLAND BIRDS from the Caribbean maintain a toehold in the Florida Keys. Only rarely do they visit the mainland.

Whitecrowns usually nest and roost in congested colonies. The one or two white eggs rest in a compact nest of twigs, roots, and grass placed in a shrub or tree, sometimes a cactus. Usually the pigeons nest on one island and commute to another to feed, flying back and forth each day in large flocks. Swift on the wing, they skim above the waves until near shore, then soar and circle as if to survey the land. They feed mainly on berries in the island jungles.

Only their loud, owl-like notes betray the whitecrowns when they hide in the treetops. The shyness of the species may result from the days of ruthless hunting which decimated the colonies.

Range: lower Florida Keys, the Bahamas, and Caribbean islands. *Characteristics:* slaty with white crown and iridescent nape. Young are brownish with grayish crown.

Ground Dove
Columbigallina passerina

WITH QUICK STEPS and nodding heads these small short-tailed doves search the ground for seeds. They hunt in fields, open woodlands, gardens, and on beaches throughout the southern United States. They venture along dusty roads and into sunny dooryards. Their mournful *coo-oo* echoes monotonously as they perch on branches, telephone wires, and rooftops.

Slow to alarm, the ground dove flutters off only at the last instant. It flies a short distance, displaying flashes of reddish brown in its wings, then slips back to earth. Near its nest it may flutter along the ground feigning lameness. A man may catch and tame one, but a Creole superstition threatens misfortune to anyone caging one of these birds.

Ground doves build flat, skimpy nests among tall weeds, in bushes, or in low trees. Occasionally they take over the abandoned nests of other birds. Both sexes incubate the two white eggs. A pair raises two or more broods during the long

Ground doves, length 6-6¾"; Paul Schwartz (also opposite)

Inca dove, length 7½-8"; Harry and Ruth Crockett, National Audubon Society

breeding season. Mysteriously, ground doves have disappeared from some areas where they had previously been abundant.

Range: S. California to S. Texas and South Carolina, south to Costa Rica; also found in Bermuda, the West Indies, and South America. *Characteristics:* small size; grayish upperparts with blackish spots on wing, reddish-brown wing patch and lining, short blackish tail; purplish underparts. Female and young are duller.

Inca Dove
Scardafella inca

MAN'S COMPANY, avoided by many birds, seems almost sought after by these fearless little doves of the Southwest. Seeking tiny seeds, they quickstep about in pastures, lawns, parks, and chicken yards. They invade cities and have rested in the shade of many an urban porch. To some listeners their insistent cooing sounds like *no hope*. These long-tailed doves are pushing their range north-

ward from the semiarid areas of the Southwest.

Though usually seen in pairs, Inca doves feed in loose flocks in winter. They place their flat nests of fibers and twigs in shrubs or trees, sometimes under house eaves. During construction the male brings a twig, perches on the back of his mate, and passes it down to her. A pair may try to hatch as many as five clutches of two pure white eggs in a single season. The parents roost huddled together on a limb. When the young can move about, they push down between the adults and join the huddle.

Range: S. Arizona to S. Texas, south along both coasts of Mexico to Costa Rica. *Characteristics:* small size, scaly gray-brown upperparts, reddish-brown wing patch and lining, scaly pinkish chest, buffy belly; long tail with white sides.

White-fronted Dove
Leptotila verreauxi

A BIRD of brushy woodlands, the white-fronted dove enters the United States only along the lower Rio Grande Valley in Texas. Solitary and retiring, it walks sedately beneath dense shrubbery in search of berries and seeds, its sole food. When nesting season nears, it perches high in leafy treetops, advertising its presence only with its soft, low-pitched cooing.

Startle a whitefront, and it may retire by swiftly walking through the underbrush. Flush it, and it will rocket off, wings whistling shrilly like those of a woodcock.

A platform of sticks and fibers in a low tree branch, a dense shrub, or a tangle of vines holds the two creamy-buff eggs.

Range: N. W. Mexico to S. Texas and S. Caribbean islands, south to S. Brazil. *Characteristics:* whitish forehead, gray-brown upperparts with iridescent nape, white tail corners; pinkish underparts, reddish-brown wing lining.

White-fronted dove, length 11-12"

Ringed turtle dove, length 12"; Bucky Reeves, National Audubon Society

Ringed Turtle Dove
Streptopelia risoria

THIS HANDSOME DOVE, originally from the Old World, has been domesticated around the globe. Those that now live in the wild in southern California and Florida stem from a few who escaped or were released from captivity. They feed primarily on seeds. Many ringed turtle doves haunt city parks, living on the generosity of the citizens.

These gentle birds apparently cannot compete with spotted doves. When both species try to nest in the same residential areas, the ringed turtle doves usually disappear, leaving the territory to their aggressive cousins.

The mellow cooing notes of ringed turtle doves rise and fall in pitch. The call begins with a single sharp note. These birds place their two white eggs on a shallow platform of sticks on a tree limb or a building.

The ancestral home of this dove remains unknown. Some geneticists believe the bird is an artificially bred variety of a wild African species. *Range:* vicinity of Los Angeles, California, and Miami, Florida; also found over much of the world. *Characteristics:* creamy tan with darker flight feathers, black band on hindneck.

Spotted Dove
Streptopelia chinensis

A NATIVE of Eastern Asia, the spotted dove was first released near Los Angeles early in the 1900's and since has flourished. It apparently drove the mourning dove from some suburbs and has become a common sight in towns and cities in southern California. Also known as the Chinese spotted dove, *chinensis* wears a half-collar of black and white spots that explains another nickname—"lace-necked dove."

Flocks of as many as 60 of these doves roam moist woodlands, feeding on seeds in usual pigeon fashion. They visit parks and yards, calling with a harsh *coo-who-coo.*

In spectacular nuptial flights they arrow up from treetops to a height of perhaps 150 feet, then spiral down. Aggressive males often flail at each other with their wings. The shallow nest of sticks, set in dense branches or on a large fork well above the ground, holds two white eggs.

Range: introduced in S. California, also Hawaii and other Pacific islands. Native to E. Asia. *Characteristics:* gray crown, spotted hindneck, brownish back and wings, white tail corners; pinkish-brown underparts. Young lack neck spots.

Spotted dove, length 13"; Herbert Lanks, Shostal

GAUDY NUTCRACKER

The Thick-billed Parrot

Family Psittacidae

Length 15-16½"
Allan Brooks

THE EMERALD FLOCKS come no more. But there was a time when great numbers of the thick-billed parrot (*Rhynchopsitta pachyrhyncha*) wandered from their Mexican breeding grounds to roam north as far as central Arizona. Then Apache hunters might have seen scores of these bright birds swirling across a pine-cloaked canyon. When the ranchers came, they sometimes heard these tropical visitors screeching outlandishly in the mountains of the border country.

The thickbill still breeds in the forests of Mexico's Sierra Madre, placing its two white eggs in tree holes. At one time this parrot depended heavily on the spacious cavities dug by the imperial ivory-billed woodpecker, now a rare species. After the thickbill young take wing, the flocks wander in search of pine cones, cracking them open with powerful beaks to get at the seeds. Destruction of northern Mexico's pines has left the birds without an avenue of approach to the United States. Arizonans may never again see them clambering through evergreens in a snowstorm.

Wild parrots in temperate North America? The brilliant macaws, lovebirds, amazons, and cockatoos among the 317 living species in the family invariably suggest the tropics. Yet our colonists found flocks of green parrots with orange-and-yellow heads. The extinct Carolina parakeet (page 194) once ranged in bottomlands from the Gulf Coast to New York and North Dakota, nesting in tree hollows and feasting on fruits and seeds. But *Conuropsis carolinensis* could not resist orchards, so farmers slaughtered them. They also were taken as cage birds, but never reached the popularity of the African and tropical American species or the tiny budgerigars from Australia, which entertainingly parrot the human voice. The last Carolina parakeet ever seen in the wild was reported from Florida in 1920. Thick-billed parrots have been seen in the Southwest since then, but only rarely.

Range: mountains of N. Mexico; may wander to Arizona and New Mexico. *Characteristics:* green with red forehead, legs, shoulder patch; yellow underwing patch.

Cuckoos, Roadrunners, and Anis

Family Cuculidae

A LIZARD SCUTTLES around a desert rock in the American Southwest. Suddenly a bird that looks like a lean, long-tailed chicken explodes from behind a prickly pear, grasps the lizard in its formidable beak, whacks it against the ground, and gulps it down headfirst. This scaly meal tucked away, the roadrunner cocks its head, raises its shaggy crest, and inspects its surroundings with a yellowish eye. Abruptly it flips its tail, then streaks away on spring-steel legs, leaving an odd series of tracks like elongated X's in the dust.

Noting these strange tracks, a Franciscan priest in California in 1790 described the bird as having four feet — "two feet going forward and two going backward"! To mislead evil spirits seeking to follow departed souls, some Pueblo Indians duplicate the confusing marks on the ground about their dead.

Southwestern folklore abounds in tales of the roadrunner, whose prowess in killing rattlesnakes recalls the cobra-battling exploits of India's mongoose. Some Plains Indians considered it "good medicine" to hang the bird's skin over a lodge door; warriors took its feathers into battle. Stagecoach drivers smiled when the roadrunner lowered head and tail and outran the horses — then suddenly put out a wing to change course and stopped short, tail raised like an exclamation point, to gawk at the passing coach. Mexicans affectionately call the bird *paisano,* or "countryman," and find the young make ever-curious, playful pets.

The X-shaped tracks help identify this desert clown as one of the cuckoo family, which spreads its 127 species around the world in tropical and temperate areas.

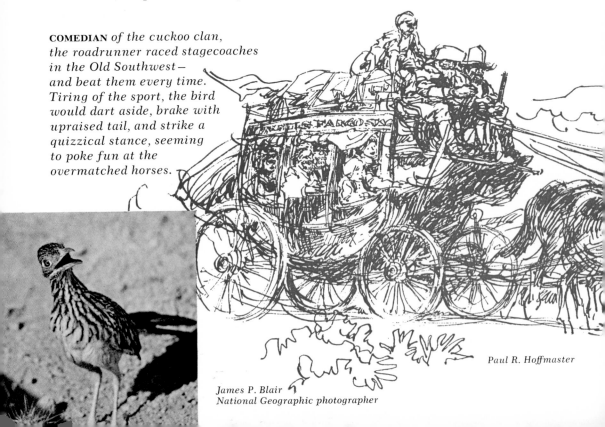

COMEDIAN *of the cuckoo clan, the roadrunner raced stagecoaches in the Old Southwest — and beat them every time. Tiring of the sport, the bird would dart aside, brake with upraised tail, and strike a quizzical stance, seeming to poke fun at the overmatched horses.*

Paul R. Hoffmaster

*James P. Blair
National Geographic photographer*

Long tails, slender form, and feet with two toes front, two to the rear comprise the quickly discernible resemblances that link the North American members.

While the terrestrial roadrunner is a solitary species, the groove-billed and smooth-billed anis are among the most gregarious of birds. They even set up cooperative nurseries and take turns incubating the eggs in community nests.

The anis fly in a loose-jointed, uncertain way, blown helplessly about in any breeze. The three North American cuckoos, in contrast, fly with speed and grace. Unlike 48 other species of cuckoos, these are not parasitic. The chuckling, gurgling calls of the yellow-billed cuckoo come more frequently when a thunderstorm is approaching—so folklore calls the bird a rain prophet.

In food, these Cuculidae have odd tastes. American cuckoos prefer hairy caterpillars, gulping them in such quantities that their stomachs get matted with bristles. And the anis pick ticks from cattle, while the roadrunner tops off a meal of snake or lizard with a scorpion or tarantula.

But for bizarre behavior, these North American birds bow to their foreign cousins. The European cuckoo always lays in a smaller bird's nest. Its eggs range from blue or green to reddish brown, plain or spotted, and each female seeks a host with eggs similar to her own. In England the cuckoo's eggs have become modified to resemble those of wagtails and pipits. On the Continent some females produce eggs like the European redstart's. Generally the cuckoo lays in the afternoon, rather than in the morning as most birds do. A warbler, for example, who lays at dawn and takes off to hunt for food in the afternoon may return to two eggs instead of one. If the nest is full, the cuckoo removes an egg to make room for her own.

After hatching, the blind baby cuckoo squirms beneath a nestmate and heaves it over the edge of the nest. One by one he gets rid of the rightful babies until he alone remains, growing so big that the small foster parents must sit on his head to feed him.

Europeans long ago named the cuckoo for its call. They saw the female sneak into other birds' nests to propagate her kind and, some say, came up with the term "cuckold" for a man whose wife was inclined to stray. They also built a clock with a wooden bird that appeared to announce the hours with the cuckoo's monotonous call. And they muttered "cuckoo" at the eccentricities of their fellow men. An early anatomist saw a similarity between the curving beak of the cuckoo and the curled rudimentary "tail" at the base of a man's spine. He borrowed the Greek word for the bird and named the bone structure "coccyx."

Truly, there is a little of the cuckoo in every one of us!

Below: mangrove cuckoo, length 12½"; Walter A. Weber, National Geographic staff artist

Mangrove Cuckoo

Coccyzus minor

SURPRISE this shy cuckoo in its Florida summer home while it is feeding in a clearing and it darts away with rapid wingbeats, heading straight for a tangled mangrove swamp. Once inside the mass of foliage the bird jumps from branch to branch. Then from the depths of the swamp comes a throaty call like that of the yellowbill.

The mangrove cuckoo, whose black mask gives it the nickname "black-eared cuckoo," eats caterpillars, other insects, and occasionally fruit. It builds a loose, almost flat nest of dry twigs for its two blue-green eggs. The race of this tropical species which migrates to Florida to breed is known as Maynard's cuckoo.

Range: W. Mexico to S. Florida and the West Indies, south to N. South America. *Characteristics:* buff-brown upperparts with grayish crown and black ear patch; buffy underparts. Young lack black "ears" and grayish crown.

Yellow-billed Cuckoo

Coccyzus americanus

THE FARMER looks up to scan the skies as hollow clucks resound from the orchard: *ka-ka-ka-ka-ka-ka-ka-cow-cow-cowp-cowp-cowp* — hurried at first, then stretching out into deliberate notes. "Rain crow," he murmurs, noting the buildup of clouds that heralds an afternoon shower.

Indeed the yellow-billed cuckoo does seem to give its guttural call most frequently when rain is in the air. But "crow"? This timid, slender bird with curving bill and soft coloring looks nothing like the bold black crow.

Try to track down the call and you quickly understand Wordsworth's lines:

> O Cuckoo! shall I call thee Bird,
> Or but a wandering Voice?

Though referring to the European cuckoo, the words apply equally to the American yellowbill. Ghosting from tree to tree in straight, fast flight, the secretive bird seldom leaves the umbrella of foliage. It sits motionless for long periods, or moves quietly and deliberately in search of prey. Scan as you may the green-hued dimness, you will seldom see *americanus* until it flutters its bronze wings or turns to look at you, revealing the yellow on its bill.

Common throughout the United States, this

cuckoo frequents fruit groves, hedgerows, and streamside thickets. Families of these birds have grown up along brush-bordered lanes within touching distance of the milkman and mailman on their suburban rounds.

Consuming large quantities of hairy caterpillars as it forages through leafy tangles, the yellow-billed cuckoo serves man well. Few other birds eat these pests that destroy the freshly grown leaves of shade and fruit trees.

Several hundred small hairy caterpillars have been found in the stomach of a single cuckoo. So many spiny hairs are swallowed that a wall-to-wall matting of caterpillar fur builds up in the stomach. At intervals the bird sheds this lining in pieces, leaving the cavity smooth and clean.

Yellowbills also eat beetles, grasshoppers, and other insects. In season they feed on wild berries and grapes.

At nesting time yellow-billed cuckoos build a frail platform of twigs and rootlets in a bush or low tree, usually four to eight feet off the ground. They line it with flower buds, moss, and perhaps a scrap of rag, but often this lining is so scanty that the three or four blue-green eggs can be seen through the bottom. A strong wind sometimes blows an egg out of this shallow nest. The mother bird, who does most of the incubating, often hangs over the edge and may knock another egg over the side when she shifts position.

The female yellowbill sometimes lays an egg in the nest of the black-billed cuckoo. The blackbill occasionally returns the compliment, and both birds have been known to lay in the nest of a catbird, chipping sparrow, yellow warbler, or wood thrush. But this is unusual as neither is a compulsive parasite like the European cuckoo.

The yellowbill mother may lay her eggs at irregular intervals, so they hatch at different times. Black and greasy looking, the baby birds sprout quill-like feather sheaths that stick out like the spines of a porcupine, hardly improving their appearance. They clamor for food; with a *curr* of contentment they accept it.

When a week old the ugly nestlings suddenly blossom. The feather sheaths split, revealing fully developed feathers inside. The quills burst so quickly that in about six hours the young birds wear soft plumage resembling that of an adult, except for the long tail.

Soon the youngsters begin clambering about the branches beside their nest. Should one fall to the ground, it climbs determinedly into the shrubbery, using feet, beak, and wings.

Range: S. British Columbia to New Brunswick, south to central Mexico and the West Indies; winters in South America. *Characteristics:* yellow lower mandible, brown upperparts, rufous wing patches; whitish underparts, long tail with large white spots.

Black-billed Cuckoo
Coccyzus erythropthalmus

GUARDIANS of the orchard, black-billed cuckoos move in to stem an invasion of tent caterpillars. They yank the hairy, tree-destroying larvae from their webbed encampments and gobble them.

Mark the black bill that distinguishes this bird from the yellow-billed cuckoo, whose feeding habits it shares; also the red eye rings that gave it the scientific name *erythropthalmus*, or "red-eye." The black-billed cuckoo is slimmer and sings more softly, many times giving voice at night. Its nest holds two or three eggs that are smaller and darker than those of its cousin. Common in New England, the blackbill tends to be more abundant than the yellowbill in the northern part of the cuckoo range.

Blackbills may raise broods as late as September. Week-old bristly nestlings "comb" away the sheaths with their bills, exposing fluffy feathers. At the age of three weeks they can fly.

Range: S. Saskatchewan to Nova Scotia, south to S. E. Wyoming, N. Arkansas, and South Carolina; winters in N. W. South America. *Characteristics:* like yellow-billed cuckoo but with black bill, red eye rings, and white crescents on tail.

Black-billed cuckoo, 11-12½"; Frederick Kent Truslow

Smooth-billed Ani
Crotophaga ani

ONLY IN FLORIDA does this strange bird with a narrow bill, parrotlike in profile, breed regularly in the United States. In tropical America it is a common sight, perched on a grazing cow, picking ticks, or running about the animal's hoofs to snatch insects stirred to flight.

Always sociable, anis go about in flocks of up to 25, uttering querulous cries, *que-lick, que-lick,* if disturbed. Often they perch shoulder to shoulder, slender tails dangling.

Several females may lay their eggs in a single bulky nest of sticks in a tree. They and their mates take turns incubating the communal clutch, up to 20 or more blue eggs with chalky white lines. The anis keep bringing nest material while the eggs are being deposited and some may be covered. These never hatch, since they are not warmed or turned regularly.

Range: S. Florida to N. Argentina. *Characteristics:* black with high-ridged bill, short wings, long loose tail. Young are sooty brown.

Groove-billed Ani
Crotophaga sulcirostris

AT A DISTANCE this dark, slender bird looks like a double of the smooth-billed ani. At close range you can see the grooves along the bill. A surer way to identify it is by locale, for in the United States the groovebill breeds only along the lower Rio Grande Valley.

With long tail strangely askew, the bird launches into flight, beating its short wings several times, then gliding. Pausing in a bush to rest, it clucks softly or calls *tee-ho, tee-ho.* Then it flaps off. In a strong wind this weak, loose-jointed flier is almost helpless.

As many as three pairs of sociable groovebills gather sticks for a single nest, lining it with green leaves. Each female contributes three or four eggs, pale blue with chalky coating. Males as well as females help incubate the colony's eggs and raise the blind, helpless, black-skinned hatchlings. The young mature rapidly and soon feed with the rest of the flock, close by the hoofs of grazing livestock.

As the cattle bed down for the night on the open range, the anis sometimes hop aboard for a late supper. Thus they earn their generic name *Crotophaga:* tick eaters. But they feed mainly on other insects, as well as on fruits and berries.

Range: S. Texas to N. South America. *Characteristics:* like the smooth-billed ani except for grooves on mandibles.

Smooth-billed ani
length 13″

Groove-billed ani
length 12″
Walter A. Weber
National Geographic staff artist

Roadrunner
Geococcyx californianus

THE YOUNG RATTLESNAKE strikes again and again, but the big bird dodges. The snake tires, and the bird dances in, stabs at the reptile's head with his long beak, thrashes it on a rock, and starts gulping it. If the snake proves too big, its tail will dangle from the beak while the "snake killer's" digestive system makes room inside.

So goes mealtime for the roadrunner, state bird of New Mexico, to whom the desert is home and almost anything there that moves may be food—lizards, scorpions, tarantulas, grasshoppers, mice, and sparrows.

Mexicans say the X-like tracks of this strange *paisano* confuse the Devil, who can't tell which way the bird has fled. Almost always it flees on foot, and some cowpokes of the Old West swore it could outrun their cayuses. For a short stretch a roadrunner can sprint 15 miles an hour.

In spring the "chaparral cock" struts and bows before his hen and pumps out throaty coos, starting on a high note with his beak low and ending vice versa. They set their stick nest in a bush or cactus plant, lining it with anything from snakeskin to dried manure. The hen lays three to six chalky white eggs at intervals, perhaps incubating the last while stuffing food into an oily black "infant dragon" hatched from the first.

Range: N. California to S. W. Kansas and N. W. Louisiana, south to S. Mexico. *Characteristics:* streaked brown upperparts, whitish underparts, long beak, shaggy crest, long white-tipped tail.

Roadrunner, length 20-24", with two lizards; Eliot Porter

ENORMOUS EYES *that gather maximum light give this great horned owl and his kin amazing night vision.*

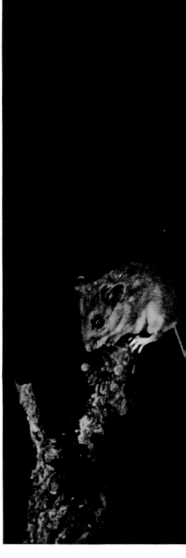

NIGHT HUNTERS ON SILENT WINGS

The Owls

Family Strigidae

By ALEXANDER WETMORE

TINY SCOURGE *of forest rodents*

THE EVENING AIR of late February in the Florida Everglades is soft and mild. Delicate scents from unseen blossoms come with the breeze; voices of myriad frogs form an incessant but attractive chorus from the marshes. Suddenly, from the moss-festooned live oaks in the background explodes demoniacal laughter, guttural and startling.

Playing the beam from my flashlight among the branches, I discover two spots of deep red—reflections from a pair of eyes. As my own eyes adjust to the dim illumination, I distinguish the shadowy form of a barred owl. Puzzled by the light, the bird stops its hubbub. But as I pass, it utters a prolonged, eerie *whoo-oo-oo-aw.*

The voices of owls are more familiar than their looks, for though they are common birds, most hunt at night. Their presence, unseen but constantly felt, has prompted fables and superstitions about them in virtually every country. The little owl of Europe, regarded in ancient Greece as a special ward of the goddess Athena, has long been an emblem of wisdom—not that an owl has any unusual intelligence, but the conformation of its head allows the eyes to look straight forward like those of

a saw-whet owl in Ohio aims dagger claws at favorite prey—a white-footed mouse.

a man. Romans, to whom Athena became Minerva, did not retain any reverence for the bird. They considered it an evil omen. An owl alighting on a housetop presaged death; its call at night aroused fear. The owl flew with witches and served as an ingredient in their unsavory brews. In the American Southwest, Pima Indians held that at death the human spirit passed into the body of an owl, and to help it along they gave owl feathers to the dying person.

Owls appear throughout the world. The order of Strigiformes includes the family of barn owls (Tytonidae) as well as that of typical owls (Strigidae). The 133 species of typical owls range in size from elf owls, no larger than sparrows, to great horned and great gray owls, up to two feet or more in length. All of them instantly identify themselves by their broad faces with prominent eyes set in feather disks, their sharp, curved beaks and claws, and their long, fluffy feathers. The feathers usually cover the lower legs and upper surfaces of the toes, bare in most birds, and plumage colors run to gray, brown, and buff—in a few to brighter colors. Owls may live to a great age. One eagle owl, an Old World species, thrived in captivity 68 years.

431

The wings of an owl have softened margins, so that the bird flies as silently as a shadow. Owls hear their prey acutely, and their large eyes can see where there is little light. But the eyes are fixed so immovably that an owl must swivel its head to alter the line of vision.

As a very small boy I was told that a perching owl would follow with its eyes a person moving around and around the perch until eventually the owl's head would twist right off! I soon had a chance to test this intriguing theory on a Florida screech owl, perched in a low pine. I walked around the bird for some time. He kept his eyes steadily on me, but his head did not fall off. Not until I conducted other experiments at a somewhat more mature age did I detect how an owl snaps its head around, giving the semblance of continuous motion in one direction.

Owls make their homes in tree hollows, in caverns, on the ground, and in stick nests built by hawks, crows, or other birds. They lay white eggs, but during incubation these may become tinted pale buff. To defend their young, owls often swoop at intruders. One evening, walking near a woodland camp in eastern Kansas, I was startled by something striking my bare head—a little screech owl! The bird had young nearby. At other times owls have knocked my hat off.

Most owls remain hidden in shaded, secluded places during the day. A few venture abroad by day as well as night. The snowy owl of the Far North must remain active in daylight since there is almost no night in the Arctic midsummer. A burrowing owl I once had in captivity loved to rest in the sun and watch hawks and other birds flying at such great heights that I could barely see them.

Though owls live mostly on animal food captured alive, they feed occasionally on rabbits freshly killed by automobiles, or on other carcasses. They regularly prey on mice, rats, and other small mammals as well as birds, and many species eat beetles, crickets, and other big insects. Great horned owls and snowy owls are fiercely predatory, killing rabbits, squirrels, and other relatively large animals. In the Dominican Republic I once saw a burrowing owl tearing at the body of a young bird of its own kind which had been killed and thrown aside by a native.

At a camp in northern Wyoming where I was collecting small mammals as specimens for the U. S. National Museum, I was puzzled by the loss of numerous traps. One day, in a low willow near camp, I found a nest of young long-eared owls. My missing traps lay scattered about. Evidently the parent owls, not averse to help in

SWOOPING IN *on muffled wings that spread four feet,*
a great horned owl strikes with deadly precision.
Acute hearing guides him to his prey.
Curved facial feathers cup sound waves into
large ear openings; wide head sets ears
far apart, helping pinpoint the source.
Downy tips on the flight feathers
eliminate the whirring sound other birds
make in flight, enabling owls to weave silently
through the night forest, glide low over meadows,
and attack small mammals and birds without warning.
Great horned owls will defend the nest vigorously.
A young great horn (below) spreads wings menacingly
and clicks his bill at a youthful naturalist in Montana.

securing food, had carried the trapped mice to the nest, where they were eaten and
the traps discarded. Owls swallow small animals whole; larger prey they tear into
pieces. The bird assimilates the flesh of the victim, while the digestive system
forms bones, fur, feathers, and other indigestible portions into compact pellets.
These the owl regurgitates to make room for another meal. Analysis of pellets found
around an owl roost provides a valuable index to the bird's diet. As with the hawks,
the usefulness of owls in destroying rodents far outweighs any injury these birds
may cause man by depredations upon chickens and game.

John Craighead. Upper: G. Ronald Austing, Photo Researchers

Screech owl, gray phase, length 8-10″; G. Ronald Austing

 ## Screech Owl
Otus asio

ALONG BAYOU LAFOURCHE, which oozes past the sugarcane plantations and the water hyacinth prairies of Louisiana's Cajun country, the mournful wail of a screech owl at night may no longer be an omen of death. But it was once. Ornithologist Edward Howe Forbush in 1927 reported that an inhabitant would creep out of bed and turn his left shoe upside down to hush the call. And if that didn't work, he would pull his left trouser pocket inside out.

The call of this misnamed bird more closely resembles a whinny than a screech. With eastern birds the quavering whistled notes rise, then fall. Western races sound the notes on a single pitch.

DINING ON A MOUSE, *a screech owl crushes the skull bones (above) before gulping the rodent whole.*

Through much of North America the haunting call is familiar to town and country dwellers who have never seen this bird of darkness.

Rather than death, the call frequently forecasts a renewal of life. These small, yellow-eyed owls with ear tufts are most vocal in mating season. The courting male sends forth his wail, hops about, flaps his wings, and bows his head. One observer reported that a perching female ignored such attentions for a long while. The male even tried winking at her. Finally she lowered her head, gazed at her persistent suitor, and approached him.

Year-round residents of open woodlands and clearings, screech owls breed in western cottonwoods, the scrub pines of the South, and the orchards of New England.

They usually nest in tree cavities, especially old woodpecker holes. Occasionally they set up house in a city park or take over a hole in the corner of a farm building. They may even tenant a martin house. Two screech owls were observed nesting in a compartment in one of these large boxes while ten purple martins occupied the other rooms. When the owl family moved out, a pair of martins promptly moved in. Screech owls furnish no nesting material for their four or five white eggs.

Many of the 18 races have two color phases, reddish brown and gray. These occur in about equal numbers without regard to sex—both phases may appear in a single brood. In the main, western subspecies are uniformly gray.

When defending their nestlings, the parents attack savagely. These birds sometimes knock the hats off townspeople who stroll along a sidewalk underneath a nest.

After dusk screech owls glide over meadows to scout for mice and course above the tree crowns to snatch large insects from the foliage or in mid-air. They also eat bats, other small mammals, crayfish, fish, reptiles, frogs, and earthworms. Included in the comprehensive diet is a variety of birds—one owl went down the chimney of a house and devoured a canary that he yanked through the bars of a cage! Screech owls even practice cannibalism.

By day *asio* roosts in cavities, hidden from the crows, jays, and cardinals that gather to harass it. If approached while perching, a screech owl compresses its feathers, freezing in an elongated, stumplike pose. The slit eyes miss nothing. If the intruder gets too close the owl squats, fluffs out its feathers, and takes off heavily without a whisper from its large wings.

Range: S. E. Alaska to Maine, south to S. Baja California and Florida. *Characteristics:* small size, ear tufts, large facial disks, yellow eyes; streaked, mottled plumage. Red phase is reddish brown or brownish. Gray phase is grayish brown.

Whiskered owl, gray phase, 6½-8"; Eliot Porter

Whiskered Owl
Otus trichopsis

THREE BOO'S, a pause, and another boo, issuing from the white oaks of an Arizona canyon, broadcast the mating call of whiskered owls. A male hearing an imitation of his notes will usually answer and may strut right up to the caller.

This small owl with facial bristles, often called the spotted screech owl, resembles *asio*. And like that bird, it has two color phases. Whiskered owls place their three or four white eggs in tree holes. They dine on large insects.

Range: S. E. Arizona to Honduras. *Characteristics:* small size, yellow eyes, long facial bristles, streaked whitish underparts, gray or reddish-brown upperparts with white spots.

Screech owl, red phase; Torrey Jackson

Flammulated owl
length 6-7"
Allan Brooks

Flammulated Owl
Otus flammeolus

FLAMMULATED? This is surely a high-sounding name for such a small bird. But it fits. In this owl's drab gray plumage, touches of reddish brown suggest a "little flame," or in Latin *flammula*. In some flammulated owls the rusty hue does not stand out. Occasionally the bright color is quite prominent, particularly about the head.

This dainty dark-eyed western mountaineer frequently breeds as high as 10,000 feet above sea level. In the ponderosa pine forests *flammeolus* may outnumber all other birds of prey.

On moonlit spring nights the male sounds a mellow hoot every few seconds for hours on end. He catches moths in flight and seizes beetles and spiders from the foliage.

For nesting, mated birds sublet a woodpecker hole and add a few feathers to the wood chips. The three or four eggs are creamy white.

Range: S. British Columbia south in the mountains to Guatemala; winters mainly south of the United States. *Characteristics:* small ear tufts, dark eyes, streaked gray upperparts tinged with reddish brown, barred white underparts.

Great Horned Owl
Bubo virginianus

DUSK steals in, chills the air, and darkens the forest. Across a glade a rabbit hops. High in an evergreen tree a great horned owl blinks its yellow eyes. Mighty wings flap silently as the big bird swoops in for the kill. Talons pierce the rabbit's back and, with a noise like someone clapping hands, the great horn snaps its bill.

If the hunting has been good, the "flying tiger" may devour just the brains, then move on to another victim. This owl seems to favor rabbits but will eat almost any animal it can kill, including squirrels, birds, rats, snakes, cats, dogs, and porcupines. But tangling with a porcupine some-

times proves to be a fatal mistake. One great horn was found dead with quills stuck in its neck, right wing, and right foot—some even had penetrated thick breast muscles. A total of 66 shafts had pierced the owl!

The varied menu includes skunks. These envelop the bird in fumes that linger, and some specimens retain the odor even after years of seclusion in a museum case.

One of the most powerful of birds, the great horn is the most widely known of our owls and the largest with ear "horns." These tufts and the catlike eyes and shape of head have earned *virginianus* the nickname "cat owl," which others in the family share.

Extraordinary endurance goes with this bird's tremendous power. One farmer, plagued by a raiding great horn, set out steel traps in the chicken yard. Caught by the leg one night, the owl broke the chain and flew off with the trap dangling. A week later the owl returned. Snared this time by the other leg, the bird broke the second chain and again escaped. With a trap on each leg it managed to live and hunt for several weeks until it caught one of the shackles on a fence and died.

Great horned owls dwell throughout the woodlands of the New World; sometimes they inhabit cliffs and gullies. In temperate regions they are year-round residents, but they abandon the colder areas for the winter. Ten races are recognized north of Mexico. Most wear dark brown plumage. One, however, the Arctic horned owl of northern Canada, may be as pale as the snowy owl.

Occasionally a great horn sends forth a spine-chilling scream. More characteristic is a deep, resonant hooting with great carrying power, a familiar and appealing sound to people who roam the woodlands. The male usually sounds four or five hoots, higher-pitched than the female's six to eight notes.

From afar these calls sound like a foghorn or a train whistle; up close, like the cooing of a dove. The great horn's notes have also been likened to the yelping of a dog and the squalling of a cat.

One of our earliest nesters, *virginianus* may breed in February in New England. In warm climes mated birds may start raising a family in late November or December. Courtship usually begins on a mild winter evening with prolonged hooting. The male bows and sidles about his mate, sometimes caressing her with his bill. One female rejected these advances until the male brought her a rabbit. After they feasted she took up the mating dance as vigorously as he.

Frequently a pair moves into the old nest of a hawk, heron, or eagle, replacing or supplementing the nest materials with breast feathers. Great horns also use tree hollows, ledges, and caves. Both sexes incubate the two or three white eggs.

436

During the four-week period snow often covers a sitting bird. The young cannot fly until they are about 12 weeks old, and feeding them all this time presents a problem for the parents. Early nesting helps because hunting is easier before summer thickens the foliage.

Generally, these versatile predators are good providers. One nest reported by ornithologist Charles Bendire contained "a mouse, a young muskrat, two eels, four bullheads, a Woodcock, four Ruffed Grouse, one rabbit, and eleven rats." The booty weighed nearly 18 pounds!

The parents strike at intruders with blows that slash through heavy clothing. Not even a fencing mask protected one observer who ventured too close to a brood. The mother clawed through the mask and gouged the man's scalp. Great horned owls have attacked men wearing fur caps, apparently mistaking the cap for prey.

Range: northern tree line in Alaska and Canada to S. South America; migratory in north. *Characteristics:* large ear tufts, yellow eyes, tawny facial disks and sides, white throat, mottled brown upperparts, barred whitish underparts.

Great horned owl, length 18-25"; G. Ronald Austing, Photo Researchers

Hawk owl, length 14½-17½; Walter A. Weber, National Geographic staff artist

Hawk Owl
Surnia ulula

POISED ATOP A TAMARACK STUB, a slender predator scans the ground for food. His yellow eyes,
peering out of facial disks, are surely those of an
owl. Yet the bright sunlight doesn't seem to bother them. Then you notice that his body angles
forward as he perches, quite unlike the straight-
up posture of other owls. His long rounded tail
also seems strange for an owl. Frequently he lifts
it at an odd angle or flicks it in the manner of a
sparrow hawk.

Without warning he pitches headlong from the
dead tree like a shrike, skims fast and low on
rapid, quivering wingbeats that suggest a peregrine falcon, then soars to hover in midair.

Owl? Hawk? Falcon? Not many bird watchers
get a chance to puzzle over this well-named
northerner. Even when its supply of mice and
lemmings runs short the hawk owl rarely leaves
the remote forests to invade the haunts of men.

A true owl despite diurnal habits, the "day
owl" spends long hours on a perch with a commanding view and occasionally sounds a melodious rolling trill. The bird shows little fear and
even may be captured by hand.

But try climbing up a decaying trunk to peer
into a hawk owl nest and both adults will probably attack without hesitation. You may get a
glimpse of three to seven white eggs in the hollow of a stub if you climb in April, or see a brood
of hissing owlets if you climb in May. But you
also may get a badly clawed scalp.

Range: forests of Alaska and N. Canada south
to S. British Columbia, central Alberta, N. Michigan, and Newfoundland; winters occasionally
to northern United States. Also found in Europe
and Asia. *Characteristics:* yellow eyes, whitish
facial disks with black "sideburns"; dark brown
upperparts and gray-brown underparts barred
with white; long tail.

438

Snowy Owl
Nyctea scandiaca

SWIRLING, diving, squawking, a mob of crows seethes round a rock jutting from a snow-draped Ohio hayfield. At the hub of the uproar a snowy owl perches like a white ghost, watching his dark tormentors through yellow eyes set in a round knob of a head.

In swoops a heckler for a closer pass. The owl crouches. Sensing a mistake, the crow veers. The owl leaps – white feet slam into the crow, black talons bite deep. On broad wings he strokes away, a dead crow dangling from his claws.

The crow's error was fatal but not foolish. Used to pestering nocturnal owls dazzled by the sun, an Ohio crow seldom meets this fierce white predator that hunts in its Arctic homeland in unbroken daylight through the summer months.

Our rare glimpses of the shy and striking "ermine owl" are closely related to the life cycle of its favorite food item, the lemming. This mouse-like creature of the tundra, multiplying into the millions upon millions, furnishes abundant fare for the snowy owls. The birds wax fat, raise bumper broods of a dozen or more, and show little urge to migrate southward when the fearsome Arctic winter begins.

Then, periodically, the lemming hordes reach a peak. As if on signal, the stubby little rodents burst from their underground cities and swarm like a living carpet over the tundra. Stalked by predators, starvation, and disease, the lemmings are almost wiped out.

Its own numbers at a peak and the larder all but empty, the snowy owl glides south, golden eyes searching for other food – a ptarmigan, a trapped weasel, a wounded duck, beached fish, even a crow if times are lean and the crows careless. No longer shy, the northerner sometimes invades cities, squats on window ledges to the delight of office workers, even lets itself be caught by hand. The snowy's swift, undulating flight on wings that span five feet has taken it as far south as California and Texas and onto ships a thousand miles at sea.

Fatigue, hunger, and trophy hunters plague the wanderers and few return. But in the Arctic fastness *scandiaca* is a marvel of adaptation. Only its eyes, talons, and the tip of its beak show through the dense blanket that warms and waterproofs the surprisingly small body and pads it out to a chunky profile. Thus equipped, this owl survives better in the frozen north than in the warm and perilous lands to the south.

Emerging from a grainy white egg in a rude hollow gouged out of the top of a frozen hillock, the owlet awakes to a world of treeless wastes raked by icy winds and strewn with swirling snow. On a vantage point nearby, the adult male keeps a sharp lookout for food and foe – just as he did while his larger mate incubated her five to eight eggs.

After a lemming "crash" few snowy owls breed. Those that do must hunt constantly. Without the parents' protection many an owlet falls prey to a fox or jaeger or wanders off and dies with sleet crusting its dark gray down.

This harsh world produces a tough and clever bird. Audubon watched a snowy owl rest at the water's edge as if asleep, then suddenly thrust a foot into the water and flap away with a fish in its claws. A wonderful bit of Eskimo folklore tells of the "great beard" that seized two hares and was torn in half when they struggled in opposite directions.

But as the lemmings increase in the Far North the snowy owl quits its fishing holes and rabbit runs and begins another cycle of feast, famine, and migration to the south.

Range: Alaska to N. Greenland, south to N. E. Manitoba and Labrador; winters to British Columbia, North Dakota, New York, and sporadically through most of U. S. Also found in Europe and Asia. *Characteristics:* yellow eyes, white plumage flecked with slaty brown. Females and young are more heavily marked with brown.

Snowy owl, length 20-27"; Karl Maslowski, Photo Researchers

Pygmy Owl
Glaucidium gnoma

UNDER AN OAK in a western canyon you sit and mimic the pygmy owl's slow, mellow whistle. High above, a gray-brown ball of fluff interrupts his sunbath, jerks his long tail, and swishes down to search for the intruder in his domain.

Others respond too. Soon the trees are a-twitter with chickadees, juncos, and other small birds eager to mob their enemy, the owl.

This boldness may cost one of them its life. For *gnoma*, far from befuddled by sunlight, often hunts by day, seizing insects and lizards, and sometimes birds and animals larger than itself. One pygmy owl was seen to claw into a gopher and ride the scampering rodent until it dropped.

Small birds attacking from ahead must face the pygmy owl's glowering yellow eyes. Mobbers converging from the rear are met by a scowling dark-eyed visage, an effect produced by two black patches on the back of the owl's head.

Similar markings earned the nickname "four-eyes" for a relative in tropical America. This bird, the ferruginous owl (*Glaucidium brasilianum*), crosses the border into Arizona and Texas.

The female pygmy owl incubates her three or four white eggs in an old woodpecker hole.

Range: S. E. Alaska to W. Alberta, south to Guatemala. *Characteristics:* yellow eyes, black patches on hindneck; gray-brown head and back spotted with white, whitish underparts streaked with black; long barred tail.

Elf Owl
Micrathene whitneyi

MOONLIGHT silhouettes the gaunt saguaros in the Arizona desert. A tiny, short-tailed owl snaps up a beetle on the wing. Unlike many of his relatives, the elf owl does not fly silently. You can hear his wings swish as he darts by or hovers to pluck insects from the desert blossoms.

On a spring night you can also hear his shrill, rapid *whi-whi-whi-whi-whi-whi*. Sometimes he and his mate join in a warbling duet while he struts before her like a tiny pigeon.

No bigger than a pudgy sparrow, this smallest of our owls inhabits the saguaro cacti of the desert plains and the oaks and pines of southwestern canyons. If you draw near its perch, the elf owl may freeze with a wing held up in front of its face. Thus shielded, the wee predator can easily be mistaken for a part of the limb. When captured, this bird often feigns death, lying limp until it spies an opportunity to take wing.

A pair usually appropriates an old nest hole dug in a spiny saguaro by a Gila woodpecker or gilded flicker. Sometimes the owls forcibly dispossess the original occupants. The three white eggs hatch after about two weeks of incubation. When a parent elf owl approaches a nestling with a bit of food – an insect, spider, or scorpion – both birds rock from side to side.

Range: S. E. California to S. Texas, south to central Mexico; winters mainly in Mexico. *Characteristics:* round head, buffy face, yellow eyes, white "eyebrows," spotted grayish-brown upperparts, mottled whitish underparts; short tail.

Burrowing Owl

Speotyto cunicularia

LIKE AN ELDERLY COUPLE enjoying the sunset on the porch, a pair of long-legged, stub-tailed owls stand on a mound of earth outside their burrow and peer into the twilight. Their heads swivel nearly full circle as they scan the plains.

They dart up to intercept passing insects and swoop low to seize mice. Between forays they call to each other with dovelike *coo-hoo* notes.

When danger threatens, the burrowing owls bow gravely and crouch as if to take off. But they don't take flight. Instead they pop into a fist-size opening and scurry along a tunnel that winds five to ten feet or more. As they dart into the hole they sound a cackling alarm note.

Though they can dig fine tunnels, the chances are that these "prairie dog owls" inherited their home from a prairie dog or some other burrowing animal of the western plains. The Florida burrowing owl, however, must dig his own, since none of his neighbors dig any that suit him.

At tunnel's end five to seven white eggs lie in a cradle of grass, roots, and dried cow dung. Both sexes share the task of incubation.

Range: S. British Columbia to S. Manitoba, south to S. South America; also central Florida to the West Indies. *Characteristics:* yellow eyes, whitish facial disks, brown upperparts and chest spotted with white, whitish breast spotted with brown; long legs, short tail.

Great Gray Owl
Strix nebulosa
(Picture on page 442)

ACROSS Lapland, Russia, Mongolia, and western North America ranges this big gray bird with the oversize head. In dense evergreen forests as far north as timberline in Alaska and Canada, it perches with small, feathered feet, often leaning top-heavily forward to scout for prey below. After a while, if nothing shows up, the hunter flaps off with labored strokes.

This is the great gray, our largest owl – at least in appearance. The bird may measure nearly three feet in length, including a foot-long tail, and its wings span five feet. But strip away the mass of fluff and you have a body no bigger than

Pygmy owls, length 7-7½"; John Craighead and (rear view)
Walter A. Weber, National Geographic staff artist
Left: elf owl, length 5-6"; Lewis Wayne Walker
Below: burrowing owls, length 9-11"; Frederick Kent Truslow

Great gray owl, length 24-33"; Frank and John Craighead

a barred owl's. The wonderfully thick dress of long, soft feathers makes the great gray immune to cold. And its sharp, slender claws penetrate the thick winter fur and feathers of small mammals and birds. But winter's slim pickings often drive this hardy owl from its northernmost haunts—sometimes as far south as Wyoming and Nebraska, and east to Massachusetts.

The 24-hour sun of the far northern summer forces *nebulosa* to hunt in daylight. One naturalist saw a great gray make a capture in the afternoon. After three unsuccessful swoops from a fir tree, the determined bird struck the ground hard on the fourth try—and crashed through the thin roof of a burrow. Then off he flew with a pocket gopher in his talons.

Sometimes the great gray bolts its food. One bird, cut open shortly after being shot, had bitten off the head of a red squirrel and swallowed the body whole. Other fare favored by this species includes rabbits, rats, and shrews.

The great gray's booming *whoo-hoo-hoo* rumbles through the woods. The bird also sounds a tremulous whistle like that of a screech owl.

A mob of cawing crows may unnerve a gray owl, but this bird seems so indifferent to people that it is sometimes caught by hand.

Great grays breed as far south as the Sierra Nevada in California, where they have been seen by visitors to Yosemite National Park. For nesting, the female and her smaller mate refurbish the abandoned home of a hawk or crow. The abode can be as high as 50 feet in the crotch of a poplar, aspen, or spruce. On a platform of sticks some two feet in diameter the owls build a bowl of twigs and moss and line it with bark strips, feathers, and sometimes hair. The two to five white eggs are more oval-shaped than those of most other owls.

Range: northern tree line in Alaska and W. Canada to Ontario, south to central California, N. Idaho, W. Wyoming, and N. Minnesota; winters to S. Minnesota and Massachusetts. *Characteristics:* large round head, lined facial disks, yellow eyes, black chin spot, dusky gray plumage with breast streaked vertically; long tail.

Spotted owl, length 16½-19"; Thase Daniel

Spotted Owl
Strix occidentalis

TWILIGHT blackens a box canyon in the southern Rockies. High above the canyon floor a brown owl with dark, spooky eyes swings off a limb of a Douglas fir and flies soundlessly to her nest in a cliff crevice. Suddenly she utters a curious whistle. Her mate, hidden in darkness, replies with a high-pitched hooting.

Naturalists who know the spotted owl do not hesitate to clamber up the cliff for a look at the young or the two or three white eggs resting on a bed of sticks and bark. For though this fierce-looking nocturnal hunter may brush a man's head as it sweeps in to look him over, it rarely fights to defend its nursery.

This western cousin of the barred owl snoozes the days away in evergreen forests and in remote timbered gorges. Unless it stirs, the spotted owl is hard to see because its mottled plumage blends with the flickering lights and shadows. Squeaking may lure this owl into view.

At sundown *occidentalis* leaves its perch to hunt. Rats and mice are favorite prey, but the bird also feeds on crickets, large beetles, bats, squirrels, and on other birds, including small owls. For their nests spotted owls choose a tree cavity, a deserted hawk's nest, or a cave.

Range: S. W. British Columbia to S. California, and from N. Arizona to central Colorado, south to central Mexico. *Characteristics:* round head, large dark eyes, brown facial disks, dark brown plumage spotted with white.

Barred Owl
Strix varia

A HAIR-RAISING CACOPHONY breaks the stillness of a lowland swamp. It may go on through the night—cackles, shrieks, and coos followed by eight wild hoots that sound like "Who cooks for you? Who cooks for you-all?"

To the barred owl this is nuptial music. As courting birds perform the serenade they bob and twist their puffy round heads.

Barred owls seek a nest site in a wooded swamp or a forest. They rarely build their own nursery; instead they usually house their two or three white eggs in a tree hollow or in a vacated nest of a hawk, crow, or squirrel.

A pudgy bird with brown eyes and a heart-shaped face framed by a barred cowl, *varia* is one of the best known owls east of the prairies. On silent wings this hunter skims the lowlands in the evening, keen eyes searching for crayfish, frogs, mice, and birds.

Range: N. British Columbia to Nova Scotia, south (east of the Rockies) to Honduras. *Characteristics:* round head, lined facial disks, barred gray-brown upperparts spotted with white, barred chest, paler belly striped vertically.

Barred owl, length 17-24"; Karl Maslowski, Photo Researchers

Long-eared Owl
Asio otus

PERCHED BOLT UPRIGHT near a pine trunk, the longear resembles a branch stub. Feathers compressed, eyes partly closed, and ear tufts erect, the bird holds its hiding pose dead still.

But this "stub" bursts into action if you venture too close to its nest. Yellow eyes blinking, beak snapping, the bird hisses, whines, squeals, and flutters about feigning injury.

Aside from such outbursts and a mellow hooting during breeding season, *otus* keeps quiet. Widely distributed through North America, the bird usually frequents dense evergreen groves. In open country it dwells in streamside timber.

A pair usually remodels an old nest of a hawk, crow, heron, or magpie. The abode of sticks and bark holds three to seven white eggs.

In the air this slim owl folds back its ear tufts — these are feather growths, not ears — and flies buoyantly on long wings. Longears feed mainly on mice. When winter cuts down the supply in their northernmost haunts, they fly south, often settling in a communal roost of up to 25 birds.

Range: S. Alaska to Nova Scotia, south to Baja California and Virginia; winters to central Mexico. Also found in Eurasia and Africa. *Characteristics:* long ear tufts, yellow eyes, rusty facial disks bordered with black; mottled gray-brown upperparts, streaked whitish underparts.

Long-eared owl, length 13-16"

Short-eared Owl
Asio flammeus

FROM HIGH in the twilight sky above the Great Plains comes a monotonous staccato of 15 to 20 low toots. Flapping and soaring, a tawny, streaked owl circles over his prospective mate. Suddenly he dives. He presses his wings beneath him and claps them together rapidly to produce a sound like the fluttering of a wind-whipped flag. Then, continuing this spectacular courtship ritual, he climbs, toots, and dives again.

Short-eared owls roam the open country — marshes, dunes, and grassy plains. They sleep and nest on the ground. The little tufts that explain their common name are seldom seen.

Under a clump of weeds, or even out in the open, mated birds prepare a thin mattress of grass for their five to seven whitish eggs. They snap their bills and sound sneezelike barks when an intruder approaches the nest; they may try a wounded bird act to draw him off.

The youngsters' hunger often forces the parents to hunt in daylight. A foraging shortear circles a few feet over a field. Sighting a victim, the bird hovers, then pounces. Shortears concentrate where mice abound, but they also dine on insects and birds. Lack of food may lead to cannibalism among the owlets. One observer watching a brood of five saw a larger nestling tug at a smaller one, then swallow it headfirst.

Range: N. Alaska to Greenland, south to S. California, N. Nevada, and Virginia; winters to S. Mexico. Also found in South America, Europe, Asia, and Africa. *Characteristics:* short ear tufts, dark facial disks, yellow eyes, streaked buffy-brown head, back, and chest, paler belly; light wing patch, dark patch on underside.

Short-eared owl, length 13-17"; Arthur A. Allen
Left: G. Ronald Austing, Photo Researchers

Boreal owl, length 8½-12"; John Craighead

Boreal Owl
Aegolius funereus

IN THE LEGENDS of the Montagnais Indians of Quebec the boreal owl was once the largest owl in the world, with a voice to match. But one day he tried to outroar a waterfall. The Great Spirit, offended, changed him into a midget with a tiny voice that sounds like water dripping from a height. The Montagnais named him *pillip-pile-tshish* — "water dripping bird." To others his liquid *ting ting ting* notes resemble the soft tolling of a high-pitched bell.

This chocolate-hued denizen of the boreal, or northern, forests is also known as Richardson's owl — having been named for Sir John Richardson, a 19th century arctic explorer.

In spring the female lays four to six white eggs on a bed of feathers and wood chips in a tree cavity. Some boreal owls remain the year round in the Far North. Others wend their way south in search of rodents and insects. These birds are so tame that they can often be captured by hand.

Range: N. Alaska to Newfoundland, south to N. British Columbia and Nova Scotia; winters to S. British Columbia and Massachusetts. Also found in Europe and Asia. *Characteristics:* yellow bill, black-rimmed facial disks, white-spotted brown head and back, streaked underparts.

Saw-whet Owl
Aegolius acadicus

THROUGH THE DAYLIGHT HOURS in the northern evergreen forests this little sleepyhead keeps out of sight, perching quietly near a tree trunk. When night falls, the saw-whet owl ventures forth to hunt — mainly mice but often rats and squirrels larger than itself.

The saw-whet was named for its two-syllable call, a rasping *skreigh-aw* that resembles the sound of a saw being filed. During breeding season — in late winter and early spring — the bird announces its presence with a whistled *too*, repeating it as many as 130 times a minute.

Seasoned bird watchers searching for saw-whet owls rap at the base of tree stubs. Often one of these birds pops up at a hole in the stub, its round face completely filling the entrance. The nest chamber, usually an old flicker hole sparsely furnished with a few chips left by the excavator, holds five or six white eggs.

When winter snows blanket the mouse tunnels many of these owls head south. But they sometimes arrive at the new haven too weak to hunt or even to eat, finding only a place to die.

Range: S. Alaska to Nova Scotia, south in the western mountains to S. Mexico, and to Oklahoma, Missouri, and Maryland; winters to Louisiana and Florida. *Characteristics:* large facial disks, yellow eyes, black bill, white-streaked head, brown back, chestnut-striped white underparts. Young are brown with white "eyebrows."

445

Length 14-20"

LORD OF THE NIGHT

♪♪ # The Barn Owl
Family Tytonidae

MANY A PRANKISH YOUNGSTER prowling on a moonless night has trembled to a chuckle in a deserted New England manse, to a snore in a colonnaded Southern ruin, to a scream in an abandoned Western mine shaft. Ghosts? No. A flashlight usually reveals the barn owl *(Tyto alba)*, the only New World member of a nearly global family comprising ten species.

With silent wingbeats this nocturnal hunter patrols the countryside for rodents. And it can catch them in total darkness by hearing alone (page 25). The barn owl tends to return every year to the same mate and nest site. Eggs and young are found together, since the five to seven white eggs are laid irregularly and incubation begins with the first egg. After nesting, barn owls may wander north or south.

Range: S. W. British Columbia to S. Michigan, S. Quebec, and N. E. Massachusetts, south to S. Chile; also found in Europe, Asia, Africa, and Australia. *Characteristics:* large tuftless head, heart-shaped white face, long wings, long feathered legs, mottled golden-brownish upperparts, pale underparts.

MICE AND MEN *shape the barn owl's world. Like the mouser opposite, most find their favorite fare near human habitation. So these pale birds dwell in barns, factories, water towers, granaries, steeples — even descend an old chimney to a boarded-up hearth (left).*

Appetite? One young bird gulped nine mice in rapid order and three hours later ate four more. Below a nest in the heart of Washington, D. C., were the remains of 225 meadow mice, 179 house mice, 20 rats, and 20 shrews.

The barn or "monkey-faced" owl has larger facial disks than the typical owls, and its long legs (upper) end in saw-edged middle claws.

Thase Daniel. Opposite and upper: H. A. Thornhill, National Audubon Society

446

Goatsuckers and Nighthawks

Family Caprimulgidae

G OATSUCKERS — the very name springs from superstition. In ancient times these seldom-seen birds with tiny bills and huge mouths were thought to suck at the udders of goats, causing the animals to go blind. Even the family's scientific name — from the Latin *caprimulgus*, milker of goats — reflects the old belief.

The family's common European name, nightjar, better suits these shadowy hunters of night-flying insects, for their weird, persistent calls certainly "jar the night." Four of the North American Caprimulgidae are named for their haunting nocturnal voices. Who has not heard the wistful plaint of the whip-poor-will, repeated over and over on a summer night? Its southern cousin, the chuck-will's-widow, has a slightly different call, as does the poor-will of the West, and the pauraque of the Rio Grande. Our two nighthawks, which are not hawks at all, prefer to perch in silence, peeping nasally as they hawk insects over city and field.

Legends surround many of the family's 67 members, which dwell in nearly every temperate and tropical land. Because of their eerie voices, some kinds are said to contain the restless souls of departed criminals. Some portend evil — though in Appalachia the whip-poor-will's cry is ominous only to a listening bachelor, for it tolls the unmarried years that are left to him. These can add up to quite a few. Naturalist John Burroughs heard one bird call 1,088 times, pause, then add 390 more!

Like other birds that hunt by night and sleep by day, the Caprimulgidae are so well camouflaged that they all but vanish into their surroundings as they sleep. With tiny feet and weak legs, they huddle motionless on the ground or perhaps perch lengthwise on a bough, looking like nothing more than a burl. Only at the last instant before danger strikes do they spread their long wings and flutter away like a moth.

HIBERNATING POOR-WILL, *discovered in 1946, rocked the scientific world. Lodged in a crevice (far right) in California's Chuckwalla Mountains, the little bundle of feathers stirred the interest of biologist Edmund C. Jaeger (in jacket, above). When the bird winked, Dr. Jaeger realized it was in a state of true hibernation as deep as any groundhog's. Next fall he found the bird at the same spot, banded it, and ran tests.*

During hibernation the poor-will's temperature sagged to 64.4° F., about 42 degrees below normal. A stethoscope revealed no heartbeat. A mirror caught no mist of breath. Strokes, shouts, and dazzling lights failed to rouse the sleeper. The bird burned its body fats so slowly that a careful weight check showed only slight losses.

The ancients thought many birds hibernated — how else to explain their absence in winter? Knowledge of migration belittled this theory. Today we know that some birds grow torpid with cold and at least one — the poor-will — hibernates.

Don Ollis

Dale Gustafson. Right: Kenneth Middleham

Whip-poor-will
Caprimulgus vociferus

"THE NOTE of the whip-poor-will, borne over the fields, is the voice with which the woods and moonlight woo me." Writing in 1840, Henry David Thoreau put into words what millions have felt as they heard this nocturnal minstrel persistently repeating the three syllables of its name, now from the ground, now perched on a tree limb, a fence post, a rock.

Three syllables? Come close to the hidden singer and you hear a fourth—a low, harsh throat-clearing sound, a *chuck* at the beginning of the call. The whip-poor-will sings most frequently in spring and summer through the evening and pre-dawn hours. In the middle watches of the night *vociferus* usually quiets down and flits about on broad wings, silent as an owl in flight. It hunts around woodland edges, its large keen eyes seeking moths, grasshoppers, crickets, caddis flies, and—happily for campers—mosquitoes. It threads the dusky trees, now sailing, now banking vertically as it feeds. Like other goatsuckers, the whip-poor-will traps flying insects with its enormous bristle-fringed mouth.

By day the whip-poor-will roosts, becoming for most eyes part of a thick branch, a piece of dead wood, a hump of leaves, a lichen-covered rock. Even the courtship of the species takes place in twilight. The birds dance and touch bills, usually making purring or grunting noises. They build no nest. The two white eggs, spotted and blotched with brown and gray, lie among leaves—on the forest floor, or in the shadow of a bush. The eggs of a southwestern subspecies, Stephens' whip-poor-will, are pure white.

Blending with the leaves in the flickering light of the woodland, the chicks have an excellent chance of passing unnoticed. To draw an intruder away from them, their mother tumbles about as if crippled, her big mouth agape, uttering strange whines and hisses.

A related species, Ridgway's whip-poor-will (*Caprimulgus ridgwayi*) of Mexico and Central America, has been found in recent years on both sides of the Arizona-New Mexico border in Guadalupe Canyon and apparently breeds there. Its buff nape band distinguishes it from *vociferus*.

Range: central Saskatchewan to Nova Scotia, south to N. E. Texas, N. Louisiana, and E. North Carolina, and central Arizona to S. W. Texas, south to Honduras; winters to Costa Rica and Cuba. *Characteristics:* mottled gray brown with whitish throat band; small bill, huge mouth, rounded tail. Tips of outer tail feathers white in male, buffy in female.

Chuck-will's-widow
Caprimulgus carolinensis

SOUTHERN VERSION of the whip-poor-will, the chuck-will's-widow is our largest goatsucker. Its name indicates how its call differs from the whip-poor-will's—more a variation of emphasis and rhythm than of melody. In areas where their ranges overlap and they sing together the result sounds more like a well-matched duet than a clashing of dissimilar airs.

In many places in the South, where people call both species whip-poor-will, *vociferus* heads north before *carolinensis* arrives to breed. On bare ground or dry leaves the chuck-will's-widow deposits two creamy eggs marbled and spotted with brown, gray, and lavender. The female lures enemies away by feigning injury. Incubation

Female whip-poor-will, length 9-10"
Hal H. Harrison, Camera Clix

Right: chuck-will's-widow, length 11-13"
Thase Daniel

takes about 20 days. The hatchlings, covered with yellowish down, lie flat on the ground at first. They grow quickly, however, and soon begin to hop about like toads, sometimes uttering strange whines. By the time the chicks are 17 days old they can fly 50 feet or more.

Into the chuck-will's-widow's cavernous maw go large insects such as June bugs and dragonflies. Occasionally this goatsucker swallows a warbler, sparrow, or hummingbird. Like its relatives, the chuck-will's-widow hunts and sings at night and sleeps in the daytime, resting on the ground or lengthwise along a bough.

Range: E. Kansas to S. New Jersey, south to central Texas and S. Florida; winters to Colombia and the West Indies. *Characteristics:* like the whip-poor-will but larger and buffier.

Poor-will
Phalaenoptilus nuttallii

THE ONLY BIRD known to hibernate, the poor-will seems somewhat lethargic even in summer. It rests all day in the cover of thick brush and hunts only for brief periods at dawn and dusk.

This little western cousin of the whip-poor-will inhabits rocky canyons and foothills from Canada to Mexico. The five races of poor-will favor open country but at times frequent low forests. These birds chase beetles and other insects along the ground or dart up in erratic flight to seize a moth in the air.

When wind, rain, and cold cut down on the movement of insects and create a food shortage, poor-wills may enter a torpid state. When insects vanish from the air in winter, the torpor deepens until it becomes true hibernation.

Poor-wills nest on bare ground, gravel, or rock, at times in full sunlight but more often in the shade of a bush. Both male and female incubate the two pinkish eggs, rarely spotted with brown.

The poor-will is named for its call—yet another version of the goatsucker serenade. As the little bird repeats it, however, it adds an extra syllable which can be heard only at close range: *poorwill-low* or *poor-will-ip.*

Range: S. British Columbia and S. Alberta to S. W. Iowa, south to central Mexico; migratory in the north. *Characteristics:* small size; grayish brown with white throat and tail tip.

Pauraque
Nyctidromus albicollis

THE GLOW of a May sunset fades from the waters of the lower Rio Grande. Now, beneath the darkened, moss-hung trees of the Santa Ana National Wildlife Refuge in Texas, two pauraques join in the rites of courtship. They face each other in a clearing and leap into the air with a flash of white-flecked wings. Returning to earth, they crouch and grovel before one another, then flutter upward once more.

Primarily a bird of South and Central America, the pauraque extends its range just north of the Mexican border. It winters along streams where thickets offer cover, but breeds in more open country. Both sexes incubate the two brownblotched pinkish-buff eggs on bare ground.

After the chicks hatch, the parents alight near them in the twilight and call with low, clucking tones. The youngsters hop, peeping, toward the voices. Finally, standing on tiptoe, they receive a regurgitated meal of insects.

The pauraque sings at night mainly in moonlight, a whistled goatsucker call rising in pitch at the end. The bird's common name, pronounced pow-*rah*-kay, supposedly stems from one of its calls, but the most typical pauraque song sounds more like *go-weeer, go-weeer.*

Range: N. Mexico to S. Texas, south to Peru and S. Brazil. *Characteristics:* gray brown with white band on rounded wings, white on sides of tail. Female shows less white.

Male pauraque, length 10-12"
Paul Schwartz

Left: poor-will, length 7-8½".
Eliot Porter

451

Female common nighthawk, length 8½-10"; B. Brower Hall, National Audubon Society

♪♪ Common Nighthawk
Chordeiles minor

THE SUN sags behind a mountain, and the land slips into repose. The breeze dies; fledgling birds twitter in their nests, then fall silent. Overhead appears a trio of dark, darting nighthawks, breaking the stillness with their nasal, buzzing calls. Rising, dipping, soaring on slender, white-banded wings, they wheel in the twilight. Gaining speed with a few leisurely wingbeats, they flick through a little cloud of flying ants, and their mouths, gaping from ear to ear, engulf great quantities of the insects.

"Nighthawk" is a misnomer. Though it looks somewhat like a hawk in flight, this bird belongs to the goatsucker family, preying only on a wide variety of insects. And it is less nocturnal than many of its relatives.

It hunts regularly by day, though mostly at twilight and dawn, and shows itself more to people than the others. We see common nighthawks perched on stumps and fence posts, on warm days panting vigorously as they fluff their feathers and turn their faces away from the sun.

In great migratory flocks these birds journey from South America in spring to seek nest sites over most of North America. In the East and South the "mosquito hawk" takes to gravelly beaches, barrens, or burned-over woodlands; in the West to sagebrush plains and sometimes to mountain slopes 10,000 feet above sea level. This species shuns the deep forests.

The male nighthawk performs a dazzling aerial courtship while the female watches from the ground. He circles and soars, then folds his wings and plummets. A few yards above the ground he pulls out of his dive. The vibrant rush of air through his flight feathers produces a sound like the plucking of a thick rubber band. The "bull-bat" continues these booming plunges at intervals throughout the nesting season.

The female selects the nest site—a gravel bar, sandspit, often a rocky pasture. One pair nested between railroad ties. Another chose the rough of a golf course. Growing cities offer the birds a new nesting habitat. Many breed on the flat gravel-and-tar roofs of office buildings, secure from the molestations suffered by ground-nesting birds. One disadvantage: In hot weather the two speckled creamy or olive eggs sometimes become trapped in the melted tar.

Range: N. W. Canada to Newfoundland, south to Panama; winters from Colombia to Argentina. *Characteristics:* mottled grayish brown with broad white wing bar, pale barring on underparts. Male has white band on throat and tail. Female, has buff throat band, lacks white on tail.

452

Lesser Nighthawk
Chordeiles acutipennis

IN THE MIDDLE of a desert road a pudgy brown bird sits amid the blown sand, watching for passing insects. Far down the heat-shimmering ribbon a glistening speck appears and quickly looms larger. Its distant hum rises to an urgent song of speed. But the bird pays no heed. On rushes the car, its driver listening to the radio in air-conditioned comfort. He never sees the bird as it dodges aside at the last split second and flies off on long wings.

This lesser nighthawk survived the encounter, but many others don't; automobiles take heavy toll of this southwestern species. Like its slightly larger cousin, the common nighthawk, this desert dweller may hunt by day but is most active in evening and early morning. It perches by day on low branches of mesquite and greasewood and seems to favor bare ground—warm and level like a road. Disturb one and before flying off it raises its head, stretches its neck, and moves its body up and down.

As the day grows hotter the lesser nighthawk turns on its cooling system. Opening its huge mouth, it rapidly flutters its throat. Moisture from the oral surfaces evaporates and the fanned air reduces the bird's body temperature.

Like its cousin, the lesser nighthawk pursues insects in the air, skimming brushy growth or rising above the trees. It strokes quickly three or four times, then sails. Sometimes it darts up from the ground to grab passing prey. Often it feeds about bright city lights.

In courtship the male chases the female in twisting flight, then soars on downcurved wings, uttering a low chuckle which ends with a rolling *cr-r-rooo*. Some of his notes sound like those of frogs. Also known as the Texas or trilling nighthawk, this bird frequently sings on the wing.

Mated pairs nest on a patch of sand under a bush, sometimes on the flat roof of an adobe house. Incubation of the two speckled gray or creamy-white eggs seems to be less a matter of warming them than of shading them from too much heat. Within a day or two after hatching, the young crawl about from place to place, seeking protection from the sun.

Range: central California to S. Texas, south to N. Chile and S. Brazil; migratory in the north. *Characteristics:* like common nighthawk but smaller and browner and with white wing bar (buffy in female) closer to the wing tip.

Female lesser nighthawk, length 8-9"; Eliot Porter

SPEED CHAMPIONS
OF THE BIRD WORLD

The Swifts
Family Apodidae

A WORLDWIDE FAMILY of about 70 species, the aptly named swifts are built for speed and show it. In normal flight they consistently hit greater speeds than other birds. Their streamlined, cigar-shaped bodies offer minimum resistance to the drag of air, and flat, narrow, swept-back wings provide maximum efficiency for sustained high-speed performance. Though a falcon stooping at prey may exceed a swift's velocity and reach 175 miles per hour, the predator maintains its top speed only during the dive.

The family's scientific name Apodidae derives from a Greek word meaning "footless." It too is fitting, for though swifts have feet and use them to grip their precipitous perches, the birds do not alight or stand on the ground. Few birds, in fact, are more totally creatures of the air than swifts. They feed and drink on the wing,

snapping up insects in midair and scooping water into their gaping mouths as they skim over the surface of a stream. Sometimes they even mate aloft. And when building their nests they gather twigs or other materials in flight and speed with them to the nest site.

All species use the same cement—saliva—to stick together the twigs, bits of bark, and other materials that form the cup. The gelatinous saliva of certain Asian species makes up the entire nest. This forms the base for bird's-nest soup, relished by Orientals. A tropical American species, the small black-and-white Cayenne swift, builds a remarkable stockinglike nest of plant fibers and down suspended from a sloping branch or cliff crevice. The birds fly in the open lower end and clamber up to the concealed shelf that holds the eggs. Some South American swifts build on the face of cliffs behind waterfalls and fly straight through the veil of roaring waters hundreds of times a day.

Swifts may course the skies in great flocks to avoid cold or wet weather and during migrations. A radar station in England tracked flocks of Old World swifts streaming 15 to 20 miles long. These birds often flew along the edges of storms, thus living up to one of their European names, "thunder swallows."

Though similar to swallows in the way they dart after insects, swifts fly differently. Instead of much gliding, they move their bowed wings with jerky, mechanical strokes. The tail is too short to serve fully as a rudder, so they steer by changing the angle of the wings. From this some observers mistakenly believed that swifts beat their wings alternately, first left, then right, then left again. High-speed motion pictures have shown that sometimes one wing may move faster than the other.

Although small birds demand almost continual feeding during early life, nestling European swifts can survive several days of near starvation. They may be forced to go on short rations during chilly, rainy summers because bad weather grounds flying insects, sole food of the family. At such times the young swift's growth slows drastically. Born naked, the nestling attains full plumage in about five weeks during a fine summer but may take eight weeks during an inclement one.

Swifts often feed both day and night. Like their close cousins, the hummingbirds, they quickly convert food into energy. "If there were continuous daylight and plenty of food in the air," writes ornithologist J. J. Murray, "it seems not impossible that the swift could spend its whole life in such continuous motion."

The chimney swift, best known of the four species found in the United States, once mistakenly was thought to hibernate in great hollow trees. The birds certainly used to roost in such trees in great numbers. Audubon estimated that a towering sycamore in Louisville, Kentucky, held 9,000 swifts at night. Some still bed down for the night in a hollow tree; others, especially the western species, may roost in the cracks between blocks of stone.

But most make full use of man-made structures—chimneys and the walls of buildings. In Maine, ornithologist Frederic H. Kennard found amid the cold ashes of a hunting lodge fireplace the crumpled nest of a swift—dashed to the hearth by a torrential rain. Contemplating the small tragedy, Kennard discovered a triumph of life. Like the legendary phoenix, a thumbnail-size hatchling stirred from the ashes. Then, naked and only hours old, it clung to the fireplace screen and inched toward the darkened shelter of the chimney above.

Man usually is only faintly conscious of his small, unobtrusive guests. Model lodgers, they sleep in seclusion and leave at break of day to hunt high in the sky. Only their chittering, peeping calls remind us of their presence overhead.

GLUED *inside a shed, a chimney swift's nest bulges with pinfeathered young. Outgrowing home, they cling to the wall with claws until ready to fly.*   455

Chimney Swift
Chaetura pelagica

IT IS a fine fall evening. The smudge of industry has washed away, leaving the city roofs to stand out stark and crisp in the sunset. But over the skyline another cloud is forming – a mass of birds swirling aimlessly, growing in size, at last gathering strength and purpose until it whirls above a brick-lined chimney. Muttering with the beat of thousands of wings, the avian whirlwind funnels into the open top. Birds stream into the dark opening by the hundreds, perhaps for 20 minutes. Then the rooftops fall silent. The migrating chimney swifts have gone to rest.

Inside, they clutch the carboned walls with tiny claws, arranging themselves to form a tight-packed mass, each bird hooked in place and braced with its spiky little tail. Like feathery shingles they cover the inside of their haven. Birdbanders in Georgia trapped and counted 7,377 swifts in a single chimney.

In the morning the chimney awakens as the birds shoot up into the light and vanish with mechanical beats of sickle-shaped wings. As they continue their southward migration they hunt far and wide for insects.

The pace of their journey seems slow and uncertain. Perhaps because of their dithering along the way, their winter goal long remained a mystery. Then late in 1943 Peruvian Indians living on the headwaters of the Amazon recovered leg bands that had been put on swifts as far away as Connecticut and Ontario.

Until settlers came to North America, chimney swifts knew only hollow trees as homes. As men felled the trees, the hardy birds discovered a perfect substitute – man-made chimneys. Today the species flourishes over much of the United States and southern Canada, one of the few birds to benefit from the arrival of the white man.

Besides chimneys, swifts settle in wells, silos, barns, even unoccupied houses where a broken window or other opening allows them to come and go freely. Farmers welcome their return in the spring, for swifts eat many insect pests.

A great chattering and twittering signals the start of breeding for the chimney swifts. Theirs is a high-speed courtship, an aerial chase accompanied by a sharpening and speeding up of the chipping notes. Three or four birds may hurtle and twist through the sky in a close line; then a pair will break free. As the pursuing male overtakes the female at blazing speed, he may raise his wings and drop toward her. Possibly the courtship culminates at this time – in midair.

Working together, male and female build their hammock-shaped nest of saliva-glued twigs. Rain may wash it off the wall or the inside of the chimney, but usually not before the four or five white eggs have hatched and the spiky nestlings are able to grip the surface.

As their wings develop, the youngsters flap from one toehold to another inside their home. As they grow they climb higher toward the exit. At last they are ready to leave the darkness and reach the open sky, which will be their hunting ground from then on.

Since they fly so speedily, swifts need have little fear of predators. But a chill summer night may be their undoing, for if a fireplace is then put to use, billowing smoke may suffocate the sleeping swifts before they can escape.

Range: S. E. Saskatchewan to Nova Scotia, south to S. E. Texas and central Florida; winters in South America in the upper Amazon basin. *Characteristics:* small bill, long curved wings, cigar-shaped body, short tail; sooty-brown upperparts, paler underparts.

Black Swift
Cypseloides niger

LARGEST of our northern swifts, the black swift remained unreported in North America until 1857. It is still rarely seen, for it flies high over western mountains and through canyons, and nests in inaccessible cliff crannies, often beside waterfalls, pounding surf, or in a hidden gorge. It takes an adventurous bird watcher to find the nest. The first one was discovered in 1901 on a southern California sea cliff.

Placed on a slight projection on a rock face, the cup of moss, fern, grass, or mud holds a single white egg. Quieter than its relatives, *niger* sounds a sharp *plik-plik-plik* call near the nest.

Range: S. E. Alaska to S. Alberta, south to S. California and S. Mexico; also in West Indies and British Guiana. Winters in tropical America. *Characteristics:* blackish with pale barred forehead; forked tail. Young have mottled belly.

Vaux's Swift
Chaetura vauxi

THIS WESTERN VERSION of the chimney swift is more old-fashioned in its nesting habits. Vaux's swift, named for the 19th century naturalist William Sanson Vaux, has only recently discovered the chimney. Smallest of North American swifts, it still breeds mainly in hollow trees, sometimes in a fire-gutted stub where the four to six white eggs lie below ground level.

Twittering weakly, Vaux's swifts cover scores of miles hunting insects for their young. A few winter as far north as Louisiana and California.

Range: locally from S. E. Alaska to British Columbia, south to Panama; also in Venezuela. Winters mainly in Central America. *Characteristics:* like chimney swift but smaller and paler.

White-throated swift
length 6-7"

Black swifts
adult, length 7-7½"
and juvenile (left)

Chimney swift
length 4¾-5½"

Vaux's swift
length 4-4½"
Allan Brooks

White-throated Swift
Aëronautes saxatalis

OF THE FOUR North American swifts, this is the finest flyer—a darting, dashing bird that "belongs to the heavens, not to earth," as George Miksch Sutton wrote. Streaking past you, a pair of white-throated swifts abruptly reverse direction and become mere black-and-white blurs. Their dazzling aerial courtship often seems to end in a nuptial embrace, the birds pinwheeling down a hundred feet before parting.

Near the Grand Canyon and on surf-pounded sea cliffs or 13,000-foot peaks, the "rock swift" nests in cracks and crevices. Flocks fly to their niches at breathtaking speed and dart into them. In near darkness one observer saw between 100 and 200 birds pour headlong into a roosting crevice and vanish in seconds.

Glued to the rocks, the nest of feathers and soft vegetation holds three to six white eggs. When they hatch, the parents keep busy hurtling after insects, the moan of wind over their wings mingling with their shrill *ji-ji-jijiji* calls. They often hunt over adjacent lowlands.

Range: S. British Columbia to W. South Dakota, south in the mountains to El Salvador; migratory in the north. *Characteristics:* blackish with white throat, white stripe down middle of the breast, and white flank patches; forked tail.

457

ANCIENT ART *attests man's long fascination with birds: Stone Age cave paintings, Egyptian carvings, Chinese tapestries. Moslems in the Middle Ages fashioned in bronze this dove-shaped vessel with a dog handle, now at St. Catherine's Monastery near traditional Mount Sinai in Egypt.*

TERN *swishes a golden tail on a fragment of cotton embroidered with wool 800 years ago in Peru.*

TOUCANS, *artfully cast in gold, seem ready to fly from this medieval Colombian staff head. Museum of the American Indian, New York.*

ST. FRANCIS *of Assisi preaches to the birds on this illuminated page in a 13th century Flemish psalter. Birds figure prominently in Christian symbolism. Pierpont Morgan Library, New York.*

SYMBOLIC BIRDS *adorn coins of the 4th and 5th centuries* B.C. *Left: eagle of Zeus on a Sicilian tetradrachm; Museum of Fine Arts, Boston. Center: owl, Athena's symbol of wisdom, on an Athenian drachm. Right: swan, associated with Apollo, on an Ionian tetradrachm; Chase Manhattan Bank Money Museum, New York.*

Acknowledgments

ONCE AGAIN the editors obtained valuable as-
sistance from scientists and collections at
the Smithsonian Institution, and from the
books of general and regional scope, field guides,
and periodicals credited in *Song and Garden
Birds of North America*. In addition, the following books of a general nature were helpful: *The
World of Birds* by James Fisher and Roger Tory
Peterson; *Handbook of North American Birds*,
Volume 1, edited by Ralph S. Palmer; *Men, Birds,
and Adventure* by Virginia S. Eifert; *Bird Migration* by Donald Griffin; *The Migrations of Birds*
by Jean Dorst; and *A New Dictionary of Birds*
edited by A. Landsborough Thomson. Other
regional books referred to for this volume
included *The Birds of Arizona* by Allan
Phillips, Joe Marshall, and Gale
Monson; and *The Birds of
Greenland* by Finn Salomonsen.

Among the many works consulted
on water, prey, and game birds
these proved particularly useful:
American Water & Game Birds by Austin
L. Rand; *Sea-Birds* by James Fisher and
R. M. Lockley; *The Ducks, Geese and Swans
of North America* by Francis H. Kortright;
The Waterfowl of the World by Jean Delacour;
Waterfowl Tomorrow edited by Joseph P. Lin-
duska; *The Art of Falconry of Frederick II* edited
by Casey A. Wood and F. Marjorie Fyfe; *Birds of
Prey of the World* by Mary Louise Grossman and

John Hamlet; *North American Birds of Prey* by
Alexander Sprunt, Jr.; *American Game Birds of
Field and Forest* by Frank C. Edminster; *A Gath-
ering of Shore Birds* by Henry Marion Hall; *Bird
Studies at Old Cape May* by Witmer Stone; and
The Pigeon by Wendell Mitchell Levi.

National Geographic Society staff members in
many departments contributed significantly to
this book. See listing on following page. The
more than 870 issues of *National Geographic*
contain a vast store of information on the life of
birds. Check the Cumulative Index.

463

ZEUS *and his legendary messenger, the eagle, grace an ancient Greek ceramic. The Louvre, Paris.*

Hints on playing your bird sound record album

MOST PEOPLE are accustomed to playing 12-inch records on their phonographs. With this handy album of six compact high-fidelity records the National Geographic Society presents an exciting way to hear bird calls. You may find the following suggestions useful as you tune in to more than one hour of delightful listening.

After placing the album on the turntable, you may find it easier to put the needle on the record if the album is not turning.

If yours is an automatic record changer, make sure that the controls are set to play manually so that the tone arm may be freely positioned by hand.

Some automatics may prove difficult to play manually. In that case the following steps may be helpful:
1. Turn the phonograph on.
2. As the tone arm swings up and starts to descend into normal playing position, place a finger under the arm to keep the needle from coming down on the turntable.
3. Gently move the tone arm in to the record playing area.

For your convenience in quickly locating a call on a record, its position is indicated by an arrowhead symbol. With most machines you will have no difficulty in placing the tone arm anywhere on the record. However, if the tone arm refuses to be carried by hand to calls on the inside of the record and kicks into automatic reject, place the arm toward the outside of the record and let it ride in to the bird call desired.